THE FIFTEENTH CENTURY
VOLUME XIV

The Fifteenth Century

ISSN 1479–9871

General Editor
Dr. Linda Clark

Assistant Editor
Dr. Hannes Kleineke

Editorial Advisory Committee
Dr. Rowena E. Archer, *University of Oxford*
Professor Christine Carpenter, *University of Cambridge*
Professor Christopher Dyer, *University of Leicester*
Dr. David Grummitt, *University of Kent*
Professor Tony Pollard, *University of Teesside*
Professor Carole Rawcliffe, *University of East Anglia*
Dr. Benjamin Thompson, *Somerville College, Oxford*
Professor John Watts, *Corpus Christi College, Oxford*

The series aims to provide a forum for the most recent research into the political, social, religious and cultural history of the fifteenth century in Britain and Europe. Contributions for future volumes are welcomed; prospective contributors should consult the guidelines at the end of this volume.

THE FIFTEENTH CENTURY
XIV

ESSAYS PRESENTED TO MICHAEL HICKS

Edited by
LINDA CLARK

THE BOYDELL PRESS

© Contributors 2015

All Rights Reserved. Except as permitted under current legislation no part of this work may be photocopied, stored in a retrieval system, published, performed in public, adapted, broadcast, transmitted, recorded or reproduced in any form or by any means, without the prior permission of the copyright owner

First published 2015
The Boydell Press, Woodbridge

ISBN 978-1-78327-048-4

The Boydell Press is an imprint of Boydell & Brewer Ltd
PO Box 9, Woodbridge, Suffolk IP12 3DF, UK
and of Boydell & Brewer Inc.
668 Mt Hope Avenue, Rochester, NY 14620-2731, USA
website: www.boydellandbrewer.com

A catalogue record for this title is available
from the British Library

The publisher has no responsibility for the continued existence or accuracy of URLs for external or third-party internet websites referred to in this book, and does not guarantee that any content on such websites is, or will remain, accurate or appropriate

This publication is printed on acid-free paper
from camera-ready copy supplied by the editor

CONTENTS

List of Illustrations	ix
Contributors	x
Abbreviations	xii
Preface	xiii
Michael Hicks: An Appreciation CAROLINE BARRON	xv
Disciplinary Ordinances for English Garrisons in Normandy in the Reign of Henry V ANNE CURRY	1
Lords in a Landscape: the Berkeley Family and Northfield (Worcestershire) CHRISTOPHER DYER	13
Hampshire and the Parish Tax of 1428 MARK PAGE	39
The Livery Act of 1429 GORDON MCKELVIE	55
An Indenture between Richard Neville, Earl of Salisbury, and Sir Edmund Darell of Sessay, North Riding, 1435 A.J. POLLARD	67
The Pursuit of Justice and Inheritance from Marcher Lordships to Parliament: the Implications of Margaret Malefaunt's Abduction in Gower in 1438 RALPH GRIFFITHS	77
The Battles of Mortimer's Cross and Second St. Albans: The Regional Dimension PETER FLEMING	91
Widows and the Wars of the Roses: the Turbulent Marital History of Edward IV's Putative Mistress, Margaret, daughter of Sir Lewis John of West Horndon, Essex S.J. PAYLING	103
Some Observations on the Household and Circle of Humphrey Stafford, Lord Stafford of Southwick and Earl of Devon: the Last Will of Roger Bekensawe HANNES KLEINEKE	117

The Treatment of Traitors' Children and Edward IV's Clemency in the 1460s JAMES ROSS	131
Edward IV and Bury St. Edmunds' Search for Self-Government ANNE F. SUTTON	143
The Exchequer Inquisitions *Post Mortem* MATTHEW HOLFORD	161
Hams for Prayers: Regular Canons and their Lay Patrons in Medieval Catalonia KAREN STÖBER	175
Production, Specialisation and Consumption in Late Medieval Wessex JOHN HARE	189
A Butt of Wine and Two Barrels of Herring: Southampton's Trading Links with Religious Institutions in Winchester and South Central England, 1430–1540 WINIFRED A. HARWOOD	207
Index	229
The Published Works of Michael Hicks, 1977–2015	243
Tabula Gratulatoria	251

LIST OF ILLUSTRATIONS

Christopher Dyer, *Lords in a Landscape: The Berkeley Family and Northfield* (*Worcestershire*)

Map 1	Location of Northfield, also showing Berkeley manors in Gloucestershire.	14
Map 2	Plan of Weoley Castle.	20
Map 3	Some Evidence for the Use of Land in Northfield.	24
Map 4	Settlements in Fifteenth-Century Northfield.	30
Map 5	Farms in 1840.	32
Map 6	Early Medieval Settlement in Northfield.	34

Mark Page, *Hampshire and the Parish Tax of 1428*

Map	The County of Hampshire.	52

Winifred A. Harwood, *A Butt of Wine and Two Barrels of Herring*

Map	Location of Religious Institutions (Andrew Murdock, APM geo ltd.)	228

CONTRIBUTORS

Caroline Barron is Emerita Professor of the History of London at Royal Holloway, University of London. She has written *London in the Later Middle Ages*: *Government and People* (Oxford, 2004) and is currently studying the reading habits of medieval Londoners.

Anne Curry is Professor of Medieval History and dean of the faculty of Humanities at the University of Southampton. She has known Michael Hicks since the 1970s and is delighted to be able to contribute to this *Festschrift*.

Christopher Dyer, Emeritus Professor of History at the University of Leicester, has written various books and articles about social, economic and landscape history. His links with Michael Hicks came about from their shared interest in the inquisitions *post mortem* and the insights that they provide into late medieval society.

Peter Fleming is Professor of History at the University of the West of England, Bristol. His research interests include later medieval English urban history, political and cultural history and the history of migration. His monograph, *Time, Space and Power in Fifteenth-Century Bristol*, is forthcoming.

Ralph Griffiths, Emeritus Professor of Medieval History, Swansea University, is honorary Vice-President of the Royal Historical Society and formerly Chairman of the Royal Commission on the Ancient and Historical Monuments of Wales.

John Hare taught history at the sixth form college in Winchester. He has had the pleasure of working with Michael Hicks at the Wessex Centre for Medieval History and Archaeology. His recent publications include *A Prospering Society*: *Wiltshire in the Later Middle Ages* (Hatfield, 2011), and co-authorship of *English Inland Trade 1430–1540*: *Southampton and its Region* (Oxford, 2015).

Winifred A. Harwood is a Visiting Research Fellow at the University of Winchester where she set up the Overland Trade Database. Under the direction of Michael Hicks she worked on the Overland Trade project for ten years and has recently contributed several chapters to the associated publication, *English Inland Trade 1430–1540*.

Matthew Holford is Research Officer for *Mapping the Medieval Countryside*, a major project dedicated to the online publication of English inquisitions *post mortem*, and curator of the medieval manuscripts cataloguing project at the Bodleian Library.

Hannes Kleineke is a Senior Research Fellow at the History of Parliament. He first encountered Michael Hicks in 1997 on top of Sandal Castle (on it). Over the years, their acquaintance has involved much good-natured historical discussion, often over a convivial pint of beer, the most memorable of which were perhaps those consumed at a conference in Windsor Castle, sitting in a flower bed (in it).

Jessica Lutkin is a Research Assistant and impact officer on the 'England's Immigrants 1330–1550' project at the University of York, funded by the Arts and Humanities Research Council. She is currently preparing a monograph about goldsmiths in medieval England. Michael Hicks supervised her undergraduate dissertation and encouraged her to pursue an academic career.

Gordon McKelvie is a Research Officer at the University of Winchester. His Ph.D. thesis on the statutes of livery was supervised by Michael Hicks.

Mark Page is Assistant Editor, *Victoria County History of Oxfordshire*, and Visiting Fellow at the Centre for English Local History, University of Leicester. From 1993 to 2000 he worked at the Hampshire Record Office in Winchester.

Simon Payling has worked for the History of Parliament Trust since 1993 as a Senior Research Fellow for the volumes covering the period 1422–1504.

A.J. Pollard, Emeritus Professor of History at Teeside University, is completing a short life of Edward IV. He has been a friend of Michael Hicks and fellow toiler in the vineyard for forty years. Despite all his efforts he has never been able to match his output.

James Ross is Senior Lecturer in Late Medieval English History at the University of Winchester. He is the author of *John de Vere, 13th earl of Oxford, 1442–1513* (Woodbridge, 2011).

Karen Stöber, researcher and lecturer at the Universitat de Lleida in Catalonia, co-directs the Monastic Wales Project and is joint general editor of the *Journal of Medieval Monastic Studies* (Turnhout), both with Janet Burton. Her Ph.D. thesis was supervised by Michael Hicks – 'hugely inspirational and wonderfully congenial' – at what was then King Alfred's College, Winchester.

Anne F. Sutton is the author of *The Mercery of London: Trade, Goods and People 1130–1578* (2005) and many articles on medieval London, the Mercers and Merchant Adventurers, with a particular interest in the Yorkist period and Richard III. She first met Michael Hicks, more years ago than she cares to remember, in the Corporation of London Records Office when they found that they were both working on Sir Thomas Cook.

ABBREVIATIONS

BIHR	*Bulletin of the Institute of Historical Research*
BJRL	*Bulletin of the John Rylands Library*
BL	British Library, London
Bodl.	Bodleian Library, Oxford
Cal. Inq. Misc.	*Calendar of Inquisitions Miscellaneous*
CChR	*Calendar of Charter Rolls*
CCR	*Calendar of Close Rolls*
CFR	*Calendar of Fine Rolls*
CIPM	*Calendar of Inquisitions Post Mortem*
CP	G.E. Cokayne, *The Complete Peerage of England, Scotland, Ireland, Great Britain and the United Kingdom*, ed. V. Gibbs *et al.* (12 vols., 1910–59)
CPL	*Calendar of Papal Registers. Papal Letters*
CPR	*Calendar of Patent Rolls*
EcHR	*Economic History Review*
EETS	Early English Text Society
EHR	*English Historical Review*
HMC	Historical Manuscripts Commission
HR	*Historical Research*
Oxford DNB	*Oxford Dictionary of National Biography from the Earliest Times to the Year 2000*, ed. H.C.G. Matthew and Brian Harrison (61 vols., Oxford, 2004)
PCC	Prerogative Court of Canterbury
PPC	*Proceedings and Ordinances of the Privy Council of England*, ed. N.H. Nicolas (7 vols., 1834–7)
PROME	*Parliament Rolls of Medieval England, 1275–1504*, ed. Chris Given-Wilson *et al.* (16 vols., Woodbridge, 2005)
RO	Record Office
Rot. Parl.	*Rotuli Parliamentorum* (6 vols., 1767–77)
RS	Rolls Series
Statutes	*Statutes of the Realm* (11 vols., 1810–28)
STC	*A Short-Title Catalogue of Books Printed in England, Scotland and Ireland and of English Books Printed Abroad, 1475–1640*, ed. A.W. Pollard and G.R. Redgrave, 2nd edn., revised by W.A. Jackson *et al.* (3 vols., 1976–91)
TNA	The National Archives, Kew
TRHS	*Transactions of the Royal Historical Society*
VCH	*Victoria County History*

Unless stated otherwise, the place of publication of books cited is London.

PREFACE

The present volume, a *festschrift* for Professor Michael Hicks, owes its existence to an initiative by one of his former students, Dr. Jessica Lutkin, and brings together some of those who have benefited from his teaching and supervision with friends and colleagues among the historians of the late Middle Ages. The essays collected here are presented to Michael with gratitude for his extensive and remarkable contribution to fifteenth-century studies.

As such, this volume displaces the usual collection of articles drawn for the most part from papers presented at the annual Fifteenth Century Conferences, the latest of which was held in September 2014 at the University of Aberdeen and ably hosted by Dr. Jackson Armstrong. The following papers were delivered at the conference; some of them will be published in future volumes of *The Fifteenth Century* series.

Katherine Basanti, '*Knighthood of the North*': *Scottish Crusade Warrior Commemoration in Walter Bower's* Scotichronicon, *1441–45*
Alex Brayson, *The Crown and the Economy in Late Lancastrian England*
Michael Brown, *Munster and the Northland*: *The Place of Regional Societies in Late Medieval Ireland and Scotland*
Christine Carpenter, *Bastard Feudalism in Fourteenth-Century Warwickshire*
Brian Coleman, *An English Gentry Abroad*: *The Case of Ireland*
Derek Crosby, *Merrymaking and Identity in Norwich*: *The Gladman Procession 1443*
Lawrence Duggan, *Ecclesiastical Moneylending in Late Medieval Germany and England*
Simon Egan, '*havyng in their mynd the grete conquest that Bruse som tyme sen to the Kyng of Scottes made in the same land*': *The Royal Stewart Interest in Fifteenth-Century Ireland*
Edda Frankot, *Popular and Official Perceptions of Crime*: *Social Control, Denunciation and Punishment in Late Medieval Kampen*
Chris Given-Wilson, *Conquest, Treason and Corruption of the Blood in Early Fifteenth-Century England*
Claire Hawes, *Legitimacy, Consent and the Public Sphere in Scotland*
William Hepburn, *The People in the Room*: *Instruments of Resignation as a Source for James IV's Chamber*
Michael Hicks, *Bastard Feudalism and Warfare in the Proofs of Age*
Tom Johnson, *Forest Administration*: *A Model of Fifteenth-Century Governmentality*?

Hannes Kleineke, *The Clergy in Parliament in the Yorkist Period*

Aleksandr Lobanov, *Anglo-Burgundian Military Co-operation after 1431: Crisis and Decline?*

Alastair Macdonald, *Fighting Talk: Exhortation in War in Late Medieval Scotland*

Elizabeth Matthew, *Scots at Piltown? The Irish 'extension' of the Wars of the Roses in 1462 Reassessed*

Alison McHardy, *Edward IV and the Old Retainers*

Gordon McKelvie, *Illegal Livery in the Fifteenth Century: The Identity of the Indicted*

Tony Moore, *England and the Foreign Exchange Market*

Athol Murray, *The Scottish Exchequer in the Fifteenth Century*

Christine Reinle, *Non-state Noble Violence ('feud') in Late Medieval England and Germany: A Comparison*

Euan Roger, *Grand Designs and Modest Means: The Poor Knights of Windsor in the Late Fifteenth Century*

Joerg Rogge, *Violence Against Kings and their Advisors in Fifteenth-Century Scotland*

Dean Rowland, *Better Not to Shoot the Messenger: Using Urban Archives to Reconstruct the Use of Proclamations by the Crown in Fifteenth-Century England*

Sheila Sweetinburgh, *Shepsters, Hucksters and Other Business Women: Economic Prospects in Fifteenth-Century Canterbury*

Sarah Thomas, *Becoming a Bishop in the Late Middle Ages*

Audrey Thorstad, *'Every mans ... home, being the theatre of his hospitality': Early Tudor Castles as the Nobleman's Stage*

Linda Clark

MICHAEL HICKS: AN APPRECIATION

Caroline Barron

This collection of essays, put together in honour of Michael Hicks, well reflects his geographical compass, since the contributions range from Yorkshire in the north to Southampton in the south, and from Wales in the west to Suffolk in the east. These essays also reflect Michael's focus on the fifteenth century and on the nobility: here we have Edward IV (who was but a nobleman with a crown), together with scions of the families of Berkeley, Neville and Stafford to represent their peers. Missing from this collection is any essay focussing on Richard III, who must surely have absorbed much of Michael's attention. But what is not reflected here, and indeed could not be, is Michael's extraordinary output.

One way of assessing Michael's contribution to historical studies might be to consider his entry in the *Bibliography of British and Irish History*. Here Michael is recorded as having published seventy-five books or articles between 1977 and 2013 – that is more than two a year – and many of these items are substantial pieces of work, not mere scraps thrown to keep our Research Excellence Framework masters at bay.[1] The *Bibliography*, however, goes beyond simply listing published works: it also provides an 'author profile' which is highly schematic but still of some interest. All the publications by a particular author are subjected to analysis in a variety of ways. A colourful pie chart demonstrates that 91% of Michael's publications related to English history, 4% related to Europe and the remaining 5% covered Britain, Wales, the Channel Islands and Scotland. Another pie chart categorises publications according to their 'discipline'. Here 32% of Michael's work is classed as 'political, administrative and legal' history, 21% as 'social history'; 'religious history' and 'events' (presumably specific battles etc.) secure 10% each, and 7% is assessed as 'economic history'. The remaining 20% of Michael's output was divided between military, medical and intellectual history, sources and historiography. Yet another pie chart reveals that 50% of his output has appeared in a remarkably wide range of scholarly journals, chief among them the *English Historical Review* and *Historical Research*. These statistics and pie charts are, of course, very blunt instruments to use in assessing Michael's outstanding contribution to the study of medieval history in England in the last forty years. But the final pie chart, entitled 'Persons Covered', does reveal

---

[1] It should be noted, however, that although the *Bibliography* is a magnificent piece of work it can make mistakes. Michael is credited with a publication listing the Manuscript Resources of the Friends' Libraries published in Philadelphia in 1960. At that time Michael would have been twelve years old and, prodigy as he is, he is unlikely to have been surveying manuscripts in libraries, let alone American libraries, before he entered his teens.

clearly the most striking characteristic of Michael's work: his focus on biography. Here the pie chart turns into a spinning pinwheel of colours: thirty different people or families have attracted Michael's historical analysis and these are only the books or articles which focus on particular people, or have a person's name in the title. Not surprisingly Richard III and Edward IV head the chart. In addition to these 'persons' recorded in the 'author profile', in 1991 Michael produced *Who's Who in Late Medieval England, 1272–1485*, which provided very many succinct biographies of famous people of the period, and he also contributed thirty-three biographies to the *Oxford Dictionary of National Biography*: biographies which ranged from fifteenth-century queens and nobles to sixteenth-century scholars such as Sir Anthony Ashley (translator of the *Mariners Mirrour*) and John Speed, an eighteenth-century physician and antiquary who lived in Southampton.

Michael himself acknowledged in the Introduction which he wrote for the volume of his collected essays, published in 1990 as *Richard III and his Rivals: Magnates and their Motives in the Wars of the Roses*, that he had a 'natural biographical bent'. In this analysis of his work up to that date (where he incidentally laments his lack of time for his own research, yet had been able to produce twenty-three books or articles in thirteen years...), he traces his evolution from his hard-nosed assessment of magnate motivation (self-interest, self-aggrandisement and financial gain), inspired by the methodology and outlook of K.B. McFarlane, to a more nuanced interpretation of magnate motives and priorities. It was the study of the wills and chantry foundations of the Hungerford family which led him to accept that fifteenth-century nobles (especially the female ones, perhaps) did indeed have personalities, preferences and pious concerns. Reading the Hungerford chantry deeds provided him with an unexpected experience like that of St. Paul on the road to Damascus (not Michael's analogy!): he abandoned his earlier view of a cynical and self-seeking world and was drawn instead to consider the idealistic element in late medieval English politics.

Yet although Michael may, in the course of his researches, have largely abandoned McFarlane's cynical view of the motivation of the men and women of fifteenth-century England, he has always retained McFarlane's insistent focus on the archival underpinning necessary for a convincing study of the people of this period, and he has been assiduous in his search for new archival sources. This commitment to reading the archives and manuscript sources he will have imbibed from his tutor at Bristol, Charles Ross, from T.B. Pugh at Southampton where he completed his M.A., and from C.A.J. Armstrong at Oxford who supervised his doctorate. Moreover, his time working on the *Victoria County History* for Middlesex (1974–8) inevitably exposed Michael to yet further record sources. This focus on the archives, whether manorial documents or chantry certificates, has been extended to include the complex history of chronicles such as the Crowland chronicle and the somewhat unappealing family histories and genealogical rolls commissioned by English aristocratic families in the fifteenth century and later. Michael's interests and scholarship certainly embrace the antiquarian writers of the sixteenth century. Furthermore, in recent years he has turned his attention to the Inquisitions *Post Mortem*, a rich source of information about the households and landowing of those who held in chief of the king, and by promoting and encouraging collaboration between the University of Winchester and the department of Digital Humanities at King's College London he has overseen a major research project dedicated to the online publication of the inquisitions, entitled *Mapping the Medieval Countryside*.

This focus on Michael's prodigious output and range of scholarly interests has so far ignored his unselfish work in many aspects of the historical field. He has been reviews editor for the journal *Southern History* for many years; he has written numerous book reviews himself; and three of the fifteenth-century conferences have been organised by him – at King Alfred's College, Winchester, in 1987, Southampton in 1999, and again at Winchester, now a University, in 2012. He took on the task of editing the papers given at the first two of these conferences (published as *Profit, Piety and the Professions* and *Revolution and Consumption*), helping younger scholars to revise their articles in an appropriate form for publication. Through teaching successive generations of students he has encouraged them to develop into confident and able historians. His relentless published output might suggest that he cuts corners, or shirks distracting administrative tasks, but this can never be said of him. Michael is generous to the young scholars whom he teaches and to the old nobility whom he studies. It is in response to this generosity of spirit, and as an acknowledgement of Michael's great contribution to the study of fifteenth-century England, that this volume has been compiled by his colleagues, friends and students.

DISCIPLINARY ORDINANCES FOR ENGLISH GARRISONS IN NORMANDY IN THE REIGN OF HENRY V*

Anne Curry

It is well known that Henry V's conquest of Normandy (1417–20) marked a major shift in English war policy. There is no earlier parallel for the occupation of territory on this scale. Although thirty years later the venture failed in a manner which did much to trigger civil unrest in England, this should not cloud the achievement of conquering and holding Normandy in the first place. By all standards, Henry V was an effective military commander. He was also astute in his political dealings with conquered peoples, carefully navigating between conciliation and control. Key to this was the maintenance of discipline in his armies. The Burgundian chroniclers, Enguerran de Monstrelet, Jean de Waurin and Jean le Fèvre (who had experienced Henry's leadership at first hand when accompanying the English army from Harfleur to Agincourt in 1415), ascribed Henry's success in France to his firmness in dealing with his soldiers. The principal reason was that he punished with death without any mercy those who went to the contrary and infringed his commands or orders, and he fully maintained the discipline of chivalry as the Romans did of old.[1]

The earliest known set of disciplinary ordinances for an English army belongs to Richard II's campaign to Scotland in 1385 but there is enough to suggest that

---

* It was at the Fifteenth-Century Conference held at the University of Bristol in 1978 that I first presented my research, at that point quite embryonic, on military organisation in Lancastrian Normandy. I was delighted to have the resulting article ('The First English Standing Army? Military Organization in Lancastrian Normandy, 1422–1450', *Patronage, Pedigree and Power in Later Medieval England*, ed. C.D. Ross (Gloucester, 1979), 193–214) published in the next year in the same volume as one of Michael Hicks's most influential papers, 'The Changing Role of the Wydevilles in Yorkist Politics'. I am equally delighted to be able to contribute to this *Festschrift*, and to have the opportunity to thank Michael for his friendship and for all that he has contributed to fifteenth-century history.

[1] '*Et la principalle cause si estoit par ce que ceulz quy faisoient le contraire et emfraignoient ses commandemens ou ordonnances il faisoit pugnir tres criminelement sans quelque misericorde, et bien entretenoit la discipline de chevallerie comme jadis faisoient les Rommains*': *A Collection of the Chronicles and Ancient Histories of Great Britain now called England, by Jean de Waurin*, ed. W.H. and E.L.C.P. Hardy (3 vols., RS, 1864–91), ii. 391; *Recueil des croniques et anchiennes istories de la Grant Bretaigne a present nomme Engleterre, par Jean de Waurin*, ed. W.H. and E.L.C.P. Hardy (5 vols., RS, 1864–91), ii. 429; *Chronique de Jean Le Fèvre, Seigneur de Saint Remy*, ed. François Morand (2 vols., Société de l'Histoire de France, Paris, 1876–81), i. 67–8. Monstrelet gives a similar panegyric but the last phrase on '*la discipline de chevallerie*' is excluded: *La Chronique d'Enguerran de Monstrelet*, ed. L.C. Douet-D'Arcq (6 vols., Société de l'Histoire de France, Paris, 1857–62), iv. 116.

Edward III had issued some ordinances in 1346.[2] That Henry V issued ordinances for his expeditionary armies of 1415 and 1417 is not doubted although we cannot be sure which of the surviving texts belongs to which date. We also have ordinances issued by Henry at Mantes in either 1419 or 1421.[3] All of these texts were for expeditionary armies serving in the field. None includes clauses in anticipation of establishing garrisons. We must ask, therefore, whether these ordinances would be useful once garrisons were established in Normandy. Some of the clauses would be applicable whatever the context. These include the ban on soldiers from attacks on churches and from raping women as well as clauses relevant to any military situation, such as obedience to a superior officer and the prevention of disputes between soldiers. Overall, the ordinances for expeditionary armies were concerned with discipline *within* the host rather than with relations between soldiers and civilians. Central to their implementation were the captains as well as the constable and marshal of the army as a whole.

Henry's systematic conquest of Normandy began in August 1417. By early 1421, at least 4,000 soldiers were held in about fifty garrisons in Normandy and the *pays de conquête* (the lands outside Normandy taken by Henry). The establishment of garrisons created regular contact between soldiers and civilians. This article explores how the English began to introduce disciplinary controls for their garrison soldiers, reflecting the specific needs created by this form of military presence. It is based mainly on the evidence of the Norman rolls, the special series of chancery enrolments created for the conquest.[4] Two key texts from the rolls, dating to 19 September 1419 and 25 April 1421, are considered in detail and are given in full in an appendix.

On the very day of Henry's landing in 1417, his eldest brother, Thomas, duke of Clarence, was appointed as constable of the army with powers to control and punish all in the army 'according to the statutes and ordinances for the rule and governing of the people of our army, and following the laws and customs of our military court'.[5] In the early months of the conquest several entries in the Norman rolls refer to these ordinances. Take, for instance, the powers given to Sir John Neville on 27 December 1417 to take fortresses into his hands and to assign soldiers and captains in his company (*comitiva*) to the guard and maintenance of watch in these places as seemed best. These included authority to punish all those in his company who were disobedient, either by imprisonment or otherwise, according to 'the form of the statutes and ordinances for the good peace, quiet rule

---

[2] M.H. Keen, 'Richard II's Ordinances of War of 1385', in *Rulers and Ruled in Late Medieval England. Essays Presented to Gerald Harriss*, ed. R.E. Archer and Simon Walker (London and Rio Grande, 1995), 33–48; Anne Curry, 'Disciplinary Ordinances for English and Franco-Scottish Armies in 1385: An International Code?', *Journal of Medieval History*, xxxvii (2011), 269–94; Rory Cox, 'A Law of War? English Protection and Destruction of Ecclesiastical Property during the Fourteenth Century', *EHR*, cxxviii (2013), 1381–1417.

[3] Anne Curry, 'The Military Ordinances of Henry V: Texts and Contexts', in *War, Government and Aristocracy in the British Isles c.1150–1500*, ed. Chris Given-Wilson, Ann Kettle and Len Scales (Woodbridge, 2008), 214–49.

[4] *Rotuli Normanniae in Turri Londoniensi Asservati Johanne et Henrico Quinto Angliae Regibus*, ed. T.D. Hardy (1835); *Annual Report of the Deputy Keeper of the Public Records*, xli (1880) and xlii (1881) [hereafter *DKR*].

[5] *Rotuli Normanniae*, ed. Hardy, 316–17.

and governance of the people of our army on this present campaign'.[6] Further references to the ordinances are found throughout 1418. In December 1418, for instance, Irishmen in the retinue of the prior of Kilmainham, deployed as scavengers in the hinterland of Rouen during the siege of the city, were ordered to conform to the regulations for the government of the army.[7]

The first formal appointment of a captain recorded in the Norman rolls is that of Richard, Lord Grey of Codnor, on 13 October 1417 for the castle of Argentan.[8] Grey was given authority to accept into allegiance any local men who wished to become the king's liegemen and to issue 'billets' under his seal. In subsequent appointments, captains and other officers were given authority to issue safe conducts to prisoners captured by members of their company (*societas*).[9] This demonstrates the embryonic development of the powers of garrison captains, but the appointments did not include any clauses on military discipline. This was because the ordinances issued at the landing in Normandy continued to apply. The desire of the king to encourage Normans to accept his rule is evident in a number of duchy-wide orders once the conquest became established. On 16 April 1418 captains were ordered not to take prisoner anyone coming to the king to swear fealty. This involved a proclamation that no Englishman should do harm to a Norman subject.[10] Even more significant was the order of 8 December 1418. This instructed each *vicomte* to proclaim that all who had suffered injury from English soldiers in garrison should appear before him to gain redress.[11]

This gives clear indication of the direction of travel which was eventually, thanks to a full set of ordinances issued by the duke of Bedford in December 1423, to bring soldiers within the administrative and judicial systems of the duchy.[12] A crucial stage was marked by the surrender of Rouen in January 1419. This ended any effective resistance to Henry's conquest and triggered his concentrated campaign to win over the hearts and minds of the Normans as a whole. On the following 14 February Henry ordered proclamation that any Norman who wished to come to the king and swear fealty, no matter what their past offence, could do so without any fear of molestation.[13] This preceded public meetings of Norman knights and esquires held by the king at Rouen on 28 February and 7 March so that they could hear 'certain royal ordinances'.[14] Henry's plan at this point was to begin negotiations with the French in the hope of having the duchy of Normandy confirmed to him in full sovereignty. It was only when talks failed later in the

---

[6] *Ibid.*, 223. There had already been an order to Neville on 14 Nov. 1417 to proclaim that all captains in his company should keep watch as required: *ibid.*, 368–9.
[7] *DKR*, xli. 720. See also the powers given to the duke of Gloucester in May 1418 for the westward advance into the Cotentin: *ibid.*, 713.
[8] *Rotuli Normanniae*, ed. Hardy, 180.
[9] For an example for Rugles, 31 Oct. 1417, see *ibid.*, 193.
[10] *DKR*, xli. 708.
[11] *Ibid.*, 720.
[12] B.J.H. Rowe, 'Discipline in the Norman Garrisons under Bedford 1422–35', *EHR*, xlvi (1931), 201–6, from BL, Birch MS 4101, f. 65.
[13] *DKR*, xlii. 754.
[14] *Ibid.* (28 Feb.); BNF, manuscrit français 26042/5365.

summer, and the French factions threatened to unite against him, that he began his march towards Paris.

In the wake of the fall of Rouen, French-style local administration in Normandy had been fully restored in both financial and judicial spheres. Although Englishmen were appointed as *trésorier-général* and as *baillis*, the administration they conducted was French in form and process and they were supported by *vicomtes* and other officials who were local men.[15] More significantly, garrison captains were accountable to the *chambre des comptes* which was fully established at Caen by February 1419, instead of to the treasurer of war and English exchequer.[16] Rather than captains being appointed by orders enrolled on the Norman rolls, indentures for captaincies were now drawn up within the administration of the *chambre des comptes*. Such indentures were definitely in place by the spring of 1419. The first known mention dates to 26 June 1419 but refers back to late February.[17] From the end of August 1419, the *trésorier général*, William Allington, who had been appointed on 1 May, was ordered to have musters carried out each quarter of all the garrisons in Normandy.[18] By July 1419 there was also a seneschal of Normandy, Sir Hugh Luttrell, although since no formal appointment is extant, we are not certain about the nature of his powers. As Newhall commented, 'not before April 1420 are there signs that Luttrell was acting as military supervisor'.[19]

The sense of permanence generated by the surrender of Rouen prompted new controls on relations between soldiers and local populations in the spring of 1419. These began to bring the military increasingly under civilian judicial authority. A highly important order was issued on 10 April.[20] This was a mandate to all *baillis* to make proclamation forbidding any soldier in castles, towns and garrisons to take goods, horses and other animals or carts without paying for them promptly and with good money. This order concerned the native population as a whole; the expeditionary ordinances had only offered protection to merchants supplying the host. The level of attention and responsiveness to the interests of local inhabitants, as well as the establishment of a systematic and centrally accountable garrison structure, is revealed by orders issued in late August 1419. These laid down that garrison captains should not allow their troops to take up quarters in towns but should ensure their residence only in the castles and fortifications of the place.[21] On 10 October captains of castles and towns were ordered to allow only such

---

[15] A whole suite of appointments was made on 12 Feb. 1419: *DKR*, xli. 730.

[16] Anne Curry, 'L'administration financière de la Normandie anglaise: continuité ou changement', *La France des principautés. Les chambres des comptes xive et xve siècles* (Paris, 1996), 91. Although it was already in existence as a *scaccarium*, it was first called a *chambre des comptes* in Feb. 1419.

[17] *DKR*, xli. 754.

[18] *DKR*, xlii. 325. Unfortunately the earliest surviving actual indenture appears to be that of 9 Dec. 1421, for Sir John Popham as captain of the town and castle of Bayeux: Caen, Archives Départementales du Calvados F 1297. Allington's first account, from 30 Apr. 1419 to 30 Apr. 1420, is TNA, E101/187/14.

[19] R.A. Newhall, *The English Conquest of Normandy, 1416–1424. A Study in Fifteenth-Century Warfare* (Cambridge, Mass., 1924), 244–5. On 17 Apr. 1420, Luttrell was given powers to superintend the *baillis, vicomtes,* receivers and other officers subject to the king in France and Normandy: *DKR*, xlii. 372.

[20] *DKR*, xlii. 313.

[21] *Ibid.*, 325.

soldiers as were necessary for defence to stay within the place.[22] There was also a ban, which captains and *baillis* were to enforce, on soldiers and English merchants buying large quantities of wine since this was considered to be detrimental to the local population.[23]

It is in this context that evidence for a set of garrison disciplinary ordinances first occurs. This was issued to the lieutenant of Rouen on 6 September 1419.[24] It remains uncertain whether these ordinances were intended for all of the Norman garrisons. The first paragraph suggests that they were, since it refers to the king and council making ordinances 'for the good governance of our captains and officials in our castles, cities and towns within our duchy of Normandy'. Yet no other recipients are listed in the enrolment, in contrast with the long list given for the second set of ordinances of 25 April 1421. Furthermore, the first clause refers specifically to Rouen. By contrast, the second set of ordinances is written in a general manner without specific mention of any one place. Even if the September 1419 orders were restricted to Rouen, they indicate what was expected at this point. The power of the captain was paramount but he was also responsible to the duchy-level officials. He exercised authority over his men in military matters, especially over booty taken in official sorties and over disputes between soldiers in the garrison. He was also to maintain a prison, presumably only for defaulting soldiers, although the wording is not explicit. A reference earlier in the text to 'debates and riotes ... that passeth not trespasse' suggests that serious cases such as murder fell under the purview of the standard judicial process. The ordinances of September 1419 are best seen as transitional. They were still largely concerned with military matters within the community of soldiers rather than with external relations. Only one clause concerns the local population. While the captain held authority over all of the defences, including the town walls, gates and ditches, he was not to cause damage to or impose burdens on the population. *Ad hoc* orders continued to be issued concerning relations with civilians. On 7 September 1420, for instance, an order was issued across the duchy forbidding provisions to be taken for the use of the garrisons without leave of their owners.[25]

By the autumn of 1420 Henry V's ambitions stretched well beyond Normandy. He had sealed the treaty of Troyes on 21 May and married Princess Katherine on 4 June. On 1 December, now recognised as heir and regent of France, he made his formal entry into Paris alongside Charles VI. He was in Rouen from late December 1420 to mid-January 1421, before crossing to England for Katherine's coronation. Before he left Rouen he put in place arrangements for his absence. These took full account of the need to ensure the good conduct of garrison troops. On 18 January 1421 the duke of Clarence was appointed as royal lieutenant and military commander in Normandy while the king was not present. On the same day Richard

---

[22] *Ibid.*, 328.
[23] *Ibid.*, 325.
[24] *Ibid.*, 325. See Appendix 1. The identity of the lieutenant is uncertain. Robert, Lord Willoughby, was in office from late Oct. 1419 (*DKR*, xlii. 329). Thomas, duke of Exeter, was captain of Rouen from Apr. 1419 to May 1422 (BNF, manuscrit français 26043/5099; *DKR*, xlii. 449).
[25] *DKR*, xlii. 390.

Wydeville was appointed seneschal of Normandy and the *pays de conquête*.[26] The terms of appointment gave Wydeville authority to oversee all captains and lieutenants of fortified towns and cities, castles and fortresses, and their victuals and equipment (including canon), and to distribute troops between garrisons. He had power to order and to take musters, to check that the numbers in indentures were being maintained, and to report on this to the *trésorier-général*. Wydeville was also to enquire into the activities (*factis et gestis*) of the captains, their lieutenants and their soldiers, how they behaved and whether they were notorious for bad behaviour, 'which we do not want to be the case (*quod nollemus*)'. He was to report on the best way of effecting improvement unless the case needed further attention by the royal council or justices. In this respect, he was not to deal personally with the correction of all defaults by soldiers. The implication is that where appropriate, these would be dealt with by standard judicial process in the duchy. Wydeville's power extended, however, to enquiring into the conduct of *baillis*, *vicomtes* and other officials, and ensuring there was no concealment of royal rights and profits.

This was a significant stage in the transition to a fully-fledged garrison-based disciplinary system, although building on the appointments of the *trésorier-général* and seneschal in 1419 as well as on the responsibility of garrison captains for the conduct of their men. The choice of Wydeville to act in the king's absence is significant. He was close to the king but he was also a professional soldier with experience in Wales, Calais and Normandy. Like Allington, who also had ample experience through service at Brest and in Gascony and Ireland, he was an esquire and representative of a distinctive class of military administrators.

Henry V's interest in garrison discipline on the eve of his departure for England was also linked to his first convoking of the Norman Estates and the first grant of local taxation. The Estates at Rouen had consented on 18 January 1421 to the levy of a *taille* of 400,000 *livres tournois* which was to be used for the maintenance of the garrisons and other troops in the duchy.[27] Once local people were paying for their own defence, their views (and complaints) on soldierly excesses had to be listened to. Meetings of the Estates offered the ideal opportunity for their voice to be heard. We do not know what views were advanced in January 1421. It is unlikely to be a coincidence that on 24 January, shortly after Henry left the Norman capital, the *baillis* were ordered to make proclamation forbidding soldiers from making any exactions whatsoever on the people, adding that a fair price should be paid for goods and that merchants should be left in tranquility.[28] More significantly, it was during Henry's absence that a fuller set of instructions for garrison captains was drawn up and distributed. These were issued on 25 April 1421, just over a month after the duke of Clarence's defeat and death at the battle of Baugé. There were clearly fears that this setback would encourage challenges to English authority. Every effort had therefore to be made to remove reasons for

---

[26] *Ibid.*, 398, printed in 'Rôles normands et français et autres pièces tirées des archives de Londres par Bréquigny, en 1764, 1765 et 1766', *Mémoires de la Société des Antiquaires de Normandie*, 3e série, xxiii (1858), no. 924. Newhall, *English Conquest*, 246, gives the incorrect date of 8 Jan.

[27] Newhall, *English Conquest*, 174; idem, 'The War Finances of Henry V and the Duke of Bedford', *EHR*, xxxvi (1921), 191.

[28] *DKR*, xlii. 409; *Foedera, Conventiones, Litterae et Cuiuscunque Generis Acta Publica*, ed. Thomas Rymer (20 vols., 1704–35), x. 56–8.

conflict between civilians and soldiers. The ordinances were issued at Rouen in the name of the king 'by the relation of the Great Council'. At this point, Thomas Montagu, earl of Salisbury, was in command in Normandy following the death of Clarence. His own interest in military discipline is revealed first by his request to Nicholas Upton to translate one of the texts of Henry V's ordinances, and secondly by ordinances he himself issued for his campaign into Maine in 1425.[29]

The ordinances of April 1421 are longer than those of September 1419. Although they are presented in the Norman rolls in Latin it must be assumed that they were communicated more widely in the vernacular. The penultimate clause gives details of a 'communication strategy' so that neither soldiers nor captains could plead ignorance. Proclamation by the *baillis* would also imply dissemination to the native population. The opening section reveals that local complaint was an influence in the drawing up of these ordinances. Some of the clauses, such as those on the watch and determination of disputes reiterate those of September 1419. What is important, however, is the addition of specific clauses on the prevention of soldiers taking goods and making impositions on civilians. In other words, previously *ad hoc* orders were being integrated into a set of ordinances for garrison discipline. Even more striking is the lengthy section against the keeping of concubines. The bad behaviour of the soldiers is ascribed to the cost of maintaining their illicit relationships with women.

Both this and the lengthy opening section are expressed in a distinctive wording which contrasts with the succinct and direct presentation of the ordinances of September 1419. The text of April 1421 emphasises that bad behaviour by captains and soldiers has not simply undermined royal authority and disturbed the local population but has also offended God. The same notion is also explicit in the section on the maintenance of illicit and adulterous relations. Although expressed in extended form here, this tone is not unprecedented in the Norman rolls. On 14 February 1418 the king had ordered the investigation of an alleged rape by soldiers in the company of Henry Styng. Their offence was against the 'statutes and ordinances for the rule and government of the army' (thereby giving another example of mention of the expeditionary ordinances where attacks on women were banned), but was also to the displeasure of God.[30]

Intriguingly, the only set of ordinances linked to Henry V which banned prostitutes from the camp were those included by Nicholas Upton in his *De Studio Militari*.[31] The ordinances which the earl of Salisbury issued for his expedition into Maine in 1425 also included a clause banning men from keeping common women within their lodgings. The penalty for the soldier in the earl's ordinances was the loss of a month's wages, which is similar, although not identical, to the punishment in the April 1421 ordinances for the keeping of concubines. It is possible, therefore, that the ordinances of April 1421 reflect the particular views of the earl of

---

[29] Curry, 'Military Ordinances of Henry V', 223–4. For Salisbury's ordinances for the conquest of Maine, see BL, Lansdowne MS 285, ff. 148–9.
[30] *Rotuli Normanniae*, ed. Hardy, 366.
[31] *The Essential Portions of Nicholas Upton's* De Studio Militari *before 1446*, ed. F.P. Barnard (Oxford, 1931), 33–48, clause 14.

Salisbury. Nicholas Upton may have had a role in their composition. This is also suggested by the similarity in tone and wording between the opening section of the 1421 ordinances and the *incipit* of Henry V's ordinances which Upton provided in his *De Studio Militari*.[32]

The successful implementation of the garrison ordinances relied on the captain and also on ensuring that all men were under his authority. Other orders were issued to facilitate this, such as that of 22 May 1421 which forbade men to leave their captains. This order was reiterated in October with clearer punishments for those who did not abide by it.[33] At base, this was the same principle that underlay the disciplinary ordinances for the expeditionary armies where captains were obliged to keep their men under control and soldiers to obey their captains. As we can see from the ordinances of September 1419 and April 1421, this core notion had been redefined within the context of an occupation of territory. Uncertainty in Normandy in the months between the deaths of Henry V and Charles VI in the autumn of 1422 necessitated *ad hoc* edicts by the duke of Bedford.[34] These included an order that all wandering soldiers should return to their captain and that those without a master should find one. By the time Henry VI became king of the double monarchy, there had already been moves towards effecting garrison discipline within the duchy of Normandy. The final stage was soon to follow. Within four months of becoming regent of France for Henry VI, Bedford, at local prompting, commissioned an enquiry into abuses committed by English soldiers, leading to a much longer and fuller set of ordinances published at the Estates at Caen on 10 December 1423.[35] These placed limitations on the authority of captains in order to ensure the interests of the civilian population were protected. This marked a new phase in garrison discipline which was to continue until Normandy was lost in 1449–50.

---

[32] Given in the original Latin and in a modern English translation in Curry, 'The Military Ordinances of Henry V', 239–40.
[33] 'Rôles normands et français et autres pièces tirées des archives de Londres par Bréquigny', nos. 995, 1039.
[34] BNF, manuscrit français 26044/5771, 5774, 5777, 5782; Newhall, *English Conquest*, 232.
[35] Rowe, 'Discipline in the Norman Garrisons', 194–208. Complaints at the Estates of 1427 about the obligations of the population to perform *guet et garde* led to an enquiry and further ordinances published at Rouen on 7 Sept. 1428; R.A. Newhall, 'Bedford's Ordinance on the Watch of September 1428', *EHR*, l (1935), 50–4, transcribed from Archives Nationales de France, KK 325 B.

APPENDIX

1. Ordinances of 6 September 1419

Enrolled: Norman rolls, 7 Henry V, part 1: TNA, C64/11, m. 24d; printed: 'Rôles normands et français et autres pièces tirées des archives de Londres par Bréquigny', no. 653; calendared: *DKR*, xlii. 325. The first paragraph is translated from Latin, the remainder left in its original Middle English.

The king to the lieutenant of the castle and city of Rouen, greeting. Certain ordinances have been made by us and our council for the good governance of our captains and officials in our castles, cities and towns within our duchy of Normandy. We send these enclosed in these current letters, ordering that you examine these ordinances and their content, and that you work to implement them to the best of your ability according to their tenor and not otherwise, and that you do not fail to do this in any way. Witnessed by the king at the castle of Rouen on 6 September.

First for the safewarde of the castel and the citee of Rouen, al maner of men being wythe ynne the castle ben obeisant to the captaine yn tyme of need.

Item that the serche of the wache and warde be governed al onlych be the capitaine and such officers as hym liketh to depute or ordeyne therto.

Item the said capitaine have governaunce and determinacion betwne soldeours and soldeours or other men goyng undirneth hym or be his auctorite oute of his garnison of alle debates for goodes that ben wonne in were in eny journey.

Item that the said capitaine and his officers have arrest and punicion of al debates and riotes made between his owne soldeours of his garnison that passeth noght trespass.

Item that the said capitaine and his officers have cognicion and determinacion of al maner covenantz and bargaynes betwixt his owen soldeours of his garnison that longeth to the were

Item that the said capitaine and his officers have al maner reule and governaunce as welle by day as be nyght of the walles, yates, issues and the dyches of the castle and cite wythe oute that thay putte eny grevaunce or imposicion to the people

Item that the said capitaine have a prison to punyssh al meffaisons of whom he hath knowlache of

Item that the said capitaine and his lieutenant withe the kynges men that thei have in governell be attendant and obeisant to the Kynges lieutenant of Normandy and to his officers and also that thei enforce the chaunceler, the tresorer and the bailly and other officers in whos bailiage thei beth ynne in execucion of ther office upon the payne of the kings indignacion

2. Ordinances of 25 April 1421

Enrolled: Norman rolls 9 Henry V: TNA, C64/16, m. 33d; printed: *Foedera*, ed. Rymer, x. 106–8; calendared: *DKR*, xlii, 428. Translated from Latin.

The king to the captain of Rouen or his lieutenant, greeting. Because several captains of our towns, castles and fortifications in the duchy of Normandy and other places of our conquest, and their lieutenants and officers have claimed and taken upon themselves in many cases, rashly and unduly, power, authority and jurisdiction which we have by no means given to them or allowed them, and have committed depredations and despoiled our liege subjects of goods and chattels, and burdened them with exactions, impositions, subsidies and *appatis*, both in cash and in victuals, and by other multifarious means, and have perpetrated and committed with impunity grave and enormous offences, crimes and excesses, and have allowed their soldiers, paid men and servants (whom they are obliged to rule and govern) to commit, to the great offence of the Divine Majesty, and our own Majesty, and to the obvious prejudice and contempt of our laws, and to the weakening and destruction of our subjects in the duchy and areas aforesaid, unless we provide a swift and appropriate remedy, as is evident from the frequent suits of our said subjects on these matters and from the evidence of the fact itself,

We therefore (as the taking on of the office of ruling obliges and compels us) wishing to avoid the aforementioned, and that justice, the mother of virtues, by which kings rule and kingdoms thrive and prosper, by which we are taught and instructed to live honourably, not to harm any other person and to do him justice, and to reign and preside everywhere in lands and places subject to us, notify you article by article by these present letters what authority and jurisdiction should belong to you by reason of your said captaincy,

And together with this, we have added certain articles which we wish and order to be observed, under penalties appropriate by law in this matter, and by other penalties specially instituted by us, and if in any of these articles a penalty is not defined, under pain of imprisonment and other greater penalty to be imposed by our own will.

First, for the safekeeping of the aforesaid places which have been placed by us in your custody, we will and decree that each and every soldier and paid man of the place, as well as others who are obliged to dwell and see to the safe and sure keeping of the place, however it relates to them, and to each of them, should obey you and be attendant to you, in every matter concerning the safe keeping and the safe and secure keeping of the place

And that to you or your officials and deputies should pertain and belong the rule and governance, by day as well as by night, of the walls, gates, entrances, ditches and look-outs of the place; and concerning the same, we order and command that you maintain watch and see to this providently, diligently and appropriately, both by day and night

And that you castigate, punish and coerce, according to the need and requirement of the case or offence, the soldiers, paid men and others who transgress, who are delinquent or who offend in any way in these matters or concerning them, although you must refrain completely from making any undue oppressions, extortions and exactions when claiming neglect of night watch or under any invented excuse.

Item, we will that you have governance and determination, and decision of every contention, litigation, or cause moved or to be moved between the soldiers of your garrison by reason of butin or gain arising out of the act of war, and that the soldiers of the garrison and others, by reason of such gain, have and obtain in their *chevauchées* or in any form of expedition or exercise of war done under you

Item, we will that you, and each and every soldier, paid man, official or minister of yours, be in all matters humbly obedient, intendant and assisting to our lieutenant of Normandy and to the chancellor, treasurer, seneschal, *baillis*, and other of our officers carrying out their office, and to assist them, and to carry out the task with armed force, when you are suitably required by them.

Item, we order and command that you do not do, nor allow to be done by your soldiers, paid men, servants and ministers, any exactions, *appatis*, prises of animals, grains or any other kinds of goods or impositions under whatever excuse, on any of our towns, parishes or subjects whatsoever, as you might wish to be accountable for this toward us and our subjects.

Item, because many soldiers of our garrisons and their servants and ministers, neither fearing God nor having respect for man, hold, as we be informed, women in concubinage and (what is worse) in adulterous and other illicit relationships, and since they do not have the wherewithal by which they can sustain their sensual and hedonistic lifestyle (which demands and requires great and inordinate costs), they plunder, steal, take away, demand and extort the goods of our lieges and subjects, thereby provoking the wrath of the divine majesty against themselves and others, and to the great danger, prejudice and harm of us and all our commonweal, and of our subjects,

We order and command that you permit no soldier or paid man of whatever rank or condition or their servants and ministers to have or hold any woman in any kind of concubinage or in any other kind of prohibited or illicit relationship and that, if you find anyone acting to the contrary, you cause him, all favour put aside, to be put in prison for at least a month or longer as the extent of the default demands and requires, during which month or period he is to lack wages and pay, nor should he be allowed to leave such incarceration until he can find reasonable security, under a certain penalty, by you determined in that respect, that he will behave and conduct himself well and honourably in the future.

Item, to the end that neither you nor any of your soldiers or paid men, in the future, may claim ignorance in these matters, we send to you particular articles enclosed with the present letters, which, according to their tenor and form, we wish to be observed, and which we will have published and proclaimed elsewhere by our *baillis*, and ordering and commanding you, under pain of our indignation, that you see to the observance of these matters faithfully and diligently, and that in no manner you usurp, or presume to exercise in any way, the ordinary jurisdiction which belongs to, or relates to, our *baillis* and other justices.

Given at our castle of Rouen 25 April 1421. By the king at the relation of the Great Council.

Similar letters were directed to the following:

The captain of Pontoise or his lieutenant, the captain of Gisors etc, the captains of Meulan, Mantes, Vernon, Pont-de-l'Arche, Louviers, Gournay, Neufchâtel and Torcy, Aumale, Etrépagny, Eu, Harfleur, Caudebec, Château Gaillard, Gaillon and Goulettes, Honfleur, Touques, Bernay, Caen, Bayeux, Carentan, Cherbourg, Avranches, Coutances, St Lô, Falaise, Vire, Valognes, Régneville, Domfront, Évreux, Conches, Verneuil, Dieppe and Poissy.

LORDS IN A LANDSCAPE: THE BERKELEY FAMILY AND NORTHFIELD (WORCESTERSHIRE)*

Christopher Dyer

Under the title 'The Lord and the Landscape' an article published a half century ago expressed the then current view that aristocratic families had a decisive effect on the landscape and society of their estates.[1] This study examines the extent to which the assumption is justified. The 1962 article investigated Wormleighton, a parish in the Feldon in south-east Warwickshire, which contained a single large nucleated village with extensive open fields for growing corn. Around 1500 the villagers were expelled, and the enclosed fields were exploited as a sheep pasture by the Spencer family, who marked their arrival by building a large brick mansion. A contrasting type of landscape is examined here, in the woodlands of north Worcestershire, where in the parish of Northfield the castle of Weoley had been founded in the twelfth century (Map 1). Here the houses of the inhabitants were scattered, and they held land in small enclosures (often called crofts) together with strips in a number of relatively small open fields. They practised mixed farming, having access to much meadow, pasture and wood as well as arable. A succession of lords, many of them assertive and powerful aristocrats of baronial rank, drew their revenues from Northfield, including William fitz Ansculf after the Norman Conquest, followed by the Paynels in the twelfth century, the Somerys in the thirteenth, and the Botetourts for much of the fourteenth.[2]

Northfield and Weoley were acquired in the early fifteenth century by the Berkeleys of Uley in Gloucestershire: Sir Maurice Berkeley III (1401–64) and his son Sir

---

* This essay began life in a lecture to the Northfield Society, and I am grateful for their invitation; at a more advanced stage it was presented to the Birmingham and Warwickshire Archaeological Society, and I acquired some useful comments and information. The staff of the Birmingham Reference Library first helped me, and later their successors in the Birmingham Archives and Heritage. The Badminton Estate Muniments are used by kind permission of His Grace the duke of Beaufort. The staff of the Gloucestershire Archives made arrangements to view them. Jane Harris and David Rymill advised on the use of the Jervoise documents at Hampshire RO. Mike Hodder supplied the records from the Historic Environment Record and Stephanie Ratkai told me about the Weoley Castle archaeological archive in the Archaeology Data Service. Helpful advice came from George Demidowicz, Peter King and Maureen Surman. Steve Linnane provided his plan of Weoley Castle. Linda Clark helped in a general way as editor of this volume, but also provided detailed information from the unpublished volumes of the *History of Parliament: The Commons 1422–61* (forthcoming). The maps were drawn by Andy Isham. Kirsty Nichol made me very welcome at Weoley Castle. The subject was chosen to please Michael Hicks, who is devoted to the study of fifteenth-century aristocrats and to mapping the medieval countryside.

[1] Harry Thorpe, 'The Lord and the Landscape, Illustrated through the Changing Fortunes of a Warwickshire Parish, Wormleighton', *Transactions of the Birmingham Archaeological Society*, lxxx (1962), 38–77.

[2] *VCH Worcestershire*, iii. 194–201; Adrian Oswald, 'Interim Report on Excavations at Weoley Castle, 1955–60', *Transactions of the Birmingham Archaeological Society*, lxxviii (1962), 61–85.

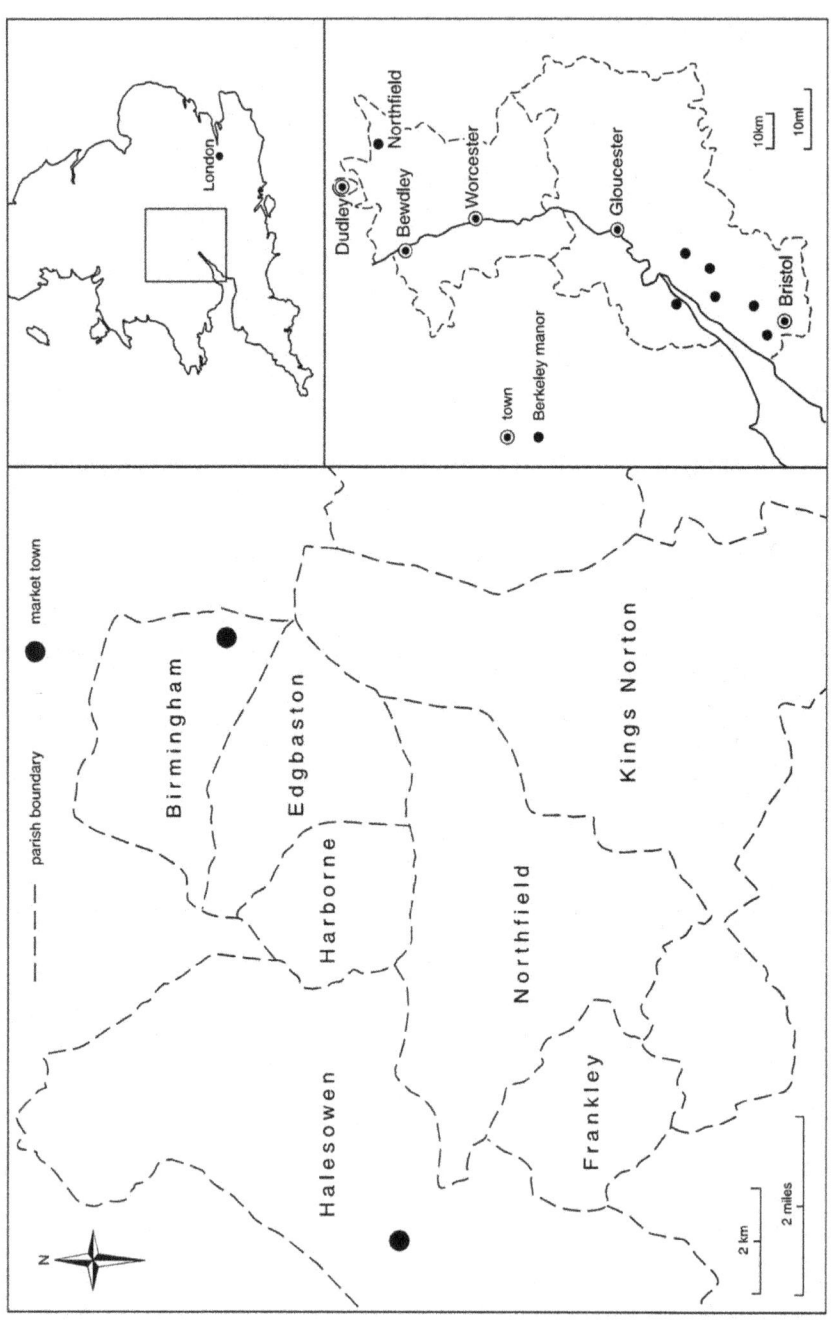

Map 1. Location of Northfield, also showing Berkeley manors in Gloucestershire, relevant towns and the river Severn.

William Berkeley (1436–1501). These wealthy knights derived most of their landed income of £250–£300 p.a. from the south Gloucestershire manors of Aylburton, Bradley, Kings Weston, Rockhampton, Stoke Gifford and Uley (Map 1). In addition they held manors in Somerset and Wiltshire.[3] Their ancestor in the fourteenth century, Sir Maurice I, had been an active soldier on Edward III's campaigns, a truly strenuous knight.[4] Did these lords direct, control, mould or influence the landscape and society of their estates?

Northfield, a large parish containing 6,000 acres (Map 1), lies on the Birmingham plateau, mostly between 500 and 650 ft above sea level. The ground slopes gently from west to east, and the topography consists of a series of stream valleys, including those of the Bourn Brook on its northern boundary and the River Rea to the south and east. There are low hills between the streams. Light soils can be found in the valleys, but there is much marl and clay.[5] The heavy soil combined with high rainfall tended to suit pastoral farming, and oats, which can cope with adverse environments, were grown in quantity in the Middle Ages.

The landscape and settlements of the parish have to be studied with the aid of nineteenth-century maps, as the whole area has been taken over by Birmingham's growth, and little survives of its rural past. Field evidence is confined to urban parks, together with finds reported from gardens and construction sites. The most striking survival from the Middle Ages, the remains of Weoley Castle, have been partly excavated and preserved as a public amenity. Selly 'manor house', which incorporates a fifteenth-century timber frame, is also on public display, but not on its original site. Fabric of the twelfth to fifteenth centuries is visible in the parish church. The written documents of the fifteenth century are kept in six different archives, and include deeds, a household account, receivers' accounts and manorial records. The duke of Beaufort's muniments, once kept at Badminton, have recently become accessible. Many documents stayed with the Jervoise family who purchased the manor in the sixteenth century, although part of their archive was deposited in chancery during a lawsuit and are now in The National Archives.[6] Richard Jervoise in the sixteenth century compiled a remarkable book of evidences, which contains copies of documents now lost.[7]

The Berkeleys could claim Northfield and Weoley because one of the Botetourt heiresses, Katherine, married the first Maurice. In the early fifteenth century they faced opposition from a redoubtable rival in the form of Joan Beauchamp, Lady Abergavenny.[8] Sir Maurice Berkeley III, who came into his inheritance of the Gloucestershire manors in 1423, can be shown to have been receiving revenues from

---

[3] Gloucestershire Archives [hereafter GA], Badminton Estate Muniments, D2700, MJ 1/4.
[4] Nigel Saul, *Knights and Esquires: the Gloucestershire Gentry in the Fourteenth Century* (Oxford, 1981), 76–7, 276, 281.
[5] J.M. Ragg *et al.*, *Soils and Their Use in Midland and Western England* (Soil Survey of England and Wales, Bulletin xii, Harpenden, 1984), 21, 23, 116–18, 168–71, 212–16, 344–8; *Legend of the Soil Map of England and Wales* (Soil Survey, 1983), 7, 9, 12, 13, 16.
[6] Birmingham Archives and Heritage [hereafter BAH]; BL, Additional Charters; GA, Badminton Estate Muniments; Hampshire RO [hereafter HRO], Jervoise of Herriard Collection; TNA, Master Blunt's Exhibits; Society of Antiquaries of London, Prattinton Collection.
[7] HRO, COPY/899/1 is a digital copy: the book is still in private hands.
[8] Christine Carpenter, *Locality and Polity: A Study of Warwickshire Landed Society, 1401–1499* (Cambridge, 1992), 373.

Northfield in the early 1430s, but only a part, and when he visited in 1432 he stayed in the rectory because the castle was occupied by Joan or her officials.[9] At that time she was collecting some of the rents and controlled at least part of the demesne. In 1437, after an arbitration by Richard Beauchamp, earl of Warwick, Sir Maurice was able to take over the whole manor, and after that the Berkeley household commonly spent time in Weoley Castle, and received all of the manorial revenues. In the accounting year 1441–2 the household was in continuous residence. When William inherited he also spent much time at Weoley, in 1467–8 for example.[10]

We might expect that a family rooted in Gloucestershire and enjoying wealth from its land there would have treated its remote Worcestershire manor as an appendage, installed a bailiff, and collected rents. Instead, they were persistent visitors to Weoley Castle, and although when Sir Maurice was mentioned in official records he was often called 'of Uley', he also appears in 1451, 1455 and 1462 as Sir Maurice Berkeley 'of Weoley'.[11] Both he and his eldest son acted as justices of the peace in Worcestershire, and William served as sheriff and MP for the county.[12] They were embroiled in the political life of the west Midlands: Sir Maurice became a retainer of the duke of Buckingham in the 1450s, and later moved in circles close to Richard Neville, earl of Warwick. William joined Neville's retinue, and in the 1470s attached himself to Edward IV's great Midland supporter, William, Lord Hastings.[13] He lost Northfield in 1485 because he fought for Richard III at Bosworth.

The Berkeleys lived at Weoley and participated in west Midland politics because of the dispute which put their tenure of Northfield and Weoley in considerable doubt. After the death of Joan Beauchamp in 1435 her grandson and heir, Sir James Butler, son of the earl of Ormond and himself later earl of Wiltshire, pressed his claims. The earlier settlement which had given Berkeley control of Northfield and Weoley in 1437 depended on the authority of Richard Beauchamp, earl of Warwick, but he died in 1439. In 1453–4 a new agreement confirmed the Berkeley control of Northfield and Weoley, but gave other Botetourt manors in the vicinity such as Bordesley and Haybarn to the earl of Wiltshire.[14] The Berkeley household's presence at Weoley asserted their claim to the manor, and deterred any hostile moves from the earl and his allies.

Northfield and Weoley (together with smaller outliers at Cradley and Oldswinford) brought in an annual income that varied between £52 and £68, more than any individual Berkeley manor in Gloucestershire and adjacent counties. The addition of the Worcestershire lands pushed the estate's income above £300 in most years.[15] Another attraction must have been Weoley Castle, a large and prestigious residence set apart from other settlements in an impressive park in tune with a current fashion

---

[9] GA, D2700 MJ1/4; TNA, C103/39.
[10] GA, D2700 MJ1/4; MJ1/5; MJ1/8; MJ17/1; TNA, C103/39.
[11] *CPR*, 1446–52, p. 534; 1452–61, p. 231; GA, D2700 MJ1/4.
[12] *The History of Parliament: The House of Commons, 1386–1421*, ed. J.S. Roskell, Linda Clark and Carole Rawcliffe (4 vols., Stroud, 1992), ii. 202; *History of Parliament: Biographies of the Members of the Commons House 1439–1509*, ed. J.C. Wedgwood with A.D. Holt (1936), 69.
[13] Carpenter, *Locality and Polity*, 459–60, 488, 492, 524–5 (Buckingham had land and influence both in south Gloucestershire and the west Midlands, exercised from his castles of Thornbury and Maxstoke).
[14] *Ibid.*, 388–9, 410, 471–2. An indenture of 1450 records an attempt to settle the dispute: TNA, C103/39.
[15] GA, D2700 MJ1/4.

(Maps 2 and 3).[16] A family of knights were gaining an income and adopting a style of life appropriate for barons.

In order to define the relationship between lords and the landscape, the ways in which the Berkeleys used and influenced Northfield and Weoley will be explored by expanding outwards from the castle to its park, and then to include the surrounding countryside. The first way in which a lord could have an impact on the topography of a manor was to choose and develop his place of residence. The lord lived at Weoley Castle, and we know something of what that meant from an account kept by William Henmershe, keeper of the household, when the household stayed at Weoley in 1441–2.[17] The lord (Sir Maurice) and his wife Eleanor made occasional journeys from the castle. The lord visited London at a total cost of £5 to deal with 'business' (*negociis*), which probably refers to a case in the king's courts at Westminster connected with the dispute with Butler. The lord and lady also travelled to Lichfield, for unknown reasons, and the lady went on a pilgrimage but not very far, as the cost came to just 18½d.

The household that remained most of the year in the castle consisted of about sixteen people, that is family members and the occasional visitor, supported by about ten servants.[18] Henmershe's account itemises expenditure under fifteen headings, of which the most important relate to the pantry (bread), buttery (ale), cellar (wine) and kitchen (mainly meat and fish). The first three of these cost about £15 each, and the kitchen £32 11s. 2d. Spending on clothing, consisting of the liveries of servants, and the wardrobe and the clothes of the lord and lady, came to almost £11, and lesser items were the chandlery (candles) and marshalsea (fodder and equipment for horses and vehicles). With other minor items and £10 on administration and legal costs, the household required an outlay of almost £134, near to half of the Berkeleys' landed income. Some costs do not appear, as most of the lord's personal spending would have come out of his privy purse. Venison from the park would not normally appear on a cash account, though hunting dogs are mentioned because they had to be fed. The scale of expenditure can be paralleled in other households. Unlike ordinary knights and esquires with incomes below £50, the Berkeleys drank wine regularly, and only members of a wealthy elite could have spent 50s. 10d. on lining two gowns (for lord and lady) with beaver fur.[19]

The lord's presence could have generated demand for foodstuffs, fodder and firewood for the local producers, but in 1441–2 at Weoley this was not the case. About twenty-five quarters of grain, out of a total of 130 quarters, came from the manor of Weoley and Northfield, and two cattle were provided by the manorial reeve as a small part of the meat consumption of twenty-six beef carcasses, twenty-five sheep and twenty pigs. The pigs and a bull travelled from the Berkeley manor of Stoke

---

[16] E.g. Briony McDonagh, '"Powerhouses" of the Wolds Landscape: Manor Houses and Churches in Late Medieval and Early Modern England', in *Medieval Landscapes*, ed. Mark Gardiner and Steve Rippon (Macclesfield, 2007), 185–200.

[17] GA, D2700 MJ1/8.

[18] The calculation of household size is based on the total paid for servants' wages, and daily ale consumption, making comparisons with other households of known size: Christopher Dyer, *Standards of Living in the Later Middle Ages: Social Change in England c.1200–1520* (revised edn., Cambridge, 1998), 64, 70.

[19] *Ibid.*, 62.

Gifford near Bristol: perhaps they walked the seventy miles, or were carried part of the way by boat up the Severn. Most of the Weoley and Northfield demesne land had been leased out to tenants, so the lord's officials could not grow crops for the household. Later, by 1467–8 under William Berkeley, the demesne had been taken back by the lord, and the lord's animals were also being grazed on former ploughed land abandoned by tenants.[20]

To return to the household in 1441–2, most of the food would have been purchased, in view of evidence from other household accounts of the period from non-local producers, either by direct negotiation at the farm gate, or from markets.[21] The malted barley and drage (a barley and oats mixture) from which the household's ale was brewed is likely to have been bought in towns. When the Berkeleys were living at Stoke Gifford their malt came from the nearby small towns of Thornbury and Marshfield, equivalent to Birmingham and Halesowen in the vicinity of Northfield.[22] The household baked and brewed for its own requirements, but occasionally needed to supplement its supplies by buying limited quantities of bread and ale, presumably from the specialist bakers and brewers living nearby. A baker is recorded selling loaves at Northfield a year or two previously, so he may have supplied the extra bread, worth 5s. 9d. while the household was living at Weoley. In the same year a dozen brewers were plying their trade in Northfield, so the household's additional purchases could have been made locally, but the quantity was limited to 249 gallons, just a fortnight's consumption.[23] The milk and eggs which were bought for 2s. in 1467–8 seem to confirm the small scale of local purchases, implying that the people of Northfield and the Berkeley household were not bound together in a close relationship by the trade in foodstuffs.

To complete the picture of the household's shopping horizons, more specialised or expensive goods came from larger towns and ports often at long distance. The Berkeley household in 1441–2 bought barrels of sprats, probably at the beginning of Lent, at Coventry, a distribution point for fish from the North Sea. Wax for candles which cost 25s. 8d. also came from the east coast, having been imported from the Baltic, which might have been bought at Coventry or at the fair at Lichfield.[24] Red wine from Gascony was shipped to Bristol, and probably upriver to Bewdley, where it would be transferred to carts, in the same way that the duke of Buckingham obtained his wine for his castle at Maxstoke in north-west Warwickshire in 1452–3.[25] The Berkeleys were familiar with Bewdley as a point of access to the Severn, as Lady Eleanor arranged for cloth to be taken from Weoley to Bristol via the river port in 1441–2 (Map 1). Sweet wines from the Mediterranean, malmsey and romney, were carried overland in barrels from London. London traders sold other luxuries to the

[20] TNA, C103/39.
[21] Arrangements by large households are discussed in J.S. Lee, *Cambridge and its Economic Region 1450–1560* (Hatfield, 2005), 142–73.
[22] GA, D2700 MJ1/8; MJ11/1/17.
[23] BAH, Weoley court rolls, 518077, 518078, 518084.
[24] Christopher Dyer, 'Trade, Towns and the Church: Ecclesiastical Consumers and the Urban Economy of the West Midlands, 1290–1540', in *The Church in the Medieval Town*, ed. T.R. Slater and Gervase Rosser (Aldershot, 1998), 61, 69.
[25] Mary Harris, 'The Accounts of the Great Household of Humphrey, First Duke of Buckingham, for the Year 1452–3', *Camden Miscellany* (Camden Society, 4th series, xxix, 1984), 15, 16, 26.

Berkeleys, such as the skinner who lined gowns with beaver fur. Five pewter vessels also came from the capital.[26]

The household depended in a very limited way on local agricultural produce, but it probably contributed more to the Northfield economy as an employer of local labour. Northfield people would have been hired for building work on the castle, to do agricultural tasks on the demesne and to provide specialist services. The number of employees was not very large. At its most active the demesne was too small to employ more than four full-time farm servants, and require any more than a few days' work from a dozen labourers, local smiths, wood workers and carters.[27]

The lords of Weoley Castle belonged to an elite of regional significance. They looked beyond the immediate vicinity to find social equals and political allies. The account of 1441–2 gives no details in its list of 'food gifts to the household from various men' which consisted of delicacies such as swans, pheasants, partridges, rabbits, piglets and poultry which could have come from such families as the Staffords of Grafton (near Bromsgrove) or the Mountforts of Coleshill in Warwickshire. We know that these prominent figures were part of the Berkeley circle because Sir Maurice had married Eleanor Mountfort, and William was to forge an alliance with the Staffords by taking Anne, daughter of Sir Humphrey Stafford, as his wife.[28] Household accounts of other lords at this time record the payments to the servant carrying the gifts, which identifies the donors and gives us an insight into a network of gift exchange. The Berkeley accounts enigmatically mention guests who visited Weoley: 'magnates, gentry and strangers'. We know the names of two of these, John Throckmorton and John Vampage, both prominent south Worcestershire gentry who belonged to the influential retinue of Richard Beauchamp, earl of Warwick, and who as councillors of Sir Maurice Berkeley provided legal advice. The office of receiver was filled by John Venor, a gentleman from the adjoining parish of Harborne. In the course of the turbulent politics of the 1440s and 1450s Sir Maurice Berkeley came into contact with a range of influential west Midland figures such as Sir William Peyto from south Warwickshire. He was also said to shelter in Weoley Castle outlaws and 'reckless people', among them no doubt ruffians like John Newhay of Nechells and Thomas Hore of Solihull, who was held to be a gentleman. Those who would not have visited Weoley included John Holt of Aston, Thomas Lyttleton from Frankley and Fulk Stafford of Harvington in Chaddesley Corbett, all of them his opponents in the dispute with the earl of Wiltshire.[29]

The Berkeleys had inherited a great house at Weoley Castle, and raised their status by embellishing it. Its origins can be traced back to the bold move of their predecessors in the twelfth century in establishing a new dwelling at Weoley more than two miles to the north of the parish church near which the original manor house was

---

[26] On the importance of London for wealthy consumers and expensive goods, C.M. Barron, *London in the Later Middle Ages: Government and People 1200–1500* (Oxford, 2004), 64–83.
[27] GA, D2700 MJ17/2.
[28] Carpenter, *Locality and Polity*, 337; *History of Parliament*, ed. Wedgwood and Holt, 69.
[29] Carpenter, *Locality and Polity*, 430, 459–60, 462. In 1449 and 1451 conflict reached such a pitch that Sir Maurice was outlawed, and he with various family members and officials were imprisoned at Worcester: *CPR*, 1446–52, p. 534. I am grateful to the History of Parliament Trust for allowing me to use information from the biography of Sir Maurice Berkeley in the forthcoming volume of *The Commons, 1422–61*.

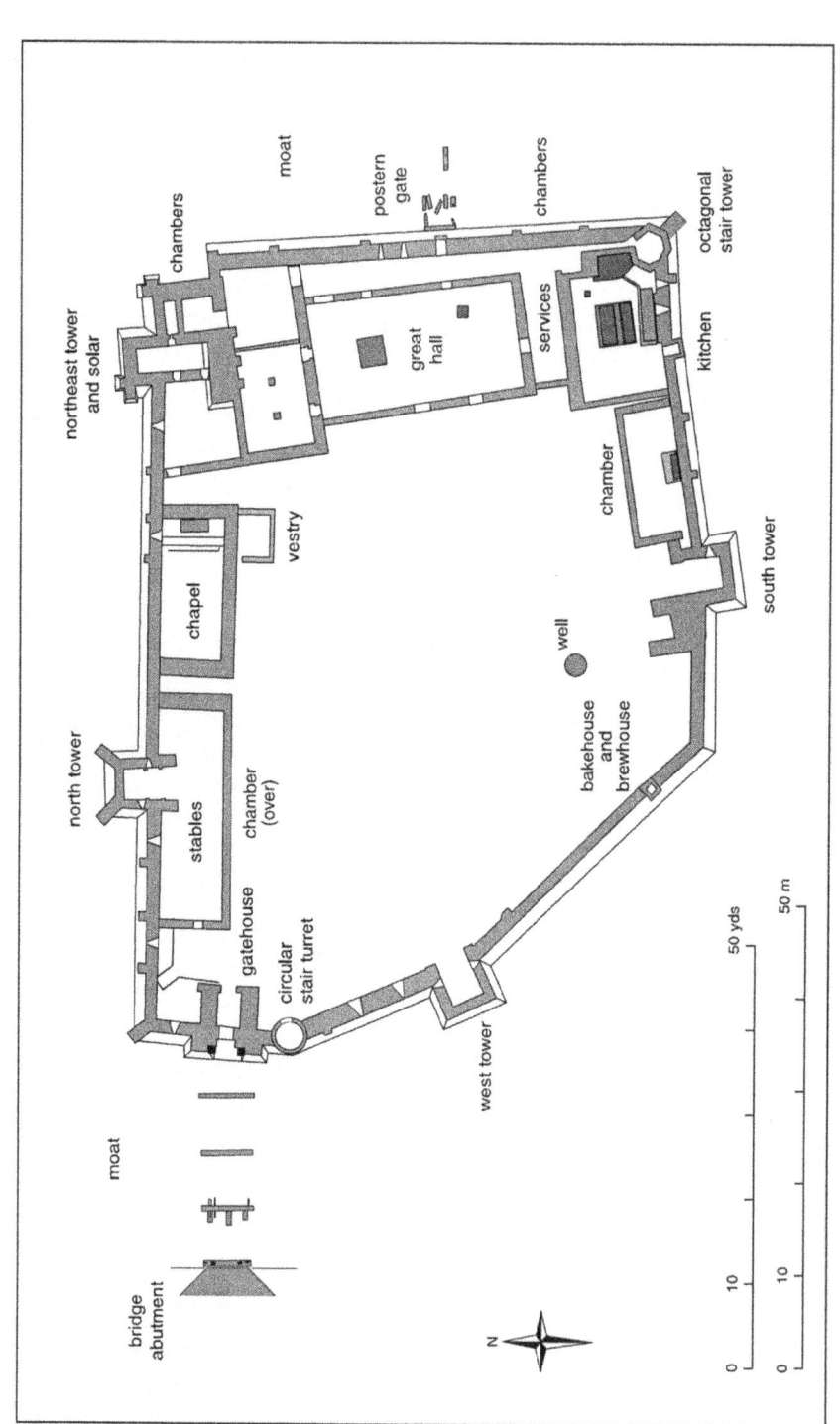

Map 2. Plan of Weoley Castle, based on an original kindly supplied by Steve Linnane, with addition information from the survey of 1424.

probably located. The Somerys in the thirteenth century elevated Weoley into a castle with a strong outer wall and towers, surrounded by a wide moat, but it lay in a stream valley, overlooked by higher ground, which prevents us from regarding it as strongly defended. Paynels and Somerys in turn exercised lordship from the hilltop fortress at Dudley, near an intersection of roads, which came by the late thirteenth century to resemble so many centres of feudal power in its combination of castle, priory, town and park.[30] Weoley by contrast was not associated with an important church or centre of population: perhaps it asserted the lord's presence at the southern end of their concentrated block of estates, but it may also have served as a retreat, where the lord and his household could enjoy the pleasures of the park. The description of 1424 lists the domestic buildings within the fortifications as a hall, chambers, chapel, kitchen, bakehouse and brewhouse, and the plans drawn by the archaeologists depict essentially the same structures (Map 2). According to the 1424 survey a stable, barns and laundry stood in the outer court.[31]

Various additions and alterations were made to this residence after 1424, according to archaeological excavation, though precise dates are lacking. A large building on the western side was built of stone with a white plaster floor. It went out of use around 1450 and on its site in the late fifteenth century a rougher building with stone walls and a mainly cobbled floor was constructed. The timber bridge on the north-west corner which was the main access across the moat was partly reframed in two phases, one in the early and the other in the later fifteenth century. The octagonal tower and buttress in the south-east corner seem to have been constructed in the fifteenth century, and also the small round tower on the western side. Around the same time, the bakehouse acquired three new ovens. The continued use of the hall and kitchen resulted in deposits of kitchen refuse in the moat, and spreads of building rubble which may relate to phases of repair or construction which have still to be identified.

The years between 1380 and 1420 have been regarded by the archaeologists as a period of building work at Weoley, with a decline in the mid-fifteenth century, but previously unknown activity is revealed by the documents. At an early stage of the new lords establishing themselves in the castle, in 1439, more than £5 was spent on 'the repair of the castle'. In 1440–1, 360 stones (assessing the quantity of stone by counting rather than in cart loads suggests that they were ashlar blocks) were quarried in the park, stone tiles were acquired, twelve quarters of lime were bought, and a carpenter was hired to work on the barn in the outer court. Work was also being carried out on the moat and pond, and the leat (called an aqueduct) that fed them. In the following year 2,000 stone tiles (we would call them slates) were bought. Most remarkable, in 1445–6 lime was again purchased for the 'work of the new hall within

---

[30] John Hunt, *Lordship and the Landscape: A Documentary and Archaeological Study of the Honor of Dudley c.1066–1322* (British Archaeological Reports, British Series cclxiv, 1997), 87–94; Oliver Creighton, *Castles and Landscapes: Power, Community and Fortification in Medieval England* (2005), 127–31, 151–67, 188–93.

[31] David Symons, 'Weoley Castle and Northfield in 1424', *Transactions of the Birmingham and Warwickshire Archaeological Society*, xciii (1983–4), 45–55; the main source used here for archaeological evidence is a document produced by Barbican Research Associates in 2011, *Weoley Castle Ruins*, with contributions on the archaeological archive, window glass and floor tiles by Steve Linnane; on the pottery and ceramic building material by Stephanie Ratkai; on the small finds by Quita Mould; on the architectural stones by R.K. Morris, consulted on 13 Dec. 2013 at http://archaeologydataservice.ac.uk/archives/view/weoleycastle_eh_2011.ADS Collection 1112.

the castle', which could mean that the hall dating from the thirteenth century was being rebuilt, or that an entirely new hall had been constructed at an unknown date.[32] These fragments of evidence record expenditure on building work by the receiver and bailiff, while the main cost would have appeared in separate building accounts which have not survived.

The household account and the evidence for the buildings (both written and archaeological) complement each other. The sixteen residents of 1441–2 and occasional guests could have found accommodation in the many chambers listed in 1424, at both ends of the hall, 'a chamber standing by itself' near the chapel, and 'a house for a chamber' on the southern side (Map 2). The chapel figures in the account because the chandlery supplied candles for religious services, and a fee was paid to a chaplain. The pantry obtained its loaves from the bakehouse, and the brewhouse supplied the buttery. Two cellars under the chamber on the north side of the hall would have stored the barrels of wine. The kitchen (with a larder) was a separate structure, and remains of the food prepared and stored have been found in the form of bones of the animals, birds and fish. These faunal remains have not been studied in detail, but they include oyster shells, whereas the household account does not mention shellfish. Public meals would have been served in the hall, and guests would have been received there. The records of the twice-yearly courts of the manor of Northfield are headed 'Weoley', so presumably on these occasions thirty or so tenants gathered in the hall of the castle.[33]

The way of life of the castle's inhabitants can be reconstructed from both written records and archaeological finds. Pewter vessels (basins and a ewer) were bought in London in 1441–2, and three pewter plates and two saucers of the fifteenth century were excavated from the moat where they had presumably been thrown by accident.[34] The accounts refer to the equipment for the stable including saddles, bridles, girths, halters and 'other harness', while the excavations have recovered a fifteenth-century horse bit and spur. Documents rarely mention pottery, but the ceramic finds from the castle reveal the routines of domestic life in the fifteenth century, with cooking pots and pipkins which would have been used in the kitchen, and jugs and cisterns in which ale would have been carried, stored and served. Pottery cups are quite rare, but small jugs would have been used as drinking vessels, and the documents refer to wooden cups. The pottery adds to our knowledge of the household's regional contacts, as some had been traded from centres of manufacture nearby (in the case of Deritend-ware made in the outskirts of the town of Birmingham), and some at a distance of twenty or thirty miles, such as the vessels from Hanley Castle in south-west Worcestershire.

Medieval castle excavations do not always produce evidence for the luxurious style of life and exotic imports that we would expect, but Weoley has been an excep-

---

[32] GA, D2700 MJ1/4; MJ1/8; MJ17/1; TNA, C103/39.
[33] BAH, 518066 and following. It is possible that courts were held at Northfield, and that there was a manorial building of some kind near the church. An inquisition of 1386 refers to a court held at Weoley and a court held at Northfield: TNA, C136/38/3. An early 16th-century deed refers to 'my court of Northfield and Weoley', and a deed was sealed 'at my manor of Northfield': TNA, C103/39.
[34] Roger Brownsword, Ernest Pitt and David Symons, 'The Analysis of Some Metal Objects from Weoley Castle', *Transactions of the Birmingham and Warwickshire Archaeological Society*, xciii (1983–4), 33–43, esp. 35–6.

tion, with its decorated pewter cruet and Syrian blue glass vessel, both earlier than the fifteenth century. From the Berkeley period comes a piece of a Valencian lustreware bowl and from the late fifteenth or sixteenth centuries two Spanish *albarelli* (drug jars), which would have been imported through Bristol, and possibly bought by the Berkeleys when they were living in south Gloucestershire. The German stoneware no doubt came through the port of London. Ceramic distilling equipment with traces of mercury, suggesting that someone was practising alchemy, adds a further flavour of out-of-the-ordinary activities in the castle in the late fifteenth century.

Many goods which the castle contained have left little trace, either in the archaeology, or in the routine purchases of a household account. Other sources mention mundane furnishings, but also prestigious possessions appropriate to a family of high status. A lawsuit of 1450 claims that ten years earlier the castle contained armour and forty yards of cloth, which may have been intended for making servants' liveries. An inventory survives of the possessions of Sir Maurice Berkeley made after his death in 1464, but to our frustration we are not given the name of the house to which it relates: it could well have been Stoke Gifford, though there is a chance that the residence with eight chambers, buttery, dairy, kitchen, brewhouse, stable and garner was Weoley. Even if the items were kept at Stoke, the list is still relevant as Weoley would have been similarly equipped. Wooden furnishings included a bedstead, casket and cupboard in the great chamber, as was appropriate for a room for sleeping and storage, but notably a trestle table and forms were also kept there, so this was a room for eating. The lord was accustomed to dine privately in his chamber, not in the hall, in an age of developing social separation between lords and their servants. All of the chambers contained bedding, much of it for servants, and some of the most valuable possessions were textiles, including bedclothes, napery (sheets and table cloths) worth £2 14*s*. 4*d*., and 'raiment for his body' which included a gown of London russet with a lining of marten fur, valued at £4. Silver plate (a goblet and a salt for example) were listed alongside the commonplace pewter table-ware and brass cooking pots. Almost half of the total value of £65 10*s*. 5*d*. consisted of livestock, mainly cattle but with some quite valuable horses.[35]

Beyond the castle, its outbuildings and water features lay the enormous park, which could have been an asset in attracting the Berkeleys to centre their lives on Weoley. The park was assessed at 1,080 acres in the sixteenth century, and its extent (amounting to 1,097 acres) can be traced from a list of fields contributing to a *modus* of 40*s*. in lieu of tithe in 1838, which was probably a survival from a late medieval agreement. Long after it had been converted to agricultural land, it is visible as a triangular space, stretching for a mile and a half from north to south, from the Bourn Brook to the road (originally Roman) leading from Worcester to Lichfield (Map 3). Parks often contained internal compartments, and in the case of Weoley some of the woods it contained are known to have been fenced to allow them to be exploited as underwood. The park was divided into sections for pasture, both for the deer and separately for cattle.[36]

---

[35] GA, D2700 MJ12/6.

[36] Acreage: David Symons, 'Further Evidence for Medieval Northfield', *Transactions of the Birmingham and Warwickshire Archaeological Society*, cxi (2007), 17–41, esp. 34; BAH, MS 20/C/7 [299990] ; Stephen Moorhouse, 'The Medieval Parks of Yorkshire: Function, Contents and Chronology', in *The Medieval Park. New Perspectives*, ed. Robert Liddiard (Macclesfield, 2007), 122–3.

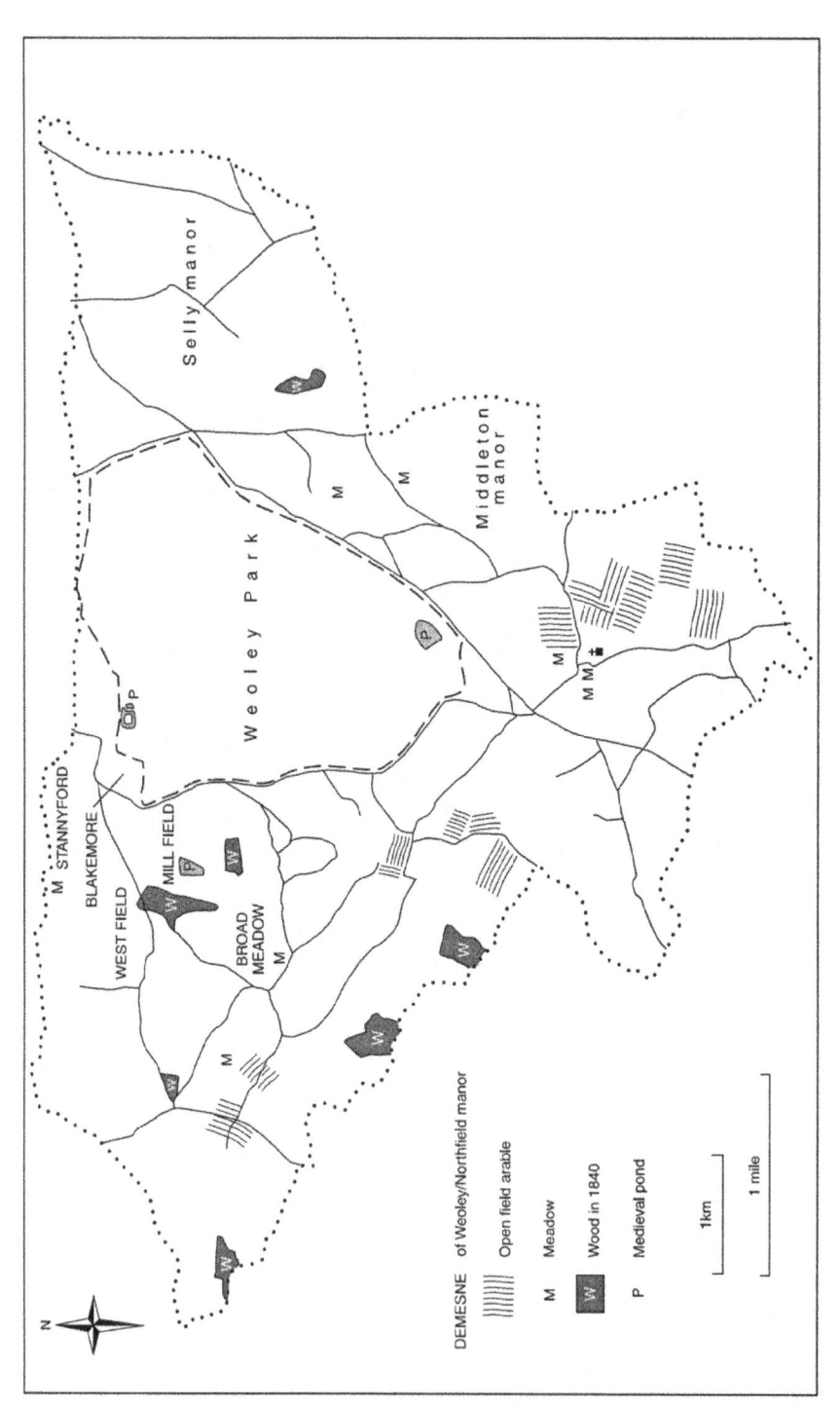

Map 3. Some evidence for the use of land in fifteenth-century Northfield. Demesne fields are in CAPITALS. The map is based on documents, the map of 1840, and surviving ridge and furrow.

Deer were kept in the park from its origins in the thirteenth century, and they posed a dilemma, expressed in a survey of the Somery estates in 1273, when the herbage (grazing) of the park was valued at £5 p.a., 'if no deer were kept'.[37] Should the park owner stock it with deer and enjoy the hunting, the consumption of venison, the companionship of visitors and supporters, and the ability to dispense patronage in the form of deer carcasses? Or should the park be exploited as a source of revenues, and above all payments for pasturing domestic animals (agistment)? If the park was subdivided the choice was not so stark, as it could have had space allocated for both the beasts of the chase and for cattle, though there was still a problem in establishing a balance between the two uses. In 1424 the survey of the manor included 'a certain park ... with deer', and in the following year an interloper from Harborne shot arrows at the deer and allowed his greyhounds to run in the park, presumably in their pursuit.[38] Part of the pasture was let in 1424 for grazing, as payments to feed domestic animals brought in £3 13s. 4d. Some cash income was needed to cover the frequent expenditure on repairing and renewing the wooden fences of the long pale.

Sir Maurice Berkeley's management of Weoley park began badly when the parker, John Broun, was found to have been failing to pay to the central administration of the estate quite large sums for agistment (more than £5 for 1437), and then left his post 'carrying off cash with him', and the small profit for the first six months on the accounting year 1440–1 was blamed on 'negligence'. A more stable and profitable arrangement began on Lady Day (25 March) 1441, when the park was leased out for five years at an annual rent of £13 6s. 8d. The term of the lease was completed in 1446, and after that revenues from the park hovered around £5 p.a. between 1454 and 1482.[39] This might suggest that the park contained few or no deer in 1441–6, and that they were then brought back, still leaving room for cattle, but this is an inference without direct evidence.

Apart from its grazing for deer and cattle, the park provided other resources. Local people paid pannage to feed their pigs on acorns and beech mast. A quarry for stone was used for building the castle, and a fish pond lay adjacent to the castle, while another is marked by a still visible dam on the southern edge of the park, probably known as Broadpool. A single reference to rabbits (which were being hunted illicitly) may mean that the park had a warren. As is found in other parks, part of the enclosed area was cultivated, as a field known as Newland was ploughed in 1444–5, though it was used as pasture in other years.[40] As the park and its facilities do not seem to have been consistently run for maximum profit, it should perhaps be interpreted as forming with the castle an ideal place, a landscape that stimulated the imagination of those who came into contact with it. The roof of one of the castle buildings in about 1400 was decorated with carved stone waterspouts, and the wide moat may have been intended to reflect the building in its surface. The castle was not just a functional structure, but was designed to be viewed and admired. The large park would have given those in the castle a sense of seclusion and set them in an 'ordered, watery,

---

[37] *The Inquisitiones Post Mortem for the County of Worcester Part 1*, ed. J.W. Willis Bund (Worcestershire Historical Society, 1894), 16–17.
[38] Symons, 'Weoley Castle', 47; BAH, 518070.
[39] GA, D2700 MJ1/4; MJ1/5; MJ17/1; TNA, C103/39.
[40] GA, D2700 MJ17/1; TNA, C103/39.

sylvan landscape'.⁴¹ In 1424 a small garden planted with vines and herbs lay within the courtyard, and two other larger gardens lay outside the walls. At that date the outer gardens were grassed over, but when the Berkeley household moved in they may have received some attention and become suitable venues for pleasurable and cultural activities, as happened in other castles. A field name recorded in the early sixteenth century refers to a lodge, which apparently stood on a hill with a view of the park. From outside, the main road from Worcester to the north Midlands ran for a mile and a half alongside the park pale. Travellers who looked beyond the fence would see the greensward of the park sweeping as far as the eye could see, and they would be impressed by the grandeur of a lord who could devote so much land to pleasure. Similar glimpses were available to those travelling northwards on the road from Northfield church to south Staffordshire.⁴²

Beyond the castle, gardens and park lay another tract of land belonging to the lord, the demesne, which consisted of Blakemore, Millfield and Westfield, a mill, and parcels of meadow such as Broadmeadow, all on the northern edge of Northfield parish, and to the west of Weoley Castle (Map 3). This compact demesne may well have originated, like the park, in the appropriation of an area of waste or common grazing land. It was a potentially important source of produce for the household, or it could have generated an income in cash. It was described in surveys attached to inquisitions of 1273–1338 as containing between 200 and 400 acres of arable, with sizeable amounts of meadow and pasture.⁴³ In about 1412, before the Berkeleys took over the manor, sixty-three and a half acres of land were being cropped as arable, and more than ninety cattle appear in the accounts. In most years between 1437 and 1479 some 'husbandry', meaning cultivation, was being practised on the demesne, but the details escape us because the documents have not survived. Two of the fields – Westfield just beyond the park, and Newland that lay within the pale – were sometimes cultivated by the lord's employees, but were also on occasion put down to grass, suggesting the type of 'convertible husbandry' which could have produced good yields.⁴⁴ Former arable fields, Westfield in 1440–1 and Millfield and Westfield in 1481–2, were rented out as pasture, for rents of £5 and more. Meadows were more consistently kept under the control of the lord, which enabled between thirty-six and sixty-one cart loads of hay to be carried to the manorial buildings for feeding the livestock kept on the demesne, including plough oxen, as well as the animals belonging to the household. In about 1412 the grazing capacity of the manor was used to gather a total of eighty cattle, which were then sold by a stock keeper or *staurarius*, apparently for £29. This does not seem to have continued in the long term, though participation in the fattening and droving trade was a feature of other west

---

⁴¹ Robert Liddiard, 'Medieval Designed Landscapes: Problems and Possibilities', in *Medieval Landscapes*, ed. Gardiner and Rippon, 201–14, esp. 213.

⁴² A field name, Middle Lodge, recalled in 1536 the existence of a lodge, the site of which may be represented by the modern place-name Lodge Hill: HRO, 44M69/E3/42; O.H. Creighton, *Designs upon the Land. Elite Landscapes of the Middle Ages* (Woodbridge, 2009), 130–1 on the lord's perception of space, here applied to the perspective of outsiders.

⁴³ *Inquisitiones Post Mortem Part 1*, ed. Willis Bund, 16–17, 36–7; *Part 2*, ed. *idem* (Worcestershire Historical Society, xxi, 1909), 113.

⁴⁴ GA, D2700 MJ17/2; TNA, C103/39 (1444–5 and 1467–8).

Midland estates.[45] In short, the demesne under the Berkeleys was subject to decision-making in two respects – should the land be directly managed by the lord, or leased out to tenants? And should the three main fields be managed as arable or pasture? The choices were by no means clear or consistent, but there would have been considerably more land under pasture than in 1273–1338.

A high proportion of the land in Northfield manor lay in tenant holdings, and most of the landscape consisted of their houses and fields. The lord's revenues came mainly from the rents and dues paid by tenants. Sir Maurice Berkeley recognised the importance of maintaining or increasing his income from this source by making a rental when he took over the manor in 1437.[46] That document has not survived, but it would not have been greatly different from the survey of 1424, which names fifty-nine tenants, of whom a number were dead or clearly absentees, so the resident landholders amounted to around fifty. This compares with thirty-nine in the rental of 1549. The rentals exclude the tenants of the smaller sub manors of Selly and Middleton, except for the lords of those manors. The figures for 1424 and 1549 represent a considerable reduction from the total of about seventy tenants around 1300, which must reflect among other factors the effects of the Black Death of 1349 and subsequent epidemics.[47]

The erosion of tenant numbers concerned Sir Maurice Berkeley and his officials. They saw vacant holdings, buildings falling into disrepair, and peasants migrating away from the manor, all of which threatened to reduce the lord's income from rents. In the period 1399–1431 there are many Northfield manor court rolls, but only three refer to the need to repair buildings. Fifteen reports of decaying buildings appear in the court rolls of 1438–58, when Sir Maurice was lord, and in order to remedy the situation new tenants were sometimes required to repair or rebuild. A tenant's entry fine might be reduced to reflect the need for repair.[48] In pursuing this problem the lord or his officials were applying lessons learnt on their south Gloucestershire manors in the early fifteenth century. No less than thirteen decayed buildings were reported to the Stoke Gifford manor court in 1424, showing that tenants neglected their duties, but also that the lord did something about it.[49]

In 1440 the Northfield manor court jury was asked to list holdings that lacked tenants, and they found eight. Four of them were headed by a toft, meaning a plot of land on which buildings had once stood.[50] If buildings were in ruins, tenants were not attracted to them, and buildings were more likely to collapse if a holding was untenanted. It was not surprising that in 1441–2 the house of Richard Wodecok, a serf, was said to be falling into ruin, as he was reported as living at nearby Harborne. Around this time another danger from the lord's point of view was revealed by an accusation

---

[45] Andrew Watkins, 'Landowners and their Estates in the Forest of Arden in the Fifteenth Century', *Agricultural History Review*, xlv (1997), 18–33, esp. 22–3.
[46] The account of 1440–1 refers to a rental made four years previously: GA, D2700 MJ17/1.
[47] Symons, 'Weoley Castle'; BAH, 382960, collated with HRO, 44M69/E1/16/12 (these are two versions of the same rental of 1549). Rentals are lists of tenants, not counts of people: in *Worcestershire Taxes in the 1520s*, ed. M.A. Faraday (Worcestershire Historical Society, new series, xix, 2003), 36–7 a list of seventy people is assessed, which includes inhabitants of Selly and Middleton, and landless people in Northfield. No doubt others were exempted.
[48] BAH, 518080, 518081.
[49] GA, D2700 MJ11/1/2.
[50] BAH, 518080.

that Odomar Walsh was appropriating selions (strips of land) from Knightes, one of the vacant holdings.[51] Holdings could disappear in this way, being added piecemeal to other inhabited tenements, and the rent lost to the lord. Berkeley countered these threats to his rent income by persuading tenants (one of them the land-hungry Odomar Walsh) to take empty holdings on seven-year leases, at rather higher rents than had previously been paid. Dawelond, for example, which Walsh accepted, was expected to yield 11s. 6d. instead of its previous rent of 10s.[52] The accounts of the manor described these new rents as *appruamentum*, or improvement, which was a bold word to use in the mid fifteenth century when rents were generally tending to fall. The seven-year leases did not all run to their full term, and when an enquiry was held into vacant holdings in 1453, six were listed, including three that had been empty in 1440.[53] When a holding lay vacant ('in the lord's hands') it did not lose all value – often a tenant was found who would take it for a year at a time for a reduced rent, or the lord would graze his animals on the abandoned land. Sir Maurice Berkeley must still be credited with a bold attempt to counter adverse tendencies, and one can find other manors which went much further downhill. As a yardstick of comparison, of the holdings described when they changed hands in the Northfield court in 1438–58, 28% were said to be headed by a toft rather than a messuage, so 72% of buildings were still standing. Tofts on other Midland manors could reach 40% of the total.[54]

Another type of improvement was attempted when a new tenant of a croft in 1447 was required to 'eradicate' the land within seven years.[55] This meant that bushes, brambles and perhaps trees had grown over the croft because a previous tenant had neglected it, or even that there had been no tenant for a time. The newcomer was expected to grub up the roots and restore it to agricultural use. A lord who took such actions was evidently aiming to restore his manor to its previously fully-tenanted and well-cultivated state, and was not at all inclined to the sort of 'improvement' pursued at Wormleighton which involved ridding the manor of tenants and planting enclosure hedges across the fields.

In order to assess the lords' management of tenancy and their consequent influence on the landscape and farming, earlier periods have to be brought into the picture. A long view can be taken of the development of the countryside by focussing on the physical survival of the medieval boundaries, roads, houses and fields. The method that has been used here is based on the 1840 tithe map, which was drawn before urbanisation and suburbanisation.[56] The map reveals much about the long-term development of the land, because areas of large irregular fields with relatively few settlements dominate in the space once occupied by Weoley Park. When the park was converted into agricultural land in the sixteenth century a distinctive type of field was imposed on its interior, with the result that the park boundary stands out clearly

---

[51] BAH, 478817, 518081, 518083.
[52] BAH, 518081.
[53] BAH, 518093.
[54] Christopher Dyer, *Lords and Peasants in a Changing Society. The Estates of the Bishopric of Worcester, 680–1540* (Cambridge, 1980), 242.
[55] BAH, 518091.
[56] Library of Birmingham, Local Studies, tithe map of parish of Northfield, LS 909/7. The apportionment was made in 1838–9.

centuries after the park ceased to exist. Similarly large fields predominate in Selly and Middleton, which must reflect the management of land and tenures by the lords of these two sub manors in modern times. They had been carved out of Northfield, in the case of Selly before 1066, and not much later in the case of Middleton, and the minor gentry who held the lordships clearly had at least an indirect impact on the evolution of the landscape (Maps 3 and 4).

In the main manor of Northfield, to the west and south of the park, but including a strip of land on the eastern side, the map of 1840 depicts a very different type of countryside, in which complex small-scale fields lie alongside twisting lanes with many farms and cottages (Map 4). We can dig deeper into the early history of these distinctive features by gathering the large number of minor place-names, of fields, farms, roads, brooks, ditches, gates, moors and heaths which appear in the medieval documents, and searching for these on the nineteenth-century map. If such a linkage is attempted in most open-field villages, of the Wormleighton type, the results can be disappointing because enclosure might have removed the local names. In the case of Northfield many medieval features and their names survived intact, allowing us to glimpse a landscape of isolated settlements, enclosures and small open fields. The 'village' as it has been known in modern times consisted of the parish church, the rectory and a cluster of houses. Apart from another group at Bartley Green, the inhabitants lived in messuages (houses with farm buildings attached) scattered at intervals along the roads and lanes. They mostly carried the names of former tenants, such as Jiggins and Hodges, or nearby fields were named after these tenants. Sometimes the name has changed, as in the case of Tinkers, which can be traced back through modern documents to the medieval Launders.[57] Some have no identifying name, but the characteristics of their plan in relation to fields and roads suggest their early origin. A late medieval house has survived at the Great Stone Inn near the church, which had an open hall and a two-storey end bay. Another is described in a court entry when John Broun (before his disgrace as a park keeper) took a nook (about eight acres of land) called Nasshes in 1440, and agreed to build a new 'hall and chamber at the front end of the hall and byre at the rear end containing in all four couples', so this was a three-bay cruck-built longhouse, measuring about forty-five feet long and sixteen feet wide. At this time and in this region, place, people and animals were not usually accommodated under the same roof, and it is clear that at Northfield as elsewhere a dwelling (usually consisting of a hall and chamber) was normally accompanied by a separate barn and another agricultural building, probably arranged around a yard. Richard Wodecok, for example, agreed to build a separate barn on his holding in 1445.[58]

These dispersed farms were often attached to one or more small closes, which are described as 'a messuage and croft and adjacent curtilage' (in 1442), or 'a cottage and adjacent croft' (1440), or 'a toft and four crofts of land adjacent' (1440), and in addition the tenants held strips of arable land in open fields. Odomar Walsh, for instance, combined his 'toft and curtilage adjacent' (and a freehold messuage in which he lived) and croft with 'parcels of land', three selions in a furlong called

---

[57] Paper by George Demidowicz on Tinker's Farm, Historic Environment Record [hereafter HER] 02948–MBM833.
[58] HER 01190–MBM139; BAH, 518080, 518089.

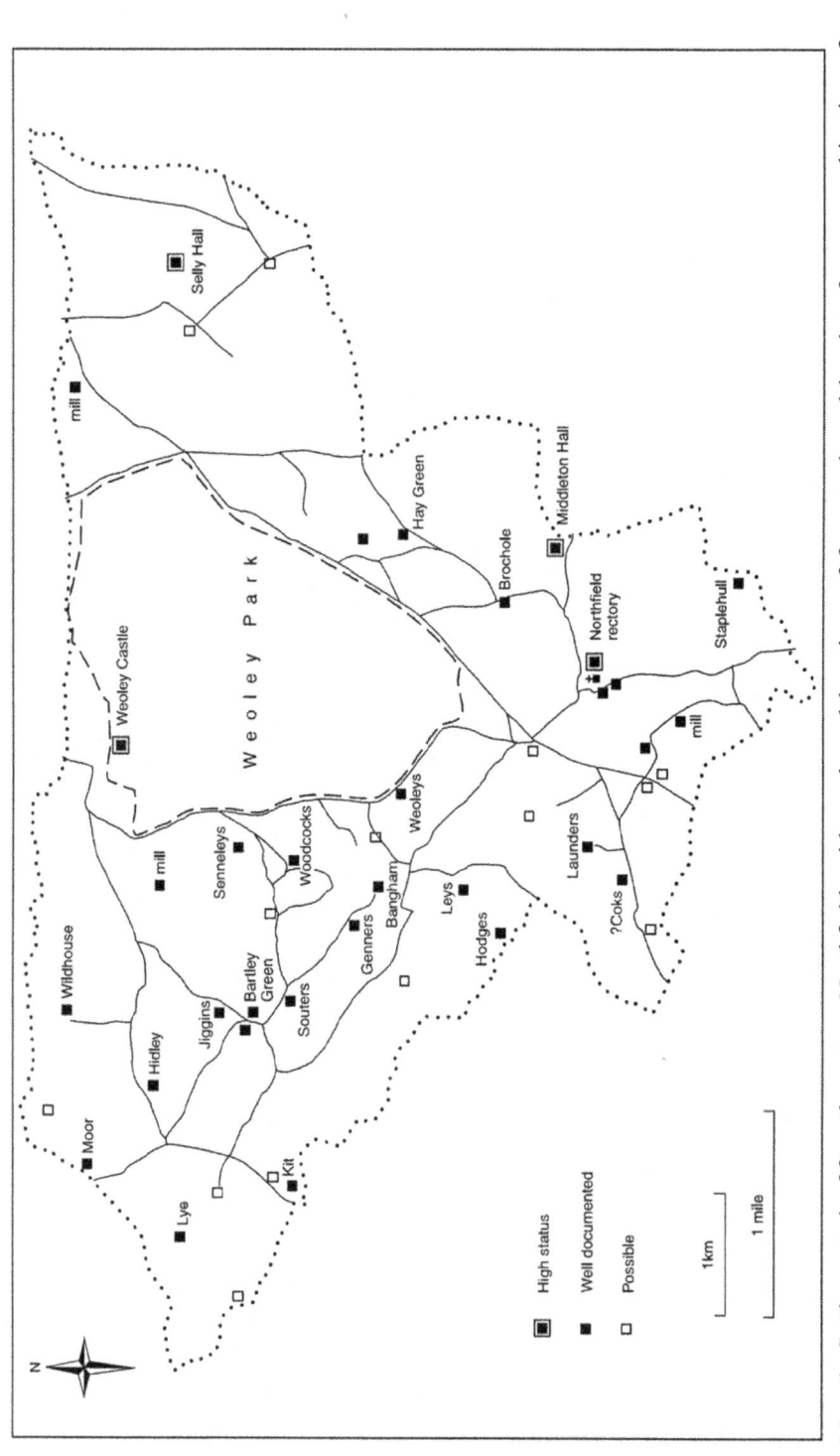

Map 4. Settlements in fifteenth-century Northfield, with roads and locations of farmsteads and hamlets from a combination of documentary sources. The location of Selly Hall is based on information from George Demidowicz.

Huswyken and four selions at Ley Hill.⁵⁹ In 1840 remnants of such arrangements survived over much of the west of the parish, with small enclosures next to farms, sometimes within a distinctively oval perimeter fence, like the group of fields south of Souters (Map 5a). In a few cases (for example near Ley Hill) open fields still consisted of unfenced strips; or long, thin fields clearly resulted from the piecemeal enclosure of an open field, preserving the shape of the strips (Map. 5b). More conventional rectangular fields had boundaries which follow the tell-tale aratral curve of the former selions. Fourteen 'fields' are mentioned in the documents (setting aside the demesne fields of Westfield and Millfield), some of which were described as common fields, and were shared by a number of tenants, such as Bradley Field, Harstone and Wyggefeld. The word field could also be used to describe land held by a single tenant, like Odrichefeld, which was 'enclosed and ditched'. Ridge and furrow still survives in modern urban parks to the east and north of the church and in Senneleys Park in the north of the parish (Map 3), but these traces of early cultivation need not always indicate the former presence of open field, as enclosed crofts would be ploughed in ridges.⁶⁰ Lanes and roads have also survived into our own time, especially in stretches of Cob Lane and Hole Lane to the south-east of the park, in the form of deeply incised holloways lined with mature trees. Numerous minor roads were essential to gain access to the scattered houses and fields.

Tenants would have had access to meadow, which was widespread across the parish, often near the brooks, and as well as pasture in enclosed crofts and curtilages they could graze animals on common land, such as West Heath, and, if they paid an agistment fee (or slipped their beasts through a hole in the fence), in the park. Woods, though poorly recorded in the medieval documents, are marked on the tithe map, such as Bromwich Wood in the south-west and a wood near Mill Field, which are likely to go back to the later Middle Ages (Map 3). Pigs could be fattened in the woods in the park on payment of pannage.

The rural landscape developed over a very long time. The layout of the parish was much influenced by the road of Roman origin from Worcester, which ran near to the south-eastern boundary of the park. Its line continues in use as the Bristol Road, a section of the A38. Ricknield Street ran north from Gloucestershire through Selly, but the problems that we now have in tracing its exact course suggests that it was of less long-term importance.⁶¹ Other minor Roman roads and boundaries may have helped to determine the shape of medieval lanes and fields, but we do not know enough about the detail of the landscape before AD 400 to be sure of this. Widely scattered finds of coins and Romano-British pottery show that part of the area was inhabited in that period.⁶² When the name Northfield was adopted (perhaps in the seventh or eighth century) it described an expanse of open land (*feld*), that is without much wood, lying to the north of Bromsgrove and Kings Norton. The nine minor

---

⁵⁹ BAH, 518080, 518081.
⁶⁰ George Demidowicz, 'Ridge and Furrow Surveys at King's Norton and Northfield, Birmingham', *West Midlands Archaeology*, xxvii (1984), 117–21; HER 20066–MBM1712; 20074–MBM1719, and author's observations.
⁶¹ R.J. and D.B. Whitehouse, 'The Roman Road between Gloucester and Birmingham, North of the Lickey Hills', *Transactions of the Birmingham Archaeological Society*, lxxxiii (1966–7), 180–7; Peter Leather, 'The Birmingham Roman Roads Project', *West Midlands Archaeology*, xxxvii (1994), 8–11.
⁶² HER contains records of ten find spots of coins, and two of pottery.

Map 5. Farms in 1840: (left) a) Souters with enclosed fields; (right) b) Ley Hill and Hoggs (Hodges) with enclosed fields and an open field.

place-names ending in -ley (O.E. *leah*) refer to woods, or pieces of open land near to woodland (see Map. 6), which does not mean that woodland was being cleared in the eighth and ninth centuries when these names were formed, but that parcels of land adjoining woods were being inhabited or farmed, or that patches of wood survived in an otherwise open landscape.[63] By the time of Domesday, Northfield was one of the most populous manors in the district, with twenty-nine tenants (and more potential tenants in the form of a priest, two male slaves and a female slave) and fourteen working ploughs. The woods can be estimated at 300–400 acres, so they provided a useful asset without dominating the landscape. A complex hierarchy of settlements and lordships is implied by the Domesday entries for no fewer than three manors called Selly, and a berewick of Bartley as well as the parent manor of Northfield.[64]

The colonising movement of the twelfth and thirteenth centuries doubled the number of tenants from rather more than thirty in 1086 to about seventy in 1323, which was not exceptional.[65] Fifteen tenants were said to be holding new land in 1323; the clearance of waste was apparently localised on the eastern and southern sides of the parish, as significant field-names such as Newland, Ridding and Stocking were concentrated there (Map 6). Around 1300 the amount of arable land in the manor was in the region of 1,000 acres, 300 in the demesne and the rest in the hands of tenants. Again, this total exceeded that of 1086, but does not represent a dramatic increase. Manors elsewhere saw the clearance of large quantities of new land, and their tenant numbers grew three-fold or more. The conclusion must be that Northfield's history does not conform with the conventional chronology of woodland settlements, in that it did not experience major expansion between 1086 and 1300, though it already had a relatively dense population before 1066.[66]

What was the lords' role in these long-term processes? The decision to enclose, enlarge and maintain 1,000 acres in Weoley Park obviously restricted settlement growth. Park creation may have removed houses and fields, but nothing survives to suggest their previous existence. The park certainly prevented the creation of new settlements, and deprived those living outside the pale from gaining free access to the common pasture that had been enclosed within its pale. Did the lords also have a role in deciding on the number and location of farms outside the park? The settlement and field pattern must date back before the Conquest, and the group of small enclosures attached to houses, especially those with an oval outline, suggest that individuals were carving out fields from the waste. Was this the result of lords making grants of land, as the wastes were supervised by the lord of the manor? In the fourteenth century Somery and Botetourt lords can be observed granting land to servants, one

---

[63] Margaret Gelling, *Place-Names in the Landscape* (1984), 198–207, 235–45; *eadem* and Ann Cole, *The Landscape of Place-Names* (Stamford, 2000), 237–42, 269–78; Della Hooke, 'Early Medieval Woodland and the Place-name term leah', in *A Commodity of Good Names: Essays in Honour of Margaret Gelling*, ed. O.J. Padel and D.N. Parsons (Donington, 2008), 365–76.

[64] *Domesday Book*, ed. Abraham Farley (1783), f. 177a and b. The estimate of woodland area is based on a formula devised by Oliver Rackham. The figures relate to Northfield manor only, not to the other places in Northfield parish, Selly and Bartley.

[65] *Inquisitiones Post Mortem Part 2*, ed. Willis Bund, 113.

[66] For comparison, J.R. Birrell, 'Medieval Agriculture', in *VCH Staffordshire*, vi. 6–7. A parallel comes from the adjoining parish: Anne Baker, 'A Study of North-Eastern King's Norton: Ancient Settlement in a Woodland Manor', *Transactions of the Birmingham and Warwickshire Archaeological Society*, cvii (2003), 131–59.

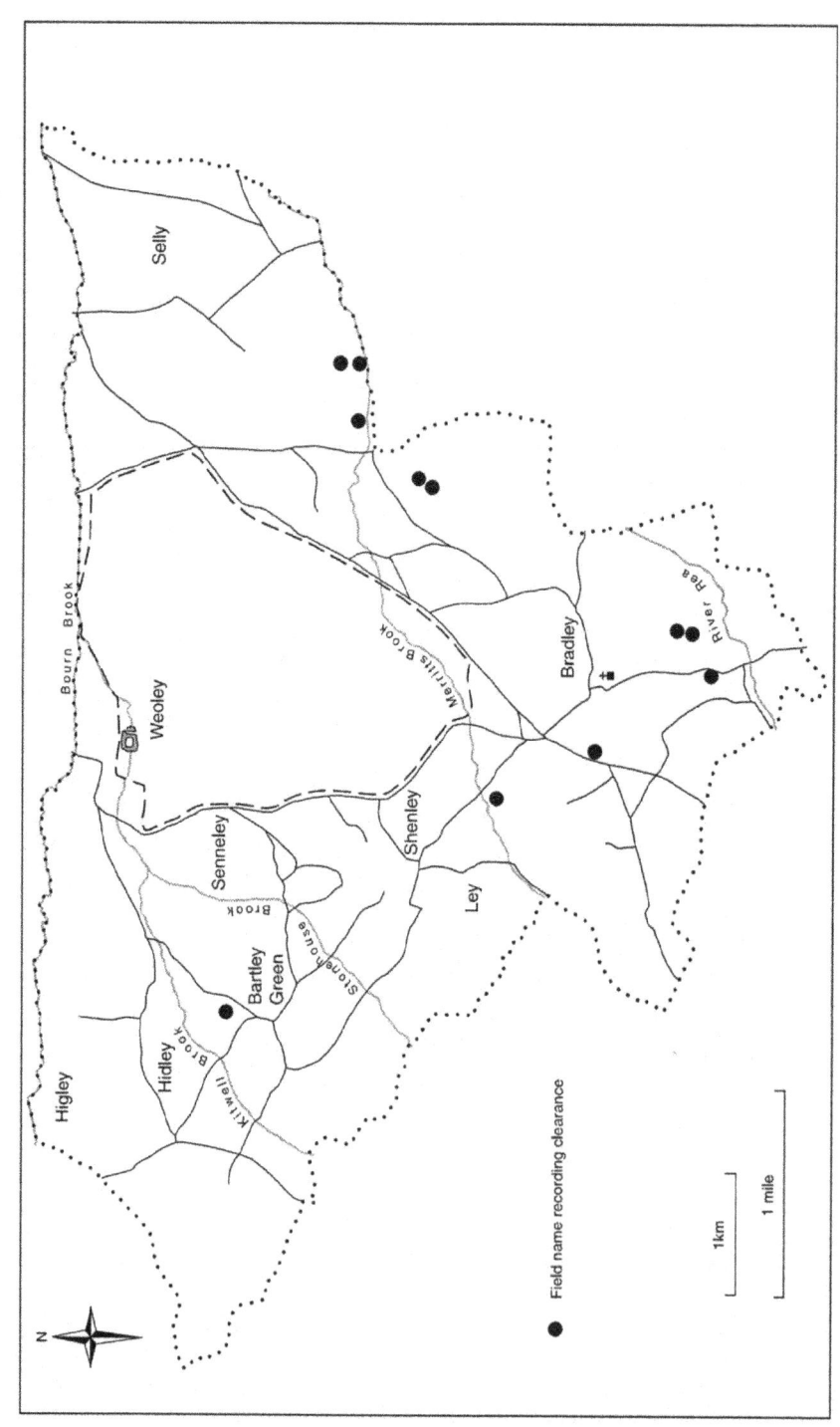

Map 6. Early medieval settlement in Northfield, showing -ley names and clearance names such as ridding and stocking.

of whom had been a baker and another a cook, but they were receiving existing holdings, not new land. A similar piece of patronage may explain the origin of the tenement called Jinners or Genners, which had been acquired by a specialist artisan who had made 'engines', a word that could include a wide range of devices including fish traps, but he may have constructed or operated siege engines for a Somery lord in the thirteenth century.[67] In earlier centuries slaves were settled on the land when they were freed, which gave lords a strong hand in the form of settlement. The irregular distribution of farms suggests, however, a good deal of individual choice by relatively independent peasants about where and how they organised their lives. Nineteen of seventy tenants in 1323 were accounted as free, and they were less likely to have been kept under the thumb of the lord.

Some light on the role of the lords in ruling over the Northfield landscape might be gained by seeing how they treated their tenants in general. Often light rents and services were encountered in a woodland environment. At Northfield, however, in a survey of 1273 a very high £19 is given for customary rents, together with tallage (an extra annual charge falling on unfree tenants) of £4 13s. 4d., and in 1323 the partly legible survey revealed that customary holdings of a yardland, that is about thirty acres, were paying near to 20s. in rent.[68] In 1424 the total of customary and bond tenants had fallen to fourteen, but free and customary tenants alike were paying substantial rents, with the majority owing between 9s. and 18s.[69] Individual serfs were still being identified in the court records as late as 1452.[70] We do not know if these obligations dated back to the granting of land to freed slaves and other settlers in a weak bargaining position before the Conquest, or whether a lord or lords at some later stage, perhaps around 1200, had imposed some quite severe conditions of tenure on the Northfield tenants. The Northfield case demonstrates that settlement forms and tenant conditions did not coincide: heavily burdened customary holdings were not necessarily organised into nucleated villages.[71]

This excursion into the centuries before the arrival of the Berkeleys at Northfield has been designed as a reminder that Northfield in the fifteenth century was already an old country, with a landscape and society that had developed under a number of influences: the woodland environment which encouraged the dispersal of settlements, the inherited landscape from before the Middle Ages, and the evolution of tenancy over many centuries. We might imagine that just as tenants were pushed and cajoled into repairing their houses in the 1440s, so earlier lords negotiated with peasants over the allocation of land, siting of houses, and forms of tenure. This legacy left the Berkeleys with limited room to make changes, and as we have seen one of their aims was to hang on to their tenants. Tenants were evidently not driven away by the relatively high rents; they perceived Northfield as an attractive place to live and farm. The Berkeleys made sure that heriots (death duties) were paid, usually in the form of quite valuable oxen and cows. They were able in 1438 to take an entry fine

---

[67] BL, Add. Ch. 49161; Symons, 'Medieval Northfield', 20; on engineers, Michael Prestwich, *Armies and Warfare in the Middle Ages: The English Experience* (New Haven, Conn., 1996), 284–6.
[68] *Inquisitiones Post Mortem Part 1*, ed. Willis Bund, 16–17; *Part 2*, 113.
[69] Symons, 'Weoley Castle', 54–5.
[70] BAH, 518092.
[71] The problem is raised in Tom Williamson, Robert Liddiard and Tracey Partida, *Champion: The Making and Unmaking of the English Midland Landscape* (Liverpool, 2013), 172–4.

as high as 40s. for a quarter yardland (about eight acres) which amounted to eight times the annual rent, presumably because they thought that the holding was desirable and the new tenant could pay.[72] The manor court attempted to impose enormous amercements for cases of trespass, but the offenders (who rarely paid) were usually outsiders: a group from Kings Norton owed 12s. 10d. for many years, and two men of Halesowen were expected to pay 20s. each for illicit tree felling.[73] In the long term the conditions of tenants became easier. The Berkeleys leased out holdings which lacked tenants, and by 1549, when a new rental was made, customary tenants and bondmen had disappeared, to be replaced by eight leaseholders, a single copyholder, and five tenants at will.[74] There was no danger of the sort of depopulation, either resulting from tenant emigration or expulsion by lords, which visited such villages as Wormleighton. Some messuages fell into disuse and ruin, as we have seen, but some tofts were often taken over by another tenant in a process of engrossing. Those who acquired more than one holding, such as the wealthy Gests, Odomar Walsh and the infamous John Broun, did not take over the community and threaten its cohesion as happened elsewhere.[75]

The scattered settlements did not prevent the people of Northfield from forming a sense of community. The manor court, though held to enforce the lord's rule, was supported by the peasants because of its value as a social regulator. The court, aided by the peasant officials who reported wrong-doing, dealt with a good number of violent incidents, and did its best to force tenants to clean ditches and keep roads open. The use of the common pastures was regulated in the court: those with enclosures were ordered to allow common grazing at the customary seasons, and trespassers were punished for invading enclosures when they had no right to graze. The later phases of building in the parish church, including a new aisle, a porch and a heightened tower in the fifteenth century, tell us something about the effectiveness of community fund raising, as the villagers rather than the lord had taken over responsibility for the church fabric.

A long-term trend of the period converted arable land into pasture, and this continued under the Berkeleys on the demesne but also among the tenants. They kept land in cultivation, for their own subsistence, but also as animal feed, as oats and peas, mainly fodder crops, figure among those grown by the Northfield peasants. In all perhaps 40% of the land was being used as arable, leaving the rest for grazing animals.[76] They specialised in cattle, which accounted for 104 of the 163 heriots recorded. Some kept beef cattle with an eye to market profits, like John Whatcrofte who had twenty bullocks in 1439.[77] Those who claimed the numerous cattle found straying in the manor, like Edmund Drover of Coventry, a Welshman from Shropshire and people from Bromsgrove and Henley in Arden, were probably taking cattle through Northfield on droving routes that connected the pastures of the

---

[72] BAH, 518077.
[73] GA, D2700 MJ17/1 (1440–1); TNA, C103/39 (1467–8).
[74] BAH, 382960; HRO, 44M69/E1/16/12.
[75] John Hare, *A Prospering Society: Wiltshire in the Later Middle Ages* (Hatfield, 2011), 137–9.
[76] Changes in farming can be seen in a final concord, dated to 1530 but likely to reflect the situation in 1485, which estimated Northfield (presumably excluding the park) as containing 1,000 acres of arable land, 100 acres of meadow, 1,000 acres of pasture and 400 acres of wood: HRO, COPY/899/1, f. 112v.
[77] BAH, 518078.

north Midlands and Wales with points south and east where the butchers and many consumers of beef lived, and Northfield peasants no doubt participated in that trade. This was done on the initiative of individuals (acting in the context of the community) who made their own decisions about farming and marketing.[78] In the same way the people of Northfield developed sidelines in trade and crafts to supplement their profits from agriculture, and we find such occupations as baker, butcher, draper, mason, smith, tailor, turner and weaver, again the result of individual choices, though no doubt the Berkeleys found it convenient to employ such specialists occasionally to shoe a horse or repair a wall.

What generalisations can emerge from a well-documented example? We can see that lords had an impact on the society and landscape of their estates in varied and complicated ways. They might live alongside the villagers, but some chose a residence (often by moving their house), in a more isolated setting, in a park if they could afford it. They often built to impress, and arranged their parks and gardens to show off their resources and the beauty of their surroundings. Land was enclosed for exclusive use, not just for parks but also to form compact demesnes for efficient agriculture, though some demesnes remained scattered and intermixed with peasant land. The households and demesnes of the wealthier lords employed some local labour, but they connected with distant markets, so they bought and sold to a limited extent among the local peasants. In the formative years, before 1250, they could have had roles in forming village landscapes, by granting parcels of waste to form dispersed settlements, or by laying out planned villages, though a process of negotiation with peasants played a part in the decision making. In the period 1100–1300 Northfield became two distinct landscapes, with a lord's section in the north and north-east, dominated by the castle, the park and the demesne, and a larger section of peasant countryside in the south and west, with its farms, fields and common pastures, which was made by colonising the waste, and no doubt processes of division and amalgamation of holdings and parcels of land. In the fifteenth century lords' policies and attitudes diverged. A minority of lords, like the Spencers, finished off villages which were losing tenants and going through problems of adjusting to post-plague economic stress. They transformed landscapes by carving up the village fields into pasture closes. The Berkeleys behaved like most lords, aiming to conserve and retain their peasants and their holdings in the expectation of the return of better times, for example by encouraging the repair of houses. They attempted through their courts to keep good order in the management of common fields and maintained a balance between individuals seeking selfish advancement and the interests of the wider community.

Lordship could have an effect on the landscape, not just when a family like the Spencers dictated a transformation in village and its fields, but in more subtle ways. The complexities of rural society, being pushed and pulled in different directions by pressures from the environment, the market, agitation from below, pressure from above, the logic of topography, and inheritance from a distant past, lay behind the landscapes of the fifteenth century. Lords and their policies could make a difference but they could rarely be the decisive or determining influence.

---

[78] Andrew Watkins, 'Cattle Grazing in the Forest of Arden in the Later Middle Ages', *Agricultural History Review*, xxxvii (1989), 12–25.

HAMPSHIRE AND THE PARISH TAX OF 1428

Mark Page

In March 1428, during the minority of Henry VI, the Commons in parliament granted a new and unusual tax for the defence of the realm. Each rural parish whose church was assessed for clerical taxes at less than ten marks was to contribute 6s. 8d., while those above that threshold were to pay at the rate of 13s. 4d. for every ten marks of value.[1] Importantly, those parishes which contained fewer than ten households were exempt from payment, and it is the listing of exempt parishes with small populations which has particularly caught the attention of historians of medieval settlement. A study of Oxfordshire's deserted medieval villages, for example, demonstrated how that county's list of twenty-five parishes certified as qualifying for exemption may be used to suggest fifteenth-century depopulation.[2] Oxfordshire provided several examples of villages abandoned in the period 1370–1520, when an estimated 2,000 were deserted in England as a whole.[3]

The fifteenth century was a period of widespread population decline, or at least stagnation, in many parts of England. Following the dramatic fourteenth-century losses caused by the Black Death and subsequent outbreaks of plague, many rural settlements shrank and an increasing number were wholly deserted as a result of migration, enclosure and other factors. The causes, extent and timing of that shrinkage and desertion have been the subject of close scrutiny over several decades of ongoing research.[4] While acknowledging regional and local variation several studies have emphasised, first, that smaller settlements were more vulnerable to depopulation than larger ones, and secondly, that many deserted or severely shrunken villages and hamlets were not abandoned until the sixteenth century or later.[5] Despite the losses of the years 1370–1520, therefore, the fifteenth century may be characterised as a period when the late medieval settlement pattern was weakened but not overwhelmed by the economic and social upheaval

---

[1] For a fuller description of the taxes levied in March 1428, Maureen Jurkowski, C.L. Smith and David Crook, *Lay Taxes in England and Wales 1188–1688* (1998), 85–6; David Dymond and Roger Virgoe, 'The Reduced Population and Wealth of Early Fifteenth-Century Suffolk', *Proceedings of the Suffolk Institute of Archaeology and History*, xxxvi (1986), 73.

[2] K.J. Allison, M.W. Beresford and J.G. Hurst, *The Deserted Villages of Oxfordshire* (University of Leicester Department of English Local History, Occasional Papers, xvii, 1965).

[3] Christopher Dyer, *Making a Living in the Middle Ages: The People of Britain 850–1520* (2002), 350.

[4] For a general survey, *Medieval Rural Settlement: Britain and Ireland, AD 800–1600*, ed. Neil Christie and Paul Stamper (Oxford, 2012).

[5] E.g. Richard Jones and Mark Page, *Medieval Villages in an English Landscape: Beginnings and Ends* (Macclesfield, 2006), 207–11, 214–21.

unleashed by the plague. By the early 1500s many settlements, even including some which eventually failed to survive, had recovered from an initial loss of population and were thriving once more. Detailed local studies, such as those provided by the *Victoria County History*, can sometimes show these varied patterns of contraction and recovery over a relatively small area.[6] For a wider region, such as a county, comparison of the list of exempt parishes in 1428 with early fourteenth-century and early sixteenth-century lists of tax-payers may offer a similarly varied picture of decline, stagnation and growth, and provide the necessary evidence to support or refute the idea that the fifteenth century was a period of underlying settlement stability.[7] In this paper the focus of attention, appropriately for a volume dedicated to Michael Hicks, is Hampshire.

I

Medieval Hampshire was a county of mixed settlement patterns. Nucleated villages predominated in the central chalk-lands, and dispersed settlement was more common in the wooded north and east, while the coastal zone (including the New Forest) encompassed a scattering of towns, villages and hamlets.[8] Fairly full inventories of the county's medieval settlements can be found in tax lists, especially those of the early fourteenth and early sixteenth centuries. In 1327, for example, around 490 places were assessed for that year's lay subsidy, to which more than 7,000 tax-payers contributed.[9] Several of the settlements listed in 1327 were subsequently deserted as a result of late medieval depopulation. Investigated examples include Northington, a village in the parish of Overton with thirteen tax-payers in 1327, whose gradual post-plague shrinkage was completed by the creation of a single farm on the village site in 1485.[10] Desertion before 1500, however, was almost certainly less common than in the sixteenth to eighteenth centuries, when landowners' creation of parks was at its height. Only one tax-payer was listed under Westbury (in the parish of East Meon) in 1327, but the settlement was still populated in 1524/5 and only abandoned in the seventeenth century following emparkment.[11] In areas of dispersed settlement, moreover, the disappearance of medieval place names may give a false impression of

---

[6] E.g. in west Oxfordshire around Broadwell and Langford: *VCH Oxfordshire*, xvii, ed. Simon Townley (2012).

[7] For a recent study of 15th-century Dorset, Mark Forrest, 'Economic Change in Late Medieval Dorset: An Analysis of Evidence from the Lay Subsidies', *Proceedings of the Dorset Natural History and Archaeological Society*, cxxxiv (2013), 68–82.

[8] Carenza Lewis and Patrick Mitchell-Fox, 'Settlement in Hampshire and the Isle of Wight', *Medieval Settlement Research Group Annual Report*, x (1995), 7–10; D.A. Hinton, 'Debate: South Hampshire, "East Wessex" and the *Atlas of Rural Settlement in England*', *Landscape History*, xxvii (2005), 71–5.

[9] These figures exclude the Isle of Wight: *The Hampshire Tax List of 1327*, ed. Patrick Mitchell-Fox and Mark Page (Hampshire Record Series, xx, 2014).

[10] John Hare, 'Northington, near Overton, and the Deserted Villages of Hampshire', *Hampshire Field Club and Archaeological Society Newsletter*, xxii (1994), 26.

[11] Michael Hughes, 'Settlement and Landscape in Medieval Hampshire', in *The Archaeology of Hampshire*, ed. S.J. Shennan and R.T. Schadla Hall (Hampshire Field Club and Archaeological Society Monograph, i, 1981), 72.

depopulation and desertion. Prallingworth in the parish of Titchfield had the same number of tax-payers – six – in 1327 and 1524/5, and covered a group of hamlets and farmsteads which still existed in the nineteenth century, but its name fell into disuse and knowledge of its location was eventually lost.[12]

The identification of more than 120 deserted settlements in Hampshire (as recognised in 1968) does not, therefore, necessarily indicate the widespread loss of villages and hamlets in the 150 years after the Black Death.[13] Although dating desertion can be difficult, the continued assessment in 1524/5 of most of the places paying tax in 1327 demonstrates the underlying stability of the pre-plague settlement pattern.[14] Nevertheless, the economic and social changes of the late fourteenth and fifteenth centuries undoubtedly encouraged migration, enclosure and other processes contributing to the shrinkage of particular settlements, which in some cases undermined their chances of long-term survival. In this context, the list of exempt parishes with fewer than ten households compiled for the 1428 tax holds considerable interest. It provides us with an opportunity to examine some of the county's least populated places and to suggest why their populations were so small. Were they formerly larger settlements fallen on hard times which were later abandoned, or had they always been inhabited by relatively few households and remained so in the sixteenth century and beyond?

II

Forty-seven places in Hampshire and the Isle of Wight were exempt from payment of the parish tax in 1428 (Appendix). The list does not survive in a contemporary account but in a large and impressive illuminated manuscript of the early sixteenth century.[15] The lack of the original record raises some unanswerable questions about the accuracy of the copy. First, it is unclear whether the list is complete, although the inclusion of parishes from every part of the county suggests that it probably is (see Map). Secondly, the spelling of some place names is uncertain, notably 'Swebrok' and 'Demstede'. Neither has been satisfactorily identified and it is not known whether the names were wrongly transcribed or refer to lost churches of which little other record has been found.[16] Another uncertainty concerns the order in which the parishes appear. The surviving list is not subdivided, but it is clear

---

[12] D.G. Watts, 'Prallingworth – A Lost Locality Identified', *Proceedings of the Hampshire Field Club and Archaeological Society*, xl (1984), 134–6.

[13] See the gazetteer in *Deserted Medieval Villages: Studies*, ed. Maurice Beresford and J.G. Hurst (1971), 188–9.

[14] John Sheail, *The Regional Distribution of Wealth in England as Indicated in the 1524/5 Lay Subsidy Returns*, ed. R.W. Hoyle (List and Index Society Special Series, xxix, 1998), 117–39.

[15] TNA, E164/4, f. 368, printed in *Inquisitions and Assessments Relating to Feudal Aids Preserved in the Public Record Office* (6 vols., 1899–1920), ii. 342. The printed edition includes one error, substituting 'Ronechirch' for 'Bonechirch', i.e. Bonchurch (Isle of Wight).

[16] In a 14th-century assessment 'Sweburk' and 'Dompstede' were among six churches in Basingstoke deanery (with Freefolk, Ewhurst, Winslade and Kempshott) exempted through poverty (*propter exilitatem*): *Wykeham's Register*, ed. T.F. Kirby (2 vols., Hampshire Record Society, xi, xiii, 1896–9), i. 375.

that it is not randomly arranged. In order to assess each parish's contribution to the 1428 tax it is most likely that the commissioners used an earlier ecclesiastical valuation (such as the ecclesiastical taxation of 1291) as the basis for their work.[17] The 1291 valuation was arranged by deanery, and for the most part the 1428 list appears to follow a similar pattern. Somborne deanery (three exempt parishes) was followed by the deaneries of Southampton (one parish), Fordingbridge (three parishes), Basingstoke (fourteen parishes including the unidentified 'Swebrok' and 'Demstede'), the Isle of Wight (three parishes), Andover (six parishes), Alresford (six parishes), Droxford (four parishes), and Alton (four parishes). Two of the final three parishes in the list, however, are not so easily fitted into this neat arrangement. They may have been added later, perhaps because they were mistakenly omitted by the fifteenth-century clerk or his sixteenth-century copyist. A further complication is that the manuscript spelling of neither place name is straightforward. 'Mappelwell' may be an uncommon or corrupted spelling of Mapledurwell (in Basingstoke deanery).[18] 'Castro Sancto Laurenco de Wath Johene' appears to be a confused rendering of St. Lawrence's chapel known as Wathe (meaning 'ford') in the Isle of Wight.[19] No such problems attend the final parish, St. Anastasius in Weeke, the only parish in Winchester deanery with fewer than ten households.[20]

A final peculiarity of the 1428 list concerns the parochial status of several of the places exempted from the tax. The taxation was based on the value of a parish's church, and it is evident that the Hampshire commissioners assessed not only independent parish churches but also dependent chapels, and not only standing parish churches but also ruined or disused churches. Pittleworth was a chapelry of Broughton, for example, and East Parley was a chapelry of Christchurch. Kempshott had formerly been a parish in its own right, but in 1393 it united with Winslade and its church was pulled down.[21] At Wallsworth, too, the chapel had fallen into ruin and in 1426 the living was united with Widley.[22] At Wanstead (in Southwick parish) the chapel was probably still standing in the 1420s although services may not have been regularly performed.[23] The inclusion of chapels and ruined churches suggests that in 1428 the commissioners used an old valuation, and probably a more detailed assessment (perhaps that belonging to Bishop Wykeham) than the one compiled in 1291.[24] Furthermore, the apparently comprehensive coverage of the 1428 assessment enhances the value of the list of exempt places. Several of Hampshire's ancient parishes covered large areas and included one or more chapelries. The exemption of some chapelries from payment

---

[17] As was probably the case in Suffolk: Dymond and Virgoe, 'Reduced Population', 74.
[18] John Hare, Jean Morrin and Stanley Waight, *The Victoria History of Hampshire*, New Series: *Mapledurwell* (2012), 5.
[19] Helge Kökeritz, *The Place-Names of the Isle of Wight* (Uppsala, 1940), 201–2.
[20] Derek Keene, *Survey of Medieval Winchester* (2 vols., Winchester Studies, ii, Oxford, 1985), i. 117, 134.
[21] *VCH Hampshire*, iv. 181, 492–3; v. 108.
[22] Roger Davey, Andrew Perrin and George Watts, 'Wallsworth: A Lost Village?', *Hampshire Field Club and Archaeological Society Newsletter*, xxxii (1999), 9–11.
[23] *VCH Hampshire*, iii. 165; *The Cartularies of Southwick Priory*, ed. K.A. Hanna (Hampshire Record Series, ix, 1988), p. lv.
[24] *Taxatio Ecclesiastica Anglie et Wallie ... circa AD 1291*, ed. Thomas Astle, Samuel Ayscough and John Caley (Record Commission, 1801), 210–13; *Wykeham's Register*, ed. Kirby, i. pp. xi–xii, 364–77.

of the tax implies that others were obliged to contribute. Thus, in the parish of Christchurch, East Parley may have been inhabited by fewer than ten households, but presumably other chapelries at Hurn and Winkton were more populous.[25] If that is correct, the 1428 list has the potential to shed light on population changes in some of the county's larger multi-township parishes such as Micheldever, where Weston Colley appears to have suffered a loss of inhabitants.[26]

III

To what extent was post-plague depopulation responsible for a parish or chapelry's inclusion in the 1428 list of places with fewer than ten households? The Appendix provides some comparative information which may help to answer this question including the number of tax-payers recorded for each place in 1327 and 1524/5. Both those taxes were assessed on heads of household with taxable wealth above a certain threshold, and an unknown number of poorer inhabitants would have been exempt. The figures for 1327 and 1524/5 underestimate, therefore, the number of households in each township, rendering direct comparison with 1428 difficult. The table nevertheless reveals some striking patterns, suggesting that the population of some places remained fairly steady between 1327 and 1524/5, while that of others rose or fell quite markedly. These patterns may be illustrated by the following examples: (1) Lomer – little or no change in its relatively small tax-paying population between 1327 (seven) and 1524/5 (six to eight); (2) Eastrop – considerable growth in its tax-paying population between 1327 (six) and 1524/5 (thirty-three); (3) Swarraton – considerable decline in its tax-paying population between 1327 (twenty-two) and 1524/5 (nine to ten); (4) Fyfield – little or no change in its relatively large tax-paying population between 1327 (seventeen) and 1524/5 (fifteen to nineteen), making its exemption in 1428 particularly notable. Parishes in each of these categories are discussed further below.

Another feature of the table in the Appendix to consider is the small geographical area of many of the places concerned.[27] Of the parishes and chapelries exempted from the 1428 tax certainly a third and possibly a half covered fewer than 1,000 acres.[28] The size of Hampshire's ancient parishes varied widely, but a disproportionate number with small acreages qualified for exemption in 1428. Among them was Bradley (670 acres), a remote chalk-land parish inhabited by six tax-payers in 1327 and six or seven in 1524/5, whose church was enlarged in about 1330. It may have suffered some depopulation as a result of fourteenth-century plagues, but if so its tax-paying population had recovered to pre-Black Death levels

---

[25] *VCH Hampshire*, v. 108.
[26] The identification of Weston Colley is uncertain because it is not known to have had a chapel; no other Weston in Somborne deanery seems to have had one either, however.
[27] A similar point is made in Dymond and Virgoe, 'Reduced Population', 74.
[28] Acreages are taken from *Census, 1841* (Parliamentary Papers (496), xxii, 1843), 272–85. Some chapelries are included in the figures for their constituent parishes, however (see Appendix).

by 1524/5, and in 1841 it accommodated 125 people in twenty-two houses.[29] Bradley's inclusion in a list of parishes with small populations is hardly surprising and cannot be taken as evidence of settlement shrinkage (still less desertion) resulting from late medieval economic and social change. Emphasis should rather be placed on its successful adaptation to the changing conditions of the post-plague economy, a characteristic it shared with several other communities exempted from the 1428 tax. Even places sometimes (misleadingly) described as deserted medieval villages demonstrated economic and social resilience in the later Middle Ages. For example, in 1327 only three tax-payers lived at West Worldham (750 acres) near Alton, and it did not contribute to the 1428 tax. By 1524/5, however, ten inhabitants were above the tax-paying threshold, and ninety-four people inhabited sixteen houses in 1841. As at Bradley, evidence of settlement shrinkage in the parish is slight.[30]

The inclusion of parishes from all parts of the county has already been mentioned as evidence of the 1428 list's completeness. The geographical spread of exempt places is not uniform, however, and some notable concentrations can be identified. Most lie on the chalk downs. The largest cluster surrounds Basingstoke and extends southwards towards the Itchen valley (see Map). A smaller group comprises the remote downland communities of Litchfield, Woodcott and Crux Easton, while further westwards lie the similarly secluded parishes of South Tidworth, Fyfield and Knights Enham.[31] The Hampshire chalk-lands were dominated by sheep and corn husbandry in the Middle Ages, but as the population fell following successive outbreaks of plague the area under tillage was reduced and sheep pastures were extended.[32] Sheep farming was not as labour intensive as cereal cropping and fewer people were needed to tend the flocks and cultivate the remaining arable. Agricultural change thus reinforced the effects of disease in keeping population low, deterring the reoccupation of abandoned holdings and encouraging the under-employed to leave. The higher chalk-lands have been identified as an area of particularly marked settlement desertion, although some deserted medieval villages, such as Polhampton and Quidhampton near Overton, were tithings (not chapelries) of larger parishes and so not eligible for assessment in 1428.[33] Several places qualifying for exemption in 1428 nevertheless exhibited some of the characteristics of the 'classic' late medieval deserted village.[34]

Among the chalk-land villages to have been deserted in the Middle Ages was Abbotstone near Alresford (eighteen tax-payers in 1327), which fell victim to post-plague depopulation possibly encouraged by non-resident lords extending their sheep pastures, its fate finally sealed in the sixteenth century when a new residence

---

[29] *VCH Hampshire*, iv. 202, 204; Nikolaus Pevsner and David Lloyd, *Buildings of England: Hampshire and the Isle of Wight* (1967), 134–5.
[30] *VCH Hampshire*, ii. 521–3; www.pastscape.org.uk s.v. Little Worldham (accessed Oct. 2013).
[31] D.A. Hinton and A.N. Insole, *Ordnance Survey Historical Guides: Hampshire and the Isle of Wight* (1988), 42–3, 45.
[32] For an overview, John Hare, 'The Bishop and the Prior: Demesne Agriculture in Medieval Hampshire', *Agricultural History Review*, liv (2006), 187–212.
[33] Hughes, 'Settlement and Landscape in Medieval Hampshire', 72; John Hare, 'Agriculture and Rural Settlement in the Chalklands of Wiltshire and Hampshire from c.1200–c.1500', in *The Medieval Landscape of Wessex*, ed. Michael Aston and Carenza Lewis (Oxford, 1994), 167.
[34] For a brief summary, Dyer, *Making a Living in the Middle Ages*, 350–2.

was built by the Paulets of Basing. Already in 1524/5 it was not separately assessed for taxation, the abandoned village was grassed over, the ruined church collapsed, and in 1589 the parish was united with neighbouring Itchen Stoke.[35] Another village suffering a similar fate was Lomer on the high chalk-lands southeast of Winchester. It seems not to have been depopulated in the fifteenth century, however: as already mentioned its tax-paying population in 1327 (seven) and 1524/5 (six to eight) remained about the same, but its small size made it vulnerable to enclosing landlords attracted by the profits from the wool trade, and it was deserted in the sixteenth century when its church was closed and the parish amalgamated with Corhampton.[36] A third less well-known example is Weston Corbett near Basingstoke (six tax-payers in 1327), which like Abbotstone was no longer separately assessed in 1524/5, and where the church fell into decay in the sixteenth century and was demolished.[37]

Such places were not typical, however, of most of the chalk-land parishes with fewer than ten households in 1428. In the area around Basingstoke several villages, judging by their tax-paying populations in 1524/5, increased in size in the fifteenth and early sixteenth centuries including Eastrop (thirty-three tax-payers), Ellisfield (nineteen), Upton Grey (twenty-two), Winchfield (twenty-four), and Worting (seventeen), while even tiny Chineham and Kempshott maintained a separate identity in the nineteenth century.[38] Similar growth evidently occurred, too, at Freefolk (twenty-two to twenty-three tax-payers in 1524/5), Greatham (nineteen to twenty), Headbourne Worthy (nineteen) and Weeke (fourteen to sixteen). Small settlements, like larger ones, had the capacity to recover from the depopulation of the later Middle Ages if their communities were given the opportunity to adapt to the new economic conditions. A further striking example from Basingstoke's hinterland was Mapledurwell (thirty-five tax-payers in 1524/5), which benefited from proximity to the town's market, a demand for wool from the local cloth-making industry, and a lack of interference by absentee landowners.[39]

Villages in the immediate vicinity of Basingstoke were better placed than the more isolated Abbotstone and Lomer to take advantage of rising urban and rural demand for agricultural produce in the fifteenth century. Similarly in the east of the county, around Alton and Petersfield, economic recovery probably encouraged the rise in population at Empshott, Greatham, Hartley Mauditt and West Worldham, where numbers of tax-payers were considerably higher in 1524/5 than in 1327.[40] Hartley Mauditt's eventual desertion was instead the result of eighteenth-century emparking by the lord of the manor.[41] Parishes with relatively large numbers of tax-

---

[35] Isabel Sanderson, 'Abbotstone: A Deserted Medieval Village', *Proceedings of the Hampshire Field Club and Archaeological Society*, xxviii (1971), 57–66.
[36] Frances Collins and J. Oliver, 'Lomer: A Study of a Deserted Medieval Village', *Proceedings of the Hampshire Field Club and Archaeological Society*, xxviii (1971), 67–76.
[37] *VCH Hampshire*, iii. 386–8.
[38] *Ibid.*, iv. 179, 231; Hinton and Insole, *Hampshire and the Isle of Wight*, 48.
[39] Hare, Morrin and Waight, *Mapledurwell*, 14–17, 29–32, 41–2, 49–50.
[40] For the market towns of Alton and Petersfield, *VCH Hampshire*, ii. 479–80; iii. 113–16.
[41] G.I. Meirion-Jones, 'Dogmersfield and Hartley Mauditt: Two Deserted Villages', *Proceedings of the Hampshire Field Club and Archaeological Society*, xxvi (1969), 111–27.

payers in 1327 and 1524/5 must have been particularly badly affected by the Black Death and its aftermath, thereby prompting their exclusion in 1428, before recovering in the later fifteenth century. South Tidworth (eighteen tax-payers in 1327 and twenty-three to twenty-seven in 1524/5), Standen (thirteen/twenty), Wallsworth (twelve/sixteen), Weston Colley (nineteen/fourteen) and Whitsbury (twenty/fourteen to seventeen) are examples in this category. Some villages which survived the economic and social turbulence of the later Middle Ages nevertheless remained small, among them Chilworth on the edge of a large common midway between Southampton and Romsey, where the tax-paying population fell from twelve in 1327 to eight in 1524/5, and Nutley (six/thirteen tax-payers) between Alresford and Basingstoke, where the church (rebuilt in 1845) was later demolished.[42] Others gradually diminished until they were no longer viable communities. North and South Charford (eleven/seven tax-payers) on the Wiltshire border both lost their churches in the eighteenth century and effectively merged with Breamore and Hale, while at Swarraton (twenty-two/nine to ten tax-payers) near Alresford the settlement's decline was probably exacerbated by the post-Dissolution development of the Grange estate. Swarraton church was eventually pulled down in 1849 and a new one built in Northington.[43]

As these examples demonstrate, the county's settlement pattern was in constant flux. Depopulation was not a feature confined to the fourteenth and fifteenth centuries and was not necessarily irreversible. Its effects were particularly marked in the chalk-lands, where late medieval sheep pastures extended across under-used arable, threatening the sustainability of some communities and creating opportunities for others. Smaller villages were more vulnerable to eventual desertion than larger ones, but under favourable circumstances even small places might remain relatively unchanged. In some cases lords were decisive in removing settlements which impeded their plans to enclose, empark or build a residence in a parish.[44]

IV

Hampshire's list of places with fewer than ten households in 1428 offers some useful evidence of the county's late medieval settlement pattern. It hints at the loss of churches or chapels (and their congregations) at 'Swebrok', 'Demstede' and Weston Colley possibly even before the Black Death. (Certainly no evidence of a church has been found at any of those places after about 1350, and in the case of 'Swebrok' and 'Demstede' the location of the settlement itself is not known.) It suggests some particularly sharp falls in population in the century following the tax of 1327, including at Abbotstone, Swarraton and South Tidworth. Other places were already small before plague struck and remained so in the 1420s, in some

---

[42] *VCH Hampshire*, iii. 369–71, 468; Pevsner and Lloyd, *Hampshire and the Isle of Wight*, 362.
[43] *VCH Hampshire*, iv. 195–6, 560, 562–3; A.M. Deveson, 'The Early History of the Grange, Northington', *Proceedings of the Hampshire Field Club and Archaeological Society*, lx (2005), 198–208.
[44] For a wider study offering comparable evidence, Richard Jones, 'Contrasting Patterns of Village and Hamlet Desertion in England', in *Deserted Villages Revisited*, ed. Christopher Dyer and Richard Jones (Hatfield, 2010), 16–27.

cases dwindling further in the late fifteenth and early sixteenth centuries, while elsewhere economic recovery was matched by an increase of population. Communities of fewer than ten households evidently remained economically and socially viable at a time of considerable disruption and upheaval, and most of the places exempted in 1428 survived into the sixteenth century and beyond.

The 1428 list does not provide us with a complete record of the county's small settlements, only those with a church or chapel assessed for ecclesiastical taxation. Many other sparsely inhabited villages and hamlets were tithings or other subdivisions of larger parishes that were subject to the same patterns of growth, stagnation and decline. They were particularly numerous in those parts of the county poorly represented among the 1428 exemptions including in the south-east around East Meon and Hambledon and in the south-west around Eling and the New Forest. These large parishes were located in parts of the county dominated by a dispersed settlement pattern of villages, hamlets and farmsteads in which population movements had a less dramatic effect in emptying the landscape than in the chalk-lands, where often a single nucleated village was surrounded by its open fields and pastures.[45] The distribution of places in the Map is fairly accurate, therefore, in showing areas of specifically 'village' as opposed to more general 'settlement' depopulation and desertion.

Maurice Beresford long ago recognised the uses and limitations of the 1428 lists for the study of population and settlement change in fifteenth-century England.[46] Their value is enhanced by the limited number of sources providing a general overview of population and settlement size between the poll tax returns of 1377–81 (which survive only patchily for Hampshire) and the lay subsidy returns of 1524/5.[47] For some counties the original records of the 1428 parish tax survive; in Wiltshire, for example, in each of the county's deaneries the value of its churches was assessed and their liability for the tax was calculated. Where a parish had fewer than ten households, as at Sopworth in the deanery of Malmesbury, an exemption was applied.[48] Although Hampshire's list of exempt parishes was extracted from a similar but no-longer extant assessment, it may usefully be compared with the ecclesiastical valuation drawn up between about 1333 and 1345 and included in Bishop Wykeham's register.[49] A considerable correlation is evident between the parishes exempted in 1428 and those not assessed on account of poverty almost a century before. The two lists are not identical, however, and as the numbers paying tax in 1327 and 1524/5 also demonstrate, communities were differently affected by the economic and social changes of the post-plague era. Abbotstone, valued at ten marks under Wykeham's predecessors, was clearly already in decline by 1428, whereas Stratfield Turgis, exempted before the Black Death, apparently contributed to the 1428 tax, was inhabited by fourteen tax-payers

---

[45] Hinton and Insole, *Hampshire and the Isle of Wight*, 82–3, 90, 98–9, 108–9.
[46] Maurice Beresford, *The Lost Villages of England* (1954), 289–90.
[47] Lists of places given tax relief in 1449 survive for some counties: Dymond and Virgoe, 'Reduced Population', 76.
[48] TNA, E179/196/91, printed in *Feudal Aids*, v. 280–98.
[49] *Wykeham's Register*, ed. Kirby, i. 364–77; Virginia Davis, *William Wykeham: A Life* (2007), 57.

in 1524/5 and accommodated 243 people in forty-eight houses in 1841.[50] Used in this way in conjunction with other evidence, the 1428 lists are a valuable source for assessing the fluctuating patterns of settlement shrinkage and recovery in many parts of late medieval England. In Hampshire, as elsewhere including East Anglia and the east Midlands,[51] some villages were irreversibly damaged by the Black Death and its aftermath, but many others (even small ones) survived its effects and remained inhabited in the sixteenth century and beyond.[52]

---

[50] It was nevertheless described as a deserted medieval village: *Deserted Medieval Villages*, ed. Beresford and Hurst, 189.
[51] Tom Williamson, *England's Landscape: East Anglia* (2006), 81–2; David Stocker, *England's Landscape: The East Midlands* (2006), 75–9.
[52] For a broadly similar conclusion, D.A. Hinton, 'Central Southern England: "Chalk and Cheese"', in *Medieval Rural Settlement*, ed. Christie and Stamper, 131.

APPENDIX

Deanery[1]	Place name (MS version)[2]	Place name (modern spelling)	Acreage in 1841[3]	No. of taxpayers in 1327[4]	No. of taxpayers in 1524/5[5]
Somborne	Weston	Weston Colley	tithing in Micheldever parish (9,340 acres)	19	14
Somborne	Pettelworth	Pittleworth	chapelry in Broughton parish (4,500 acres)	4	included in Broughton (112–14)
Somborne	Eldene	Eldon	extra-parochial (276 acres in 1851)	16 (including Compton)	2
Southampton	Chelworthe	Chilworth	1,400 acres	12	8
Fordingbridge	Wycchebury	Whitsbury	1,850 acres	20 in 1332[6]	14–17[7]
Fordingbridge	Chardeford	Charford	850 acres (570 acres in North and 280 acres in South Charford)	11 (including Hale)	7 (2 in North and 5 in South Charford)
Fordingbridge	Estperle	East Parley	chapelry in Christchurch parish (24,640 acres)	included in Hurn (20)	included in Hurn (15–16)
Basingstoke	Worthyng	Worting	1,070 acres	8	17
Basingstoke	Upton	Upton Grey	2,310 acres	8	22
Basingstoke	Asshe	Ashe	2,310 acres	1	5–6
Basingstoke	Estrop	Eastrop	440 acres	6 (including Lickpit)	33
Basingstoke	Ullesfeld Sancto Martini	Ellisfield	2,360 acres	9	19
Basingstoke	Chynham	Chineham	520 acres	11	included in Monk Sherborne (34)
Basingstoke	Wynterslode	Winslade	880 acres	7	9
Basingstoke	Kympshete	Kempshott	330 acres	3	included in Winslade (9)
Basingstoke	Weston Corbet	Weston Corbett	extra-parochial (440 acres)	6	?included in Upton Grey (22)

Basingstoke	Frifolke	Freefolk	800 acres + tithing in Whitchurch parish (7,330 acres)	12	22–23
Basingstoke	Swebrok	not known	not known	not known	not known
Basingstoke	Demstede	not known	not known	not known	not known
Basingstoke	Iwnest	Ewhurst	820 acres	4 (including Pitt)	?included in Wolverton (17)
Basingstoke	Wynfeld	Winchfield	1,760 acres	12	24
Isle of Wight	Wodyton	Wootton	530 acres	14	12
Isle of Wight	Staundon	Standen	included in Arreton parish (8,270 acres)	13	20 (16 in East and 4 in West Standen)
Isle of Wight	Bonechirch	Bonchurch	150 acres	?included in Whitwell (22)	?included in Whitwell (26)
Andover	Fyfhyde	Fyfield	2,210 acres	17	15–19
Andover	Thodeworth	South Tidworth	2,170 acres	18	23–27 (including Sarson)
Andover	Leueshull	Litchfield	2,900 acres	14	8
Andover	Wodecote	Woodcott	1,350 acres	8	23 (including Crux Easton)
Andover	Crokeston	Crux Easton	950 acres	7	23 (including Woodcott)
Andover	Enham	Knights Enham	2,490 acres	12	13–17
Alresford	Chilton	Chilton Candover	2,190 acres	8	15
Alresford	Bradlegh	Bradley	670 acres	6	6–7
Alresford	Wordy Comitis	Headbourne Worthy	1,650 acres	9	19
Alresford	Swareton	Swarraton	1,710 acres	22	9–10 (including Godsfield)
Alresford	Nuttele	Nutley	1,210 acres	6	13
Alresford	Abboteston	Abbotstone	included in Itchen Stoke parish (2,850 acres)	18	included in Itchen Stoke (24–32)
Droxford	Wallesworth	Wallsworth	included in Widley parish (950 acres)	12	16
Droxford	Lomere	Lomer	included in Exton parish (2,210 acres)	7	6–8
Droxford	Cornhampton	Corhampton	2,410 acres	7	11

Droxford	Wanstede	Wanstead	included in Southwick parish (4,950 acres)	included in Southwick (25)	4–5
Alton	Hertlegh	Hartley Mauditt	1,550 acres	9	18–20
Alton	Imbeschete	Empshott	1,320 acres	9	18–21
Alton	Worldham Minor	West Worldham	750 acres	3	10
Alton	Gratham	Greatham	4,230 acres	9	19–20
Basingstoke	Mappelwell	Mapledurwell	730 acres	8	35
Isle of Wight	Castro Sancto Laurenco de Wath Johene	St. Lawrence	350 acres	17	?included in Whitwell (26)
Winchester	Sancto Anastasio	Weeke	1,190 acres	5	14–16

[1] *Taxatio Ecclesiastica Angliae et Walliae*, ed. Astle, Ayscough and Caley, 210–13.
[2] TNA, E164/4, f. 368; printed in *Feudal Aids*, ii. 342.
[3] *Census, 1841*, 272–85.
[4] *The Hampshire Tax List of 1327*, ed. Mitchell-Fox and Page.
[5] Sheail, *Regional Distribution of Wealth*, ed. Hoyle, 117–39.
[6] *The Wiltshire Tax List of 1332*, ed. D.A. Crowley (Wiltshire Record Society, xlv, 1989), 17–18.
[7] Sheail, *Regional Distribution of Wealth*, 373.

Map: The County of Hampshire

Key to Map of places with fewer than ten households in 1428

a) By place-name

Abbotstone	36
Ashe	10
Bonchurch	24
Bradley	32
Charford	6
Chilton Candover	31
Chilworth	4
Chineham	13
Cornhampton	39
Crux Easton	29
'Demstede' (not shown)	19
East Parley	7
Eastrop	11
Eldon	3
Ellisfield	12
Empshott	42
Ewhurst	20
Freefolk	17
Fyfield	25
Greatham	44
Hartley Mauditt	41
Headbourne Worthy	33
Kempshott	15
Knights Enham	30
Litchfield	27
Lomer	38
Mapledurwell	45
Nutley	35
Pittleworth	2
St. Lawrence	46
South Tidworth	26
Standen	23
Swarraton	34
'Swebrok' (not shown)	18
Upton Grey	9
Wallsworth	37
Wanstead	40
Weeke	47
Weston Colley	1
Weston Corbett	16
West Worldham	43
Whitsbury	5
Winchfield	21
Winslade	14
Woodcott	28
Wootton	22
Worting	8

b) By map reference

1. Weston Colley
2. Pittleworth
3. Eldon
4. Chilworth
5. Whitsbury
6. Charford
7. East Parley
8. Worting
9. Upton Grey
10. Ashe
11. Eastrop
12. Ellisfield
13. Chineham
14. Winslade
15. Kempshott
16. Weston Corbett
17. Freefolk
18. 'Swebrok' (not shown)
19. 'Demstede' (not shown)
20. Ewhurst
21. Winchfield
22. Wootton
23. Standen
24. Bonchurch
25. Fyfield
26. South Tidworth
27. Litchfield
28. Woodcott
29. Crux Easton
30. Knights Enham
31. Chilton Candover
32. Bradley
33. Headbourne Worthy
34. Swarraton
35. Nutley
36. Abbotstone
37. Wallsworth
38. Lomer
39. Cornhampton
40. Wanstead
41. Hartley Mauditt
42. Empshott
43. West Worldham
44. Greatham
45. Mapledurwell
46. St. Lawrence
47. Weeke

THE LIVERY ACT OF 1429

Gordon McKelvie

Ever since K.B. McFarlane's work on the ties of lordship known as 'bastard feudalism', historians have concentrated on the potential for social cohesion they offered. This is in stark contrast to older interpretations which emphasised the disruptive nature of noble affinities.[1] Bastard feudalism was the system in which lords retained men by grants of annuities and livery, enabling them to obtain the administrative, military and domestic service they required. For those retained, service was an avenue for social and economic advancement.[2] The relationship also offered a potential benefit for medieval governments which might utilise these connections for the effective administration of the localities.[3] As James Ross has noted, the emphasis of recent scholarship has been on 'the durability and loyalty of magnate affinities, not their fickleness or instability'.[4] The acceptability of certain forms of retaining should not, however, disguise the reality that retaining also had the potential to facilitate disorder. Retaining did not in itself lead to lawlessness and rebellion, but might be a method of recruitment employed by the nobility for such purposes. Regulation was required and came in the form of several statutes passed between 1390 and 1504 that attempted to restrict retaining by grants of livery, and from 1468 onwards by indentures of retainer, to members of a lord's family, his estate officials and immediate household.[5] These Acts have been used by historians to illuminate the politics of the periods in which they were passed. The first Act, of 1390, has been examined in relation to problems regarding

---

[1] K.B. McFarlane, *The Nobility of Late Medieval England: The Ford Lectures of 1953 and Related Studies* (Oxford, 1973); idem, *England in the Fifteenth Century: Collected Essays*, intro. G.L. Harriss (1981). For earlier work see in particular John Fortescue, *The Governance of England*, ed. Charles Plummer (Oxford, 1885), 15–16, 25; William Stubbs, *Constitutional History of England in the Middle Ages* (3 vols., Oxford, 1880).

[2] This is a central theme of Michael Hicks, *Bastard Feudalism* (1995).

[3] W.H. Dunham, *Lord Hastings' Indentured Retainers, 1461–83: The Lawfulness of Livery and Retaining under the Yorkists and Tudors* (Transactions of the Connecticut Academy of Arts and Sciences, xxxix, 1955); C.D. Ross, *Edward IV* (1974), 331–41; James Ross, *John de Vere, Thirteenth Earl of Oxford (1442–1513): 'The Foremost Man of the Kingdom'* (Woodbridge, 2011), 114–49; Sean Cunningham, 'Henry VII, Sir Thomas Butler and the Stanley Family: Regional Politics and the Assertion of Royal Influence in North Western England', in *Social Attitudes and Political Structures in the Fifteenth Century*, ed. Tim Thornton (Stroud, 2002), 241.

[4] James Ross, 'A Governing Elite? The Higher Nobility in the Yorkist and Early Tudor Period', in *The Yorkist Age: Proceedings of the 2011 Harlaxton Symposium*, ed. Hannes Kleineke and Christian Steer (Donnington, 2013), 111.

[5] For the Act of 1390: *PROME*, vii. 147–50; for that of 1468, *ibid.*, xiii. 384–6; and for that of 1504 *ibid.*, xvi. 365–8.

Richard II's retaining policy;[6] a dispute between the Commons and Lords regarding the lawless activities of magnates and their retainers;[7] and as a 'by-product of [the gentry's] concern for their own social position' through the restriction of those entitled to distribute liveries.[8] Similarly, the retaining laws passed during Henry VII's reign, and in particular the Act of 1504, which introduced licenses to retain, have been viewed as central to understanding that monarch's policy towards the nobility.[9]

Michael Hicks's primary contribution to our understanding of livery laws is his article on the statute of 1468, which demonstrated that this formed part of Edward IV's professed commitment to law and order made in parliament on 17 May that year, and was provoked by a series of prosecutions for illegal livery linked to recent disturbances in Derbyshire. He also discovered that magnates such as the dukes of Norfolk and Suffolk were indicted for illegally granting livery shortly after the Act was passed.[10] The present discussion will focus on the livery Act of 1429, which expanded existing statutory law by introducing new procedures and defining their scope and terms more rigorously than previous Acts.[11] Contemporary chroniclers do not seem to have been particularly interested in this Act or the petitions which prompted it, unlike the Acts of the late fourteenth century, which did catch their attention.[12] Nor has it attracted much attention from historians of the period. In their overviews of the livery and retaining statutes, W.H. Dunham and J.M.W. Bean concentrated on the more famous Acts of 1390, 1468 and 1504.[13] Yet this lack of interest may be unjustified. It is the contention of this article that the Act of livery of 1429 was important for two reasons: first, it demonstrates that unrestricted retaining was viewed as a threat to public order during the 1420s; second, it was part of the long-term development and increasing sophistication of the livery laws. Although the Act was not as radical or as wide-ranging as others, when examined in detail in conjunction with surviving judicial records, it sheds light on the evolution of parliamentary legislation during the fifteenth century.

---

[6] Christopher Given-Wilson, *The Royal Household and the King's Affinity: Service, Politics and Finance in England, 1360–1413* (London and New Haven, Conn., 1986), 234–45.

[7] R.L. Storey, 'Liveries and Commissions of the Peace, 1388–90', in *The Reign of Richard II*, ed. F.R.H. Du Boulay and C.M. Barron (1971), 131–52.

[8] Nigel Saul, 'The Commons and the Abolition of Badges', *Parliamentary History*, ix (1990), 302–15, quotation on p. 313.

[9] See in particular Sean Cunningham, *Henry VII* (2007), 209–15; Alan Cameron, 'The Giving of Livery and Retaining in Henry VII's Reign', *Renaissance and Modern Studies*, xviii (1974), 17–35; Dominic Luckett, 'Crown Office and Licensed Retinues in the Reign of Henry VII', in *Rulers and Ruled in Late Medieval England*, ed. R.E. Archer and Simon Walker (1995), 223–38.

[10] M.A. Hicks, 'The 1468 Statute of Livery', *HR*, lxiv (1991), 15–28. For the relevant cases, see TNA, KB29/99, rots. 31–2.

[11] *PROME*, x. 402–3.

[12] For reports of livery legislation and petitions in late fourteenth-century parliaments: *The Westminster Chronicle, 1381–1394*, ed. and trans. L.C. Hector and B.F. Harvey (Oxford, 1982), 83, 354–7, 365–7; *The Chronicle of Adam Usk, 1377–1421*, ed. and trans. Christopher Given-Wilson (Oxford, 1997), 82–5.

[13] J.M.W. Bean, *From Lord to Patron: Lordship in Late Medieval England* (Manchester, 1989), 200–30; Dunham, *Lord Hastings' Indentured Retainers*, 67–89.

I

The parliament of 1427 was, as far as the surviving parliamentary records go, the first to pass legislation about liveries since that of 1411.[14] A Commons' petition complained that the earlier statutes regulating the distribution of livery had not been upheld because many who contravened the Acts could not be indicted owing to 'the great maintenance' they enjoyed.[15] The petition requested that justices should have the power to award writs of attachment and distraint against those alleged to have contravened the statutes. These truncated procedures which, in theory, 'shifted the advantage to the prosecution',[16] would enable justices of the peace to arrest suspects, interrogate them and convict them without resort to a jury. To ensure that any new Act would not invalidate earlier statutes, the petition asked that older legislation should not be repealed. It was also requested that the laws should be enforced in the palatinates of Cheshire and Lancashire. Finally, certain people were to be exempt from the Act, namely mayors while in office, sergeants and those entering the universities. Yet the petition proved unsuccessful, with the response being: '*Soient les estatutz devaunt ces heures en ceo cas faitz, tenuz et gardez et mys en due execucioun*' (Let the statutes made before this time in this regard be upheld and observed and duly enforced). Accordingly, no new legislation resulted.

Even though the Commons were unable to obtain a new statute regarding liveries, earlier statutes continued to be enforced. In 1428 fourteen cases of illegal livery in Cheshire, in which 104 men were indicted, were heard before Humphrey, duke of Gloucester, at that time the protector and defender of England.[17] Several of these cases have already been briefly discussed by Jane Laughton in the context of lawlessness within the city of Chester,[18] but they have not been considered in their broader national context. Fourteen was a comparatively large number of indictments for illegal livery. There had been three cases of illegal livery in Yorkshire in the early 1420s,[19] but the only previous substantial cluster of prosecutions occurred in Staffordshire in 1414, when there were twenty-one indictments connected to the disorder in the region.[20] A similar context was evident in Cheshire in the 1420s where 'a multitude of feuds had sprung up among the local gentry', particularly involving the families of Egerton and Brereton.[21] The fact that a high number of illegal livery cases in the palatinate were heard by the

---

[14] *PROME*, viii. 547–8.
[15] For this paragraph, unless stated otherwise, see *ibid.*, x. 354–5.
[16] Hicks, '1468 Statute of Livery', 16.
[17] TNA, CHES25/12, mm. 16–17.
[18] Jane Laughton, *Life in a Late Medieval City: Chester, 1275–1520* (Oxford, 2008), 97.
[19] TNA, KB27/642, rex rot. 31; KB29/56; 57, rot. 5.
[20] TNA, KB9/113, mm. 2, 11, 28, 40–3; KB27/613, rex rots. 39–40. Several of these cases are calendared in 'Extracts from the Plea Rolls of the Reigns of Henry V and Henry VI', ed. George Wrottesley, *William Salt Archeological Society*, xvii (1896), 6–7, 9–10. For violence in Staffordshire prior to the 1414 indictments, Edward Powell, *Kingship, Law and Society: Criminal Justice in the Reign of Henry V* (Oxford, 1989), 208–24.
[21] R.A. Griffiths, *The Reign of Henry VI: The Exercise of Royal Authority, 1422–1461* (1981), 137.

duke of Gloucester himself indicates that this was part of a determined attempt by central government to restore order to the locality.

A year after the indictments in Cheshire the Commons again raised the issue of unregulated liveries when they petitioned the king and Lords. They complained, as they had done in 1427, that previous statutes had 'not been duly observed' due to the great maintenance enjoyed by those who breached them.[22] Much of the petition repeated requests made at the parliament of 1427, but then made certain additions, including a proviso that permitted the distribution of livery in times of war. This was a broader exemption than that already enjoyed by the wardens of the March, whom it was recognised needed to be able to retain men quickly for the purposes of defending the border with Scotland.[23] The purchasing of a lord's livery in order to secure his 'support, aid or maintenance in any dispute, or in any other way whatsoever', was to be prohibited. This was the first occasion in which a distinction was made in the law between those illegally wearing a lord's livery with his knowledge, since he had bestowed it upon them, and those who wore the livery of a lord without his knowledge. They could either have continued to wear it after being dismissed from their lord's service or have obtained it by some other means such as theft or making the livery themselves. Finally, women were to be bound by the statutes. In contrast to that of 1427, this petition was successful, obtaining the response: *Soit fait come il est desire par la petitioun* (Let it be done as it is desired by the petition).

It is not obvious why the petition of 1427 failed and the one submitted two years later succeeded. The disturbances in Cheshire and consequent livery indictments may have been a factor, but a better explanation probably lies in the context of the parliament of 1429. When writs of summons were issued on 12 July plans had probably already been made for the coronation of the eight-year-old Henry VI (which indeed took place at Westminster Abbey on 6 November, during the first session); yet a crisis in Lancastrian rule in France, arising from the crowning of Charles VII at Rheims on 17 July in the aftermath of Joan of Arc's success at the siege of Orléans, made it necessary for a military expedition to be mounted to escort Henry across the Channel to confirm his sovereignty there.[24] Added to this crisis was the growing personal animosity between the king's great-uncle Cardinal Henry Beaufort, and his uncle Humphrey, duke of Gloucester. Five months prior to the opening of this parliament Gloucester raised the question about whether Beaufort's retention of the see of Winchester, despite being elevated to the ranks of the cardinals, made him susceptible to accusations of *praemunire*.[25] At the same time, however, Gloucester's own powers were being diminished, for the coronation of Henry VI also required the duke's resignation as protector of England.[26] The fact that leading nobles were about to embark on a potentially lengthy expedition to France may have focused the attention of parliament on the urgent need to deal with problems of lawlessness at home, in a manner akin to that of Henry V prior to

---

[22] *PROME*, x. 402–3.
[23] *Ibid.*, viii. 38.
[24] Malcolm Vale, *Charles VII* (1974), 45–6, 56–7.
[25] On the personal quarrel between Beaufort and Gloucester in the years leading up to this parliament see in particular G.L. Harriss, *Cardinal Beaufort: A Study of Lancastrian Ascendancy and Decline* (Oxford, 1988), 134–90.
[26] *PROME*, x. 280.

his expedition to Normandy in 1415.[27] One petition in particular harked back to Henry V's reign, for it requested the upholding of a statute from the parliament of April 1414 for the imposition of justice regarding 'murders, homicides, robberies, batteries, assemblies of large numbers of people in the manner of insurrections, and of various other rebellions and lawlessness'.[28] The impending absence of the king and, more importantly given Henry's youth, of many magnates and gentry, necessitated strict provisions for the government of England while they were away. This probably predisposed the king's council to accept more readily petitions from the Commons for rigorous enforcement of the law. The seeming ease with which the Act was passed is evident in the surviving bill. The formula '*soit baille aux seigneurs*' at its head indicates that the legislation was indeed introduced in the Commons and the text of the bill itself is unaltered in the parliament roll.[29] It is therefore likely that the petition was successful and passed with relative ease because of the need for a definitive statement against lawlessness before the coronation expedition embarked.

This requirement was evident on other occasions during the parliament. In his opening speech the chancellor, John Kemp, archbishop of York, stressed the need for the restoration of justice within the kingdom.[30] Several of the Acts of the parliament were connected to problems associated with public order, including the famous Act restricting the franchise of the shires to freeholders with land worth at least 40*s*. (a statute which was not to be repealed until the Great Reform Act of 1832).[31] There had been three disputed elections to the parliament – in Cumberland, Buckinghamshire and Huntingdonshire.[32] Hannes Kleineke has argued that these troubles were instrumental in the passing of the electoral statute,[33] presumably since restricting the numbers who could vote would, in turn, mean that fewer people would be present at elections, reducing the chance of their disturbance by threats and intimidation. Legislation designed to regulate the distribution of livery and reduce the potential for violence at parliamentary elections addressed different forms of the abuses that might be facilitated by ties of lordship.

Three further petitions touched on such abuses of lordship and the excesses of bastard feudalism. The statutes of livery restricted the size of noble affinities and the number of men permitted to wear magnates' livery. The problems associated with large groups of men being retained by members of the nobility, and therefore potentially shielded from justice, were a further cause for complaint in a petition regarding the criminal activities of soldiers going to France via Kent and Sussex, who seized food and other supplies from local inhabitants without payment. Yet

---

[27] This is the central theme of Powell, *Kingship, Law and Society*.
[28] *PROME*, x. 419–20.
[29] TNA, C49/19/8. For the procedure of law-making in medieval English parliaments, see P.R. Cavill, *The English Parliaments of Henry VII, 1485–1504* (Oxford, 2009), 146–53.
[30] *PROME*, x. 376.
[31] *Ibid.*, 404–5.
[32] *Parliamentarians at Law: Select Legal Proceedings of the Long Fifteenth Century Relating to Parliament*, ed. Hannes Kleineke (Oxford, 2008), 132–67; J.S. Roskell, *The Commons in the Parliament of 1422: English Society and Parliamentary Representation under the Lancastrians* (Manchester, 1954), 15–21.
[33] *Parliamentarians at Law*, ed. Kleineke, 13.

this particular petition, which asked that any solider who had been underpaid, or not paid at all, should complain to his captain instead of taking from the land, proved unsuccessful, with the response being '*Le roi s'advisera*'.[34] Maintenance was a further aspect of bastard feudalism attacked during this parliament. Another petition complained that forcible entries into lands and property were not being properly dealt with because the perpetrators bribed lords with '*douns, feffementz et discontinuances*' (gifts, feoffments and discontinuences) to gain their support.[35] During the second session of the parliament new guidelines for the royal council were approved. One of their eighteen provisions touched closely on the abuses of bastard feudalism, in stipulating that no lord of the council was to keep in his household, support or give livery to any known criminal or outlaw.[36] The likely impetus for this ordinance was the feud that had developed between two members of the council, John Mowbray, duke of Norfolk, and John Holand, earl of Huntingdon. One chronicler stated that the quarrel between them led to a proclamation during this parliament that no member of either household was to carry weapons within the royal palace.[37] This particular provision therefore related specifically to royal councillors, rather than to members of the nobility in general, yet despite its possible origins in a personal quarrel, it also formed a part of a broader campaign by parliament to combat potential disorder in the kingdom encouraged by noble affinities prior to the coronation expedition. A third petition referred to recent robberies and acts of arson in the town of Cambridge as well as the counties of Cambridgeshire and Essex. It successfully requested that any incident of arson committed since the beginning of the reign should be classed as high treason.[38] Clearly, the livery Act of 1429 was not passed in isolation, but was one of several measures taken by a parliament attempting to deal with problems of public order and perversions of justice.

II

In the long-term history of livery legislation, the petitions of the late 1420s occupy a point mid-way between the earlier 'Commons-driven' legislation of the reigns of Richard II and Henry IV and the later 'Crown-driven' legislation of the Yorkist and Tudor eras. Like the earlier statutes, the Act of 1429 had its origins in petitions from the Commons. The first statute in 1390 was passed in response to complaints about the abuses of liveried retainers.[39] Petitions in 1393, 1397, 1401 and 1406 all asserted that previous legislation had not been upheld and demanded action.[40] The records of the king's bench give credence to these complaints, as only one indictment is recorded on the *rex* side of the plea rolls before Henry V's reign. This, made in 1393, concerned a group of men who wore the same livery 'by corrupt

---

[34] *PROME*, x. 409–10.
[35] *Ibid.*, 412–14.
[36] *Ibid.*, 372–3, 394.
[37] John Amundesham, *Annales Monasterii St Albani*, ed. H.T. Riley (2 vols., RS, 1870, 1871), i. 42–3. On the quarrel between Norfolk and Huntingdon see Griffiths, *Henry VI*, 135.
[38] *PROME*, x. 404–5.
[39] *Ibid.*, vii. 147–50.
[40] *Ibid.*, vii. 239–40, 313–14; viii. 148–9, 400–1.

allegiances and confederacy, each of them maintaining the other in all plaints, true or false, against whomever should wish to complain against them or any one of them'.[41] A similar lack of enforcement was evident prior to the parliament of 1427. There were only four cases of illegal retaining between the cluster of indictments at the start of Henry V's reign and the petition delivered in 1427, three of which concerned events in Yorkshire (in the successive years from 1421 to 1423),[42] and the other criminal activity in Shropshire in 1421.[43] The petitions of 1427 and 1429 were following a clear trend by complaining about ineffectual enforcement of the statutes, which was why the petitioners believed a new law, with new truncated procedures, was required. Indeed, the only Act regarding livery which was passed apparently without the prompting of a preceding Commons petition belonged to Henry IV's first parliament in 1399, and this placed a distinct emphasis on royal retaining.[44] The peculiar nature of this particular Act, in contrast to other pre-Yorkist livery Acts, owed everything to political circumstances. It was a response to the final years of Richard II's reign, in which that king's retaining practices had become the subject of intense criticism. They were one of the thirty-three charges for which Richard II was deposed.[45]

III

In order to assess the significance of the legislation it is necessary to consider the effect it had on the enforcement of the statutes. It transpires that there was little sustained enforcement of the Act after its passing in 1429. The first two cases of illegal livery prosecuted after the statute passed, in 1432, concerned the activities in Cheshire of two obscure gentlemen, George Werle and Richard Wehelok, who were indicted for illegally distributing livery of cloth, respectively to four and twenty-two yeomen.[46] This was followed a year later by two cases in Somerset,[47] and in 1434 by fourteen in Derbyshire.[48] The Derbyshire cases were brought before a commission of *oyer et terminer* in the aftermath of the murders of Henry Longford and William Bradshaw on 1 January that year and the maiming of their patron Sir Henry Pierrepoint. These events were entangled within various quarrels in the county and the commission heard a number of indictments for murder, assault, rape and theft.[49] As in Staffordshire in 1414 and Cheshire in 1428, illegal

---

[41] KB27/528, rex rot. 35; printed in *Select Cases in the Court of King's Bench Under Richard II, Henry IV and Henry V*, ed. G.O. Sayles (Selden Society, lxxxviii, 1971), 83–5.
[42] KB27/642, rex rot. 31; KB29/56, rot. 25; 57 rot. 5.
[43] KB27/640, rex rot. 7; 642, rex rot. 7.
[44] *PROME*, viii. 38.
[45] *Chronicles of the Revolution, 1397–1400: The Reign of Richard II*, ed. Christopher Given-Wilson (Manchester and New York, 1993), 174. See also Nigel Saul, *Richard II* (1997), 392–4, 431, 444–5, 460; J.L. Gillespie, 'Richard II's Archers of the Crown', *Journal of British Studies*, xviii (1979), 14–29; Given-Wilson, *King's Affinity*, 212–26.
[46] CHES25/12, m. 25.
[47] KB29/66, rot. 28; 67, rot. 4.
[48] KB29/68, rots. 4d–5, 9d–10d, 17d, 20; KB9/11, mm. 15, 17.
[49] S.M. Wright, *Derbyshire Gentry* (Derbyshire Records Society, viii, 1983), 128–33.

livery figured in several indictments related to wider instances of disorder. There were five other indictments for illegal livery during the 1430s: in Kent in 1435,[50] Warwickshire in 1436,[51] Sussex in 1437,[52] and in London and Yorkshire in 1439.[53] These were followed in 1440 with another in Oxfordshire.[54] These six cases, however, were isolated in character and were not apparently discovered as a consequence of a general campaign against serious disorder in a particular locality. By contrast, many of the cases from the 1450s can be connected with wider problems of public order and its deterioration into open civil war.[55] The enforcement of the statutes after the passing of the Act of 1429 was therefore sporadic, until needed as a response to disorder on a very large scale.

Furthermore, it is difficult to ascertain the rigour with which this specific Act was enforced, or its long-term consequences, because few indictments cite specific statutes, instead stating that offences had been committed against the form of the 'statutes of livery'. While it must be assumed that the latest statute tacitly over-rode the rest, the only case discovered which explicitly cited the statute of 1429 referred to events in Rutland many years later in 1510, when two husbandmen, Robert and Nicholas Greenham, were indicted for illegally wearing the livery of Thomas Howard, earl of Surrey.[56] This case was similar to several others from Henry VII's reign when various people were indicted for wearing the livery of prominent peers such as the duke of Buckingham, the earls of Arundel, Derby, Essex, Northumberland and Oxford, and even the king's mother, Margaret Beaufort.[57] Although it was the Act of 1429 that first outlawed the purchasing and fraudulent wearing of a magnate's livery, these sixteenth-century cases are best understood within the context of Henry VII's relations with the nobility and his attempts to combat illegal retaining, which is beyond the remit of the present article.[58] During the 1420s and 1430s the indictments were focused on lords giving livery to men who were not family members, estate officials or legal counsel. It was not until the Tudor era that those who wore livery without the consent of the lord whose livery it was became the target of prosecution. The 1429 Act only had a short-term impact on the enforcement of the legislation, at best. Its long-term significance was in introducing laws regarding the fraudulent wearing of a magnate's livery that were enforced with greater rigour during the reign of Henry VII.

---

[50] KB29/68, rot. 11d.
[51] KB29/69, rot. 19.
[52] KB29/70, rot. 16.
[53] KB29/72, rots. 22d, 30d.
[54] KB29/74, rots. 3, 14.
[55] E.g. Herefordshire in 1452 (KB9/34/1, m. 5) and 1457 (KB9/35, mm. 6, 67–9); and Yorkshire in 1454 (KB9/149/1, mm 20–1, 49, 53). For the contexts of these indictments see especially Ralph Griffiths, 'Local Rivalries and National Politics: The Percies, the Nevilles, and the Duke of Exeter, 1452–55', *Speculum*, xliii (1968), 589–632; Alisa Herbert, 'Herefordshire, 1413–61: Some Aspects of Public Disorder', in *Patronage, the Crown and the Provinces in Later Medieval England*, ed. R.A. Griffiths (Gloucester, 1981), 103–22.
[56] KB27/1013, rex rot. 8d.
[57] KB9/390, m. 47; 434 mm. 9, 14, 21; 436, mm. 7–8.
[58] See in particular Cunningham, *Henry VII*, 209–15; Cameron, 'The Giving of Livery and Retaining', 17–35; Luckett, 'Crown Office and Licensed Retinues', 223–38.

IV

Rather than producing sustained enforcement of earlier legislation, the primary significance of the 1429 livery Act is the light it sheds on the evolution of late medieval parliamentary statutes. Previously, it was believed that the Act was significant in that it extended the legislation to the palatinate counties.[59] Yet the fourteen indictments in Cheshire in 1428,[60] coupled with an earlier case in 1415,[61] indicate that the laws were already being enforced in that palatinate county prior to 1429. Instead, the Act codified existing practices in law, which highlights the ambiguous constitutional position of Cheshire during the late medieval period. As a palatinate county it enjoyed administrative independence and a high level of autonomy. By the mid fifteenth century the myth was being propagated that before the Norman Conquest there had been a representative assembly in Cheshire which had full powers to make laws and grant subsidies. In terms of taxation, a principle had been established that Cheshire was exempt from liability to contribute to subsidies granted in parliaments summoned by the king.[62] In general, the late medieval parliament respected Cheshire's liberties and made allowances for them.[63] Thus, another petition presented to the parliament of 1429, regarding false indictments, explicitly stated that the proposed law should *not* extend to that county.[64] Two apparently contradictory conclusions therefore seem to emerge from the indictments of 1428. First, that the statutes of livery were always enforceable in the palatinate of Cheshire, despite there being no explicit mention of Cheshire in the statutes themselves. Second, that parliament was generally respectful of Cheshire's autonomy. In order to understand this apparent contradiction it is necessary to consider the relationship between other cases from the 1420s and the 1429 Livery Act.

In addition to the palatine counties, the Act stated that women were to be bound by the legislation.[65] Aristocratic women were heads of their own households and had their own servants; therefore, the fact that they were bound by the statute should not be surprising, given that women are known to have distributed livery previously. A notable example is Elizabeth de Burgh, who gave livery to 338 people in 1343.[66] The first known prosecution of a woman is found in Yorkshire in 1422, seven years before the law was explicitly declared to apply to women. Elizabeth, Lady Neville, the daughter-in-law of Ralph, earl of Westmorland (*d*.1425), was accused of illegally distributing livery to three yeomen on 2

---

[59] Tim Thornton, *Cheshire and the Tudor State, 1480–1560* (Woodbridge, 2000), 2, n. 5, 120, n. 3; Griffiths, *Henry VI*, 134.
[60] CHES25/12, mm. 16–17.
[61] CHES25/25, m. 14.
[62] P.H.W. Booth, *The Financial Administration of the Lordship and County of Chester, 1272–1377* (Manchester, 1981), 116–17. For the longer historiographical tradition of Cheshire being separate from the rest of England see Philip Morgan, *War and Society in Medieval Cheshire, 1277–1403* (Chetham Society, 3rd series, xxxiv, 1987), 1–8.
[63] Thornton, *Cheshire and the Tudor State*, 119–20.
[64] *PROME*, x. 415.
[65] *Ibid.*, 402–3.
[66] E101/92/23; J.C. Ward, *English Noblewomen in the Later Middle Ages* (1992), 129–42.

December 1420.[67] Her indictment indicates that the clause may have been inserted as a means of clarifying existing practices in statute. The first woman to be indicted after the passing of the Act of 1429 was Joan Beauchamp, Lady Abergavenny, who was charged in 1434 with giving illegal livery to two gentlemen from Derbyshire, Thomas Makworth and Richard Broun, on 13 April 1433.[68] There is considerable evidence pointing to Lady Joan's encouragement of disorder in the Midlands. Back in 1418 she and her followers had been responsible for major civil disturbances in Warwickshire, and she had been required under pain of £1,200 to keep the peace. This, by her active incitement of violence in Birmingham in 1431, she blatantly failed to do, thus forfeiting her bond. After paying £1,000 at the exchequer, on 8 July 1433 she was pardoned the rest of the fine.[69] Even so, she had clearly remained incorrigible. Yet even here any connection between Lady Joan's activities and the inclusion of the clause binding women to the statute is tenuous. Her indictment for illegal livery is best explained within the context of the commission of *oyer et terminer* sent into Derbyshire in 1434. Both of the gentlemen to whom she had given livery were also indicted for receiving livery from Ralph, Lord Cromwell, in April 1431, and in addition Broun had also been given livery by Sir Richard Vernon – who himself had received it from Cromwell – in the same month.[70] Thus, Lady Abergavenny had given livery to two men who were caught up in a web of illegal retaining relationships in Derbyshire during this period and are likely to have been connected to the lawlessness occurring in the county at that time. It would appear, therefore, that neither the indictment of Lady Neville nor the activities of Lady Abergavenny can realistically be linked directly to the petitions of 1427 and 1429. In the case of both women and the palatinate counties it is clear that, instead of expanding the law, parliament was clarifying the existing legislation.

Other legislation enacted by the parliament of 1429 suggests that the assembly was intent on a process of codification of the laws. This process is evident in the Act restricting the franchise to forty-shilling freeholders. Like the Act of livery, the electoral Act of 1429 was building on and codifying existing legislation, which, in the case of parliamentary elections stretched back to 1406. Four other petitions also seem to be the product of a parliament with a legalistic agenda. One referred to the improper conduct of escheators holding inquisitions *post mortem*,[71] which had been a problem considered in previous parliaments.[72] Legislation was also passed concerning due legal process and jurisdiction,[73] and correcting errors in writs.[74] Thus the awarding of writs of attachment and distraint to sheriffs in cases of illegal livery, which the livery Act introduced,[75] seems to provide further indication of the level of expertise in the law provided by the Members of the Commons. As the

---

[67] KB27/645, rex rot. 8; KB29/56, rot. 25d; *CP*, xii (2), 548–9.
[68] KB9/11, m. 15.
[69] *CPR, 1429–1436*, p. 295.
[70] All the relevant indictments are found in KB9/11, m. 15.
[71] *PROME*, x. 422–3.
[72] *Ibid.*, 260–2. For the relevant inquisitions, *CIPM*, xxii. 443–6.
[73] *PROME*, x. 430–1.
[74] *Ibid.*, 416–17, 421–2.
[75] *Ibid.*, 402–3.

fifteenth century progressed the numbers of lawyers in the Lower House rose,[76] although a detailed analysis of the composition of each parliament needs to be made before the impact of lawyers on parliamentary business may be properly judged. Even though the petition requesting that weights and balances be standardised across the realm indicates the redress of grievances of the mercantile community who represented many boroughs (rather than directly concerning abuses of lordship),[77] its focus on standardisation and clarification fitted in with a distinct theme of this parliament's legislation.

V

This examination of the Livery Act of 1429 and the context in which it was passed has implications for our understanding of attempts to regulate the excesses of bastard feudalism and of the development of late medieval laws. In the narrow terms of the evolution of the statutes of livery, the Act marked the last of the Commons' petitions regarding the problem. Later livery legislation was the product of the professed campaigns of Edward IV and Henry VII against disorder. The Act itself was one of a series of measures against lawlessness in the localities prior to the coronation expedition, in a manner akin to Henry V's attempt to pacify disruptive elements in England before the Agincourt campaign. Restricting those to whom a lord could distribute his livery had, at least in the eyes of the Commons, the potential to diminish the lawlessness associated with noble affinities. By explicitly stating that women were to be bound by the statutes and that the laws were to apply in the palatine counties (even though in practice women were already bound by the statutes and cases of illegal livery had already been prosecuted in Cheshire), the Act also sheds light on the legal processes. Parliament was clarifying existing legislation in response to recent events. The statute of livery of 1429 did not radically alter existing laws (like the statutes of 1468 and 1504 were to do); rather, it refined their provisions, defined precisely who was bound by the statute and while demonstrating a concern from the Commons that the statutes were not being enforced offered a plausible remedy. In the same way that labour laws of the fourteenth and fifteenth centuries have been shown to have evolved and been modified over time,[78] so too did Parliament enable the gradual evolution of laws to control retaining. Further research that juxtaposes acts of parliament with the surviving legal records is required to determine whether this was a standard practice of late medieval parliamentary law-making or whether the practices identified here were unique to either illegal livery or the parliament of 1429.

---

[76] Simon Payling calculated that in 1395 around 15% of MPs could be classed as lawyers, compared to 20% in 1442 and 24% in 1491: S.J. Payling, 'The Rise of Lawyers in the Lower House, 1395–1536', in *Parchment and People: Parliament in the Middle Ages*, ed. Linda Clark (Edinburgh, 2004), 104–5.

[77] *PROME*, x. 403–4.

[78] Christopher Given-Wilson, 'Service, Serfdom and English Labour Legislation, 1350–1500', in *Concepts and Patterns of Service in the Later Middle Ages*, ed. Anne Curry and Elizabeth Matthew (Woodbridge, 2000), 24–5.

AN INDENTURE BETWEEN RICHARD NEVILLE, EARL OF SALISBURY, AND SIR EDMUND DARELL OF SESSAY, NORTH RIDING, 1435[*]

A.J. Pollard

Michael Hicks has done more than any other historian since K.B. McFarlane to elucidate the world of bastard feudalism. He has drawn our attention away from the narrow confines of the indenture of retainer to emphasise the wider context of service in which the formal legal ties between lord and man existed.[1] But the indenture and the payment of annuities remain the most visible form of clientage in the fifteenth century. We seldom see behind the formal contract to the reasons for its existence, the personal relationships, or the motivation especially of a retainer in actually making this solemn undertaking. Even more rarely do we know how the relationship develops, the tensions that might arise, and how they might be resolved, short of the cancellation of a fee. A tantalising and frustratingly incomplete glimpse of one dispute between lord and man is revealed in a revision of an existing indenture of retainer between the earl of Salisbury and Sir Edmund Darell of Sessay in the North Riding in 1435, which is transcribed below.

The Dawnay Archive in the North Yorkshire Record Office contains one box, ZDS 1/2/1, listed as 'Sessay'. It contains some seventy-six documents covering the period from c.1150 to 1503. The contents of the box are not fully catalogued. The name is misleading, for the collection focuses not on Sessay, one of the properties that passed from the family of Darell to that of Dawnay in 1503, but is in essence the remnant of what was once a vast Darell archive. It is a miscellaneous collection, no doubt weeded out by later generations. There is no knowing why particular documents were kept, but some must be there to 'prove' possession, such as the one court roll for Sessay and Dalton from the reign of Richard II and two enfeoffments of 1423 and 1431 encompassing virtually the whole of the Darell inheritance.[2] No doubt this remnant itself survived through the eighteenth and

---

[*] I would like to thank the referees for their comments, which have significantly helped improve this essay.
[1] See in particular 'Bastard Feudalism: Society and Politics in Fifteenth-Century England', in *Richard III and His Rivals: Magnates and their Motives in the Wars of the Roses* (1991), 1–40; *Bastard Feudalism* (1995) and *English Political Society in the Fifteenth Century* (2002), ch. 8, pp. 141–63.
[2] North Yorkshire RO, Dawney MSS, ZDS 1/2/1, 7 Aug. 1423, 14 May 1431. The files containing each document are kept in strict chronological order, each file dated. Here and elsewhere I have identified the individual file by its date. A handful of other documents originally in the collection were deposited with the Yorkshire Archaeological Society, but are being moved to the Leeds Archive Service. This paper derives from my involvement in the Heritage Lottery funded Sessay

nineteenth centuries out of antiquarian curiosity. Among these papers is the indenture between Richard Neville, earl of Salisbury, and Sir Edmund Darell.

The Darells were a long-established and substantial North Riding family, whose estates were focussed on a compact block of land around Sessay, between Thirsk and Easingwold. They held property in at least a dozen places as well as in the neighbourhood of York.[3] From this estate, excluding Thirkleby, Brodsworth and property in York itself, settled on feoffees by Sir Edmund's father, Marmaduke, in August 1423, an annuity of fifty marks was granted by the feoffees a month later to his mother, Joan, immediately following the elder Darell's death.[4] This provision for Joan's widowhood is likely to have been her dower to the value of a third of the deceased estate. A conveniently rounded sum, it suggests an estimated evaluation then of a landed income of £100, excluding properties in the three places named above that were probably held at the time by Marmaduke's own mother. Such an inheritance put the Darells in the top rank of the North Riding gentry.

Sessay and other immediately adjacent properties were held of the Percys as mesne tenures by knight's service of the lordship of Topcliffe, three miles to the north. One might thus have expected a close relationship between the Darells and the earls of Northumberland. However, the family had a long-standing connection with John of Gaunt, duke of Lancaster. Gaunt's manor of Easingwold was almost as close to Sessay as Topcliffe. Edmund's great-great-grandfather William, who had died in 1365 (many of the Darell men died young), had served with John of Gaunt in 1359–60. A John Darell, possibly his younger son, may have been the man who was Gaunt's receiver of Richmondshire before 1372 and was still in office in 1383–4, when the earldom was once more in royal hands.[5] Marmaduke Darell, who inherited in 1398, appears not to have been politically engaged, but it was possibly the older connection which led his younger brothers (Sir Edmund's uncles) John and William, into the service of Ralph Neville, earl of Westmorland, after his marriage to Gaunt's daughter Joan Beaufort. John was a trustee for the settlement of Sheriff Hutton on Joan and Ralph jointly and their heirs in 1398. He moved to London, where he secured employment in the exchequer, although continued to serve the earl as his metropolitan agent, becoming one of the executors of his will in 1425 and active thereafter in its administration. He established himself in Kent, for which county he was an MP seven times between 1407 and 1429. He died in 1438.[6] William, John's younger brother, followed him into a career in the exchequer. He acquired property in Wiltshire, which he represented three times as MP from 1431, and where he was active in the local service of Richard Neville, earl of Salisbury, Westmorland's eldest son by Joan Beaufort. But he retained his links with his Yorkshire kinsmen. He was the

---

Archive project. An account of the Darell family in the fifteenth century will appear in *Essays from Sessay*, ed. Janet Ratcliffe (Sessay Local History Society, Easingwold, forthcoming). I am grateful to Janet Ratcliffe, Cris Connor and others for advising me on many aspects of the history of the village and for helping to locate ancillary documents.

[3] North Yorkshire RO, ZDS 1/2/1, 7 Aug. 1423; 14 May 1431.
[4] North Yorkshire RO, ZDS 1/2/1, 3 Sept. 1423.
[5] M.J. Devine, 'Richmondshire, 1372–1425' (Teesside Univ. Ph.D. thesis, 2006), 33; *VCH North Yorks*. i. 446–9; Bolton Castle, Bolton MSS 409, MH/15, f. 11.
[6] *History of Parliament: The Commons, 1386–1421*, ed. J.S. Roskell, Linda Clark and Carole Rawcliffe (4 vols., Stroud, 1992), ii. 752–5.

principal trustee of his nephew Sir Edmund's estates from 1431, and after his death continued to assist his widow Isabel, being an administrator of her affairs after her death in 1448. He himself died in 1450/1.[7] Given these family connections and, as we shall see, the proximity of Sessay to the Neville property of Raskelf, it is not surprising that Edmund himself came to be retained by the Countess Joan and her son, the earl of Salisbury.

The document itself is brief and cryptic in the extreme. It is an agreement, dated 20 August 1435, between the earl and Darell, confirming that he was retained for life with the earl and his mother and that he thereby agreed to the reduction of his fee from £10 to £5 and, in certain circumstances, even to its withdrawal altogether, while he would nevertheless continue to serve them. The indenture adds another name to those who are known to have been retained by the earl of Salisbury. Seven original indentures of retainer made by Richard Neville between 1426 and 1456 have survived. Furthermore, by 1457 Salisbury was also paying a total of twenty fees to retainers charged to the lordship of Middleham, in addition to an annuity paid to his brother William, Lord Fauconberg. This was the core of a significant body of indentured retainers beholden to the earl, recruited predominantly in the northern counties.[8]

The date of the original indenture, the original terms, and the source of the fee are not recited in this subordinate contract. Another subordinate indenture, similarly varying the terms of an earlier one, was sealed by Richard Neville on 1 May in the same year, to an indenture of retainer also made jointly by himself and his mother Joan, countess of Westmorland. In this contract the date of the original indenture is given, 1 March 1435. The conventional clause that the retainer, Robert Eure, is 'bilast and withholden against all other saving his liegance' is also repeated. This is because the variation, sealed but two months later, concedes that Robert may be of 'consail and helping' with his brother Sir William Eure and his children against the countess and earl if any difference in law happened to fall between them ('which God defend'). The well-documented context of this is the conflict between the two branches of the Neville family over the possession of their inheritance in Durham.[9] While the retaining of Robert Eure in 1435 is to be

---

[7] I am grateful to the trustees of the History of Parliament for allowing me to see drafts of the articles on Sir Edmund Darell of Sessay (by Jonathan Mackman) and William Darell of Littlecote (by Linda Clark) that will appear in the forthcoming *History of Parliament: The Commons, 1422–1461*, ed. Linda Clark, from which I have drawn for this and the following two paragraphs. William of Littlecote's son and heir, George, was retained by Richard, duke of York, in 1453, fought against his cousin and namesake George at Towton, and subsequently prospered in the reign of Edward IV.

[8] 'Private Indentures for Life Service in Peace and War, 1278–1476', ed. Michael Jones and Simon Walker, *Camden Miscellany XXXII* (Camden Society, 5th series, iii, 1994), nos. 117, 120, 121, 126, 127, 128, 132; A.J. Pollard, 'The Northern Retainers of Richard Nevill, Earl of Salisbury', *Northern History*, xi (1976 for 1975), 66–8; Hicks, *Richard III and His Rivals*, 357–8.

[9] A.J. Pollard, 'Provincial Politics in Lancastrian England: the Challenge to Bishop Langley's Liberty in 1433', in *People, Places and Perspectives: Essays on Later Medieval and Early Tudor England*, ed. Keith Dockray and Peter Fleming (Stroud, 2005), 71–5; *Oxford DNB*, xl. 521–2; C.D. Liddy, *The Bishopric of Durham in the Later Middle Ages: Lordship, Community and the Cult of St Cuthbert* (Woodbridge, 2008), 213–19; G.L. Harriss, *Cardinal Beaufort: A Study in Lancastrian Ascendancy and Decline* (Oxford, 1988), 267–8.

seen in the context of Durham politics, the contract agreed with Sir Thomas Dacre, son and heir of Lord Dacre, by the earl of Salisbury on his own on 22 April in the same year, was almost certainly linked to the defence of the West March. It may well have been part of a plan by which Salisbury would himself resign and his place be taken by Dacre, his new retainer, who put in a bid for the office. But while Salisbury resigned in July, the wardenship was in fact granted to the earls of Northumberland and Huntingdon jointly.[10]

It is unlikely that the original contract with Sir Edmund Darell dates from 1435, or was linked with either the Neville family dispute or the defence of the West March. All this variation of the terms states is that Edmund accepts an immediate halving of his fee to £5 during the countess's lifetime and that if a resolution be reached in a dispute between him and the tenants of Raskelf the full fee of £10 would be cancelled and thereafter Darell would continue to serve the countess and earl for life without fee. The actual wording of the passage concerning the dispute is

> and if so bee it that accorde and ende be had bitwix the said countesse and Erle or that one hem on that one parte And the said Sir Edmond on that other parte of the variaunce, iniuries and wronges that the said Sir Edmond pretendes to be done to hym by the tennauntes of Raskell that thene fro thensforth the paiement of the said X li cesse and be relessed and the said countesse and Erle therof discharged.

Why should he agree to that?

Raskelf, an outlying member of the lordship of Sheriff Hutton belonged to the countess for the term of her life by joint enfeoffment with her husband, the late earl of Westmorland. The halving of the fee during her lifetime would have reflected the fact that the fee was charged to her lordship. The earl of Salisbury inherited it on her death in 1440.[11] It is possible that the dispute might have arisen from the collection of the fee from the issues of Raskelf. In three of the surviving original indentures payment was to be made by the receiver of a designated lordship (Pontefract and Penrith twice), in two from the issues of a manor or lordship (Humburton and Barnard Castle), presumably by the bailiff and receiver respectively, and in one the source of the fee is unspecified.[12] But in May 1429 Salisbury retained John Hotoft '*de concilio*' for four marks to be drawn from specified rents from various lands and tenements in Ware to be collected by him or his assigns. In another contract between Thomas, Lord Roos, and Sir John Cressy, in the same year, Cressy was empowered to distrain for his fee if it were not paid by the local offficers.[13] It is thus conceivable, though unlikely, that Darell's fee had been assigned to Raskelf, and that he or his assign had been authorised to collect it

---

[10] R.A. Griffiths, *The Reign of King Henry VI: The Exercise of Royal Authority, 1422–61* (1981), 161.

[11] In the contract between Salisbury and Sir Thomas Dacre sealed in April 1435 it was specified that Sir Thomas would receive a fee of twenty marks during the countess's life and £20 after her death: 'Private Indentures', ed. Jones and Walker, no. 20.

[12] *Ibid.*, no. 116 (Pontefract), 128, 132 (Penrith), 126 (Humburton), 127 (Barnard Castle), 120 (unspecified).

[13] *Ibid.*, nos. 117, 118.

from designated tenements and that the injuries and wrongs Darell claimed to have been done to him derived from a dispute over the collection of the fee.

There is another possible explanation. Raskelf lies three miles south of Sessay and the lands of the two manors bordered each other between two areas of common waste called Pilmoor (part of Sessay) and Raskelf Moor, divided by a stream called 'sun beck'. An endorsement in a sixteenth-century hand on the indenture might hold a clue. It reads 'An [*sic*] Indentures for noyances in Raskall [crossed out] in Sessey by the tenauntes versus ['vss'] Raskall'. This would suggest that this indenture was preserved, while the original was discarded, because it referred to a dispute that still had potential contemporary significance when the endorsement was made. One might thus speculate that the dispute was over the boundary running through one large area of common waste between the two settlements and the rights to graze on them. Uncertainties over the boundaries running through, and rights over, common grazing land were common, and in some places led to open conflict. The long-running quarrel over rights in the fens between Spalding and Pinchbeck on the one side and Deeping on the other led to violence and murder in 1449–50.[14]

The document might thus possibly record what was in effect a bond for good behaviour on behalf of his tenants given to the earl by Sir Edmund pending the settlement of a dispute. One may note, however, that only *his* claim that injuries and wrongs had been done by the tenants of Raskelf is acknowledged: no reference is made to any counter 'noyances', or claims for injuries made by the countess or earl. If there had been a negative at the beginning of the fifth line, if it had read 'if so bee that *no* accord be had', the issue might have been more explicable. But the fee is to be removed altogether if final agreement *is* reached, not if it is *not*. Although one cannot rule out the possibility, it is highly unlikely that a scribal error would have been left uncorrected in a legal instrument such as this, especially the copy kept by Darell. It is inconceivable that he would have been prepared both to accept that he and his tenants were in the wrong and that he would be willing to surrender his fee if an agreement were reached. Another possibility is that his willingness to accept a reduction of his fee and ultimately waive it while still serving the earl was the price he was prepared to pay for a redrawing in his favour of the boundary between the two manors, or confirmation of the rights of his tenants over common pasture on the moorland lying between them. If an agreement of this kind had been reached a formal deed of conveyance or confirmation would have been executed which spelled out in detail the nature of the dispute that had led to 'noyances'. But none has survived. It may be therefore that the issue was not in fact resolved before Sir Edmund's death a year later and that the subsequent endorsement reflects the fact that it subsequently remained a bone of contention.

---

[14] Jonathan Mackman, '"To Theire Grete Hurte and Finall Destruction": Lord Welles's Attacks on Spalding and Pinchbeck, 1449–50', in *Foundations of Modern Scholarship: Records Edited in Honour of David Crook*, ed. Paul Brand and Sean Cunningham (York and London, 2008), 183–95.

Disputes between lord and retainer could drag on for years without resolution. In 1392 Sir Ivo Fitzwaryn had granted to Ralph Brit his property in Antioch in Stalbridge and a property called 'Le Wythe' in Caundel Marsh near Sherborne in Dorset as the fee for his service for life, Brit taking his livery as his esquire in war and peace. Subsequently Fitzwaryn re-entered the lands, and in 1403 Brit brought a case of *novel disseisin* against him. Brit claimed that Fitzwaryn had expelled him from his household, and refused to give him his livery. Fitzwaryn counter-claimed that he had repossessed the property because Brit had refused to do him service. The dispute only ended with Sir Ivo's death in 1414, which effectively closed the case.[15]

Relationships did not deteriorate as far between Darell and the Nevilles as between Brit and Fitzwaryn. Darell, as agreed in 1435, did continue to give service. In 1436 he sailed to France in Salisbury's company as part of the army taken out that year by Richard, duke of York. It was probably not the first time he had served in France with the earl. In the spring of 1431 Richard Neville had indented with the crown to raise reinforcements for the army that had crossed the Channel with the boy king the previous year. He contracted to serve with 199 men-at-arms and 600 archers for six months.[16] Sir Edmund may have been in their number. On 14 May 1431, not long before the expedition sailed, he drew up a will. It is contained in a deed, which rehearses an enfeoffment of his estates that he had already made. This is recited in the third person before switching to the first person to express Darell's last will and instructions to his feoffees for the disposal of his property in the event of his death. The second part is not the will itself, but being in the first rather than the third person, as one would expect in such a deed, reads like an extract from it.[17] It is possible, therefore, that the original indenture between him and Neville was drawn up before this expedition. Between sailing to France in 1431 and 3 October 1432 Darell was knighted, and in the summer of 1433 he was returned to parliament as one of the knights of the shire for Yorkshire. It was before that assembly in July that the dispute between Thomas Langley, bishop of Durham, and his Durham subjects over the bishop's palatine rights was aired. Also sitting in the house of Commons was Sir William Eure, who presented a petition countering Langley's plea for the confirmation of his regality. The matter was referred to the king's council, which ruled in Langley's favour. Darell's return for Yorkshire for this one parliament may well have been in the Neville interest to ensure at least one voice in the house in support of Langley.[18]

In 1436, now as his man with a reduced fee (or possibly none at all), Darell accompanied Salisbury to France again. This time he was part of a retinue of 240 men-at-arms and 1,040 archers. It is possible that he subcontracted with Salisbury

---

[15] 'Private Indentures', ed. Jones and Walker, no. 81, n. 188.
[16] A.R. Bell, Anne Curry, Andy King and David Simpkin, *The Soldier in Later Medieval England* (Oxford, 2013), 34.
[17] North Yorkshire RO, ZDS 1/ 2/1, 14 May 1431, transcribed in *Essays for Sessay*, ed. Ratcliffe. If Darell were in Salisbury's army (unfortunately no musters have survived) he may have been present at the coronation of Henry VI as Henri II of France in Paris on 16 December and returned with his captain early in 1432.
[18] Pollard, 'Provincial Politics', 75; Liddy, *Bishopric*, 221–2; Jonathan Mackman, 'Sir Edmund Darell' in *The Commons, 1422–61*, forthcoming.

to lead his own contributory retinue.[19] The lost indenture with the earl may have specified the number of men that Sir Edmund was to bring with him in time of war, though none of the other surviving Neville indentures contain such detail.[20] On 18 April Darell renewed the 1431 enfeoffment of his estates, but he did not draw up a new will before sailing.[21] The army landed on 7 June at Honfleur. In August it laid siege to Fécamp, which had fallen to the French in the previous year. Thomas Basin later wrote in his *Histoire de Charles VII* that such was the shortage of supplies in the district and so hot the weather that many died of hunger and disease and thus the siege had to be abandoned. Other accounts suggest Fécamp was taken, but lost again soon after; it was not securely back in English hands until later in the year.[22] But one of the victims of disease (rather than hunger one might suppose), or a casualty in a skirmish, was Darell. He made a new short will at, rather than outside, Fécamp on 6 September and died soon afterwards.

Darell conventionally committed his soul to God Almighty, the Blessed Virgin Mary and all the company of saints and his body to be buried in the church at Sessay. He gave the customary mortuary of his 'best beast' to the rector, provided seven marks for an honest chaplain to sing masses for a year after his death for his and his parents' souls, a small amount for alms, and candles to be burnt before the image of the Virgin in the church. There were no other specific bequests; the inheritance had already been settled. The residue of his goods was to be distributed for the salvation of his soul by his executors.[23] Sir Edmund was probably only in his mid-thirties when he died. His remains were brought home from Normandy (no doubt just his bones after the body had been boiled down), and were buried, as he willed, in the church at Sessay. On 12 November 1436, almost as soon as news of his death was received, Sir Edmund's feoffees, as instructed in 1431, settled all the estates they held on his widow Isabel; and she on the same day appointed attorneys to receive seisin. On 26 February 1437 dower was assigned from the remaining Darell lands.[24] The will itself was not proved until 5 July that year and the executors completed administration in June 1438.[25] In the meantime the wardship of Sir Edmund's heir, George, who was born in or about 1430, was assigned. An inquisition *post mortem* was probably begun, but in the Hilary term of 1437 Henry

---

[19] Bell, Curry, *et al.*, *Soldier*, 34.
[20] *The History and Antiquities of the Counties of Westmorland and Cumberland*, ed. Joseph Nicholson and Richard Burn (1777), i. 96 ascribes to the Walter Strickland of Sizergh who was retained by Salisbury in 1448 ('Private Indentures', ed. Jones and Walker, no. 128) a list of 290 men on whom he could call, particularly for border service. But Daniel Scott, *The Stricklands of Sizergh Castle. The Records of Twenty-Five Generations of a Westmorland Family* (Kendal, 1908), 70, shows that this retinue of 290 men in fact belonged to a later Walter Strickland, who died in 1569.
[21] Yorkshire Archaeological Society, MD182/54, printed in *Yorkshire Deeds*, IX, ed. M.J. Hebditch (Yorkshire Archaeological Society, Record Series, cxi, 1948), no. 386, pp.149–50.
[22] Thomas Basin, *Histoire de Charles VII*, ed. Charles Samaran (2 vols., Paris, 1933, 1944), i. 249–51; Juliet Barker, *Conquest: The English Kingdom of France in the Hundred Years War* (2010), 250.
[23] Borthwick Institute of Historical Research, Univ. of York, Probate Register 3, f. 498.
[24] North Yorkshire RO, ZDS 1/2/1, 12 Nov. 1437; *Yorkshire Deeds*, IX, ed. Hebditch, no. 387, p. 150; *Yorkshire Deeds*, X, ed . M.T. Stanley Price (Yorkshire Archaeological Society, Record Series, cxx, 1955), no. 150, p. 56.
[25] Borthwick Institute, Probate Register, 3, f. 498; North Yorkshire RO, ZDS 1/2/1, 12 November 1437; *Yorkshire Deeds*, IX, ed. Hebditch, no. 386; X, ed. Stanley Price, no. 150.

Percy, earl of Northumberland, sued William Pickering in the court of common pleas to surrender the boy, whose wardship pertained to him as his mesne lord.[26] He was successful. By April 1440, when the manor of Brodsworth was settled upon the couple, George was married to Margaret, the daughter of the earl's retainer Sir William Plumpton.[27] George subsequently entered Percy service and the long family attachment to the Nevilles was severed.

Sir Edmund Darell died serving his lord, the earl of Salisbury, a year after he renegotiated his indenture of retainer. As Michael Hicks has emphasised, indentures of retainer were entered into in the light of existing obligations.[28] In this case we know little more of the relationship before the formal contract was first entered than we do of the reasons why it was modified in 1435. It is apparent, however, that loyalty to the earl, a family commitment over two generations, was more significant than payment. For Sir Edmund it was a matter of personal honour that, in the words of one of those initial indentures of retainer made by the earl that have survived, he was 'bylaste and withholden with' the earl and his mother. It seems likely that he had also agreed that he would be 'wele and convenably horsed, armede and arrayede and alway redy to ryde come and goe with to and for the said Erl at al tymes and into al places on this side and beyonde the see aswele in tyme of paix as of were'.[29] It was going beyond the sea, horsed, armed and arrayed, in his lord's company that he met his premature death.

---

[26] TNA, CP40/704, rot. 143d. William Pickering was probably a relation of Sir Richard Pickering (d.1441), of Oswaldkirk, who was one of the witnesses to Darell's enfeoffment of 18 April 1436. He was not the escheator. One can only speculate as to why he had custody of the boy.
[27] *Yorkshire Deeds*, IX, ed. Hebditch, no. 100, pp. 45–6.
[28] Hicks, 'Bastard Feudalism', 38.
[29] 'Private Indentures', ed. Jones and Walker, no. 128 (Walter Strickland, 1 Sept. 1448).

APPENDIX

North Yorkshire RO, ZDS I 2/1

20 August 1435.

This endenture made bitwix Richard Erle of Sarum on that one parte and Sir Edmond Darell knighte on that othere parte bereth witnesse that where the said Sir Edmond is bilast / and withholden with Johane countesse of westmorland and the Erle for time of lyve taking yerely for his fee ten pound of money under certein form thendenture / thereupon made conteined neverthelesse the said Sir Edmond wol and grauntes be thies that the paiementes of C.s. yerely of the said X li cesse and no wise be rered / during the lyve of the said countesse and that the said countesse and Erle for that tyme of the paiement of the said C.s. bee discharged for ever and if so bee that accorde and / ende be had bitwix the said countesse and Erle or that one hem on that one parte And the said Sir Edmond on that other parte of the variaunce, iniuries and wronges that the / said Sir Edmond pretendes to be done to hym by the tennauntes of Raskell that thene fro thensforth the paiement of the said X li cesse and be relessed and the said countesse and Erle / therof discharged and the same Sir Edmond that notwithstanding bee their man without fee or anuite taking of theim. In witnesse of which thing the said / parties to the parties of this endenture entrechangeably have sett thir sealx. Gifen the xx day of August the yere of the Reyne of king henry sext after the / conqueste thirtened.

Dorse (in a later, sixteenth-century hand)

An [*sic*] Indentures for noyances in Raskall [crossed out] in Sessey / by the tenauntes versus [vss] Raskall.

THE PURSUIT OF JUSTICE AND INHERITANCE FROM MARCHER LORDSHIPS TO PARLIAMENT: THE IMPLICATIONS OF MARGARET MALEFAUNT'S ABDUCTION IN GOWER IN 1438

Ralph Griffiths

The marcher lordship of Gower in south Wales rarely rated a mention in the proceedings of the medieval English parliament. However, it achieved notoriety when the Commons and the Lords met in the winter of 1439–40: they were treated to a harrowing story with Gower at its centre. A petition was submitted to the Commons, either in the parliament's first session at Westminster between 12 November and 21 December 1439, or more likely in the second session held at Reading between 14 January and the third week of February 1440, on behalf of a young widow, Margaret Malefaunt. Her husband, Sir Thomas Malefaunt, had died in London on 8 May 1438, and the petition described how, in the course of her journey to London some weeks later from the Malefaunt estates in Pembrokeshire, she was abducted in Gower, and then taken to the neighbouring lordship of Glamorgan where she was raped and forced into marriage by her husband's former servant, Lewys Leyshon. The purpose of the petition was to secure the arrest and punishment of Leyshon: it accordingly related Margaret's view of the incident and proposed certain legal procedures by which he could be brought to justice.[1]

Sir Thomas and Margaret Malefaunt were lord and lady of the manors of Upton and Pill in the lordship of Pembroke and of the manors of Wenvoe and St. George in the Vale of Glamorgan. In 1438 they were, therefore, mesne tenants of both Humphrey, duke of Gloucester and earl of Pembroke, and Richard Beauchamp, earl of Warwick and lord of Glamorgan. The incident in Gower, whose lord was John Mowbray, duke of Norfolk, casts light on several aspects of society and the law in fifteenth-century England and Wales: on relationships – including judicial relationships – between three marcher lordships and between them and the crown, on the availability of justice (including for women), on relations between marcher lords and their prominent tenants, and on the interconnections of the English and Welsh gentry and their links with the royal household.[2]

---

[1] The following paragraphs are based on the petition (TNA, SC8/27/1316) and the copy recorded on the parliament roll, *Rot.Parl.*, v. 14–16; the English of the latter is modernised in *PROME*, xi. 271–3. There is a brief notice of the petition in *Calendar of Ancient Petitions relating to Wales*, ed. William Rees (Cardiff, 1975), 38.

[2] These are among themes explored in Michael Hicks's writings, most recently in *The Wars of the Roses* (New Haven, Conn., and London, 2010), for example ch. 4 ('Problems with the System').

Doubtless in the light of advice available to Margaret from her relatives, friends and attorneys, the first part of her petition recounts what happened in Gower and Glamorgan in June 1438. At the time of her husband's death in London, Margaret, who was well advanced in pregnancy, was staying at their fortified manor house of Upton Castle, situated on a tidal inlet of Milford Sound a few miles north of Pembroke.³ The cause of Sir Thomas's death is unknown, though it may have been pestilence, for during 1437–8 there was great scarcity of corn and a food shortage in England; according to one chronicler, 'moche worthy peple deyed in the yere of pestilence, and of oþer commune peple of men, women and childern, thurghout the Ream'.⁴ According to the petition, Lewys Leyshon (or Lleision in modern Welsh orthography), also known as Lewys Gethin (the swarthy), was one of Sir Thomas's personal servants who was with him when he died. Lewys was related to the Lleision family of Baglan near the coast in western Glamorgan, where the personal name of Lleision is uniquely common. It is not easy to locate him in the genealogies of the Welsh lords of Afan and Baglan, but he may have been a young, possibly illegitimate, member of the family.⁵ Lewys may have been recruited to the Malefaunt household at Wenvoe and St. George not far to the east. These two Glamorgan manors were acquired by the Malefaunts by marriage in the later fourteenth century. St. George may have been the more favoured residence: there are substantial remains of a fifteenth-century hall-house, and in her will (1445) Margaret Malefaunt made a bequest to the small yet handsome church there.⁶

On learning of Sir Thomas's death, Margaret Malefaunt's mother, Jane Astley, who had been Henry VI's head nurse from 1422 and still had a close connection with the royal household, took urgent steps to convey the sad news to her

---

³ The Malefaunts had been important tenants of the lordship of Pembroke since the thirteenth century. For Upton's fortified manor house, much of which still stands, see Thomas Lloyd, Julian Orbach and Robert Scourfield, *The Buildings of Wales: Pembrokeshire* (New Haven, Conn., and London, 2004), 488–9. Several Malefaunt tombs are in Upton's tiny chapel close by.

⁴ *The Brut or The Chronicles of England*, ed. F.W.D. Brie (2 vols., EETS, cxxxi, cxxxvi, 1906, 1908), ii. 473.

⁵ TNA, C67/39, m. 22 refers to him as a gentleman of Baglan when he was pardoned in 1446 (a reference kindly provided by Dr. Roger Thomas). See G.T. Clark, *Limbus Patrum Morganiae et Glamorganiae* (1886), 79–81; Mr. Barry Davies confirms the difficulty of locating Lewys in the Baglan genealogies. Interestingly, the poet Ieuan Gethin ab Ieuan ap Lleision of Baglan was a contemporary member of the family, though he does not allude to Lewys Leyshon in his surviving poems. See *Gwaith Ieuan Gethin*, ed. A.P. Owen (Aberystwyth, 2013); I am grateful to Dr. Owen for verification. For the castle at Plas Baglan, which may have been occupied in the fifteenth century, see *An Inventory of the Ancient Monuments in Glamorgan, Vol. III, Part 1a: The Early Castles from the Norman Conquest to 1217* (Royal Commission on Ancient and Historical Monuments in Wales, 1991), 149–52.

⁶ London Metropolitan Archives [hereafter LMA], commissary ct. wills, DL/C/B/004/MS09171/4, f. 166; I am grateful to Dr. Christian Steer for bringing the will to my notice. Thomas was born c.1400: A.V. Mellefont, 'Draft Copy of History of Malefant Families' (privately published, Killarney Vale, New South Wales, 1983, available at the Glamorgan RO, DX 978), no pagination. For the Malefaunts' genealogy, see Clark, *Limbus Patrum*, 419; P.C. Bartrum, *Welsh Genealogies, A.D. 1400–1500* (18 vols., Aberystwyth, 1983), viii. 1256. For the remains of the Malefaunts' late medieval manor house at St. George, see *An Inventory of the Ancient Monuments in Glamorgan, Vol. III, Part 1b: The Later Medieval Castles, from 1217 to the Present* (Aberystwyth, 2000), 494–9. Nothing survives of a late-medieval house at Wenvoe, but for an earlier castle, *ibid.*, 494–501. See also John Newman, *The Buildings of Wales: Glamorgan* (1995), 562–3, 644–5.

daughter.⁷ Margaret's father, Thomas Astley of Leicestershire, had died several years earlier and so Jane took matters in hand. She entrusted Lewys Leyshon with the task of bringing Margaret from Pembrokeshire to London, supplying Lewys with personal letters addressed to Margaret and with tokens of identification, and having received Lewys's assurance that he was a married man and therefore a fit and proper person to act as the pregnant widow's escort on the lengthy journey across south Wales and southern England. Lewys, however, evidently had his eye on Margaret, suddenly become a rich widow, 'by subtle and unlawful means, planning and scheming to ravish' and marry her. He accordingly destroyed Jane Astley's letters and replaced them with counterfeit letters in Sir Thomas Malefaunt's name as if the latter were still alive and wanted Margaret to join him in London as quickly as she could because he was so ill.

When he arrived at Upton Castle on 1 June 1438, Lewys warned Margaret that the ill-disciplined Carmarthenshire squire, Gruffudd ap Nicholas of Newton and Dinefwr, and several others, were lying in wait for her along with other of her enemies but assured her that he, Lewys, would conduct her safely to London or else die in the attempt.⁸ Margaret was taken in by this assurance, and (her petition stressed) she was anxious to comfort her supposedly sick husband; straightaway she and several of her servants left Upton in Lewys's company. They travelled all that day and part of the next until, on 2 June, they came to the edge of the extensive deer park at 'Park of Prys' within Parc le Breos in Gower, in the demesne manor of Lunnon which belonged to John Mowbray, duke of Norfolk and earl marshal of England. There a large band of armed men was waiting for them 'at the plan and command of the said Lewys'.⁹ Margaret's party was ambushed and in the scuffle swords were drawn; Margaret was wounded on the arm and her servants were beaten. Lewys apparently did nothing to help, though he continued to insist that he would protect her. In fear of her life, she left her servants and agreed to go with him. She was taken into the mountains (presumably in northern Gower close to the border with the lordship of Glamorgan), where she was kept without meat or drink for more than a week, except for some watery milk at various places where they halted, until 'she was nearly dead'. All this was rehearsed before the Commons in parliament.

According to the petition, on 10 June Lewys took Margaret to the house at Tythegston, situated near Ewenni Priory in Glamorgan and not far from the

---

⁷ R.A. Griffiths, *The Reign of King Henry VI* (2nd edn., Stroud, 1998), 51–2. Jane's original annuity of £20 was doubled in 1427 and continued to be paid thereafter: for example, TNA, E403/661, m. 7 (20 May 1423); 681, m. 3 (22 May 1427); 727, m. 4 (14 May and 1 June 1437). See also *CPR, 1422–9*, p. 178; 1436–41, p. 127; 1446–52, p. 550.

⁸ For the ruthless Gruffudd ap Nicholas, and his power on or close to the land route which Margaret would need to take, see R.A. Griffiths, 'Gruffydd ap Nicholas and the Rise of the House of Dinefwr', *National Library of Wales Journal*, xiii (1964), 256–68, reprinted in *idem, King and Country: England and Wales in the Fifteenth Century* (1991), ch. 11, and see most recently *idem, Sir Rhys ap Thomas and his Family: A Study in the Wars of the Roses and Early Tudor Politics* (2nd edn., Cardiff, 2014), 12–17.

⁹ Parc le Breos extended inland from close to the southern coast of the Gower peninsular; part of it was known as 'parke ap Rice' in 1551 and as 'Parke Price' by 1650. I am grateful to David Leighton for guidance on the deer-park; see also his 'A Fresh Look at Parc le Breos', *Gower*, l (1999), 71–9.

Lleision property at Baglan, which belonged to Gilbert Turberville. The Turbervilles were lords of the mesne lordship of Coety, a little to the east. Margaret recalled that by this stage she was greatly confused and hardly of sound mind or capable of sound judgement; she was imprisoned and threatened that unless she married Lewys he would take her back to the mountains without any of her friends or relatives 'to the shortening of her life'. As a result of these threats, and with the connivance of Gilbert Turberville and his wife, and having enlisted the offices of Hugh, vicar of Tythegston, a Turberville appointee, and many others to form a congregation, on 16 June Margaret was forcibly taken to Tythegston church in order to be married to Lewys Leyshon. She refused, and privately and publicly told the vicar that she would never agree to the wedding; indeed, at this stage she may not have been aware of her husband's death. Nevertheless, they compelled her to go through a ceremony, she being pregnant and 'greatly confused and not of sound mind' but resolutely refusing to agree to, or even utter, 'any words of matrimony'. Lewys thereupon took her back to Turberville's house at Tythegston, into a chamber in its strong tower, and there he 'ravished her and feloniously lay by her against her will, she crying at all times for help and succour though she could have none'.[10] Margaret, whose unborn child survived this torment, was kept at Tythegston until 27 June when 'with wise governance' (and perhaps in the light of news that her husband was indeed dead) she was released and eventually made her way to London to her mother, Jane Astley.

How she was rescued or escaped or released is not explained in the petition. This omission is not, however, sufficient to cast decisive doubt on Margaret Malefaunt's version of the incident or to suggest – as was not unknown in other instances of abduction, rape and enforced marriage among well-to-do families – that Margaret may have colluded in the abduction and marriage to the outrage of her family and friends who subsequently induced her to submit the petition in the interests of the Malefaunt inheritance.[11] Aside from the circumstantial detail, including the threat posed by Gruffudd ap Nicholas whose ambitions in Carmarthenshire and Pembrokeshire were well known beyond south Wales by 1439–40, and the impending birth of Margaret's son, Edmund, who was regarded

---

[10] For Gilbert Turberville of Tythegston, see Clark, *Limbus Patrum*, 456; P.C. Bartrum, *Welsh Genealogies, A.D. 300–1400* (8 vols., Cardiff, 1974), iv. 923. Tythegston Court, with its surviving fourteenth-century tower, is described in *An Inventory of the Ancient Monuments in Glamorgan, The Later Medieval Castles*, 434–42, esp. 437. For connections between the neighbouring Lleision and Turberville families, see the grant by Ieuan Gethin ab Ieuan ap Lleision, presumably the poet (see above n. 5), of land in the small town of Kenfig, not far from Baglan, which was witnessed by Gilbert Turberville's son John on 21 Sept. 1441, in *Cartae et alia Munimenta quae ad Dominium de Glamorgan Pertinent*, ed. G.T. Clark (2nd edn, 6 vols., Cardiff, 1910), iv. 1579–80.

[11] For such alleged collusion, see Caroline Dunn, *Stolen Women in Medieval England: Rape, Abduction and Adultery, 1100–1500* (Cambridge, 2013), esp. 95–6 on Margaret Malefaunt; but Gwen Seabourne, *Imprisoning Medieval Women: The Non-judicial Confinement and Abduction of Women in England, c.1170–1509* (Farnham, 2011), 145–51, is more sceptical that collusive and consensual legal cases predominated. Nonetheless, it was important in Margaret's petition to avoid any suggestion that she had consented to marriage with Lewys Leyshon in order to avoid being deprived of any dower, jointure and inheritance, according to the act of 1382: J.B. Post, 'Sir Thomas West and the Statute of Rapes, 1382', *BIHR*, liii (1980), 24–5; E.W. Ives, '"Agaynst taking awaye of women": the Inception and Operation of the Abduction Act of 1487', in *Wealth and Power in Tudor England: Essays presented to S.T. Bindoff*, ed. E.W. Ives, R.J. Knecht and J.J. Scarisbrick (1978), 21–44, esp. 23.

as her and her late husband's heir, it may be thought unlikely that she and Lewys had connived at an elopement in the three weeks or so immediately following Sir Thomas Malefaunt's death and when Margaret was in Pembrokeshire, more than 200 miles from London.[12]

Significantly, the Lleision of Baglan family and the Turbervilles were near-neighbours. Moreover, the plot had been sprung in Parc le Breos, which belonged to the lord of Gower, John Mowbray, duke of Norfolk, a man in his twenties who had a wild reputation; he was in London jousting about the time Sir Thomas Malefaunt died.[13] Not only might Mowbray have been aware of Lewys's mission to Pembrokeshire, but Lewys is likely to have been known to one of Mowbray's tenants in Gower, the eighteen-year-old Philip Mansell, whose lands lay close to Parc le Breos and whose family was – or would soon become – related to both Gruffudd ap Nicholas and the Turbervilles.[14] If, then, Margaret Malefaunt's account is to be believed, she emerges as a brave and determined woman – and a victim. To complain so publicly and in such a forum as parliament in an attempt to secure justice and to neutralise the scandal caused to her family, her baby and herself, and any future marriage that she might contract (and perhaps also to counter any wagging tongues), was very unusual. Moreover, her experience touched the interests of a number of influential landowners in south Wales, not to speak of the marcher lords of Pembroke, Gower and Glamorgan. Nevertheless, it should be noted that no response to the charges is known from Lewys Leyshon, apart from his flight from justice.

Several features of the parliamentary procedure employed by Margaret Malefaunt are extraordinary. The parliamentary commons in 1439–40 adopted her petition which requested that the king, acting with the advice of the lords spiritual and temporal and by the authority of parliament, should issue a writ of proclamation to the sheriff of Somerset so that Lewys Leyshon might be arrested and appear before the king and his justices to answer the twin charges of felony and rape. Somerset was acknowledged to be the nearest English county to Glamorgan and Lewys may already have fled there. Although the alleged offences had been committed in Gower and Glamorgan, the petition requested that Somerset's sheriff should execute the writ within two months on pain of £100. If Lewys did not appear before the king's justices, he should be condemned of high treason and attainted, and the lords of the marcher lordships where his lands were situated – Glamorgan and Gower – should take possession of his property as escheat. Margaret further petitioned that if he were declared attainted, a privy seal

---

[12] Their first son, Henry, was evidently dead by the time of Edmund's birth; Margaret's will of 1445 suggests that he was buried beside his father in St. Bartholomew's hospital, London: LMA, DL/C/B/004/MS09171/4, f. 166.

[13] *Oxford DNB*, *sub nomine*.

[14] Philip Mansell inherited his family's Gower estates, including the manor of Nicholaston and nearby properties, when his grandfather died in 1435; his grandmother was a Turberville: *Cartae et alia Munimenta*, ed. Clark, iv. 1554–6. For the relationships, see also Griffiths, *Sir Rhys ap Thomas*, 31, 62, 248, 253–4, 256, 274, 278, 280; J.B. Smith and T.B. Pugh, 'The Lordship of Gower and Kilvey in the Middle Ages', in *Glamorgan County History, Volume III: The Middle Ages*, ed. Pugh (Cardiff, 1971), 251–2.

letter should appoint appropriate persons to arrest him and bring him before the king wherever he might be found, whether in England or in Wales – or indeed elsewhere. She asked that when Lewys appeared before the justices, she or her attorney should be able to appeal him of rape in Somerset, regardless of the marriage having taken place at Tythegston in Glamorgan.

In his acceptance of the petition, Henry VI deliberately noted that this was an extraordinary case and that the writ of proclamation should not prejudice the rights of marcher lords in similar cases in the future.[15] Aside from the proximity of Somerset to Glamorgan and Gower, there may have been another reason for instructing the sheriff of Somerset to arrest and arraign Lewys Leyshon. Although cases from Wales (and other royal dominions) had been heard in the court of king's bench in the past, uncertainty was sometimes expressed as to whether this was an appropriate procedure; transferring responsibility to the sheriff of Somerset would certainly reduce the scope for legal challenge. Accordingly, Henry VI addressed his writ to Walter Rodney, sheriff of Somerset, on 8 March 1440, ordering him on pain of £100 to make proclamation for the arrest of Lewys Leyshon and to produce him before the justices in king's bench by 5 June; failure to attend would result in his condemnation of high treason and the forfeiture of his property, provided (of course) that this did not prejudice the rights of the marcher lords.[16]

Rodney discharged his duty at the county court held at Ilchester on 28 March, the next meeting to be held after receipt of the king's writ, and he did so again on 25 April, so that Lewys should attend on 5 June to answer the charges of felony and rape. Margaret attended the court on 5 June in person but Lewys did not do so, and accordingly he was attainted of high treason against the king, his crown and dignity. On 22 June Henry VI instructed the justices to enrol and implement Margaret Malefaunt's petition in king's bench and ordered that privy seal letters should be sent to certain persons, to be named by the sheriff, so that they could bring Lewys to Westminster from wherever he might be found. If he appeared, the king stated, Margaret should indeed have her right of appeal of rape by writ or by bill either in person or through her attorney; and this appeal should be heard before the king's justices, even though the rape had occurred in Glamorgan and despite any celebration of marriage that may have taken place there.[17]

Why the entire incident and its aftermath were aired in parliament requires explanation. Anthony Musson's perceptive judgement provides a context: 'The historian must consider the appropriateness of the forum to the case in question and be aware of the procedural advantages to be gained or the restrictions evident in different courts, as well as their ability to award damages or the scope of

---

[15] The king's caveat was duly appended to the petition and recorded on the parliament roll: *Rot. Parl.*, v. 16.

[16] R.A. Griffiths, 'The English Realm and Dominions and the King's Subjects in the Later Middle Ages', in *Aspects of Late Medieval Government and Society: Essays presented to J.R. Lander*, ed. J.G. Rowe (Toronto, 1986), 99, reprinted in Griffiths, *King and Country*, 52–3. Walter Rodney was sheriff of Somerset and Dorset and keeper of Somerset's county gaol at Ilchester in 1439–40: *History of Parliament: Biographies of the Members of the Commons House 1439–1509*, ed. J.C. Wedgwood with A.D. Holt (1936), 720–1.

[17] The case is fully recorded in the crown section of the king's bench plea roll, TNA, KB27/717, rex rot. 31, and in the *recorda* file, KB145/6/18 (partly illegible). The exceptional features of this plea in king's bench – treason and safeguarding marcher privileges, and perhaps the king's personal interest – are reflected in its appearance in the 'rex' section of the plea roll.

punishments available to the particular court.'[18] Margaret Malefaunt's abduction took place in the lordship of Gower and her rape and enforced marriage in the lordship of Glamorgan. The lords of both lordships had jurisdiction in all pleas of the crown, both civil and criminal, whether initiated on behalf of women or men, without intervention by the king's judicial officers except in special circumstances: in short, the king's writ did not normally run in these lordships. Seigneurial jurisdiction was exercised in the county court of each lordship, held at Swansea for Gower and at Cardiff for Glamorgan. Unfortunately, there is little surviving evidence for the practical operation of this jurisdiction and none from the 1430s. Consequently, it is not known whether or not Margaret Malefaunt availed herself of the county court of either lordship.[19]

To secure a conviction in a case of rape was no easier in the early fifteenth century than it appears to be in the twenty-first century: according to the researches of Edward Powell, of 280 men indicted of rape in the three Midland shires of Derby, Leicester and Warwick between 1400 and 1429, not a single one was convicted.[20] Circumstances in the marcher lordships of Glamorgan and Gower in 1438–9 may have been even less propitious. The suitors of the county courts in both lordships included the principal mesne tenants, and these numbered relatives or allies of the Lleisions and Turbervilles, as well as friends and neighbours of the Malefaunts. Moreover, there was an absence of personal lordship in Glamorgan that might otherwise have ensured a swift and effective hearing in the county court for such an important case. During 1437–9, Richard Beauchamp, earl of Warwick, was serving in France where he was the king's lieutenant-governor of France and Normandy; he died there on 30 April 1439. Warwick was close to King Henry VI: he had been the king's guardian and tutor and is likely to have recruited Jane Astley as Henry's nurse in 1421–2; he might have been expected to interest himself in Margaret Malefaunt's case if he had been available to do so. His son and

---

[18] Anthony Musson, 'Crossing Boundaries: Attitudes to Rape in Late Medieval England', in *Boundaries of the Law: Geography, Gender and Jurisdiction in Medieval and Early Modern Europe*, ed. idem (Aldershot, 2005), 88. He could appropriately have added Wales to this chapter's title.

[19] Michael Althschul, 'The Lordship of Glamorgan and Morgannwg, 1217–1317', in *Glamorgan County History, Volume III*, ed. Pugh, 51, 57, 67, 72; Smith and Pugh, 'The Lordship of Gower and Kilvey in the Middle Ages', *ibid.*, 239–40, 251–2; W.R.B. Robinson, 'The Government of the Lordship of Gower and Kilvey in the early-Tudor Period', *ibid.*, 266–9. See also R.R. Davies, *Lordship and Society in the March of Wales, 1282–1400* (Oxford, 1978), 78, 97–8, 151–4, 156–7. For cases of assault and rape against individuals and against the king's peace tried in the seigneurial courts of the lordship of Dyffryn Clwyd in the mid-fourteenth century, and in the lordships of Newport (1476) and Brecon (1503), sometimes involving abduction, see M.F. Stevens, *Urban Assimilation in Post-Conquest Wales: Ethnicity, Gender and Economy in Ruthin, 1282–1348* (Cardiff, 2010), 209–12, and T.B. Pugh, *The Marcher Lordships of South Wales, 1415–1536: Select Documents* (Cardiff, 1963), 90, 126–7. For general comment on the legal avenues available to women in the later fifteenth century, see Deborah Youngs, '"She hym fresshely folowed and pursued": Women and Star Chamber in early Tudor Wales', in *Women, Agency and the Law, 1300–1700*, ed. Bronach Kane and Fiona Williamson (2013), 73–87.

[20] Edward Powell, 'Jury Trial at Gaol Delivery in the Late Middle Ages: the Midland Circuit, 1400–1429', in *Twelve Good Men and True: The Criminal Trial Jury in England, 1200–1800*, ed. J.S. Cockburn and T.A. Green (Princeton, N.J., 1988), 100–4.

heir, Henry Beauchamp, was fourteen years old at the time of his father's death, and on 16 May 1439 the Beauchamp estates, including Glamorgan, were committed to eight trustees on behalf of the earl's executors and his widow; she died later in 1439, on 27 December. When he was sixteen Henry Beauchamp received seisin of the lordship as a special favour from the king, but this was well after Margaret Malefaunt had decided to petition parliament.[21]

At the same time, the young lord of Gower, John Mowbray, duke of Norfolk (born 1415), was acquiring a reputation as a notorious ruffian. He was in London at the time of Sir Thomas Malefaunt's death, and he does not seem to have taken much active interest in his lordship to exercise control over some of his tenants. His large deer-park, Parc le Breos, where the abduction took place, lay near the property of Philip Mansell, whose family were suitors of the county court of Gower. Nor could there be any guarantee that suits in the county court of either lordship – even meetings of the courts themselves – would not be bought off by a fine offered by one or both of the parties involved.[22] Even more open to abuse in particular cases was the use of so-called 'letters of March' to gain for an accused tenant in one lordship judicial immunity in another lordship, even to enable his return if he were arrested elsewhere. Without effective supervision by the lord himself this too could prove an obstacle to pursuing a complaint.[23] Thus, in the absence of the responsible marcher lords, there was a strong possibility that the accused might escape trial. In Margaret Malefaunt's case, such an eventuality would have damaged Margaret's reputation and might have made it difficult to challenge her status as a widow allegedly forced into marriage.

Despite the independent powers enjoyed by marcher lords in their lordships, in exceptional circumstances it was open to a complainant of sufficient standing, or a marcher lord himself, or in circumstances where a marcher lord was under age, to seek justice directly from the king. Moreover, if a case could be construed as treason, the crown had exclusive jurisdiction. It is significant that the conclusion in Lewys Leyshon's case was that he merited being attainted and declared a traitor.[24] It is not known whether Margaret Malefaunt had rejected the possibility of obtaining redress through the judicial system of the march, but when Henry VI responded to her petition, he was careful to state that his decision – which might lead to a charge of treason – should not prejudice the customary rights of marcher lords. In any case, petitions from Wales and other dominions of the crown had long been dealt with in parliament. It is also possible that Margaret and those who counselled her were encouraged to submit her petition to the Commons by a not dissimilar case that had arisen in the previous parliament which met at Westminster

---

[21] T.B. Pugh, 'The Marcher Lords of Glamorgan, 1317–1485', in *Glamorgan County History, Volume III*, ed. *idem*, 191–2.

[22] For this practice, which was becoming common in the fifteenth century, see Pugh, *The Marcher Lordships of South Wales*, 37–40; Davies, *Lordship and Society*, 173, 166–7.

[23] Davies, *Lordship and Society*, 245–7; Stevens, *Urban Assimilation in Post-Conquest Wales*, 211.

[24] Robinson, 'The Government of the Lordship of Gower and Kilvey', 267–8; Davies, *Lordship and Society*, 151–2, 217–18. Early in the sixteenth century, the crown's ultimate jurisdiction could be exercised in the prerogative courts such as Star Chamber: see Youngs, 'Women and Star Chamber in early Tudor Wales', 78–9, 80–3, for other cases arising in the ill-disciplined borderland between Gower and Glamorgan. J.G. Bellamy, *The Law of Treason in England in the Later Middle Ages* (Cambridge, 1970), ch. 5 ('The Scope of Treason'), does not specifically deal with these implications of jurisdiction in treason cases.

between 21 January and 27 March 1437, when Margaret's brother, Thomas Astley, represented Leicestershire.[25]

On that occasion the Commons were presented with two petitions on behalf of Isabel Boteler, the widow of Sir John Boteler of Bewsey in the county palatine of Lancaster. The first petition stated that on 23 July 1436 William Pulle (or del Pole), a Cheshire gentleman from Birkenhead, along with many others had broken into her house at Bewsey where William raped Isabel and then fled with her to Wales. He was indicted before the king's justices of the peace at Lancaster on 15 October, and at the request of her friends who appeared before the king's council ten days later, the king appointed a commission under the great seal to arrest William and two accomplices, and to take Isabel into safe custody. William thereupon sought refuge elsewhere in Wales where the king's writ did not normally run in order to avoid arrest by the commissioners. Sir Thomas Stanley, one of the commissioners (and Isabel's cousin), was at least able to locate Isabel at William's house in Birkenhead and he took her to Chester. This petition was designed to clarify the legal process by which William could be brought to justice since two county palatines, each with exclusive jurisdiction, and Welsh lordships or counties were involved. Isabel accordingly sought by authority of parliament a writ of proclamation from the chancery at Lancaster so that the sheriff of Lancashire could summon William before the justices of the county palatine to answer the felonies of which he was accused. If he failed to appear, then he should stand attainted of high treason, the petition adding that he was already a murderer and that the rape of Isabel was especially cruel.

That a second petition on Isabel's behalf was presented to the same parliament suggests that the complexity of jurisdictions and their procedures might obstruct justice. This petition related the same violent rape at Bewsey, but it identified William Pulle (or del Pole) as a gentleman of Liverpool, also in Lancashire; he then took Isabel to Birkenhead in Cheshire and in the parish church of Bidston induced her to marry him against her will and under threat of death, and then he raped her again at Birkenhead. In this petition, Isabel sought specific royal authority to have an appeal of felony against William and his accomplices in Lancashire, since ordinarily neither county palatine had jurisdiction over inhabitants of the other. Both petitions were adopted by the Commons and endorsed by the king.

Isabel Boteler's case raised some issues that arose a few years later in Margaret Malefaunt's. William Pulle was abetted by a number of men from Flintshire as well as Cheshire and Lancashire. The commission for William's arrest had been issued under the king's great seal rather than under the seal of the county palatine of Lancaster, and William was able to exploit the independent jurisdictions of the

---

[25] Griffiths, 'The English Realm and Dominions', *King and Country*, 52–3; *Rot. Parl.*, v. 495–6; S.H. Payling, 'Thomas Astley', in *The History of Parliament: The Commons 1422–61*, ed. L.S. Clark (forthcoming). I am grateful to the trustees of the History of Parliament Trust for sight of this unpublished biography. Both cases are briefly discussed, albeit in the context of 'a steady (if not a "massive") decline in the effectiveness of the judicial system' under Henry VI, especially in border regions, in S.A. Sinclair, 'The "ravishing" of Isabel Boteler: Abduction and the Pursuit of Wealth in Lancastrian England', *The Ricardian*, xi (1997–9), 546–7.

two county palatines and their county courts, not to speak of the courts of Welsh lordships or Flintshire to which he seems to have fled. A plea of rape was eventually heard at Lancaster on 13 March 1437. William Pulle's arrest was duly ordered by the sheriff of Lancashire, and Sir Thomas Stanley undertook to deliver three of the accused (but not William Pulle) from Flintshire and Cheshire to the chancery at Westminster; yet William continued to evade capture and to challenge the legal process. Accordingly, on 30 June 1439 the king instructed the chancellor of the county palatine of Lancaster to issue a new commission under the palatinate's seal; William was eventually outlawed and further writs for his arrest were still being issued in February 1440.[26] This long-running case was fresh in the mind when the parliament of 1439–40 considered Margaret Malefaunt's petition. Moreover, in addition to Thomas Astley, MP for Leicestershire in 1437, Sir Thomas Stanley, controller of the king's household where several of Margaret's relatives served, was elected as knight of the shire for Lancashire in 1439; while Humphrey, duke of Gloucester, the king's uncle and earl of Pembroke, headed the commission to arrest William Pulle. They – and doubtless others – could have brought their knowledge of the first case to bear in dealing with the second.[27]

Many abduction and rape cases were pursued by the victim's nearest relatives, as the act of 1382 recognised. Margaret Malefaunt's husband and father might be dead, but her grandfather, Sir Thomas Gresley, was alive and she had a clutch of brothers, as well as contacts in the royal household through her well-connected mother, Jane Astley. Behind the scenes, Margaret and her family may have been encouraged to air her experience in south Wales by her connections with the household of the young king.[28] Although Henry VI had outgrown the nursing ministrations of Margaret's mother, the latter was still in the king's favour. When Henry was in Paris in 1430–1 for his coronation as king of France, Jane and her husband, Thomas Astley, were in his entourage; so too was Thomas Malefaunt.[29] Malefaunt and his wife may have been introduced to the king's household by either

---

[26] *Rot. Parl.*, iv. 495–8; TNA, SC8/27/1305 (the first petition); KB9/232/2/6–13; KB145/6/18. The clerk of chancery of the county palatine reported that he had eventually issued the appropriate writ. Perhaps significantly, Thomas Haryngton, Isabel's brother, was knight of the shire for Lancashire in 1437. For Stanley's commission to take Isabel into safekeeping at Chester, see TNA, E28/82/59–60; *CPR*, 1436–41, p. 83; *CCR*, 1435–41, pp. 114–15, 121, 162. For Sir John Boteler (1403–30) of Bewsey, see J.S. Roskell, *The Knights of the Shire for the County Palatine of Lancaster, 1377–1460* (Chetham Society, new series, xcvi, 1937), 161–2. The independent nature of the Cheshire and Lancashire counties palatine, and the powers of their county courts, are discussed in D.J. Clayton, *The Administration of the County Palatine of Chester, 1442–85* (Chetham Society, 3rd series, xxxv, 1990), 3–11, and Robert Somerville, *History of the Duchy of Lancaster, Volume One, 1265–1603* (1953), 59–60, 142–3. There is relevant comparative comment in Paul Worthington, 'Royal Government in the Counties Palatine of Lancashire and Cheshire, 1460–1509' (Univ. of Wales Ph.D. thesis, 1990), ch. 5 ('The Link with Westminster').

[27] Roskell, *The Knights of the Shire for the County Palatine of Lancaster*, 164, 190, for Stanley.

[28] For general comment on the role of male relatives, in the absence of a husband, in assisting a woman in an abduction case, see Lisabeth Johnson, 'Married Women, Crime and the Courts in late Medieval Wales', in *Married Women and the Law in Pre-modern Northwest Europe*, ed. Cordelia Beattie and M.F. Stevens (Woodbridge, 2013), 74–5. Compare also *Paston Letters and Papers of the Fifteenth Century*, ed. Norman Davis (2 vols., Oxford, 2004), i. no. 45, for the reaction of relatives and friends to an incident of abduction and ravishment in 1452.

[29] As esquires of the royal household, Thomas Astley and Thomas Malefaunt were contracted to serve the king in France for a year in the first instance: TNA, E101/408/11; E403/695, m. 3; E404/46/206, 219; each was accompanied by three archers.

Humphrey, duke of Gloucester, or Richard Beauchamp, earl of Warwick, or both, from whom Thomas Malefaunt held, respectively, his Pembrokeshire and Glamorgan lands. It is an intriguing possibility that the marriage between Malefaunt and the Astleys' daughter was arranged while the two families were in France. It is even possible that Nurse Jane's daughter and the king were known to one another as the king grew up – and, moreover, at the court from time to time was the teenaged Henry Beauchamp, earl of Warwick and lord of Glamorgan.

Thomas Malefaunt remained close to the king's household. He had been knighted by 12 February 1438 when, as 'late of Windsor', he was pardoned of his outlawry for not appearing before the king's justices to answer a plea of debt owed to a London mercer. This did not affect his reputation, for two days later Sir Thomas, described as a knight of Gloucestershire, and John Burgh of Surrey were accepted as pledges for John Solers, esquire, when the latter was granted for twenty years all the lead mines bearing gold and silver in Devon, the king retaining one-fifteenth of the profits. All three – Malefaunt, Burgh and Solers – had been together in the royal expedition to France in 1430–1 as esquires of the household.[30]

Sir Thomas Malefaunt was buried in the church of St. Bartholomew's hospital, London, before the high altar, where a brass commemorating him, his wife and his sons, Henry and Edmund, was placed on his tomb, possibly by Margaret or her mother, Jane Astley.[31] Jane evidently maintained her own contacts with the king's household and, it might be thought, retained the king's affection. Although her husband, Thomas Astley, the Leicestershire esquire, had died in 1432, she continued to receive her generous annuity, and her income was protected even when Acts of Resumption in the 1450s threatened the incomes of others: following the resumption in 1450 she was re-granted fifty marks per annum, which she retained until the resumption of 1455, when she was allowed to keep forty marks of it until the end of her life because she was 'so stricken with age'. Even more remarkably, a £40 life-annuity was granted to her by the new king Edward IV on 14 July 1461.[32] Jane's father, Sir Thomas Gresley, an important Derbyshire knight, lived until 1445, while her sons, Thomas, John and Richard Astley, also joined Henry VI's household. In short, Margaret Malefaunt as a widow had access to significant familial support in royal circles following her experience in 1438.[33]

---

[30] *CPR*, 1436–41, pp. 107, 291, 566; *CFR*, xvii. 25; TNA, E403/695, m. 4; E404/46/219; and for Burgh, see E404/46/228, 48/311.

[31] For notice of the burials, see John Stow, *Survey of London*, ed. C.L. Kingsford (2 vols., Oxford, 1908), i. 22. For the inscription and a brief description of the monument, see John Strype, *A Survey of the Cities of London and Westminster* (2 vols., 1720), i. bk. 3, p. 232, and F.W. Weever, *Ancient Funeral Monuments* (1631; repr. Amsterdam, 1979), 435, kindly brought to my attention by Dr. Christian Steer.

[32] *Rot. Parl.*, v. 278, 316; *CPR*, 1461–7, p. 122; TNA, SC8/28/1383 (her petition for the continuance of the annuity in 1455). Jane's annuities were drawn on the revenues of Warwickshire and Leicestershire, with which her family was closely associated.

[33] Margaret's brother, John Astley, was fast making a reputation for himself as a champion at feats of arms (by 1438), and after the famous encounter with an Aragonese knight in Henry VI's presence at Smithfield in January 1442, he was knighted by the king: F.B. Barnard, *Edward IV's Expedition of 1475* (Oxford, 1925), 42–7; *Gothic: Art for England, 1400–1547* ed. Richard Marks and Paul Williamson (2003), 212–13 (including a depicture of the Smithfield joust, with St. Bartholomew's

To judge by the number of Margaret Malefaunt's relatives who received bequests of personal or domestic items in her will, drawn up on 21 May 1445, she probably looked to them for assistance after the death of her husband and her own abduction. The will was proved on 21 June. St. Bartholomew's hospital seems to have been important to the Astley and Malefaunt families, certainly after the burial there of Sir Thomas Malefaunt. Jane Astley, herself a widow, was renting a tenement there above the Smithfield gate and a garden within the hospital's precinct by 1456, and possibly well before that.[34] Her daughter Margaret may have lived there too after the death of her husband, to judge by benefactions in her will and her employment of Robert Forster, one of the brothers at the hospital, as her confessor. Margaret willed that her body should be buried with that of her husband and either she or her mother raised the Malefaunt tomb in the choir before the high altar. Her first-born son, Henry, was already dead and her will instructed that prayers should also be said for him. Margaret's devotion to the hospital, and to the Carmelites and Carthusians of London, is apparent. As to her family, she made bequests to her mother and her grandfather, Sir Thomas Gresley, who died some months after Margaret, in September 1445; and to her five brothers, Sir John Astley, Thomas, William, Richard and Henry Astley, as well as to several Gresley kinsmen. She was close, too, to her eldest sister Elizabeth, probably the widow of Andrew Sackville of Essex, and her sister Joan, the wife of John Clay of Hertfordshire; her third sister, Katherine, seems to have been unmarried in 1445. Further bequests were made to her kinsman, Sir Roger Fiennes, who had become treasurer of Henry VI's household on 9 April 1439, and to her Glamorgan neighbour, David Mathew, both of whom had a role to play in the custody of her surviving son and heir, Edmund Malefaunt. To Edmund, with whom she had been pregnant in 1438, she left devotional items as well as rich hangings and other household items listed in an inventory and which were temporarily in her mother's possession. The executors of Margaret's will were drawn from this extended family: John Astley, Margaret's son Edmund and Elizabeth Sackville, who were supervised by Sir Roger Fiennes and Sir Thomas Gresley, the two most senior of her kinsmen.[35]

In this social and familial environment, Margaret Malefaunt's plight may have roused sympathy at court and in high places among those with an interest in south

---

church in the background, made under Astley's supervision). Thomas was certainly a member of the household by Easter 1437 and his younger brothers John and Richard soon followed him: Payling, 'Thomas Astley'.

[34] *Cartulary of St Bartholomew's Hospital: A Calendar*, ed. N.J.M. Kerling (1973), 153–4. For the suggestion that a number of well-connected widows were attracted to the hospital, see E.C. Roger, 'Blakberd's Treasure: A Study in Fifteenth-Century Administration at St. Bartholomew's Hospital, London', in *The Fifteenth Century XIII: Exploring the Evidence: Commemoration, Administration and the Economy,* ed. Linda Clark (Woodbridge, 2014), esp. 98–100.

[35] LMA, DL/C/B/004/MS09171/4, f. 166; *The History of Parliament: The Commons, 1386–1421*, ed. J.S. Roskell, Linda Clark and Carole Rawcliffe (4 vols., Stroud, 1992), iv. 274 (Sackville); iii. 70–3 (Fiennes), 236–9 (Gresley); *History of Parliament: Biographies*, ed. Wedgwood and Holt, 187. It is relevant to note that the cousin of Margaret Malefaunt, also called Joan, the daughter of Sir William Astley, was the widow of Reynold, Lord Grey of Ruthin (died 1440); they too could have supported Margaret after 1438: TNA, C139/133/4; *CP*, vi. 158–9. Other bequests were made to younger members of the Astley and Gresley families; Margaret also mentioned a daughter Katherine who is not otherwise known.

Wales, a concern for seigneurial rights and the securing of landed inheritances among marcher tenants. Here too was an opportunity to highlight the lawless activities of landowners of the region like Gruffudd ap Nicholas, Philip Mansell and Gilbert Turberville.[36] Members of this circle were enlisted to protect the Malefaunt inheritance even before parliament met in November 1439. Following Sir Thomas Malefaunt's death in May 1438, Humphrey, duke of Gloucester, as lord of Pembroke, would have received custody of his Pembrokeshire estates. On 17 September 1439, when Margaret's son, Edmund, can hardly have been more than a year old, Gloucester assigned wardship of the baby to the treasurer of the king's household, Sir Roger Fiennes, Margaret's kinsman. He was also MP for Sussex during the parliament of 1439–40 in which her petition was submitted.[37]

After Henry VI endorsed Margaret's petition and began the proceedings to apprehend Lewys Leyshon, formal steps were taken to safeguard Margaret's position and that of her young son by securing the support of several landowning families of south Wales, among them the Mathew family of Llandaff, and arranging for the future marriage of young Edmund to David Mathew's daughter, Katherine. On 28 March 1441, a group of influential knights and esquires mainly from the lordships of Glamorgan and Pembroke swore a solemn oath to do so at Ewenni Priory, in Glamorgan, in the presence of Thomas Frankelen, abbot of the nearby Cistercian monastery of Margam, both leading monasteries in south Wales situated close to the Turberville and Lleision estates. Led by Sir William ap Thomas of Raglan, a Beauchamp retainer and one of the most prominent knights of the region, Sir Edward Stradling of St. Donat's who was scarcely less influential, and Sir Henry Wogan of Wiston, in Pembrokeshire, one of the duke of Gloucester's retainers, they included Thomas Botiller of Dunraven, a neighbour of the Malefaunts in Glamorgan, and three of the Mathew family, David, his brother Lewis and John the elder of Llandaff.[38] May this ecclesiastical involvement have

---

[36] J.G. Bellamy, *The Criminal Trial in Later Medieval England: Felony Before the Courts from Edward I to the Sixteenth Century* (Stroud, 1998), 168–73, stresses the potential danger to public order that might be posed by cases of abduction and rape among the gentle classes.

[37] *CCR, 1435–41*, p. 479, recording that Fiennes paid £100 for the wardship. Although in her will Margaret Malefaunt described Fiennes as '*consanguineus*', the relationship is unclear apart from her grandfather's use of Fiennes as a feoffee since 1411: *The Commons, 1386–1421,* ed. Roskell, Clark and Rawcliffe, iii. 71–2, 238. The lordship of Glamorgan was in the hands of trustees following the death of Richard Beauchamp, earl of Warwick, earlier in the year.

[38] *CCR, 1435–41*, p. 468; Bartrum, *Welsh Genealogies, 1400–1500*, viii. 1256 (which gives Edmund Malefaunt's wife as Margaret, daughter of David Mathew). Ewenni Priory was near Tythegston and enjoyed Turberville patronage; the Lleision family of Baglan was among donors to Margam Abbey. Sir William ap Thomas headed the list of trustees of the Beauchamp lands after Warwick's death: M.A. Hicks, 'Between Majorities: the "Beauchamp interregnum", 1439–49', *HR*, lxxii (1999), 27–43. For Stradling's prominence and earlier connection with the Malefaunts, see R.A. Griffiths, 'The Rise of the Stradlings of St Donat's', *Morgannwg: Transactions of the Glamorgan History Society*, viii (1963), 22–6, reprinted in *idem, Conquerors and Conquered in Medieval Wales* (Stroud, 1994), 33–5, and *Cartae et alia Munimenta*, ed. Clark, iv. 1536–7. For Sir Henry Wogan, see R.A. Griffiths, *The Principality of Wales in the Later Middle Ages: The Structure and Personnel of Government: South Wales, 1277–1536* (Cardiff, 1972), 150–1, and *idem*, 'The Extension of Royal Power, 1415–1536', in *Pembrokeshire County History, Volume II: Medieval Pembrokeshire*, ed. R.F. Walker (Haverfordwest, 2002), 233. The Mathews would have been all too familiar with the Turbervilles and the Baglan family since they had property in the vicinity of their houses: J.B.

been intended to buttress Margaret Malefaunt's assertion that she had not willingly entered into marriage with Lewys Leyshon? No landowner from either Carmarthenshire or Gower was invited to take part, and the formal ritual at Ewenni Priory signalled to the Turbervilles and Lleisions that they were beyond the pale.

A fortnight earlier, on 16 March, in London, this group had entered into a bond of £200, payable by 24 June, towards Margaret Malefaunt, Sir Roger Fiennes, his brother James Fiennes, Sir Thomas Gresley and Margaret's brothers Thomas and John Astley, to ensure that they duly discharged their obligations. The bond may have been paid well before its designated term, for on 26 May 1441 Sir Roger Fiennes granted to David and his son John the younger, in return for 210 marks, the wardship and marriage of Edmund Malefaunt, so that they could look after the baby and maintain the Malefaunt properties and in due time marry him to David's daughter.[39] As for Lewys Leyshon, he remained beyond the reach of justice and lay low. The safeguarding of the Malefaunt inheritance in 1441 and the death of Margaret Malefaunt in 1445 offered an opportunity for him to recover his social standing and to bring the case against him to a practical, if not a legal, conclusion. Lewys took advantage of the general pardon granted by the king on 18 May 1446 for those accused of offences committed before the previous 9 April. Described as a gentleman of Baglan, on 16 October 1446 he received his pardon. 'The crown, it could be said, was cutting its losses by permitting people who might in any case have escaped the penalty of their crimes to resume ordinary lives.'[40]

The abduction in Gower in 1438 sheds an unflattering light on the behaviour of certain landowning families of Gower and western Glamorgan, and also on the growing dominance of Gruffudd ap Nicholas and his family in south-west Wales. The vulnerability of Margaret Malefaunt exposed rifts and loyalties among families and neighbourhoods, underscored the obligations of lordship and the bonds of tenantry and service, and demonstrated the extent of social and legal relationships in the kingdom at large as well as in the marcher lordships. Such relationships might also be enhanced by service to the crown and in the king's household.

Davies, 'The Mathew family of Llandaff, Radyr and Castell-y-Mynach', in *Glamorgan Historian, XI*, ed. Stewart Williams (1975), 175–8.

[39] *CCR, 1435–41*, p. 479. Because Edmund Malefaunt was so young, the agreement also provided that should Katherine Mathew die without issue before he came of age, he should be returned to Sir Roger Fiennes's custody within three months and the 210 marks repaid provided two months' notice was given, presumably to allow time for the money to be raised. Sir Roger and the Mathews concluded bonds of £200 to observe these agreements. In her will, Margaret left a gold ring inscribed with her initial (could it have been used as a signet seal?) to Sir Roger Fiennes, together with £10 that was owed her by David Mathew: LMA, DL/C/B/004/MS09171/4, f. 166.

[40] R.L. Storey, *The End of the House of Lancaster* (1966; reprinted Gloucester, 1986), 215 (the quotation). Lewys received a pardon again on the following 24 Nov.; eight days earlier, William Gethin (otherwise known as William Leyshon), perhaps his brother or his father, also received a pardon and may have been involved in Margaret's abduction: TNA, C67/39, mm. 12, 22 (references provided by Dr. Roger Thomas); Clark, *Limbus Patrum*, 80–1.

THE BATTLES OF MORTIMER'S CROSS AND SECOND ST. ALBANS: THE REGIONAL DIMENSION

Peter Fleming

That the campaigns surrounding the battles of Mortimer's Cross and Second St. Albans of February 1461 were crucial to the accession of Edward, earl of March and newly-minted duke of York, as King Edward IV the following month hardly needs emphasising. With his father, Richard, duke of York, killed at Wakefield at the end of December 1460, had Edward not won the first battle, then the earl of Warwick's defeat at the second might well have led to a Lancastrian occupation of London and, quite possibly, the decisive collapse of the Yorkist challenge. As it turned out, of course, London refused entry to the whole Lancastrian army and Margaret of Anjou and her other commanders decided to head north, allowing Edward to be proclaimed king in the capital on 4 March and then to inflict a bloody defeat on them at Towton twenty-five days later.[1] Also obvious is the importance of London in these manoeuvres. Both sides were attempting to secure London and Westminster, and thereby their symbolic and very real bureaucratic and financial power. The Lancastrians' refusal to attempt to force their way into London, and their retreat northwards, can easily be seen, in hindsight, not only as an admission of defeat in the south, but also as a move that rendered their defeat a virtual inevitability.

Less obvious is the reason for the Lancastrian surrender of the south of England to the Yorkists in February–March 1461. Clearly, they had more support in the north than the Yorkists, but given that until very recently the west Midlands – or, at least, the area around Coventry, Tutbury and Kenilworth – had played host to the Lancastrian 'court', it might be thought that a retreat to this area would have made more sense. From here, they could draw upon their reserves of support in the Midlands and Wales, and be able to threaten Yorkist control of London. Another question, which is linked to this one, concerns the support that Edward was able to garner in the Welsh marches, and that enabled him to win at Mortimer's Cross. How, and why, had he been able to draw upon these reserves, and to what extent was the army that followed him to London – and beyond – composed of men from

---

[1] A recent summary of these events is provided by Michael Hicks, *The Wars of the Roses* (New Haven, Conn., and London, 2010), 160–3. For London's role, see C.M. Barron, 'London and the Crown, 1451–61', in *The Crown and Local Communities in England and France in the Fifteenth Century*, ed. J.R.L. Highfield and Robin Jeffs (Gloucester, 1981), 88–109; J.L. Bolton, 'The City and the Crown, 1456–61', *London Journal*, xii (1986), 11–24. For an account of the second battle of St. Albans from the point of view of a London chronicler, see Hannes Kleineke, 'Robert Bale's Chronicle and the Second Battle of St. Albans', *HR*, lxxxvii (2014), 744–50.

the march and the west Midlands? The two questions are linked, it is argued, because a significant Yorkist presence in the west Midlands had been built up – perhaps quite rapidly – by early 1461, probably exploiting Edward's powerbase in the marches.

Answering these questions is not straightforward. The first tempts one to adopt the role of 'armchair general', for which earlier generations of military historians have been justly criticised. Not being privy to the deliberations of Margaret and her commanders, we simply cannot know why they acted as they did; but we can make educated guesses. To answer the second definitively would also require the consultation of non-existent evidence, but the records of two towns and one city within this region do throw some light on this problem. The towns are Bristol and Shrewsbury, and the city is Coventry. All three were of considerable strategic importance. Coventry's importance is obvious, at one level, since it was part of the west Midlands region apparently chosen by Queen Margaret as her centre of operations in the later 1450s.[2] Bristol, while just on the outside of both the Welsh march and the west Midlands, was the largest provincial town or city in southern England, and controlled the routes from those regions to London. Shrewsbury dominated the central march; it is also less than forty miles north of Mortimer's Cross. All three have usable records for the appropriate period. Coventry's *Leet Book* and Bristol's *Red Books* contain civic ordinances, guild records and other materials from which some sort of political narrative can be reconstructed, and both places produced local chronicles that add something to these accounts.[3] Shrewsbury has financial accounts, a category of records lacking in the other two places, and from these it is possible to get some sense of the factional loyalties of the municipal leadership.[4] Other towns in the region lack such relatively adequate records, although those of Gloucester do offer some tantalising glimpses of its factional affiliations in the 1450s and 1460s.[5]

---

[2] R.A. Griffiths, *The Reign of King Henry VI: The Exercise of Royal Authority, 1422–1461* (1981), 777–85.

[3] *The Coventry Leet Book or Mayor's Register*, ed. M.D. Harris (EETS, original series, cxxxiv–v, cxxxviii, cxlvi, 1907–13, in 1 vol.); *The Great Red Book of Bristol: Text*, ed. E.M.W. Veale (4 vols., Bristol Record Society, iv, viii, xvi, xviii, 1933–53); *The Little Red Book of Bristol*, ed. F.B. Bickley (2 vols., Bristol and London, 1900). For the town chronicles, see: Peter Fleming, *Coventry and the Wars of the Roses* (Dugdale Society Occasional Papers, 1, Stratford-upon-Avon, 2011), 24–35; *The Maire of Bristowe is Kalendar*, ed. Lucy Toulmin Smith (Camden Society, new series, v, 1872).

[4] D.R. Walker, 'An Urban Community in the Welsh Borderland: Shrewsbury in the Fifteenth Century' (Univ. of Wales Ph.D. thesis, 1981), provides a thorough analysis of the town and its records in this period.

[5] *VCH Gloucestershire*, iv: *The City of Gloucester*, 17, 23, 38–9, 44–5; R.A. Holt, 'Gloucester: an English Provincial Town During the Later Middle Ages' (Birmingham Univ. Ph.D. thesis, 1987). For the towns of the region as a whole, see Christopher Dyer and T.R. Slater, 'The Midlands', in *The Cambridge Urban History of Britain, Vol. I, 600–1540*, ed. D.M. Palliser (Cambridge, 2000), 609–38; Christopher Dyer, 'Small towns, 1270–1540', *ibid.*, 505–37; R.A. Griffiths, 'Wales and the Marches', *ibid.*, 681–714. This discussion draws on the following individual studies of the four places, but seeks, by reassessing the evidence on a regional basis, to offer new perspectives: Peter Fleming, 'Politics and the Provincial Town: Bristol, 1451–1471', in *People, Places and Perspectives: Essays on Later Medieval and Early Tudor England*, ed. Peter Fleming and Keith Dockray (Stroud, 2005), 79–115; *idem*, *Coventry and the Wars of the Roses*; Holt, 'Gloucester: an English Provincial Town'; Walker, 'An Urban Community'.

All three places were close to estates held by the duke of York or Richard Neville, earl of Warwick. In Coventry's case, Warwick, the earl's principal seat, was less than ten miles away. In right of his wife, Anne Beauchamp, the earl was the dominant landowner in the south-west Midlands.[6] Through Anne, Warwick also held the manor and hundred of Bedminster, and the hundreds of Portbury and Hartcliffe, all just south of Bristol, and Bristol's Earl's Court, or Great Court of the honour of Gloucester, and the manor and hundred of the Barton, also known as Barton Regis, comprising the lands attached to Bristol castle that extended over two hundred acres to the north and east of the town.[7] York held estates in Wiltshire, Gloucestershire and Somerset, including the manor of Easton-in-Gordano, just to the south of Bristol, and extensive estates in southern Shropshire and the central Welsh marches, close to Shrewsbury.[8]

All three places demonstrated support for the Yorkists before Edward's accession on 4 March 1461, but the point at which such support becomes evident varies considerably. Powerful factions within the ruling elites of both Bristol and Shrewsbury showed themselves to be supporters of the duke of York from near the beginning of the 1450s. In Bristol, this came about through one of the town's members in the parliament of 1450–1, Thomas Young, who sponsored a petition calling on York to be recognised as heir to the crown after the death of Henry VI.[9] For his presumption he spent a spell in the Tower. A prominent lawyer, Young had been York's steward of Easton-in-Gordano since 1447, and also one of the duke's English attorneys during his sojourn in Ireland. He was half-brother to his fellow Bristol MP in this parliament, William Canynges, the wealthy ship-owner and merchant. Canynges would also show himself to be a stalwart Yorkist (at least until the Readeption), but, while it is hard to believe that he was unaware of Young's intentions, Canynges was as yet not willing to commit to such a public, and dangerous, show of support.

William Burley appears to have been Thomas Young's equivalent in Shrewsbury. A successful lawyer, he had been steward of the town from the 1420s, and steward of some of York's Welsh estates. He was present in the same 1450 parliament in which Young's ill-fated petition was presented, and in 1455 Burley was appointed by the Commons to lead their delegation to the Lords to ask for

---

[6] Michael Hicks, *Warwick the Kingmaker* (Oxford, 1998), 49–50; A.J. Pollard, *Warwick the Kingmaker: Politics, Power and Fame* (2007), 98–105.

[7] Hicks, *Warwick the Kingmaker*, 46–9, 123; Michael Ponsford , 'Bristol Castle: Archaeology and the History of a Royal Fortress' (Bristol Univ. M.Litt. thesis, 1979), 180–92; *Accounts of the Constables of Bristol Castle in the Thirteenth and Early Fourteenth Centuries*, ed. Margaret Sharp (Bristol Record Society, xxxiv, 1982), pp. xxiv, xxxvi–lxiii. For Anne Beauchamp as heiress to the Barton, see *CPR*, 1441–6, pp. 391, 400, 434, 443.

[8] P.A. Johnson, *Duke Richard of York, 1411–1460* (Oxford, 1988), 14–15; M.A. Hicks, 'The Career of George Plantagenet, Duke of Clarence, 1449–1478' (Oxford Univ. D.Phil. thesis, 1975), 308, tables xvi and N; Walker, 'An Urban Community', 385.

[9] This paragraph is drawn from Johnson, *Duke Richard of York*, 63, 73, 98–100; Griffiths, *Henry VI*, 671, 674, 692, 704, n. 61, 748; A.F. Pollard, 'Young, Sir Thomas (c.1405–1477)', revised by Nigel Ramsay, *Oxford DNB*; Clive Burgess, 'Canynges, William (1402–74)', *ibid.*; Fleming, 'Politics and the Provincial Town', 81, and *passim* for Bristol's involvement with the politics of this phase of the Wars of the Roses.

York's appointment as Protector.[10] There is a temptation to see Young and Burley as part of a strategy on the part of York or his counsellors to cultivate influential individuals in crucial towns, with a view to their development of pro-Yorkist networks.

Both Bristol and Shrewsbury received letters from York calling for their support in his unsuccessful – as it proved – armed demonstration at Dartford in 1452. The mayor and common council of Bristol had the letters read aloud and then passed them on to the king. Bristol's dominant governing elite at this point seems to have been unwilling to show itself as Yorkist supporters.[11] The reaction in Shrewsbury was very different. Here, in response to the letters, a group of townsmen staged an armed demonstration at York's stronghold in Ludlow in support of the duke, and at least one man accompanied York to the debacle at Dartford. The Ludlow demonstration was led by a former bailiff and a former common serjeant.[12] Shrewsbury was left exposed by York's failure at Dartford, and the town had to spend a good deal of money to avoid suffering the full consequences of its support for the disgraced duke.[13] From 1452 to 1458, Shrewsbury seems to have very overtly hedged its bets, with frequent visits by, and concomitant payments to, Lancastrian magnates like the dukes of Exeter, Somerset and Buckingham, and the earls of Shrewsbury and Pembroke, as well as playing host to the duke of York and his supporter, Lord Grey of Powys. In the words of David Walker, 'The actual motives of visitors and of townsmen remain undisclosed, though appearances suggest either that the loyalties of the townsmen were in the balance or that they were deliberately seeking to appear uncommitted.'[14]

While Shrewsbury's ruling elite had got their fingers badly burnt in 1452, and seem to have spent the next six years carefully cultivating a position of neutrality, Bristol appears to have been more cautious in that year. However, there are indications that by 1454 the town's loyalty to the Lancastrian monarchy was widely suspected. In that year an approver claimed that a group of prominent Bristol men had been casting spells to bring about King Henry's descent into mental illness. While the approver's claims were dismissed, and he was executed, that he chose Bristol as the imagined venue for these activities suggests that it was by then sufficiently notorious that he judged that the association with the town would have made his tale the more believable. Evidence from the granting of pardons to prominent Bristolians also suggests strong Yorkist support, at least among a faction within the ruling elite.[15]

Judging by Shrewsbury's bailiff's account roll for October 1458 to October 1459, the town was no longer regularly frequented by Lancastrian magnates in this year, but *was* visited by the earl of March, and was being courted by York, at least if this is the inference to be drawn from a letter the duke sent to the town, the contents of which are unknown. If York was expecting significant aid from

---

[10] Walker, 'An Urban Community', 385; *The History of Parliament: The Commons, 1386–1421*, ed. J.S. Roskell, Linda Clark and Carole Rawcliffe (4 vols., Stroud 1992), ii. 432–5.
[11] *Great Red Book, Text*, part 1, p. 136.
[12] Walker, 'An Urban Community', 384–7.
[13] *Ibid.*, 387–8.
[14] *Ibid.*, 389.
[15] TNA, KB9/273, m. 2; KB27/776, rex rot. 4d; Anthony Gross, *The Dissolution of the Lancastrian Kingship* (Stamford, 1996), 21–2; Fleming, 'Politics and the Provincial Town', 82–5.

Shrewsbury, then he appears to have been disappointed. Shrewsbury men watched, but did not intervene in, the manoeuvres in September 1459 that led to the clash at Blore Heath and the show-down at Ludford Bridge. Their one active response appears to have been to strengthen the town's defences.[16]

Meanwhile, Coventry found itself at the centre of the Lancastrian concentration of power in the west Midlands. From 1456 to 1460 the city was, according to one historiographical tradition, chosen as the seat of Margaret of Anjou's headquarters, she, along with other members of the Lancastrian leadership, feeling that London was no longer safe, since it had shown itself to be overwhelmingly Yorkist in sympathies.[17] Certainly, the city was frequently visited by the king and queen in these years. Between September 1456 and June 1460 the royal couple made numerous appearances, and councils were probably held there on three occasions. In addition, the Parliament of 1459, where the Yorkist leaders were condemned as traitors, was held in Coventry.[18] Coventry had also benefited from the king's particular favour, having been granted a charter in 1451 that elevated it to the status of a county, and its special relationship with the crown was recognised in 1456 by the city's adoption of the title of 'Prince's Chamber'.[19] Indeed, the Lancastrian attachment to Coventry in the 1450s seems to have been reciprocated by its civic leadership. Most of Coventry's MPs during this period were connected to the royal household or were royal bureaucrats, and Professor Griffiths has described its citizens as being 'fiercely loyal to the Lancastrians'.[20] However, there are indications of some tension between citizens and Lancastrian courtiers and their followers in the later 1450s. In the autumn of 1456 it appears that the duke of Somerset had to be shielded from the wrath of some Coventry men following a fatal altercation between some of his followers and the city watch. The following year Queen Margaret's insistence on what some regarded as quasi-regal ceremonial during her visit caused friction between her household and the mayor and councillors.[21]

More importantly, Professor Hicks has called into doubt the notion that Coventry did play host to a Lancastrian 'court in exile' in the period 1456 to 1460. He has shown that, while Margaret did indeed spend much of this period in the west Midlands, most of her time was divided between her castles of Kenilworth and Tutbury rather than Coventry, and government business continued to be carried out in Westminster, probably under Henry's independent direction. For Hicks, the traditional version, that Margaret moved the king and his government into the west Midlands in order the more completely to dominate both, away from

---

[16] Walker, 'An Urban Community', 389–91.
[17] Griffiths, *Henry VI*, 777–85.
[18] Henry VI's visits to Coventry are listed in the itinerary compiled by Bertram Wolffe in his *Henry VI* (New Haven, Conn., and London, 1981), 369–71. For Margaret's visits see *Coventry Leet Book*, ed. Harris, 285–92, 297–301.
[19] *VCH Warwickshire*, viii. 263; Christian Liddy, 'The Rhetoric of the Royal Chamber in late Medieval London, York and Coventry', *Urban History*, xxix (2002), 323–49, at 340.
[20] Griffiths, *Henry VI*, 778.
[21] H.E. Maurer, *Margaret of Anjou: Queenship and Power in Late Medieval England* (Woodbridge, 2003), 141–2, 144; *Coventry Leet Book*, ed. Harris, 298–9.

potential challengers based in London and Westminster, reflects the hostile view of the queen as a manipulative 'she wolf' whose part in English politics was largely illegitimate and destructive.[22]

While both Coventry's role as the home of the Lancastrian 'court in exile' and its unquestioning loyalty may be doubted, there is no reason to believe that the Lancastrian leadership were in any way mistaken in treating it as a safe haven in the period 1456 to summer 1460. That it was also in the centre of the traditional Beauchamp-Warwick sphere of influence in the west Midlands was perhaps no coincidence. Probably, the Lancastrian concentration of power in this area in the later 1450s was partly intended to subvert the Warwick lordship. The Neville earl did indeed suffer a number of desertions from his west Midlands connection during this period.[23] This may supply the necessary context for understanding an ordinance recorded in the *Leet Book* for Michaelmas 1456, designed to curtail the activities of outsiders who had acquired 'meyntenaunce of mighty men of straunge shires', who were exercising undue influence within the city. In other words, this may be evidence of a Lancastrian-dominated civic government trying to exclude Neville influence.[24]

The tumultuous events of 1460 naturally had their impact on Bristol, Coventry and Shrewsbury. In Bristol, the year opened with Thomas Young spending another spell in the Tower after a priest alleged that he had committed treason. He was released on bail in March, but the case was not closed until November, when the Yorkists were in control of the levers of justice. At the root of this accusation may have been communications with the duke of York, then in exile in Ireland.[25] Young's alleged treason found something of a counterpoint in Coventry, where, in February, a royal letter was received requiring the punishment of certain inhabitants who had lately been criticising the king and favouring 'our supersticious traitours and rebelles nowe late in our parlement there attaincted'.[26] In January a commission of array, issued on 21 December and sent to Coventry to raise men to aid the Lancastrian resistance, had mysteriously gone missing, so that it was not until over a fortnight after its arrival, on 5 February, that it reached the new mayor, William Wilgrise. While this may have been the result of simple carelessness, it took another fifteen days before forty men were finally raised, and this looks more like reluctance to support the Lancastrians on the part of Coventry's governing elite.[27]

That Thomas Young should have remained under suspicion is not surprising, and it certainly does not prove that Bristol's governing elite as a whole were in any sense 'Yorkist' in the opening months of 1460. Indeed, in January Bristol's former gauger and water bailiff, John Burgh, a yeoman of the crown, was rewarded for his good service against the rebellious Yorkists.[28] However, as we have seen, it is possible that a faction of Yorkist sympathisers was growing within the town. More surprising, perhaps, is the Coventry evidence, where it would seem likely that the

---

[22] Hicks, *Wars of the Roses*, 125–30, a view shared by Maurer, *Margaret of Anjou, passim*.
[23] Hicks, *Warwick the Kingmaker*, 49–50; Pollard, *Warwick the Kingmaker*, 98–105.
[24] *Coventry Leet Book*, ed. Harris, 294.
[25] TNA, C67/45, m. 7; *CCR, 1454–61*, pp. 419–20; 1461–8, p. 150.
[26] *Coventry Leet Book*, ed. Harris, 309.
[27] *Ibid.*, 308, 310–11; *CPR, 1452–61*, p. 561.
[28] *CPR, 1452–61*, pp. 275, 329, 350, 354, 579.

Lancastrian hold on the city was beginning to loosen. If so, then the speed with which this happened is notable: the Coventry Parliament, after all, had only been dissolved on 20 December 1459.[29]

In July 1460 Queen Margaret was at Coventry when she heard the news that the Yorkists had secured victory at the battle of Northampton. She immediately left, with her son, Prince Edward, the duke of Exeter and a handful of attendants.[30] With her departure, and the collapse of Lancastrian authority in the south consequent upon Northampton and Henry VI's capture at the battle, Coventry would have been left wide open to a Yorkist takeover. Unfortunately, however, the local sources are frustratingly silent for the rest of 1460. This is despite the fact that the duke of York passed through the city in September, on his way to London, and that the Lancastrian duke of Somerset and earl of Devon and their army passed through in December. Probably, the governing elite of Coventry tried to maintain a neutral stance, avoiding overt commitment to either side.[31]

For much of 1460, this also seems to have been the approach of their equivalents in Shrewsbury. The town responded to the Lancastrian demand for troops issued in December 1459 and supplied sixty-one men for the Northampton campaign six months later. Shrewsbury only committed itself to the Yorkist cause later in the year. In early September 1460 the duke of York returned from Ireland, and made a leisurely progress through the marches, holding sessions and raising support at Shrewsbury, as well as Ludlow, Hereford and Gloucester. At Shrewsbury he was joined by the earl of Warwick and it may have been here that he discussed with the earl his plan to make himself king: whether or not Warwick agreed, let alone then prepared the way for York's coronation, is a moot point. In any case, at Ludlow York seems to have been requested to take the throne by a group of local gentry, and such public events may have been stage-managed along the route to London, perhaps starting in Shrewsbury.[32] York arrived in London in October accompanied by a substantial contingent from the marches.[33] Only after the duke's visit does Shrewsbury appear as anything like an enthusiastic supporter of the Yorkists. In order to counter growing Lancastrian pressure in Wales, led by Jasper, earl of Pembroke, Edward, earl of March, was dispatched from London to the marches in December, and he spent Christmas at Shrewsbury, where he was well entertained.[34] Forty fully-equipped soldiers were sent to join the duke of York in Yorkshire.[35]

The reactions of Bristol's governors in the first nine months of 1460 may have been less guarded. According to a Chancery petition presented by the masters of two ships, the *Marie* of Bayonne and the *Marie* of La Rochelle, in July 1460 their vessels were seized by the Yorkist John, Lord Clinton, at the behest of the mayor

---

[29] Hicks, *Wars of the Roses*, 146.
[30] Maurer, *Margaret of Anjou*, 187; Griffiths, *Henry VI*, 866; C.L. Scofield, *The Life and Reign of Edward the Fourth* (2 vols., 1923), i. 98.
[31] Scofield, *Edward the Fourth*, i. 117.
[32] Johnson, *Duke Richard of York*, 210–12.
[33] H.T. Evans, *Wales and the Wars of the Roses* (Stroud, 1998), 72.
[34] Johnson, *Duke Richard of York*, 220 and n. 133.
[35] Walker, 'An Urban Community', 391–2.

of Bristol, Thomas Roger, and the sheriff, Robert Jakkes, to form part of the flotilla which would bring the duke of York back from Ireland that September, despite both masters having letters of safe conduct from the earl of Warwick. The clear imputation behind this allegation was that the mayor, sheriff and other burgesses of Bristol were acting on York's behalf.[36] By the year's end Bristol appears to have been split along factional lines, but a commission issued to the mayor in August to suppress riots and disturbances suggests that this may have occurred earlier.[37] From Michaelmas 1460 the mayor was William Canynges, half-brother to Thomas Young and a committed Yorkist. While the town's governing elite may now have been under firm Yorkist control, the same could not be said of the wider body of Bristolians beyond the mayor and common council. One burgess, Henry May, had already been conspiring with John Judde, master of the king's ordnance, to secure the town's stock of gunpowder for the Lancastrians, but had been foiled in this attempt by the mayor, acting on orders from the duke of York. May was also prevented from supplying the Lancastrian army led by the duke of Somerset and the earl of Devon that passed close by Bristol on its way north in December. This was the same army that passed through Coventry, and it also visited Bath, Cirencester and Evesham. That it did not include Bristol on its itinerary suggests that the Lancastrian commanders believed that their reception there would have been hostile.[38] December also saw attempts by the former sheriff of Devon and Lancastrian diehard Sir Baldwin Fulford to incite Bristolians to take action against the duke of York.[39]

The impression created by the examples of Bristol, Coventry and Shrewsbury, of governing elites trying to balance their dynastic loyalties with their survival instincts, while the populace over which they ruled showed signs of antagonism along factional lines, is probably correct, not just for these three places, but for the south-west Midlands and the southern and central Welsh marches as a whole in 1460. The Yorkist presence in this area in September 1460 appears to have marked a sea change at Shrewsbury, and to have consolidated their support in Bristol. Coventry's stance is obscure, but, again, the activities of the duke, and possibly of Warwick too, in September may have brought about a decisive shift in loyalties throughout the region.[40]

York's death at Wakefield at the very end of 1460 shook the kaleidoscope once again in this region, as it did nationally. Edward, now duke of York, was either at Gloucester or Shrewsbury when he heard of his father's defeat and death. He immediately prepared to meet the victorious Lancastrian army as it marched towards London. Edward's force was composed largely of men from the marches,

---

[36] *Cal. Inq. Misc.* viii. 162–3.
[37] *CPR*, 1452–61, pp. 517, 608.
[38] *Great Red Book*, *Text*, part 1, pp. 136–8; TNA, C1/29/542. This episode is discussed at greater length in Fleming, 'Politics and the Provincial Town', 87–8.
[39] According to charges made against Sir Baldwin at his treason trial in Bristol in Sept. 1461: TNA, KB9/297, mm. 134–5.
[40] The Act of Accord of 24 Oct. 1460, by which York was recognised as heir to the throne, may have made it easier for these urban governing elites to square their support for York with their consciences, and to sell this stance to those they governed, but the evidence for this agreement having had a significant effect on the local politics of these towns is lacking. For the Accord, see Hicks, *Wars of the Roses*, 157–62.

including, presumably, some from Shrewsbury. However, he was diverted from this course of action by other unwelcome news. Jasper Tudor, earl of Pembroke, and James Butler, earl of Wiltshire, were leading a Lancastrian army through Wales, heading for Hereford. Edward resolved to meet them.[41] The clash came at Mortimer's Cross, between Wigmore, site of one of Edward's castles, and Leominster, on 3 February, and the Lancastrians were routed. Two weeks later, however, came the second battle of St. Albans, at which the Yorkists, led by Warwick, were defeated by the Lancastrian army that had come down from the north. London now lay before Queen Margaret and the other Lancastrian leaders, but the hostility of the citizens dissuaded them from forcing an entrance and instead they retreated. On 19 February they fell back on Dunstaple. Meanwhile, Edward had remained in the marches, dividing his time between Hereford and Gloucester. At Gloucester, on the 19th, he heard of Warwick's defeat and set off towards London. Warwick had fled west, and the duke and the earl met on 22 February in Oxfordshire. Five days later they entered London unopposed. On 4 March Edward was proclaimed king, and nine days later he left with an army in pursuit of the retreating Lancastrians, upon whom he inflicted a massive defeat at Towton on 29 March.[42]

On 12 February 1461 Edward had been commissioned to raise troops in Bristol and the marches, and Bristol supplied sixty men at a cost to the town of £160.[43] These men doubtless accompanied him on his march to London, and were probably present at Towton, along with an additional Bristol contingent.[44] Such overt partisanship did not go unnoticed by the Lancastrians, at least if we are to believe a near-contemporary chronicler, who alleges that shortly after the second battle of St. Albans, 'The quene with her counsell had graunted and yeve leve to the northurmen forto spoyle and robbe ... the townes of Couentre, Brystow, and Salesbury wyth the shyrys withynne rehersed, as for payment and recompense of theyre sowde and wages, as the comon noyse was among the peple at that tyme.'[45]

Why Coventry should have attracted Margaret's ire is explained by events in that city that followed soon after St. Albans.[46] Within hours of their victory, the Lancastrian leadership dispatched a contingent to Coventry. They carried a letter written in the name of Prince Edward and addressed to the mayor and aldermen, who were thereby required to assist three local Lancastrians, Sir Edmund Mountfort, Sir Henry Everingham and William Elton, esquire. When the party reached Coventry they were led into St. Mary's Hall, where the letter was read before the mayor, aldermen and some of the citizens. Then, Sir Henry's priest, who had delivered the letter, added that his master needed to know that he would be safe if he came to Coventry. If he received such an assurance, 'he wylle come to helpe to kepe the cyte when the northeryn men comyn downe to you fro the felde

---

[41] Evans, *Wales and the Wars of the Roses*, 74–6.
[42] *Ibid.*, 76–80; C.D. Ross, *Edward IV* (1974), 31–7.
[43] Evans, *Wales and the Wars of the Roses*, 77.
[44] Griffiths, *Henry VI*, 882, n. 96; *Great Red Book, Text*, part 3, pp. 77–8.
[45] *An English Chronicle, 1377–1461: A New Edition*, ed. William Marx (Woodbridge, 2003), 98.
[46] This and the next paragraphs are based on Fleming, *Coventry and the Wars of the Roses*, 12–17, 33–5.

and entrete thayme to do yow favour'. However, 'when the lettre was redde in Saynt Mary halle the comyns were so meved ayens the preest and hys men had not the mayre conveyed thayme owte of the fraunches thay wold a smytt of the prestes hed and hys men also'.[47] Instead of rendering the requested assistance to the Lancastrians, Coventry raised £100 to pay for a detachment sent to accompany Edward to London. For their assistance, the men of Coventry were singled out for thanks in a letter from Edward, written on 5 March, the day after his proclamation as king. The letter also urged them to resist further Lancastrian 'rebels'; a similar plea was sent to thirty-three other counties, but this had to wait until 7 March. A week later King Edward requested more soldiers from Coventry, which supplied an additional one hundred men. By this time the earl of Warwick was himself in Coventry, where he executed the Lancastrian, Thomas Holand, the illegitimate son of John Holand, duke of Exeter, before leading off a city detachment that would join their fellows at Towton.

The speed with which both the Lancastrians dispatched a contingent from St. Albans in a vain attempt to secure the loyalties of Coventry, and King Edward acknowledged the great service that the city had done him by refusing their blandishments, demonstrates the strategic importance of the place in February 1461. The thinly-veiled threats uttered by Sir Henry Everingham's priest, that, basically, if he was not allowed to enter safely, then the city would be left to its fate at the hands of the ravening hordes of northerners, may have prompted the spontaneous anger of the men gathered in St. Mary's Hall, but it is more likely that the audience was already heavily infiltrated by Yorkists. The raising of troops for Edward could not have occurred until after 21 February, given that it would have taken at least thirty-six hours for a message to reach Coventry from Gloucester, where Edward heard about St. Albans on the 19th, and these troops joined the march to London, which was reached on the 27th. This makes it very likely that there was already a Yorkist presence in the city before the arrival of the Lancastrian detachment, and that preparations were being made to raise troops by then. Edward had been busily recruiting men in the marches since December, and those two months would have given him ample time to secure Coventry. On his return from Towton King Edward visited Coventry, where he was presented with £100, and in June a further forty men were provided by the city, at a cost of £40, to help Warwick suppress Lancastrian resistance in the north. However, pro-Lancastrian sentiment remained. In July the mayor was ordered to demand obedience from the citizens, and to condemn any plots to free prisoners and the wearing of livery and badges. In October the mayor was joined by Warwick himself on a commission of enquiry into treasonous insurrections in the city.

The faction-fighting that occurred in Bristol and Coventry may have had its counter-part in Gloucester.[48] From 1460 to 1464 the position of Prior Hayward of Lanthony Priory was challenged by John Schoyer. The canons appear to have been split between pro-Hayward and pro-Schoyer factions, and these divisions were reflected beyond the walls of the priory, with the townsmen of Gloucester backing

---

[47] These two quotations come from 'The Coventry Annals', or 'Aylesford Annals', the original of which is Finch-Knightley of Packington Hall MSS, LH1/1, in the possession of the earl of Aylesford. A photocopy is held at Coventry RO: PA 351/1.

[48] This paragraph is based on Holt, 'Gloucester: an English Provincial Town', 274–7.

Hayward while, across the River Severn, Schoyer found support in the Forest of Dean. There were outbreaks of serious violence between the rival supporters. Significantly, Hayward and his faction were backed by the earl of Warwick, and eventually Edward IV expelled Schoyer and restored Hayward. Meanwhile, in 1463 a crowd of country people searched out one of the bailiffs of Gloucester, John Doding, dragged him from his hiding place in St. Peter's Abbey infirmary, and hacked him to death under the High Cross. The mob placed his head on the West Gate and left, only to return a few days later with the intention of murdering other burgesses. Warwick persuaded them to allow him to adjudicate on their grievances (concerning which we are not informed), and he acceded to their demands. This looks like a temporary attempt to placate the mob until greater force could be brought to bear, which it was in the following year, when Edward IV himself visited the town, with a large number of armed men, and the ringleaders were executed and their heads replaced the head of John Doding. In his treatment of the two episodes, Richard Holt suggests that unspecified antagonisms between the laity and clergy, or economic differences between town and country, may have been to blame, but is unable to account for them beyond these suggestions. Given the murderous passions involved, however, and the direct involvement of the earl of Warwick in both episodes (and these two episodes may in any case have been connected), it is perhaps more likely that they too were local manifestations of the factionalism apparent in Coventry and Bristol, and as such were provoked by rival Lancastrian and Yorkist partisans.

Factional disorder continued in the region after Edward's accession, but there seems little doubt that the key urban centres were in Yorkist control by the beginning of 1461. The presence of the duke of York in September 1460 seems to have suppressed much Lancastrian opposition, and to have persuaded local elites of the wisdom of supporting the Yorkists. This opinion was greatly strengthened by Edward, earl of March and then duke of York between December and February, so that by the time of Mortimer's Cross and the second battle of St. Albans this was a securely Yorkist area. While both Coventry and Bristol were within Warwick's sphere of influence, and Shrewsbury close to important possessions of the dukes of York, the experience of Coventry in the later 1450s indicates that this was not a factor that could be relied upon to guarantee the continued Yorkist adherence of their inhabitants. After an impolitic demonstration of Yorkist enthusiasm in 1452, Shrewsbury spent much of the rest of the decade cautiously hedging its bets. While both Coventry and Bristol seem to have experienced growing factionalism in the later 1450s, it was not until the winter of 1460–1 that they came out as unmistakably Yorkist, to provide significant support for Edward, in quick succession as earl of March, duke of York and then as king. Neither side was in any doubt of the strategic significance of this area. In particular, the importance with which both Margaret and Edward regarded Coventry indicates that it may have been key to their opposing strategies in the first three months of 1461. Control of the Coventry region, alongside control of Bristol and the central marches, was crucial. In addition to ensuring supplies of men and finances from this area, Yorkist domination here presented a barrier to Jasper Tudor and the largely Lancastrian west Wales. More importantly, it prevented the re-establishment of Lancastrian domination of Coventry and the west Midlands in the immediate aftermath of the rebuff given by London in February 1461. News of the hostile reception afforded by Coventry to the detachment sent out from the battlefield of St. Albans would have come as a sore blow to the Lancastrian leadership, since it meant that there was no safe, and strategically suitable, haven for them in the south, once London had shown itself as hostile. The Lancastrian decision to relinquish the core of the English realm can be seen as sowing the seeds of their eventual defeat at Towton. To maintain that the Lancastrians were doomed to inevitable defeat by the events of February 1461, not just in London but also in the west Midlands, may not be unreasonable.

WIDOWS AND THE WARS OF THE ROSES: THE TURBULENT MARITAL HISTORY OF EDWARD IV'S PUTATIVE MISTRESS, MARGARET, DAUGHTER OF SIR LEWIS JOHN OF WEST HORNDON, ESSEX[*]

S.J. Payling

Soon after the death of her husband, John Talbot, second earl of Shrewsbury, at the battle of Northampton on 10 July 1460, his widow, Elizabeth, sister of James Butler, earl of Ormond and Wiltshire, presented a petition to Pope Pius II. She recalled how her vulnerability in the wake of her husband's death had led her to make undertakings that she was now anxious to repudiate. Her husband had fallen on the defeated Lancastrian side, and so, fearing the loss of her lands and goods, she had pretended a readiness to marry one of the victors, Walter Blount of Barton Blount in Derbyshire. Blount was, as she rightly insisted to the pope, 'unequal and inferior to her in nobility and wealth'. Yet she felt her situation was desperate, and Blount's influence offered protection 'from the attacks of her enemies and the perils which threatened'. Now that the danger had passed, she asked the pope to release her from her promise.[1] Her plea illustrates an obvious point: the normal hazards facing the wealthy widow were amplified in times of acute political dislocation, particularly if, like Elizabeth Butler, they found themselves alone in the world, with neither parents nor adult children to support them.[2] Such widows had one obvious recourse, namely to marry into the new political establishment. Elizabeth contemplated that solution but found unpalatable the social derogation that, in her case, it entailed.[3] Other widows were offered what were, at least in

---

[*] I am very grateful to the Trustees of the History of Parliament Trust for their permission to draw here on material to be published by the History in *The Commons, 1422–61*, ed. L.S. Clark (forthcoming).

[1] *CPL*, xii. 150–1; *CP*, xi. 705n. The grant to her on 31 Oct. 1460, during the parliament of which Blount was a member, of a life interest, in allowance of her dower, in the castle of Sheffield and other valuable Talbot property, was presumably one of the fruits of her suitor's support: *CPR*, 1452–61, p. 635. For Blount her rejection proved a blessing in disguise, materially at least. By the spring of 1466, he had married a much wealthier widow, Anne, a daughter of Ralph Neville, earl of Westmorland, by Joan Beaufort, and the widow of another victim of the battle of Northampton, Humphrey Stafford, duke of Buckingham: *CPL*, xii. 522; *CP*, ix. 336.

[2] Widows could sometimes find protection within their own families. John Tiptoft, earl of Worcester, for example, secured a grant to the advantage of his sister, wife of the attainted Thomas, Lord Roos, an example of a Yorkist lord protecting a Lancastrian widow: *CPR*, 1461-7, p. 87.

[3] She may also have been personally disinclined to remarry. On 19 July 1460, only nine days after her husband's death, John, bishop of the Isles, was commissioned to veil her, and although, on 6 Feb. 1464, she sued out a licence to marry free of the constraints usually imposed on the widows of tenants-in-

appearance, better options, none more so than Elizabeth Wydeville, widow of Sir John Grey of Groby (Leicestershire), a Lancastrian who fell at the second battle of St. Albans on 17 February 1461. Her marriage to Edward IV in May 1464 is the ultimate example of a Lancastrian widow finding a Yorkist protector. This paper concerns one of two women who may, as Michael Hicks has suggested in his *Edward V*, have unsuccessfully taken the path Elizabeth later followed. One of these is well known. Eleanor, daughter of John Talbot, first earl of Shrewsbury (*d*.1453), and sister-in-law of Elizabeth Butler, was the widow of another Lancastrian, Sir Thomas Butler, son and heir-apparent of Ralph, Lord Butler of Sudeley. It was to her that, according to the *Titulus Regius* of 1483, Edward IV had been pre-contracted, to the invalidation of his subsequent marriage to Elizabeth Wydeville.[4] This paper concerns the second less well-known mistress of the early part of Edward's reign. Sir Thomas More, unaware of the content of *Titulus Regius* and presumably following a now-lost text or tradition, identified the lady to whom the new king had been pre-contracted as 'Dame Elizabeth Lucy', by whom he is said to have had a child. As no such woman can be identified in the contemporary record, Michael has plausibly suggested that More is in error in respect of her Christian name, and that the subject of this story was Margaret, widow of Sir William Lucy, who had fallen on the Lancastrian side at Northampton. Since More is the only source, such an identification is, as Hicks concedes, beyond proof.[5] None the less, even if it is to be rejected, Margaret's remarkable marital history is worth recounting. Not only is it more than usually well-documented, particularly in a chancery suit of the mid-1460s, but it illustrates the difficulties and dangers faced by widows during the turmoil of the Wars of the Roses. Their hands, most particularly if their husbands had fallen in a losing cause, could become the object of a competition in which the normal social rules were in abeyance. On a rare occasion that suspension of the rules favoured the widow, as it did for Elizabeth Wydeville, but routinely it did not. Hence Walter Blount could aspire to the hand of a widowed countess and eventually obtain that of a widowed duchess, and Margaret could become the victim of the unwelcome advances of a lawyer, Thomas Danvers, seeking to marry above himself.

Margaret, born in the late 1430s, was of distinguished birth. Although her father, Sir Lewis John, 'a Welshman of dubious origin', had largely made his own way in the world, her mother was of high aristocratic rank, a daughter of John Montagu, earl of Salisbury (*d*.1400).[6] Her mother's high status was further exemplified by marriage, soon after Sir Lewis's death in October 1442, to John Holand, duke of Exeter (*d*.1447).[7] In the late 1450s Margaret's aristocratic connexions and youth recommended her to Sir William Lucy of Dallington (Northamptonshire), who was old enough to have been her grandfather. One of the richest gentry in England, he

---

chief, she remained unmarried until her death in 1473: *Testamenta Eboracensia*, iii (Surtees Society, xlv), 335; *CPR*, 1461–7, p. 300; *CP*, xi. 705.

[4] M.A. Hicks, *Edward V: The Prince in the Tower* (Stroud, 2003), 31–4.
[5] *Ibid.*, 34.
[6] *The History of Parliament: The Commons, 1386–1421*, ed. J.S. Roskell, Linda Clark and Carole Rawcliffe (4 vols., Stroud, 1992), iii. 494–8. Her date of birth can only be inferred. Her parents married in about 1433 and she was the youngest of the three daughters of the marriage. She is named in the will her father made on 2 June 1440: TNA, PROB11/1, f. 107.
[7] *CP*, v. 210.

had had a long and distinguished career both in France and at the royal court.⁸ His marriage to Margaret had both a personal and political context. Although he had been twice-married, he was still childless and a young bride offered him a new opportunity to perpetuate his ancient line. Much more interesting, however, is the marriage's place in a series of matches made in the late 1450s that created marital links among a group of adherents of the Lancastrian court. Three such marriages occurred within a brief space of time among Lucy's immediate circle: his nephew, William Vaux of Great Harrowden (Northamptonshire), married an attendant of Queen Margaret, shortly before 22 December 1456, when the bride had letters of denization;⁹ Lucy's own marriage to Margaret took place shortly before 10 March 1457, when the crown retrospectively licensed a jointure settlement;¹⁰ and on 19 January 1458 a contract was drawn up for the marriage of the daughter and heiress-presumptive of Lucy's friend and neighbour, Henry Green of Drayton, to John, third son of Humphrey Stafford, duke of Buckingham.¹¹ To these matches is probably to be added a fourth, that of Margaret's paternal half-brother, Henry Fitzlewis, to a sister of Henry Beaufort, duke of Somerset, although this cannot be dated accurately.¹² These marriages, linking Lucy, as a prominent Lancastrian knight, with other Lancastrian families, are to be seen in the same context as other more important ones of the late 1450s, most notably that of the duke of Somerset's first cousin, Margaret Beaufort, dowager-countess of Richmond, to Buckingham's second son, Henry.¹³ The number of such matches in so brief a period suggests a conscious policy pursued by the Lancastrian regime in the strife-torn late 1450s to create a closely-related Lancastrian elite.

---

⁸ To his patrimony, lying in four counties, with its principal properties at Dallington (Northamptonshire) and Cublington (Buckinghamshire), he united a maternal inheritance that comprised a significant part of the inheritances of the knightly families of Talbot of Richard's Castle (Herefordshire) and Archdeacon of Ruan Lanihorne (Cornwall): *CP*, i. 187–8; viii. 261–2; *CIPM*, xvi. 771–8; xviii. 64–7; xx. 762–4; TNA, C139/130/13. He also had a life interest in the valuable manor of Gainsborough (Lincolnshire), the inheritance of his second wife, Elizabeth, daughter and coheir of Sir Henry Percy (*d*.1432) of Atholl: TNA, CP25(1)/293/72/351. It is worth observing that his name had enough posthumous currency to be assigned by Shakespeare to a soldier in *Henry VI, Part I*. For a detailed discussion of his career: S.J. Payling, 'Sir William Lucy', in *The Commons, 1422–61*, ed. Clark (forthcoming).
⁹ *CPR*, 1452–61, p. 342; *CP*, xii (2), 216–17.
¹⁰ *CPR*, 1452–61, p. 352. The marriage cannot have taken place before the autumn of 1455, when Lucy's second wife, Elizabeth Percy, died: C139/192/16. It is sometimes misdated to before October 1453 on the basis of a wrongly dated jointure settlement in Margaret's inquisitions *post mortem*: TNA, C140/20/29.
¹¹ *CP*, xii (2), 736. Lucy was a feoffee of Green in 1453: *CPR*, 1452–61, p. 85.
¹² A daughter, Mary, who later married Anthony Wydeville, Earl Rivers, was born to this couple on 30 May 1467: *Archaeologia*, xxviii (1840), 458; *CP*, xi. 24. But it is probable that they had been married for some years by that date. Margaret's maternal half-sister, Anne Hankford, also married into a leading Lancastrian family: as early as the mid-1440s she took as her husband Thomas, brother of James, earl of Wiltshire, and of Elizabeth Butler: *CP*, x. 132.
¹³ This series of marriages and its importance is noted in R.A. Griffiths, *The Reign of Henry VI* (1981), 802–3. To the examples he cites is to be added the marriage, in about April 1458, of Elizabeth Butler's brother, the earl of Wiltshire, to (like Fitzlewis) a sister of the duke of Somerset: *CP*, x. 128–9.

If, however, Margaret Lucy's marriage had an important political dimension, it was the personal one that informed the generous marriage settlement made in the young bride's favour. With no issue to disappoint, Lucy could afford to be lavish, and he made her an extensive jointure settlement. On 10 March 1457 the Crown, for the payment of £20, retrospectively licensed the settlement of five scattered manors upon the couple in fee-tail, and, by his death, Lucy had added seven further manors, including, most significantly, that of Dallington, his principal residence. Precise valuations are hard to assign, but it would be surprising if these dozen manors were not worth approaching £200 p.a., a jointure more fitting to an earl's daughter than an earl's granddaughter.[14] This promised the young Margaret a wealthy widowhood, but it was to prove a mixed blessing. Indeed, the generosity of her elderly husband may even have been a factor in the brevity of their marriage as it certainly was in the difficulties she faced in the early 1460s.

Like the second Talbot earl of Shrewsbury, Lucy fell on the Lancastrian side at the battle of Northampton, but not seemingly in the normal course of battle.[15] The apparent circumstances of his death were so remarkable as to attract the notice of at least two contemporary chroniclers. The London chronicle identified with William Gregory, mayor of London in 1451–2, provides the best account: 'And that goode knyght Syr Wylliam Lucy that dwellyd be-syde Northehampton hyrde the goone schotte, and come unto the fylde to have holpyn the kynge, but the fylde was done or that he come; an one of the Staffordys was ware of hys comynge, and lovyd that knyght ys wyffe and hatyd hym, and a-non causyd hys dethe.'[16] The other chronicle, the *Annales Rerum Anglicarum* wrongly attributed to William Worcestre, is terser, although it identifies more particularly the villain of the piece: '*In fine belli servientes Johannis Stafforde, armigeri, occiderunt Wyllelmum Lucy, militem, cijus uxorem idem Johannes sibi maritavit cito postea.*'[17]

There are some curiosities in the first more detailed account of Lucy's death. Why, as a prominent Lancastrian, was he not in the king's army at the outset of the battle, coming there only when he 'hyrde the goone schotte' and arriving only after the conflict was over? Further, if he was near enough to have heard the sounds of battle, why did he fail to reach the field until after the conflict was over? The story of the Gregory chronicler is probably not to be taken literally, but is rather intended to emphasise the element of treachery in the knight's death. That death occurred after the battle was over, a statement reflected in the account of the pseudo-

---

[14] *CPR*, 1452–61, p. 352; C140/1/16; 20/29.

[15] His inquisitions *post mortem*, held in five counties, all give the date of the battle as the date of his death: C140/1/16.

[16] *Historical Collections of a Citizen of London*, ed. James Gairdner (Camden Society, 2nd series, xvii, 1876), 207. The appearance of this story in the chronicle offers some slight support to Thomson's suggestion that the continuator of the chronicle (after 1452) was a cleric, Thomas Eborall, master of Whittington College, who was named by Gregory as the supervisor of his will: J.A.F. Thomson, 'The Continuation of Gregory's Chronicle: a Possible Author?', *British Museum Quarterly*, xxxvi (1972), 92–7. Eborall had Northamptonshire connexions, indirectly at least, through his kinsman (probably his brother), John Eborall, rector of Paulerspury, who, according to one source, was the priest who married Edward IV to Elizabeth Wydeville: TNA, E163/29/11, m. 5; Hicks, *Edward V*, 41.

[17] *Letters and Papers Illustrative of the Wars of the English in France during the Reign of Henry VI*, ed. Joseph Stevenson (2 vols. in 3, RS, xxii, 1861–4), ii (2), [773]. McFarlane has shown that Worcestre was not the author: K.B. McFarlane, 'William Worcester: a Preliminary Survey', in *England in the Fifteenth Century: Collected Essays*, ed. G.L. Harriss (1981), 209–10.

Worcestre that it happened at the battle's end. Further, it was provoked not by the differing political allegiances of killer and killed but by a base personal motive on the part of the former (and perhaps one unsuspected by the latter). The chronicler's description of the murderer as 'one of the Staffordys' may be intended to imply a further element of treachery. The author either believed, or was inviting the reader to believe, that the perpetrator was a near kinsman of the duke of Buckingham, who fell on the Lancastrian side at the battle. Such an identification implies that Lucy, who had 'come unto the fylde to have holpyn the kynge', was killed by one of his own side. More persuasive is the identification, in the pseudo-Worcestre's account, of the murderer as John Stafford. Here the common-law records produce a crucial piece of evidence, and indirectly implicate Margaret in her husband's death. In pleadings of Trinity term 1466 she is described as the widow of John Stafford, thus corroborating the statement of the pseudo-Worcestre that such a marriage took place.[18]

One possible explanation for these events is that Margaret had, in her first husband's lifetime, begun a liaison with Stafford. Stafford is an obscure figure, and he was certainly not closely related to the duke of Buckingham.[19] He has tentatively been identified as the son of another John Stafford, an esquire with minor landed interests in Worcestershire and Staffordshire who died in August 1421. Aged only four at his father's death, he was brought up in the wardship of Joan Beauchamp, Lady Abergavenny.[20] No more is certainly known of him before the battle of Northampton and his subsequent marriage to Margaret. That marriage made him a wealthy man, and there can be little doubt that her extensive jointure, on the assumption that he was aware of it, added to her attractions in his eyes. For Margaret the advantages of the match are less obvious. Later evidence shows that Stafford must have been in the Yorkist ranks at Northampton, and thus that the implication of the Gregory chronicler (that Sir William died at the hands of one of his own side) is false. Yet it seems unlikely that, in marrying him, Margaret was explicitly seeking a protector from the victorious side. Had this been the case she would surely have had status and wealth enough to have found a more important man. In short, there seems little reason to doubt that, as the seemingly well-informed London chronicler comes close to stating explicitly, she and Stafford were having an affair before Lucy's death.

Whatever the precise circumstances of Margaret's second marriage, it was to be even briefer than her first. A marriage that began with death in battle quickly ended in the same way. Stafford enjoyed a brief period of prominence due to Margaret's lands, sitting as MP for Worcestershire in the Yorkist Parliament of October 1460 before being killed in the Yorkist ranks at the battle of Towton in the following March.[21] If she did have an affair with the new king, Edward IV, that affair

---

[18] TNA, CP40/820, rot. 488d.
[19] For an account of his career: C.E. Moreton, 'John Stafford II', in *The Commons, 1422–61*, ed. Clark (forthcoming).
[20] *CFR*, xiv. 440; *CIPM*, xxi. 434.
[21] *Paston Letters and Papers of the Fifteenth Century*, ed. Norman Davis, Richard Beadle and Colin Richmond (3 vols., EETS, supplementary series, xx–xxii, 2004–5), i. 165.

probably, as Hicks has suggested, dates from the first year of the reign.[22] It is possible that rumours of this affair explain the interest of the two chroniclers in the circumstances of her first husband's death, although the scandal of a marriage to the suspected murderer of an earlier husband might be taken as explanation enough for that interest.

Later rival accounts give no clear chronology of events after her second husband's death, but there is no doubt that, leaving aside all question of a possible affair with the king, she then found herself courted by at least two suitors. One of these was Thomas Danvers, an Oxfordshire lawyer with strong Lancastrian connexions.[23] Her relationship with Danvers appears to have begun by 4 November 1462 when, according to a suit brought by Danvers and pleaded in the court of common pleas in Trinity term 1466, she borrowed £300 from him, and it may be that this loan stands at the beginning of his courtship of her.[24] A chancery case, on a petition presented by Danvers in about 1466, gives two contradictory accounts of the course of this courtship. Danvers complained to the chancellor, the earl of Warwick's brother, George Neville, archbishop of York, that he had made a lawful contract of marriage with Margaret, but that this contract had been subverted by the duplicity of her half-brother, Sir Henry Fitzlewis.[25] Fitzlewis, he claimed, had 'caused and stered' his sister to write him a letter 'of her owne hond'. This letter asked her suitor to agree to 'such appoyntmentes' as Sir Henry would declare to him 'by modethe'. Fitzlewis told him that Margaret had denied her contract with Danvers, 'to my lord of Warrewyk and other estates of her kynne'; and that therefore Danvers should himself confirm that denial, 'in savyng of her wurship'. Yet he promised that this would only delay the completion of the match, offering to be bound, jointly with his sister, to Danvers in £1,000 that the marriage would be made within six months. He also, according to Danvers's petition, took a further precaution: he asked Danvers's lord, William Waynflete, bishop of Winchester, 'to move your said besecher to applye to the forsaid desires and not to trouble with his said suster, promyttyng his loythe and undertakyng unto the said buysshop that she shuld perfourme the said maryage'. As a result Danvers did as he was asked, and even paid Fitzlewis twenty marks as reward for his good offices. Sir Henry had then, in contradiction of his undertakings, 'stured and moved' Margaret to make a contract of marriage with Thomas Wake and 'with his owne hondes ensured hem to geder and after that cownceyled and caused hem to be wedded to geder contrary to the lawe of god to the open shame and hurte of his said suster and to the extreme trouble and undoyng of your said besecher'. Danvers asked the chancellor to summon Fitzlewis by *subpoena* and that he be compelled to repay him not only the twenty marks but also the £1,000 forfeited on the bond and 'to make amendes' for the damages the petitioner had suffered by 'menes of his unknyghtly demenyng'.

Fitzlewis replied to Danvers's accusations in a detailed rejoinder. He portrayed Danvers as an importunate suitor whom he had attempted to assist until it became clear that Margaret had no desire to marry him. He claimed that, in either January or February 1463, Danvers had paid him ten marks to act as his intermediary,

[22] Hicks, *Edward V*, 35.
[23] For his career: L.S. Clark, 'Thomas Danvers', in *The Commons, 1422–61* (forthcoming).
[24] CP40/820, rot. 488d.
[25] TNA, C1/31/298.

telling him that he loved Margaret 'as muche as was possible for eny erthely man to love a woman and that he coude thinke she was estraungyd from hym by sum persones abowght her and other not his wel willers and wolde be othir wyse disposid to hym yf he myght speke with her, almost dayly laboring and desyring the said Harry to fynde sum meane that the said Thomas Danvers myght speke with the said Margret'. But Sir Henry, despite his best efforts on the suitor's behalf, had found his sister determined not to meet Danvers and prepared only to write a letter to him. This Sir Henry duly delivered, knowing nothing of its contents save for what its recipient later told him of them. With it he also brought a verbal message from his sister. That message was unequivocal. She said that 'she merveylid gretly' that Danvers 'coude fynde in his harte to trouble defame or noyse her wrongfully and under suche forme as he dyd', that is, presumably, by falsely claiming a contract of marriage with her. None the less, Sir Henry, on his own account, continued to press Danvers's unwelcome suit, eventually bringing them together 'to speke and comyn to gedre as long as hem goodly lykyd'. The bishop of Winchester then, in this account, intervened on Danvers's behalf, sending for Sir Henry and willing him 'to be ffrendely' to Danvers in the matter of the marriage. Sir Henry told the bishop that the 'ouermuche bisines and sclawnderus labours' of Danvers, 'so sore vexing and troubeling the said Margret in the conseite of the said Harry myght neuer engendre hartly love but cause muche hatred'. He added that if Danvers 'had suche affection and love to the said Margret as he had oftyn tolde to the said Harry', and if he 'entended verily to gete the love and goode wille of the said Margret' that he should 'surces of his ouermuche bysines and sclawnderus labours' and resort instead to 'honest and soft deling'. Only when it became clear to Fitzlewis that Margaret would not have the marriage and that there had been no promise of marriage on her part, did he join 'other kynnysmen frendes and counsell of the said Margret' in promoting the marriage to Wake.[26]

Other evidence adds a little to these accounts. Danvers's indignation over his failed suit had led him, before he sought financial redress against Sir Henry by his petition to the chancellor, to take action against Margaret herself. After her marriage to Wake, he issued proceedings against her in the consistory court of John Chedworth, bishop of Lincoln, in whose diocese she resided, alleging that she had contracted marriage with him *per verba legitime de presenti*. Chedworth committed the matter to George Neville, then still bishop of Exeter (he was not raised to the archbishopric of York until 15 March 1465), who excommunicated her for contumacy when she failed to appear before him. Like the dowager-countess of Shrewsbury before her, although in somewhat less favourable circumstances, Margaret was obliged to sue for papal redress. She claimed, in a petition to Pope Paul II, that she had not appeared because she had been summoned to 'an unsafe and distant place', to which she dared not go on account of the power of Danvers and his friends (a standard plea in such circumstances). On 23 August 1465 the pope instructed the bishops of Winchester, Salisbury and Lincoln to

---

[26] TNA, C4/2/6.

investigate.²⁷ This investigation was presumably still pending when, on the following 8 October, a powerful commission, headed by Edmund Grey, earl of Kent, was issued for the arrest and appearance in chancery of Margaret, her new husband Thomas Wake and Thomas Pachet, a Worcester lawyer who had, according to Danvers's complaint, conspired with Sir Henry to frustrate the match.²⁸ It is tempting to see the issue of this commission as a result of Danvers's chancery petition, but the petition postdates the commission. In any event, it is unlikely that the commission was acted upon.²⁹

Danvers next turned to the common law, bringing a suit against Margaret in the court of common pleas, of which his half-brother, Robert Danvers, was one of the judges, in Trinity term 1466, alleging that she had failed to repay him £300 borrowed in November 1462. Margaret responded that at the day the writ was sued she was the wife of Thomas Wake, and not, as named in the writ, the widow of John Stafford, and at the same time she and Wake brought a plea against Danvers for a forcible entry into her property at Dallington.³⁰ Whatever the rights and wrongs of the case, Margaret was soon spared further trouble. Her eventful life ended on 4 August 1466, hopefully after she had succeeded in having the sentence of excommunication lifted. Although she had had three husbands, she was only about twenty-eight at her death and the probability is that she died of complications arising from childbirth. A son, John, had been born to her and Wake only three months before she died.³¹ Interestingly, as far as it can be reconstructed, the memorial inscription on her brass, which survives in the church of Ingrave in Essex (having been moved from the church of West Horndon), remembered none of her husbands (although her three marriages were reflected in armorial bearings). Instead she was described only in terms of her parentage and, in a contrived way of asserting her rank to posterity, her mother's third marriage to the duke of Exeter.³²

The chancery petition may have been presented shortly before Margaret's death, but the probability is that it was presented soon afterwards. All that can be said with certainty is that the petition postdates the promotion of its addressee to the archbishopric of York on 15 March 1465. Two considerations, however, imply that it was many months later. First, it mentions Pachet's part in aiding Fitzlewis but does not ask for a *subpoena* against him. This implies that the petition postdates Pachet's death, which occurred between 9 December 1465 and 23 January 1466.³³

---

²⁷ *CPL*, xii. 405.

²⁸ *CPR*, 1461–7, p. 491. Pachet numbered among his clients both Margaret Lucy and her maternal half-sister, Anne Butler: *CPR*, 1461–7, p. 265; PROB11/5, ff. 90v–92. For his career: S.J. Payling, 'Thomas Pachet', in *The Commons, 1422–61* (forthcoming).

²⁹ Although, however, the commission was not issued as a result of Danvers's petition to the chancellor, its composition leaves no doubt that it was issued at his suit. Among those commissioned were his stepfather, Sir William Mauntell of Heyford (Northamptonshire), and William Fiennes, Lord Say and Sele, the brother of his late first wife.

³⁰ CP40/820, rots. 488d, 533.

³¹ C140/20/29.

³² H.L. Elliot, 'Fitz Lewes, of West Horndon, and the Brasses at Ingrave', *Transactions of the Essex Archaeological Society*, new series, vi (1898), 39–41. Her brass bears three shields of arms. The interpretation of three of these is clear: one represents the marriage of her parents and two of the others her own marriages to Lucy and Wake of Blisworth. The fourth would appear to relate to her other marriage, impaling the arms of Fitzlewis with the arms 'crusilly, a cross'.

³³ PROB11/5, ff. 90v–92. It may be that Danvers had petitioned the chancellor against Pachet on an earlier occasion, but that this petition is now lost. On 5 Nov. and 4 Dec. 1464 Pachet had entered

Second, no *subpoena* is asked for against Margaret, yet her alleged undertaking to marry him is the basis of Danvers's case against her half-brother. If, however, the petition does postdate her death, it can be no later than 8 June 1467, when Neville lost the chancellorship.[34]

This is as much of Margaret's story as can be obtained from the contemporary record. It is clear that about eighteen months after the death of her second husband at the battle of Towton she became the subject of Danvers's advances. As a husband, he had little obvious attraction for her. Socially, she could expect to do better (although she had disparaged herself in making a second marriage and her social stock may have been diminished by the controversial circumstances of that liaison), and Danvers was still, in the early 1460s, compromised by his Lancastrian past (as he was to be even more in the late 1460s).[35] Yet Danvers's pursuit of her in the church court and then of her half-brother in chancery implies that she may have committed herself to him in some way (even perhaps a 'contracte of lawfull matrimony' but that must be doubtful). She seems quickly to have repudiated that commitment, yet the question arises of whether she did so because she had come to think better of it or because she had come under pressure from her 'kin' to marry elsewhere (or at least not to marry Danvers). This, in turn, raises the most interesting of the allegations in Danvers's chancery petition, namely, his claim that Sir Henry Fitzlewis and Thomas Pachet had concocted a story to make him defer his suit. It is worth paying attention to the precise wording of the petition: Danvers attributed the story to Fitzlewis and Pachet and left open the possibility that Margaret was unaware of their ruse. She was 'caused and stered' to write a letter, but that letter did not set out the reason why the marriage must be delayed, it only asked Danvers to be guided by what Fitzlewis should tell him. It was Fitzlewis, seemingly acting on his own initiative, who told him that his sister had been obliged to deny 'to my lord of Warrewyk and other estates of her kynne' that she was promised to Danvers. Whether or not Fitzlewis did employ this as an excuse, the story has credibility. The chancellor to whom the petition was addressed was the earl's brother, who would either know or could easily discover what the earl would have thought about any marriage between Margaret and Danvers. Danvers is

---

bonds to Chancellor Neville to appear before him. Since any sums forfeited on these bonds were to be levied in Wake's county of Northamptonshire rather than Pachet's of Worcestershire, it is probable that this appearance was connected with the dispute over Wake's marriage: *CCR*, 1461–8, pp. 271, 273.

[34] The dispute between Danvers and Wake continued after Margaret's death, although the litigation adds nothing to Margaret's story. Wake sued an action of maintenance against Danvers, claiming that, on 28 Nov. 1466, he had illegally maintained at Northampton an appeal of robbery against him by one Roger Plummer. Danvers replied with a more interesting action of his own, alleging that Wake had breached the Statute of *Praemunire* by having him summoned to appear in the papal curia (seemingly on matters unconcerned with the late Margaret): CP40/824, rots. 286, 337; KB27/826, rot. 85d. The dispute was brought to an end in February 1468 when Sir John Catesby, acting as an arbiter at the instigation of William, Lord Hastings, awarded Danvers 100 marks in return for the discontinuance of the action of *praemunire*: C1/90/34.

[35] In June 1468 he was committed to the Tower of London on suspicion of being in treasonable correspondence with Queen Margaret's court in exile, but he was soon released: *Wars of the English*, ii (2), [789–90].

unlikely to have made up a story that could easily be proved to be false, therefore it is fair to assume that, whether or not Fitzlewis pleaded the earl's disapproval as an excuse for delaying the marriage, the earl did disapprove of the match. But why should he have any interest in the matter? Margaret was indeed his kinswoman: through her Montagu mother she was his first cousin, once removed. That relationship seems to have had meaning, for Margaret's mother had named Warwick as the supervisor of the will she made in 1457. Further, it is possible that, in the early months of the new reign, Margaret was (as Michael Hicks has suggested) living in the earl's household at Warwick castle. When she sued out a pardon on 5 February 1462 (probably before Danvers had begun to court her) and perhaps at the time she was having her affair with the king, the town of 'Warwick' is given as one of her addresses.[36] The earl's interest is also manifest in the marriage she did make, to Thomas Wake of Blisworth, the head of a leading Northamptonshire family.[37] By the late 1460s Wake numbered among the earl's close adherents, and there is no reason to doubt that he was already the earl's man when he married Margaret (probably in 1464).[38] It is, therefore, not unlikely that the earl's hand lay behind Margaret's marriage to Wake, just as it did behind the third and grandest of Wake's marriages, in the early 1470s, to Elizabeth, the elderly widow of Warwick's uncle, the deranged George Neville, Lord Latimer, and one of the three daughters of Richard Beauchamp, earl of Warwick, by the Berkeley heiress.[39]

On this reading of the evidence, the earl of Warwick was responsible for Danvers's marital disappointment, as Danvers was probably aware. Seeking, however, to blame someone against whom he might obtain some redress, he chose to make allegations of fraud against Fitzlewis, whom neither the earl nor Chancellor Neville had any reason to protect.[40] When Danvers commissioned him

---

[36] Hicks, *Edward V*, 35; TNA, C67/45, m. 34. According to the Tudor chronicler, Polydore Vergil, it was rumoured that the young king had, early in his reign, 'assayed to do some unhonest act in the earles howse': *Three Books of Polydore Vergil's English History*, ed. Henry Ellis (Camden Society, xxix, 1844), 117. Margaret's possible residence in the earl's household raises the possibility that she was the victim of this 'unhonest act', although this may be to carry speculation too far.

[37] The possibility cannot be entirely discounted that Margaret's husband was Thomas Wake's son, Thomas, who was of age in the late 1460s: *CCR*, 1461–8, p. 407; TNA, C241/254/12, 34. The probability is, however, that the groom was the elder Thomas, the subject of the common-law action brought by Danvers after Margaret's death. He was said to be 24 'or more' at the death of his own father, another Thomas, in 1458, but, if he was a father himself by the mid-1440s, he must have been some years older: C139/172/19; 177/43. His first wife, Margery, was a minor Somerset heiress: BL, Add. Ch. 28894.

[38] In November 1461 Thomas was appointed to the Northamptonshire shrievalty and his brother John to the office of escheator in Cambridgeshire and Huntingdonshire. Later, in July 1469, Wake's son and heir, probably the Thomas mentioned above, met his death in the earl's cause in the battle of Edgecote, and Wake himself was one of those implicated in the murder of the earl's enemy Earl Rivers: John Warkworth, *Chronicle of the First Thirteen Years of the Reign of Edward IV*, ed. J.O. Halliwell (Camden Society, x, 1839), 7; M.A. Hicks, *False, Fleeting, Perjur'd Clarence* (Gloucester, 1980), 48. He also, no doubt as an agent of Warwick, made a malicious allegation of witchcraft against Rivers's widow: *Rot. Parl.* vi. 232; *CPR*, 1467–77, p. 190.

[39] *CP*, vii. 480. Latimer died in the last days of 1469, and it may be that Elizabeth's marriage to Wake took place during the Readeption and was the earl's way of forwarding a favoured retainer.

[40] Although the earl was clearly no friend of Danvers, the lawyer enjoyed much better relations with the archbishop. A window in the church of Waterstock (Oxfordshire), where Danvers was buried,

to act as his intermediary in the first months of 1463, Fitzlewis was still in the process of leaving his Lancastrian past behind him. He had been attainted in the first parliament of the new reign and had remained in arms in the Lancastrian cause until as late as 27 December 1462, when he was one of the garrison that surrendered Dunstanburgh castle. Thereafter, however, he very quickly won redemption: on 7 May 1463 he received a general pardon, and his attainder was reversed, along with that of his brother-in-law, the duke of Somerset, soon afterwards.[41] Yet, when Danvers petitioned against him, he may have still been tainted by his past loyalties in the eyes of the Nevilles, if not in those of the king. But what case did Danvers have against him? It would hardly have been worthwhile bringing the chancery case but for the £1,000 bond that Fitzlewis had allegedly entered that his sister would complete the marriage. Here there is a flat contradiction. Danvers claimed that 'the copyes of which obligacionz wryten with the propre honde of the said Thomas Pachet and by hym delyuered to the said Sir Harry your said besecher hathe redy to shewe'. But how could the petitioner have the copies of the obligations 'redy to shewe' if they were in Sir Henry's hands? Further he later complained that Sir Henry had failed to seal the obligations. Fitzlewis denied the fact of the bonds. The bonds are hard to believe in. Why should Fitzlewis have bound himself in so great a sum, just to persuade Danvers that the marriage must be delayed? Danvers's own account of them is incoherent. All he had was his own assertion of an undertaking by Sir Henry to be bound.

The story of Margaret's marital adventures in the early 1460s, as far as they are revealed in the chancery proceedings and other incidental references, do little to either support or contradict the notion that she was briefly Edward IV's mistress and that she had a child by him. One can only speculate upon whether any of the actions of the principals in this affair were motivated by the knowledge of this supposed affair. It might be argued that Danvers's energetic pursuit of her implies that she was not and had not been the king's mistress, but it may be that he was simply unaware of that relationship. The same point could be made of Wake's subsequent willingness to marry her. More revealing, perhaps, is the earl of Warwick's attitude, if that attitude is correctly represented in Danvers's petition. If Margaret was indeed resident for a time in his household at Warwick, he was probably aware of her relationship with the king (and, even if she were not, he was better placed to be so than Danvers or Wake); it might be supposed that he would have been keen to have her married, and thus that any suitor would meet with his approval. On this line of reasoning, his opposition to Margaret's proposed marriage to Danvers contradicts that idea of a royal affair. On the other hand, he might have opposed it because he was assured that she would be married to his man, Wake.

Better indirect evidence against the affair might be derived from a close look at Margaret's own situation in the early 1460s. Michael Hicks speculates that the

joins the archbishop's name with that of Bishop Waynflete and himself in a request for prayers: F.N. Macnamara, *Memorials of the Danvers Family* (1895), 166.

[41] M.A. Hicks, 'Edward IV, the Duke of Somerset and Lancastrian Loyalism in the North', in *Richard III and his Rivals* (1991), 149–52, 162–3. He soon won Edward IV's trust. On 2 July 1463 the treasurer and chamberlains of the exchequer were ordered to pay him 100 marks for the wages of soldiers, 'appoynted to attend vpon our persone': TNA, E404/72/3/46.

affair was an attractive possibility to her because she found herself 'needing royal favour' to secure the great jointure settled upon her by Lucy and the dower to which she was entitled in the rest of the Lucy estate. He draws this inference from the delay in the completion of the formalities necessary to give her that security: not until 24 November 1461 (sixteen months after Lucy's death) were the escheators of Worcestershire and Bedfordshire ordered to give her livery of seisin of two manors in those counties settled in jointure and held in chief; and her dower was not assigned until the following March. He also argues that her position was threatened, potentially at least, by the attainder in the first Parliament of the reign of Lucy's nephew and coheir, William Vaux.[42] This is one reading of the evidence, but there is a contrary one. It should be noted that Margaret had no need for a royal grant of livery of seisin in the bulk of her jointure, which was not held in chief, and there is no reason to suppose that she did not enjoy it from the time of Lucy's death. The delay in the formal livery to her of two of the jointure manors held in chief was simply the result of another, namely that in holding Sir William's inquisitions *post mortem*, the last of which was delivered into chancery only on 21 November 1461. Neither delay can, in themselves, be cited as evidence that she had difficulty establishing her rights.[43] Nor is there any evidence that Vaux's attainder caused the crown to seize what should have been hers: none of the grants made by the crown of Vaux's share of the Lucy inheritance included lands held by Margaret in jointure.[44] If there was ever any threat to her possession of what Lucy had given her, it probably predated the king's accession, and was posed not by the crown but by Lucy's heirs, Vaux and another of his nephews, Walter Hopton, who had every reason to resent his generosity to her. On 26 August 1460, with the Yorkists in control of government, the two heirs had been granted licence to take seisin without suing livery or paying relief.[45] This was a mark of favour to Hopton, who was a servant of the house of York, and, potentially at least, gave the heirs the pretext to enter Margaret's jointure lands. There is, however, no evidence that they did so, and in any event, if Hopton posed any threat to Margaret, that threat ended with his childless death in February 1461.[46] The most that Margaret can be said to have gained from Edward IV's accession was the belated issue of writs of *diem clausit extremum* in respect of Sir William, the issue of which had been forestalled by the grant of 26 August 1460. These were issued on 6 July 1461 and allowed her jointure settlement to be recorded and her dower assigned, but these were mere formalities and if there was then any danger to her possession it is difficult to see where that danger lay.[47] It seems fair to conclude that her vulnerability in the wake

---

[42] Hicks, *Edward V*, 35; *CCR*, 1461–8, p. 5; C140/8/33.
[43] C140/1/16. The assignment of dower made to her in March 1462 concerned only Lucy's lands in Worcestershire, and those assigned to her were of little value, for she already held in jointure the bulk of the Lucy lands in that county. Not until 16 Nov. 1463 did she trouble to have the assignment delivered into chancery (by the hand of Thomas Pachet), another indication that the assignment was a mere bureaucratic formality: C140/8/33.
[44] *CPR*, 1461–7, pp. 153, 195, 220, 369, 434, 456–7, 486–7.
[45] *CPR*, 1452–61, pp. 597–8.
[46] C140/5/42. For Hopton as a servant of York: *CPR*, 1452–61, p. 552. It may be significant here that both Margaret's second husband, John Stafford, and her lawyer, Thomas Pachet, were elected to the parliament which met on 7 October 1460. If her interests had needed protecting, as MPs they would have been well placed to do so.
[47] C140/1/16.

of Edward IV's accession lay in the general uncertainties of the time rather than the particularities of her own situation. On balance, therefore, the story of the affair is not supported by any unusual need on her part for royal favour.

One further doubt is also to be raised as to Margaret's identification with More's 'Dame Elizabeth'. In the English version of his *History of Richard III* More contents himself with remarking that the king had 'gotten' Elizabeth 'with child', but in the Latin versions he adds a further detail. He implies that she was a virgin when the affair began, or at least may have been: '*Eam forte virginem rex deuirginaverat*'.[48] If he believed this to be true, then it is unlikely that he had the twice-widowed Margaret in mind as the king's mistress. The identity of his 'Dame Elizabeth Lucy' is, it seems, to be sought elsewhere.[49]

---

[48] *The Yale Edition of the Complete Works of St. Thomas More*, ed. R.S. Sylvester (15 vols., New Haven, Conn., 1963–97), ii. 139.

[49] For unpersuasive arguments in favour of identifying 'Dame Elizabeth' with the daughter of a Hampshire gentleman, Thomas Wayte: John Ashdown-Hill, 'The Elusive Mistress; Elizabeth Lucy and her Family', *Ricardian*, xi (1999), 490–505.

SOME OBSERVATIONS ON THE HOUSEHOLD AND CIRCLE OF HUMPHREY STAFFORD, LORD STAFFORD OF SOUTHWICK AND EARL OF DEVON: THE LAST WILL OF ROGER BEKENSAWE*

Hannes Kleineke

If we disregard the opprobrium heaped upon the 'new men' who – at least in the opinion of Richard Neville, earl of Warwick – came to dominate Edward IV's first reign, the young king's friends and associates in this early period remain somewhat shadowy figures.[1] While modern biographies outlining the public careers of many leading members of the Yorkist court have been, or are about to be, published,[2] detail beyond births, marriages and deaths, and lists of official appointments, is available only for a few of the greatest men of the age, such as the 'Kingmaker' earl of Warwick, or the monarch's younger brother, George, duke of Clarence.[3] Testamentary materials have been used with some success to gain a measure of individual members of the Yorkist court, but the limited snapshot provided by an

---

* I am grateful to Dr. Linda Clark and *The Fifteenth Century*'s anonymous referees for their helpful comments on an earlier version of this essay, and to the trustees of the History of Parliament for permission to draw upon the unpublished draft articles prepared for the 1422–1504 section of the *History*.

[1] *The Politics of Fifteenth-Century England: John Vale's Book*, ed. M.L. Kekewich, Colin Richmond, A.F. Sutton, Livia Visser-Fuchs and J.L. Watts (Stroud, 1995), 213; D.A.L. Morgan, 'The King's Affinity in the Polity of Yorkist England', *TRHS*, 5th series, xxiii (1973), 1–25, at 9–10; J.R. Lander, 'Marriage and Politics in the Fifteenth Century: the Nevilles and the Wydevilles', *BIHR*, xxxvi (1963), 119–52, repr. in *idem*, *Crown and Nobility 1450–1509* (Montreal, 1976), 94–126, esp. 94–5, 108–9, 124–5; Michael Hicks, *The Wars of the Roses* (New Haven, Conn., and London, 2010) 189, 191.

[2] Biographies of Humphrey, Lord Stafford of Southwick and earl of Devon, William, Lord Herbert and earl of Pembroke, Richard Wydeville, Earl Rivers, John Neville, earl of Northumberland and marquess of Montagu, John Tiptoft, earl of Worcester, William, Lord Hastings, Walter Blount, Lord Mountjoy, Walter Devereux, Lord Ferrers of Chartley, and Sir John Fogge, treasurer of Edward IV's household, among others, are found in the *Oxford DNB*. More comprehensive entries for, among others, Blount, Devereux, Herbert and Stafford will appear in *The History of Parliament: The Commons 1422–61*, ed. L.S. Clark (forthcoming).

[3] See e.g. A.J. Pollard, *Warwick the Kingmaker: Politics, Power and Fame* (2007); Michael Hicks, *Warwick the Kingmaker* (Oxford, 1998); *idem*, *False, Fleeting, Perjur'd Clarence: George, Duke of Clarence, 1449–1478* (Gloucester, 1980); *idem*, 'Dynastic Change and Northern Society: The Fourth Earl of Northumberland, 1470–89', *Northern History*, xiv (1978), 78–107; *idem*, 'The Career of Henry Percy, Fourth Earl of Northumberland, with Special Reference to his Retinue' (Southampton Univ. M.A. dissertation, 1971); Anne Crawford, *Yorkist Lord: John Howard, Duke of Norfolk, c.1425–1485* (2010).

individual's will offers, at best, a selective picture.[4] By virtue of the survival of two sets of his household accounts, John Howard, later Lord Howard and duke of Norfolk, is perhaps the Yorkist peer of whose daily life most is known;[5] the library of John Tiptoft, earl of Worcester, lends a cultural varnish to the image of the 'Butcher of England';[6] while the wider retinue of Edward IV's chamberlain, William, Lord Hastings, was studied in detail by William Dunham more than half a century ago.[7] That aside, little can be said of the composition or size of the establishments of the greater men of Yorkist England, or of where and how the members of these households were recruited.[8] The information (however limited) on the household of Humphrey Stafford, Lord Stafford of Southwick and briefly earl of Devon, that may be gleaned from the will of Roger Bekensawe (d.1468), a cleric closely associated with him in the 1460s, is thus of some interest.

I

Humphrey was a descendant of a cadet branch of the Stafford family, earls of Stafford and dukes of Buckingham, that had become established in Dorset in the second half of the fourteenth century. His father, William, an esquire of Henry VI's household, had been murdered during the rebellion of 1450, and he had subsequently been taken into the household of his guardian, William, Lord Bonville. Like Bonville, he became identified with the Yorkist cause, and in the autumn of 1460, after the Yorkist victory at the battle of Northampton, was entrusted with the shrievalty of the counties of Somerset and Dorset. He developed an affinity, perhaps even a friendship, with the young Edward, earl of March, and after the earl's accession as Edward IV was elevated to a barony as Lord Stafford of Southwick, soon becoming the young king's principal lieutenant in the south-west. He established himself at Tiverton, formerly the seat of the attainted Courtenay earls of Devon, with many of whose estates he was endowed, and in 1469 he was granted the comital title itself, only to be executed just weeks later

---

[4] Hannes Kleineke, 'The Five Wills of Humphrey Stafford, Earl of Devon', *Nottingham Medieval Studies*, liv (2010), 137–64.

[5] *The Household Books of John Howard, Duke of Norfolk, 1462–1471, 1481–1483*, intr. Anne Crawford (Stroud, 1992).

[6] See e.g. H.B. Lathrop, 'The Translations of John Tiptoft', *Modern Language Notes*, xli (1926), 496–501; Roberto Weiss, 'The Library of John Tiptoft, Earl of Worcester', *Bodleian Quarterly Record*, viii (1935–7), 157–64; R.J. Mitchell, 'A Renaissance Library: the Collection of John Tiptoft, Earl of Worcester', *The Library*, iv (1937), 67–83; Joachim Rühl, 'Regulations for the Joust in Fifteenth-Century Europe: Francesco Sforza Visconti (1465) and John Tiptoft (1466)', *International Journal of the History of Sport*, xviii (2001), 193–208.

[7] W.H. Dunham junior, *Lord Hastings' Indentured Retainers, 1461–1483: The Lawfulness of Livery and Retaining under the Yorkists and Tudors* (New Haven, Conn., 1955), and now see also Theron Westervelt, 'William Lord Hastings and the Governance of Edward IV, with Special Reference to the Second Reign (1471–83)' (Cambridge Univ. Ph.D. thesis, 2001).

[8] Some observations on the establishments of the higher cathedral clergy of late medieval England may be found in Hannes Kleineke and Stephanie Hovland, 'The Household and Daily Life of the Dean in the Fifteenth Century', in *St Paul's: The Cathedral Church of London 604–2004*, ed. Derek Keene, Arthur Burns and Andrew Saint (2004), 167–8.

after suffering a crushing defeat at the hands of Robin of Redesdale's rebels in the battle of Edgecote.[9]

Scattered references indicate that, as might be expected, Stafford spent time at Edward IV's court, interacted as an equal with other courtiers, like Sir John Howard (to whom he lost 4*d*. at 'pykynge' in 1464), and took part in important events such as the tournament held in 1467 to mark the visit of the Great Bastard of Burgundy, an event celebrated with pageantry on a grand scale.[10] Information about his household and affinity is equally sparse. There are isolated references to some of the men who served under him in his various offices, such as Rawlyn Bayne, one of his deputies as keeper of Dartmoor,[11] Simon Glyn, another duchy of Cornwall official,[12] William Plush, probably his servant as deputy constable of Taunton castle,[13] and his officers as sheriff, Clavilsey and John Jewe of Ilchester.[14] Among those who sought his good lordship was William Forster, who in January 1461 granted to Stafford an annuity of 26*s*. 8*d*. to the end '*quod erit bonus dominus*' to him,[15] while the cities and towns of the south-west plied him with the customary gifts of wine and victuals.[16] These urban communities also provided some of the armed members of the retinues that Stafford periodically led to the defence of Edward IV's throne. The names of a few of Stafford's servants and associates around the time of his death may be gleaned from his will. There was Henry Hake, who kept the key to the coffer at Tiverton which contained this document. There was Master Nicholas Gosse, vicar of Kilkhampton and chancellor of Exeter cathedral, to whom Stafford wrote from Cirencester on 21 July 1469, just days before his death, instructing him secretly to collect his plate and muniments from Tiverton.[17] There was the vicar of Powerstock, Robert Olyver, who was entrusted with a sealed parcel of other writings to take to Gosse.[18]

More difficult to evaluate is Stafford's relationship with the men who served as feoffees of his estates. Customarily, a man's feoffees included not only trusted

---

[9] For Edgecote, see P.A. Haigh, *The Military Campaigns of the Wars of the Roses* (Stroud, 1995), 97–103, and Barry Lewis, 'The Battle of Edgecote or Banbury (1469) Through the Eyes of Contemporary Welsh Poets', *Journal of Medieval Military History IX: Soldiers, Weapons and Armies in the Fifteenth Century*, ed. Anne Curry and A.R. Bell (Woodbridge, 2011), 97–109. Specifically on the disputed date of the engagement see also W.G. Lewis, 'The Exact Date of the Battle of Banbury, 1469', *BIHR*, lv (1982), 194–6.

[10] *Household Books of John Howard*, intr. Crawford, pt. 1, p. 250; *Excerpta Historica or Illustrations of English History*, ed. Samuel Bentley (1831), 210; Theron Westervelt, 'Royal Charter Witness Lists and the Politics of the Reign of Edward IV', *HR*, lxxxi (2008), 211–23, at 219; J.R. Lander, 'Council, Administration and Councillors, 1461 to 1485', *BIHR*, xxxii (1959), 138–80, repr. in *idem*, *Crown and Nobility*, 191–219, at 213–14.

[11] TNA, C1/44/259.

[12] Cornw. RO, Launceston borough records, B/Laus/158.

[13] TNA, CP40/810, rots. 129, 307.

[14] *Somerset Medieval Wills 1383–1500*, ed. F.W. Weaver (Somerset Record Society, xvi, 1901), 196–7; L.S. Clark, 'John Jewe', in *The Commons 1422–61*, ed. Clark (forthcoming).

[15] *Bridgwater Borough Archives 1445–1468*, ed. T.B. Dilks (Somerset Record Society, lx, 1948), no. 828.

[16] *Ibid*. nos. 824, 830; Devon RO, Exeter receivers' accts. 1–9 Edw. IV.

[17] *Somerset Medieval Wills*, ed. Weaver, 199–200.

[18] Olyver, vicar of Teffont Evias from May 1458, exchanged that benefice for Powerstock in Oct. 1460: Wilts. RO, Reg. Beauchamp (Salisbury), vol. 1, ff. 62, 80.

associates, but also individuals whose local standing or legal expertise made them undesirable opponents for anyone wishing to challenge the descent of an estate in the law courts.[19] This was true of Humphrey Stafford's feoffees, who were mostly drawn from the ranks of the Somerset and Dorset gentry and also included a few well-connected local lawyers. William Kayleway of Sherborne, John Mohun of Hammoon and Thomas Martin of Athelhampton had been feoffees of the Stafford family estates since the days of Humphrey's grandfather. Mohun and John Jewe had been associates of his father, William, during the latter's quarrels with his niece's husband, James Butler, earl of Wiltshire, in the 1440s. Others were more recent recruits, like William Browning of Melbury Sampford (who in the 1440s had taken Butler's side against William Stafford, but who by the 1460s had come to terms with his son), George Middleton, Henry Hull of Ashill, John Byconnell and John Filoll.[20]

Among Stafford's most trusted friends and servants, it is reasonable to assume, were the men appointed his executors. These were headed by the bishop of Winchester, William Waynflete, and included, apart from two of his cousins and heirs (John Cheyne and Sir John Willoughby), the Bridgwater merchant John Kendale, who seems to have doubled up as Stafford's factotum,[21] Richard Gyldon, probably a member of a Devon family from Bridgtown Pomeroy, who had been associated with William, Lord Bonville, and after his death had been among the administrators of his goods, and a cleric, Roger Bekensawe.[22] Bekensawe did not live to carry out his master's testamentary instructions, but he left a will of his own which had much to say about Earl Humphrey's household at the end of his life.

II

Born in Croston in Lancashire, Roger Bekensawe came from a family that took its name from the neighbouring hamlet of Beckinsall. By contrast with many of his Lancashire neighbours in this period, who found advancement in the Church through the patronage of three members of the Booth family of Barton (all three of whom rose to the episcopate in the mid fifteenth century and whose role in providing benefices to many of their younger relatives is well known), Bekensawe seems to have found his patron elsewhere.[23] If he did indeed owe his advancement

---

[19] It was not uncommon for men to appear in court and plead ignorance of ever having been enfeoffed of a particular estate: see e.g. TNA, C1/32/61; 55/42–43, 103; 76/49.

[20] L.S. Clark, 'William Kayleway', 'John Mohun', 'Thomas Martin', 'John Jewe', 'William Browning I', 'George Middleton', 'John Byconnell' and 'John Filoll', and H.W. Kleineke, 'Henry Hull', in *The Commons 1422–61*, ed. Clark (forthcoming).

[21] *Bridgwater Borough Archives 1468–85*, ed. R.W. Dunning and T.D. Tremlett (Somerset Record Society, lxx, 1971), pp. xiii–xiv; A.F. Sutton, 'John Kendale: A Search for Richard III's Secretary', *The Ricardian*, v (1981), 320–2, 367–9, 404, 438–47; vi (1982), 27, repr. in *Richard III: Crown and People*, ed. James Petre (Gloucester, 1985), 224–38, at 226; *The History of Parliament: Biographies of the Members of the Commons House 1439–1509*, ed. J.C. Wedgwood and Anne Holt (1936), 512–13.

[22] Devon RO, Seymour MSS, 3799M–0/ET/3/22–24, 45, 57; Hants RO, Jervoise of Herriard MSS, 44M69/C751; *Registrum Thome Bourgchier*, ed. F.R.H. Du Boulay (Oxford, 1957), 198.

[23] *The Estate and Household Accounts of William Worsley, Dean of St Paul's Cathedral 1479–1497*, ed. Hannes Kleineke and S.R. Hovland (Donington, 2004), 3–4; and also see A.C. Reeves, 'William

to a Lancashire connexion, it may have been one with the baronial family of Harington, who in the reigns of the Lancastrian kings forged ties of marriage in the south-western region, where he would find ecclesiastical preferment. The tie was probably first established by Elizabeth Courtenay, a daughter of Edward, earl of Devon, who in her youth married John, Lord Harington (c.1384–1418), before returning to her native south-west to become the wife of Sir William, later Lord Bonville (1393–1461), in 1423. Some two decades later, the tie between the Bonvilles and Haringtons was further strengthened by the marriage of Elizabeth's niece of the same name, the daughter and sole heir of William, the last Lord Harington (c.1390–1458), to her stepson, Bonville's son William.[24]

It is impossible to be certain about the date at which Bekensawe first arrived in the south-west. In chronological terms, it is possible that he came as part of the entourage of either of the two Ladies Harington, and he was probably a member of the Bonville household for some years, before being presented to the Cornish rectory of Kilkhampton by its patron, William Grenville, Bonville's son-in-law, in March 1449. Almost five years later, in January 1454, Bekensawe added to this the rectory of Combpyne in Devon, the patronage of which belonged to Bonville himself. Roger had evidently been promised additional preferment some time previously, as in July 1453 he had procured a papal licence to hold two incompatible benefices. A further preferment by Bonville to St. Mewan in Cornwall in December 1455 may never have taken effect as there were questions over the patronage of the church.[25] He thus did not acquire his final benefice, the rectory of Burton Bradstock in Dorset, until August 1466.[26] Bekensawe apparently remained close to his patron throughout the 1450s. He was among the feoffees of the lands assigned to Bonville's bastard son John (*d*.1499), the son of Isabel Kyrkeby, probably on the occasion of his marriage to Alice, daughter of William Denys,[27] and in July 1461 was included among the men to whom Archbishop Bourgchier entrusted the administration of Lord Bonville's goods, as the peer had left no will when he was executed on Queen Margaret's orders after the second battle of St. Albans in February of that year.[28]

Booth, Bishop of Coventry and Lichfield (1447–52)', *Midland History*, iii (1475–6), 11–29; *idem*, 'William Booth, Bishop of Coventry and Lichfield, Archbishop of York', in *idem*, *Lancastrian Englishmen* (Washington, D.C., 1981), 265–362; *idem*, 'Lawrence Booth: Bishop of Durham (1457–76), Archbishop of York (1476–80)', in *Estrangement, Enterprise and Education in Fifteenth-Century England*, ed. S.D. Michalove and A.C. Reeves (Stroud, 1998), 63–88; *idem*, 'Bishop John Booth of Exeter, 1465–78', in *Traditions and Transformations in Late Medieval England*, ed. Douglas Biggs, S.D. Michalove and A.C. Reeves (Leiden, 2001), 125–44.

[24] For the Bonvilles and Haringtons see *CP*, ii. 218–19; vi. 317–20.

[25] *The Register of Edmund Lacy, Bishop of Exeter (AD 1420–1455)*, ed. F.C. Hingeston-Randolph (2 vols., London and Exeter, 1909), i. 338, 382; *Registrum Bourgchier*, ed. Du Boulay, 155–6; *CPL*, x. 121; xi. 553–4. Bekensawe resigned Combpyne at an uncertain point before Oct. 1459, when rector Stephen Bilton, probably his successor, for his part resigned the benefice: Devon RO, Reg. Neville, f. 12.

[26] Wilts. RO, Reg. Beauchamp, vol. 1, f. 124.

[27] *CIPM Henry VII*, ii. 266.

[28] *Registrum Bourgchier*, ed. Du Boulay, 198.

Lord Bonville's execution extinguished the principal male line of the Bonvilles, since his son and grandson had both been killed at the battle of Wakefield in the previous December. The heiress, Bonville's great-granddaughter Cecily, was a mere infant. Bekensawe now formed an attachment to Edward IV's favourite, Humphrey, Lord Stafford of Southwick, who rapidly adopted the mantle of the new regime's leading supporter in the south-west. Their connexion was evidently a close one: Bekensawe left a bequest of money to be distributed among Stafford's household servants at their master's discretion; and he asked Stafford to assist his executors in their task. Stafford for his part, as we have seen, named him among the executors of his own testament. This latter task Bekensawe would never carry out, for he died, probably in London, within days of making his will on 29 May 1468. Probate of his will was granted on 4 June, and four days later Master Nicholas Gosse, chancellor of Exeter cathedral and another member of Lord Stafford's circle, was presented in his stead to the church of Kilkhampton.[29] The circumstances of Bekensawe's death are unclear, but his request for burial in the undistinguished parish church of Lambeth, with which he cannot otherwise be connected, his complaint of having been deserted in his 'grete sekenesse' by all his 'felawship', except for the priest John Wode, and his bequest to that cleric of the 'horse, sadell and bridell which I rode on to London', may suggest that he had been struck down in the capital by a severe and possibly infectious disease.[30]

In their majority, the provisions of Bekensawe's will were commonplace. There were the usual bequests to parish churches and individuals, in return for prayers and masses. His connexions in the south-west aside, Bekensawe preserved close links to his native Lancashire, where he left legacies not only to the church of Croston, where he had been baptised, but also to a number of friends and neighbours, including members of the Molyneux and Hurdleton families.[31] Central to the concerns expressed in the will were a number of provisions relating to Lord Stafford of Southwick's household with which the testator was clearly intimately familiar. There were bequests both to Lord Stafford himself ('xx oxen beyng in the parke at Hoke [Hooke, Dorset] for and to thentent to supporte and maynteyne myn executours to the perimplisshement of this my testament and last will'), and to his wife, Lady Elizabeth, the daughter of Sir John Barre ('a blakke hamelyng colt beyng in the parke of Tyuerton'). To an aristocratic young member of the household, John Bonville the younger, went Bekensawe's best horse,[32] while John

---

[29] Devon RO, Reg. Booth, f. 13. For Gosse, and the theft of Stafford's jewels from his custody, see Kleineke, 'Five Wills', 149, 158, 160–4. A day later, on 9 June, a new incumbent was also admitted at Burton Bradstock: Wilts. RO, Reg. Beauchamp, vol. 1, f. 139.

[30] I am grateful to Dr. Christian Steer for his comments on Bekensawe's choice of burial place.

[31] The Robert Hurdleton remembered in Bekensawe's will may perhaps be identified with Robert, son and heir of Nicholas Hurdleton of Hurdleton, who married Agnes, daughter of Henry Scarisbrick: Lancashire RO, Scarisbrick MSS, DDSC 43A/168, 169, 175.

[32] The identification of this individual and his relationship to Lord Bonville presents some difficulties. It is unlikely that the John Bonville in question was either Lord Bonville's bastard son, who had been married to Alice Denys and endowed with part of her inheritance in 1453 (*Pedes Finium commonly called Feet of Fines for the County of Somerset, Henry IV to Henry VI*, ed. Emanuel Green (Somerset Record Society, xxii, 1906), 116; TNA, C140/72/67; *CIPM Henry VII*, ii. 266), or his nephew, the son of his brother Thomas, who by 1468 was over 50 years old (TNA, C140/22/46). The most likely candidate would seem to be John Bonville (c.1458–1493), of Dillington, who was probably the son of Lord Bonville's first cousin of the same name, and grandson of the peer's

Molyneux 'w^t my said lord' was to have a colt. Twenty marks were to be distributed among Stafford's household servants at their lord's discretion. Bekensawe's proximity to Stafford is further emphasised by the location of many of his goods and chattels in the comital parks and residences at Colcombe and Tiverton. Clearly, these were places with which the testator was as familiar (or, indeed, more so) than with his benefices in Cornwall and Dorset.

III

Within the Stafford household, Bekensawe formed part of a distinct grouping, that we may perhaps term the 'Bonville connection', an identifiable group of former Bonville men who had found employment with Stafford after the death of their lord. Their transition may in some respects have been a natural one, since in the aftermath of his father's murder at the hands of Jack Cade's rebels in 1450 Stafford had himself been raised in Bonville's household as his ward. Following Bonville's execution in February 1461 and the consequent extinction of the principal male line of the family, the Bonville estates were split up between his widow, Elizabeth, who was awarded a substantial dower settlement,[33] Lord Bonville's younger brother Thomas, who claimed those of the family lands entailed in tail male (some of which were included in his sister-in-law's dower),[34] Lord Bonville's bastard son, John, who benefited from a settlement made by his father in his lifetime,[35] and Lady Katherine Harington, the widow of his grandson, to whom the king granted the wardship of her infant daughter and custody of her lands.[36] Lord Bonville's household was dispersed, and those of its members who did not remain with the dowager Lady Bonville were left to find a new master. Regional candidates were in short supply: the dukes of Somerset and Exeter, the earls of Devon and Wiltshire, and the barons Hungerford were all under attainder, the duchy of Cornwall was vested in the Crown, and the focus of the Lords Stourton lay too far east, in Somerset and Wiltshire. Stafford, who must have been a figure familiar to many members of his late guardian's circle, and who was increasingly establishing himself as Edward IV's principal lieutenant in the south-west, provided an obvious focal point. It was thus that Lord Bonville's young kinsman John Bonville was taken into his household, and that a number of former Bonville clients, including Bekensawe, Richard Gyldon, and probably John Molyneux, also came to join it.

---

paternal uncle Thomas: James Davidson, 'Documents relating to the Estate of Sir William Bonville, of Shute, co. Devon, temp. Edw. III.', *Collectanea Topographica et Genealogica*, viii (1843), 237–47, at 240, 245; *CIPM*, xxi. 874; TNA, C141/2/17; *CIPM Henry VII*, iii. 585.

[33] *CPR*, 1461–7, p. 108.

[34] Thomas Bonville's male line came to an end with the death of his son John in 1494. John left two surviving daughters, Florence, the wife of Sir Humphrey Fulford, and Elizabeth, wife of Sir Thomas West, and under the terms of the entail the lands which had come to Thomas at his brother's death should have reverted to Cecily Harington, but in the event it was only after a protracted dispute lasting for more than ten years that a settlement was agreed: Devon RO, Petre MSS, 123M/TB519–523.

[35] *CIPM Henry VII*, ii. 266.

[36] *CPR*, 1461–7, p. 118.

The wholesale, or at least large-scale, transfer of the Bonville connection to Humphrey Stafford had its parallel in other noble affinities deprived of their patron by the executioner's axe: as a footnote to his account of the judicial murder of William, Lord Hastings, in 1483, penned just days after the event, Simon Stallworth reported to Sir William Stonor that '[a]ll þe lord Chamberleyne mene be come my lordys of Bokynghame menne'.[37]

In the standard historiography of the period, the story of the south-west of England in the 1440s and 1450s is that of the political rivalry between the Bonvilles and the Courtenays of Tiverton.[38] This rivalry came to an apparent end with the executions of Lord Bonville and Thomas Courtenay the younger respectively at St. Albans and Towton in early 1461. Humphrey Stafford's quest for regional dominance crowned by the comital title provides an epilogue to this narrative. After Edward IV's accession and the earl of Devon's execution in the wake of Towton, as is well known, Stafford was endowed with many of the principal manors of the formerly comital Courtenays. He established his principal seat at the earls' castle of Tiverton and even had been granted Thomas Courtenay's chapel furniture and artillery train.[39] None of this was lost on popular opinion which maintained that in the second half of 1468 Stafford himself engineered the arrest and execution of the heir to the earldom, Henry Courtenay, because he desired the comital title for himself.[40] Yet, royal grants went only so far. In the west, long-established loyalties to the Courtenays ran deep, and even after Henry Courtenay's execution there were living claimants to the earldom in the persons of the last earl's youngest brother, John Courtenay, then in exile with Queen Margaret of Anjou at Koeur, and – closer to home – in his cousin Hugh Courtenay of Boconnoc (whose son Edward would indeed achieve restoration to the family title in 1485).[41] On the eve of the battle of Tewkesbury in 1471 the Courtenays were said to be raising the west for Queen Margaret,[42] and it was in that engagement that both John and Hugh Courtenay met their deaths. During the 1460s, the surviving Courtenays had provided a focal point for the former members of the earl of Devon's retinue,[43] and Edward IV's relative clemency towards the heirs of the

---

[37] *Kingsford's Stonor Letters and Papers, 1290–1483*, ed. Christine Carpenter (Cambridge, 1996), 417.

[38] R.L. Storey, *The End of the House of Lancaster* (2nd edn., Gloucester, 1986), 84–92, 165–75; Martin Cherry, 'The Struggle for Power in Mid-Fifteenth-Century Devonshire', in *Patronage, the Crown and the Provinces in Later Medieval England*, ed. R.A. Griffiths (Gloucester, 1981), 123–44; R.A. Griffiths, *The Reign of King Henry VI* (2nd edn., Stroud, 1998), 574–7, 753, 755.

[39] *CPR*, 1461–7, pp. 116, 323, 358; TNA, C140/22/48; 32/30.

[40] *A Chronicle of the First Thirteen Years of the Reign of King Edward the Fourth by John Warkworth D.D.*, ed. J.O. Halliwell (Camden Society, original series, x, 1839), 6.

[41] M.L. Kekewich, 'The Lancastrian Court in Exile', in *The Lancastrian Court: Proceedings of the 2001 Harlaxton Symposium*, ed. Jenny Stratford (Donington, 2003), 95–108, at 98–9; J.A.F. Thomson, 'The Courtenay Family in the Yorkist Period', *BIHR*, xlv (1972), 230–46, at 232–5. The receiver's account of the city of Exeter shows that Sir Hugh Courtenay was at the battle of Edgecote, but he may not have been on Stafford's side: Devon RO, Exeter receiver's acct. 8–9 Edw. IV, m. 2.

[42] *Historie of the Arrivall of Edward IV in England and the Finall Recouerye of his Kingdomes from Henry VI. A.D. M.CCCC.LXXI*, ed. John Bruce (Camden Society, original series, i, 1838), 23; *Chronicle by John Warkworth*, ed. Halliwell, 17–18.

[43] So, for instance, the earl of Devon's former servant John Brigham became Henry Courtenay's receiver: BL, Add. Chs. 64717, m. 3; 64808.

lords attainted in 1461 may have held out some hope, however vague for the time being, for a future restoration of the old dynasty.[44]

If it was the Courtenays' position in the south-west to which Stafford aspired, to a large extent with the collusion of his friend, the king, his and his household's tradition was a different one, and one that dated from his own youth and adolescence. Yet although many of the members of his household had previously been in the service of William, Lord Bonville, in whose household he had himself been raised, Stafford's grip on the Bonville affinity was not complete: some of its members drifted into the orbit of other rising Yorkist magnates. The earl of Devon's cousin, Sir Philip Courtenay (*d.*1463) of Powderham, head of a line of the comital family established in the late fourteenth century, had formed a close friendship with Bonville in the 1420s, became perhaps his closest ally in his well-known struggle with the earl of Devon, and in 1455 had been subjected to a spectacular siege and bombardment of his castle at Powderham on the Exe estuary. By the end of the 1460s, Sir Philip's sons, Sir William, Sir Philip the younger, Humphrey and Walter, as well as a further sibling, Peter, the long-serving archdeacon and later bishop of Exeter, had formed an attachment to the young Edward IV's heir presumptive, George, duke of Clarence, whose proximity to the throne must – with the benefit of hindsight somewhat ironically – have made him seem a more certain bet than the ambitious climber Stafford. In 1470 they staged a rebellion in Devon in support of the simultaneous rising orchestrated by Clarence and the earl of Warwick in the north, and after its failure they provided the duke and the earl with an escape route to Calais. They benefited from this attachment during the Readeption, when Peter Courtenay served as secretary to the restored Henry VI, and it subsequently provided them with a way back into the allegiance of the victorious Edward IV.[45] Like the elder Sir Philip, several other earlier Bonville associates also died in the first years of Edward IV's reign. They included men like Walter Raleigh (*d.*1464) of Fardel, and William Champernowne of Modbury, neither of whom can be shown to have built up any rapport with Stafford. Nevertheless, Warwick's characterisation of Stafford as an upstart and '*homo novus*' with no roots in his region was a caricature. The new earl of Devon's political ascendancy in the south-west during the 1460s was built on foundations at least as long-established as those of many other noble families. Humphrey Stafford's contemporaries were in no doubt as to the significance of his acquisition of Tiverton castle and its furnishings for his future ambitions. It is probable that they were equally aware that the move of the young man raised in the Bonville household into the Courtenay earl's residence represented – at least in one of its dimensions – nothing less than the victory of Bonville over Courtenay in a rivalry that dated back to the 1420s.

In the longer term, however, neither Bonvilles nor Courtenays were to emerge as winners. Humphrey Stafford's execution after Edgcote left the young Cecily

---

[44] S.J. Payling, 'Edward IV and the Politics of Conciliation in the Early 1460s', in *The Yorkist Age: Proceedings of the 2011 Harlaxton Symposium*, ed. Hannes Kleineke and Christian Steer (Donington, 2013), 81–94.

[45] Thomson, 'Courtenay Family', 236–43.

Harington to take the Bonville tradition along with the baronial title to her husband, Edward IV's stepson Thomas Grey, marquess of Dorset, and their descendants,[46] even as one by one the junior cadet lines of the Bonvilles came to an end. Cecily's branch of the family was destined for even greater prominence as a result of the marriage of her grandson Henry Grey, duke of Suffolk, to Henry VIII's niece, Frances Brandon, but it was terminated in the male line with the duke's execution on Tower Hill on 23 February 1554, eleven days after the beheading of its (briefly) most distinguished offshoot, Suffolk's daughter, Queen Jane.[47] The restored Courtenay earls of Devon proved as inept at negotiating the treacherous waters of Tudor politics as their Bonville-Grey counterparts – if not more so – and, further encumbered in Henry VIII's eyes by the marriage of Earl William to his aunt Katherine, suffered repeated attainders, forfeitures and imprisonment until the childless death in 1556 of the last Earl Edward finally saw their line also brought to an end.[48] In the event, thus, the great Bonville-Courtenay quarrel was ended, like the senior lines of the two families, not by the victory of one side or the other, but by the paranoia and executioner's axe of the Tudor monarchs.

---

[46] After her first husband's death Cecily married his cousin, Henry Stafford, earl of Wiltshire (*d*.1523): *CP*, xii (2), 738–9.

[47] *CP*, ii. 219; iv. 419. While the barony of Bonville is deemed to have become extinct with the duke's execution, Henry Grey left two further daughters, one of whom carried the Bonville blood forward into later centuries: *CP*, iv. 421.

[48] *CP*, iv. 329–32; Margaret Westcott, 'Katherine Courtenay, Countess of Devon, 1479–1527', in *Tudor and Stuart Devon: The Common Estate and Government*, ed. Todd Gray, Margery Rowe and Audrey Erskine (Exeter, 1992), 13–38, at 20–23; Maria Hayward, 'Clothed by the Tudors: Yorkist Prisoners in the Tower of London 1485–1547', in *The Yorkist Age*, ed. Kleineke and Steer, 64–80.

APPENDIX

The Will of Roger Bekensawe

In the following text, common abbreviations have been expanded, capitalisation and the use of v and u modernised and a degree of punctuation introduced. Interlinear insertions are indicated by angular brackets (< >), editorial interventions by square brackets ([ ]).

TNA, PROB11/5, ff. 251v–252

In the Name of God Amen. The xxix[th] day of the moneth Maij in the yere of our lord Jehesu Crist m[l] cccclxviij and in the yere of the Reigne of King Edward the iiij[th] the viij[th]. I, Sir Roger Bekensawe, parson of the parissh chirch of Kilkeham<p>ton[49] and Birton[50] in my goode and hoole mynde beyng, thanke be almyghty God, do ordeyne and make this my present testament in this fourme: In the first I biqueth and recommend my soule to all myghty God, my creature and savyour, and to his blissed modir, our lady Saint Mary the virgyne, and to all sayntes, my body to be buried in the parissh chirch of our lady of Lamehith in the counte of Surrey in the chauncell there afore the high auter. Also I biqueth to the high auter of the said chirch xijd. Also I biqueth to þe chirches werk there to thentent my body to be buried w[t]in þe same chirch vjs. viijd. Also I biqueth to a seculer preest to sey masse for my soule and all cristen soules in the parissh chirch of Kilkehampton aforsaid by the space of ij yeres after my decesse xvj marcs of lawfull money of England. Also I biqueth and gif to þesame chirch of Kilkehampton xij marcs sterlinges to thentent to by a masse boke there to abide for ever, that the parisshens there may specialy have me in mynde. Also I biqueth to John Simond, my servaunt, xxs. over all his expensez and wages to hym dieu. Also I biqueth to Sir William, my parissh preest, xiijs. iiijd. and my best gowne ther beyng. Also I biqueth to Robert Hurdelton all my beddynge, pottez and pannez and peauter vessellez perteynyng to my houshold. Also I biqueth to the same Robert a bay colt beyng at the Sokke. Also I biqueth to the parissh chirch of Byrton to the makyng of the rode soler there v marcs. Also I biqueth to a seculer preest to say masse for my soule and for all Cristen soules by an hoole yere after my decesse w[t]in the same chirch viij marcs. Also I biqueth to my lord Humfrey Stafford xx oxen beyng in the parke at Hoke for and to thentent to supporte and maynteyne myn executours to the perimplisshement of this my testament and last will. Also I biqueth to my lady Elizabeth Stafford, his wif, a blakke hamelyng colt beyng in the

---

[49] Kilkhampton, Cornw.
[50] Burton Bradstock, Dorset.

parke of Tyverton. Also I biqueth to John Bonevile the yonger, dwelling w^t my said Lord Stafford, my best horse in the parke of Rameshome. Also I biqueth to Sir John Wode, preest, for his tendre and diligent labour havyng about my body whan all my felawship forsoke me in my grete sekenesse, and also to and for thentent that he specialy pray for my soule during his liff in his memento, xx li. of lawfull money of England, xij silver spones, a saute seller of silver, a flatte cuppe of silver, my horse, sadell and bridell, which I rode on to London. Also I biqueth to Robert Milleholme ij beddes w^t þe best coveringez, blankettes and shetes and ij bolsters. Also I biqueth to Thomas Hurdelton a bay colte in Wyscombe park.[51] Also I biqueth to my servant John Walsshe a horse at Colkome[52] or els xls. to by hym a horse w^t all. Also I biqueth to the same John j olde shepe beyng in Byrton. Also I biqueth to the same John all my gownes in my place at Byrton. Also I biqueth to Richard, my servaunt there beyng, xx shepe. Also I biqueth to Sir John, Sir Thomas at Birton, John Clerke and his wife ther beyng iiij marcs in money. Also I forgyf the said Sir John all the dettez which he oweth me to thentent that he shall specialy pray for my soule and all Cristen in his memento. Also I biqueth to the servauntez of my said lord of Stafford daily in his houshold abiding xx marcs in money tobe departed amongez theim by the discrecion of my said lord. Also I biqueth to William Estcote[53] x s. Also I biqueth to Sir John Colly vj silver spones. Also I biqueth to Sir Robert Olyver[54] vj silver spones. Also I biqueth to Sir William Cassy[55] vj silver spones. Also I biqueth to John Molyneux w^t my said lord a colte at Byrton of iij yere age. Also I biqueth to Robert Hyrdelton ij payre shetez next the best in my cofre at Tyverton. Also I biqueth to þe parissh chirch of Croston, where I was bourne, a chalys, price of iiij marcs, to thentent the parisshens there to pray for my soule. Also I biqueth to the said parissh chirch of Lamehith, where my body restith, iiij grete torches there tobe spende in theworship of the blissed Trinitee. The residue trieuly of all my singuler goodez, catellez and dettes, whersuever theybe, after my dettez paied, my funerall expensez perimplisshed, maade and done, and this my present testament fulfilled, I gyf and biqueth hooly to the said John Bekensawe, Roger Bekensawe and to John Bekensawe, their brodir, and to everych of theym, to thentent þat they dispose therof for my soule in meke usez and dedez of charite, such as they best suppose may best please God and my soule the more proufite, as they afore the high juge at þe day of Dome shall answere. And over that to the fulfilling of this my testament I ordeyne, make and sett my principall executour the said Sir John Wode and his coexecutouris I ordeyne and make William Estcote, Raulyn Bayne and John Bekensawe thelder, to thewhich my said executouris I biqueth and gyf to everych of theym cs. and all theyre expensez aslong and during the tyme and space they labour about the perimplisshement of this my testament and last wille. And also I wole and charge

---

[51] Wiscombe Park, in Southleigh, Devon.
[52] Colcombe, Devon.
[53] Probably the lawyer of this name from Bideford in northern Devon, son of Robert Estcote of the same: TNA, CP40/818, rot. 115; Gloucestershire Archives, Sotheron-Estcourt MSS, D1571/E156; Plymouth and West Devon RO, Yonge of Puslinch MSS, 107/471–2; *Wilts. Notes and Queries*, ii (1896 8), 14–15.
[54] In 1466 Robert Olyver, the vicar of Powerstock, served as Bekensawe's proctor at his installation as rector of Burton Bradstock: Wilts. RO, Reg. Beauchamp, vol. 1, f. 124.
[55] William Cassy, rector of Corscombe from Dec. 1459: *ibid.*, f. 73.

my said executouris that they see all my singuler dettez in which of right I stande bounde to pay to any dettour be well and trieuly paide for the discharge of my soule. In wittnesse wherof to this my present testament I have sett to my seale the day and yere abovesaid. Thiez witnesshyng Maister Thomas Edmond, Sir John More, Chapleyn w^t my lord Cromwell,[56] Sir Pyers White, priestes, William Purdeney, John Bothe and other. Also I biqueth to Thomas Hurdelton a bay colt in Wyscum parke of iiij yere age.

Probatum fuit suprascriptum testamentum apud Lamehith iiij^{to} die mensis Junij anno domini m^{l}cccc^{mo}lxviij^{uo} ac approbatum etc. Et commissa fuit administracio omnium et singulorum bonorum et debitorum dicti defuncti Willelmo Escote executori etc. de bene administrando etc. ac de pleno et fideli inventario omnium et singulorum bonorum etc. citra festum omnium sanctorum proximo etc. ac de plano compoto etc. iurato etc. Reservata potestate etc.

---

[56] Humphrey Bourgchier, Lord Cromwell (*d*.1471): *CP*, iii. 554.

THE TREATMENT OF TRAITORS' CHILDREN AND EDWARD IV'S CLEMENCY IN THE 1460s[*]

James Ross

Edward IV's reputation for clemency remains intact amongst modern historians. Charles Ross wrote 'His record of mercy to his enemies is quite remarkable in a ruthless age', Christine Carpenter has argued that 'a remarkable degree of mercy was shown', and while Simon Payling, focussing more on the gentry and the attainders of 1461, has recently questioned the level of conciliation, he does describe a 'politic but limited magnanimity'.[1] There is also general agreement as to why Edward behaved in the way he did: Ross argues that 'clemency was also dictated by policy, by the need to widen the basis of support for his regime, especially amongst the baronage', Michael Hicks has discussed the importance to Edward of winning over erstwhile Lancastrians, while Rosemary Horrox has argued 'Given the narrowness of his power base in 1461, such a policy had obvious practical advantages, but it perhaps also marked a deliberate attempt by the king to restore political life to normality after the factionalism of the previous decade.'[2] In discussing this policy of conciliation, historians have tended to focus on the restorations of estates and titles to those who had taken up arms against the Yorkists, such as Henry Beaufort, duke of Somerset, or those who were of age, or near enough, to succeed their traitorous fathers, such as John de Vere, earl of Oxford. Less attention, because less is known, has been paid to young noble children and adolescents, both heirs and younger sons, who lost their fathers in the carnage of the civil war of 1459–61. A little light is shed upon the fate of three such boys by a warrant surviving amongst the remnants of the documents of the privy seal office, now housed at The National Archives. One of these boys is, appropriately, Henry Percy, the subject of Michael Hicks's M.A. dissertation.[3]

The document is a damaged warrant from the king, dated 9 March 1463 and addressed to Robert Stillington, keeper of the privy seal, ordering him to draw up

---

[*] I am very grateful to Dr. R.E. Archer for reading and commenting on an early draft of this paper, and for the comments of *The Fifteenth Century*'s referees.

[1] C.D. Ross, *Edward IV* (1974), 65; Christine Carpenter, *The Wars of the Roses* (Cambridge, 1997), 159; S.J. Payling, 'Edward IV and the Politics of Conciliation in the Early 1460s', in *The Yorkist Age: Proceedings of the 2011 Harlaxton Symposium*, ed. Hannes Kleineke and Christian Steer (Donington, 2013), 81–94 (quotation p. 94).

[2] Ross, *Edward IV*, 65; M.A. Hicks, 'Edward IV, the Duke of Somerset and Lancastrian Loyalism in the North', in his *Richard III and his Rivals* (1991), 149–63, esp. 156–8; Rosemary Horrox, 'Edward IV (1442–1483)', *Oxford DNB*; Hannes Kleineke, *Edward IV* (Abingdon, 2009), 53, 210.

[3] M.A. Hicks, 'The Career of Henry Percy, Fourth Earl of Northumberland, with Special Reference to his Retinue' (Southampton Univ. M.A. dissertation, 1971).

letters to the treasurer and chamberlains of the exchequer to pay £87 11*s*. 6*d*. to John Tiptoft, earl of Worcester, for his expenses in looking after Henry Percy, son and heir of Henry, third earl of Northumberland, who had been killed at Towton in 1461, and two younger sons of John, earl of Oxford, executed for treason in February 1462.[4] Regrettably, much of the detail of the expenses was contained in a schedule once attached to the warrant, but now lost, nor can this be supplemented by details from the archive of the exchequer, as no trace of this payment can be found among the warrants for issues or on the issue rolls.[5] However, the warrant did set out future payments for the diets of the boys – 6*s*. 8*d*. a week each – and for their servants, two gentlemen, allowed 6*s*. 8*d*. together and five yeomen, allowed 8*s*. 4*d*. Worcester's custody of Percy and the two de Vere boys is not otherwise known, and the substantial sum expended on the adolescent boys might also indicate something of King Edward's own attitude towards these traitors' children.

Henry Percy was born about 1449, and was therefore in his early teens in 1463.[6] His grandfather had died at the first battle of St. Albans in 1455, his father at Towton, and the latter had been posthumously attainted in Edward IV's first parliament in the same year. It is not known when Edward took Percy into his custody; a later tradition, found in the chronicles of Grafton and Hall, states that Henry Percy was in Scotland at the time of the battle of Hexham in 1464, but this is disproved by the warrant.[7] It can be presumed that Edward would have seized Henry as soon as he could, not least because the youth's great-uncle Ralph, the effective head of what was left of the Percy retinue, was active in the north – three times turning his coat and finally rejecting Edward IV before dying at the battle of Hedgeley Moor in 1464.[8] By 17 March 1465 Percy had been moved from Worcester's custody to that of the keeper of the Fleet prison, Elizabeth Venour,[9] although, as this was primarily a debtors' prison, it was presumably less secure than the Tower. When in the Fleet, Venour was granted 26*s*. 8*d*. a week for Percy's expenses and diet, and those of his servants, a greater sum than had been allowed while he was in Worcester's custody. A further payment for his apparel (£7 8*s*. 10*d*.), and in regard for his four servants at 6*d*. a day increased the total. Indeed, £69 14*s*. 1*d*. was paid to Elizabeth for Percy's expenses over a period from mid-

---

[4] TNA, PSO1/23, no. 1215A, printed in the Appendix below.
[5] TNA, E403/827A, 828; E404/72/3. No teller's roll survives for Edward's third regnal year.
[6] For his career see Hicks, 'Career of Henry Percy'; *idem*, 'Dynastic Change and Northern Society: the Career of the Fourth Earl of Northumberland, 1470–1489', *Northern History*, xiv (1978), 78–107; S.G. Ellis, 'Percy, Henry, fourth earl of Northumberland (*c*.1449–1489)', *Oxford DNB*; *CP*, ix. 717–18.
[7] 'After this victory, king Edwarde returned to Yorke, where, in despite of the Erle of Northumberlande, which then lurked in the realme of Scotland, he created syr Iohn Neuell, Lorde Montacute, Erle of Northumberland': *Grafton's Chronicle; or History of England* (2 vols., 1809), ii. 4; Edward Hall, *Hall's Chronicle; Containing the History of England during the Reign of Henry the Fourth and the Succeeding Monarchs* ..., ed. Henry Ellis (1809), 261 (identical wording).
[8] P.W. Hammond, 'Percy, Sir Ralph (1425–1464)', *Oxford DNB*.
[9] Elizabeth was the widow of William Venour, keeper of the Fleet, who died around 1461. She held the office until at least 1466 (*CPR, 1461–7*, p. 512). She was the subject of a well-known legal case, described in detail in C.H. Williams, 'A Fifteenth-Century Lawsuit', *Law Quarterly Review*, xl (1924), 354–64. Her first name is given as Alice in at least one source in relation to Henry Percy (E404/73/1, no. 124B), but this is presumably a clerical error.

March to early November 1465.¹⁰ However, two further small payments indicate the complexity of his position. He was given 6*s*. 8*d*. in silver, presumably for personal expenses, but one of his servants, William Tunstall, was paid directly a further 40*s*. for his unspecified expenses, indicating not only rather greater financial freedom, but perhaps also that those attendant on Percy were the king's servants rather than his own.¹¹ He was, however, allowed to mingle with his fellow prisoners: John Paston, in the Fleet for debt in 1465, wrote a 'cunnyngly wrought' rhyme to his wife Margaret in which he claimed 'My Lord Persy and all this house / Recomaund them to yow, dogge, catte, and mowse.'¹² By Michaelmas 1467, Percy had been moved from the Fleet into the custody of William Herbert, Lord Herbert and later earl of Pembroke, whose daughter he subsequently married: 100 marks were allowed annually for his sustenance and that of diverse people attendant upon him.¹³ While this was less than Venour had received, it may be that the integration of Percy into a noble household, rather than having a separate establishment in the Fleet, achieved economies. However, Percy had been returned to direct royal custody by October 1469, probably as a result of the battle of Edgecote on 26 July that year, when Herbert had been captured and executed. It was from the Tower that he was released on 27 October, having taken an oath of fealty to Edward and given bonds totalling £8,000.¹⁴ His release was intended to counter-balance the power of the disloyal Neville family in the north.

The presence of two of the younger sons of the twelfth earl of Oxford in the custody of the earl of Worcester is of little surprise. Not only were the earl of Oxford and his eldest son Aubrey tried for treason before Worcester, as constable of England, between 13 and 20 February 1462, but it had been he who, in company

---

¹⁰ TNA, E405/42, rots. 1, 4; E404/73/1, no. 124B; C.L. Scofield, *The Life and Reign of Edward the Fourth* (2 vols., 1923), i. 335, 491, 505. For comparisons with allowances for sixteenth-century noble prisoners, see *Calendar of State Papers Domestic, Mary I, 1553–8*, ed. C.S. Knighton (1998), no. 238, cited in Maria Hayward, 'Clothed by the Tudors: Yorkist Prisoners in the Tower, 1485–1547', in *The Yorkist Age*, ed. Kleineke and Steer, 68, and more generally on clothing supplied: Hayward, 'Clothed by the Tudors', 64–80.

¹¹ TNA, E405/42, rots. 1–2. This William Tunstall might have been the younger brother of Sir Richard Tunstall of Thurland. William had been a Lancastrian but by 1465 he was in receipt of annuities of £20 from both Edward IV and Warwick: A.J. Pollard, *North-Eastern England During the Wars of the Roses: Lay Society, War and Politics, 1450–1500* (Oxford, 1990), 302. However, William may have been of too high a social status to act as a 'servant' to the powerless Percy. Percy's other servants are named on rot. 2 as John Wilson, Roger Hall and Walter Wyntor. Wilson and Hall might be the men of the same names appointed within a month of each other in 1465 as gaugers in the ports of Bristol and Southampton respectively: *CPR*, 1461–7, p. 386.

¹² *Paston Letters and Papers of the Fifteenth Century*, ed. Norman Davis, Richard Beadle and Colin Richmond (3 vols., EETS, Special Series, xx–xxii, 2004, 2005), i. 145. Margaret responded in more sober prose, asking that she be recommended to Lord Percy: *ibid.*, 322.

¹³ TNA, SC6/1236/11, m. 1, account of John Milewater, receiver-general of various crown lands in Wales, 7–8 Edward IV. The assignment of 100 marks was allowed from the farm of Haverfordwest, then in the hands of Herbert. No such allowance had been made in the previous year (SC6/1236/10).

¹⁴ *CCR*, 1468–76, pp. 100–1; Ross, *Edward IV*, 144. Scofield notes a last payment to Percy for clothing while in the Tower, but cites a source ('Roll of Treasurer's Accounts, 9 Edw. IV') that cannot now be traced: *Edward the Fourth*, i. 505, n. 2.

with Lords Ferrers and Herbert, had arrested them in Essex on 12 February.[15] The youngsters were probably continuously in Worcester's custody from then onwards; this is reinforced by a reference to a date in February in the damaged text of the warrant. The damage to the text has also obliterated the name of the first of the two de Vere boys. The second name is legible and is that of Thomas, the earl's fourth son, who would have been in his mid-teens at this date.[16] The most likely of the earl's other sons to be in custody was George, who had been presented by his father in 1459 at the early age of sixteen to the wealthy benefice of Lavenham, Suffolk, but subsequently gave up a projected career in the Church, in later years loyally serving his brother, the thirteenth earl, on the battlefield, and twice marrying.[17] It is also possible, however, that the missing name from the warrant was that of the youngest son, Richard, perhaps just into his teens at this date.[18]

What the king intended to do with the title and estates of the earldom of Oxford is less clear than his policy regarding the earldom of Northumberland. Some estates pertaining to the latter were quickly granted to Richard Neville, earl of Warwick, in 1461, and more, along with the title of earl, were bestowed on Neville's brother John in 1464. No act of attainder was passed on the twelfth earl of Oxford, though his estates were considered forfeit by rebellion, and his widow, Countess Elizabeth, was pardoned for any involvement in her late husband's conspiracy on 28 May 1462.[19] She was thus at liberty, and it may be that the youngest of her sons, Richard, was allowed to live with her, although almost all the de Vere estates were granted in tail-male in the following August to King Edward's young brother Richard, duke of Gloucester. It appears that the intention at this stage was that the de Veres would not be restored; yet within a year George Neville, bishop of Exeter, was granted their lands during the minority of John de Vere. The whereabouts of the latter, the eldest surviving son of the late earl, is unknown. If in custody he would seem to have been separated from his brothers, since Worcester was only paid for two de Vere boys. It is more likely that he was in the company, if not the custody, of Warwick the Kingmaker, for at some point, probably in 1463, he was married to Neville's sister Margaret, a marriage which Michael Hicks has argued 'probably helped [him] to recover his family earldom of Oxford'.[20] While separating the four de Vere sons was a sensible precaution, one wonders if Worcester's custody of two of the younger ones was therefore a

---

[15] 'John Benet's Chronicle', ed. G.L. Harriss and M.A. Harriss, *Camden Miscellany XXIV* (Camden Society, 4th series, ix, 1972), 232. For the political background see James Ross, *John de Vere, Thirteenth Earl of Oxford, 1442–1513* (Woodbridge, 2011), 38–46. Tiptoft had only been appointed constable five days earlier: *CPR, 1461–7*, p. 74.

[16] For what little is known about Thomas (*d.*1478 or 1479), see Ross, *John de Vere*, 78.

[17] *Biographical Register of the University of Cambridge to 1500*, ed. A.B. Emden (Cambridge, 1963), 608; *CPL*, xi. 546; Claude Morley, 'Catalogue of the Beneficed Clergy of Suffolk, 1086–1550', *Proceedings of the Suffolk Institute of Archaeology*, xxii (1934–6), 81. On 18 July 1462 the king presented one John Walter to the parish church of Lavenham, void by the resignation of George Vere: *CPR, 1461–7*, p. 193. For his subsequent career, see Ross, *John de Vere*, 77, 203–4.

[18] Richard's date of birth is unknown; he was studying for his M.A. at Cambridge in 1469–70: *Biographical Register of the University of Cambridge*, ed. Emden, 608; Ross, *John de Vere*, 78–9.

[19] TNA, C81/791, no. 957.

[20] M.A. Hicks, *Warwick the Kingmaker* (Oxford, 1998), 234; A.J. Pollard, *Warwick the Kingmaker: Politics, Power and Fame* (2007), 16, 63; Ross, *John de Vere*, 50–1.

measure taken to ensure the good behaviour of the eldest surviving son and his mother.

Worcester's custody of the boys did not last more than another year or two after the warrant was issued in March 1463. By 17 March 1465 Percy had been transferred to the Fleet prison; and on 18 January 1464 the de Vere boys' elder brother John was given licence to enter his estates and title – his brothers would surely have been released at that point if not before.[21] What is not stated in the document is in what capacity Worcester was placed in charge of the three boys. No formal grant of custody of either Percy or the de Veres appears on the patent roll, and the lack of a definite term is suggested in the warrant's arrangements for payment of future charges 'during the tyme þat it shal please us that they or any of theym shal continue in þe gouernance of our said cousin'. Personal grants of custody were usually enrolled, and would often also include control of the ward's estates.[22] If it was not a personal grant, then Worcester held two offices by virtue of which he might have assumed custody of the children. Having been appointed constable of the Tower of London on 2 December 1461, it could well be that his responsibility for Percy at least was as constable of the most secure royal prison.[23] However, such custody and mundane matters such as food and clothing were usually delegated to a deputy of the constable; a few months later expenses totalling £52 for the subsistence of Edmund Beaufort, brother and heir to the duke of Somerset, and his servants for fifty-one weeks were paid to Robert Malory, esquire, Tiptoft's lieutenant constable of the Tower, rather than to the earl himself.[24] The case for the de Vere boys is perhaps a little different. It was as constable of England that Tiptoft had executed their father the earl of Oxford, and his custody of the two probably dated from that time; it may even have dated from 12 February, the day that Worcester arrested the earl and his eldest son.[25]

The earl of Worcester gained no personal benefit as custodian of the boys. The attainder of the third earl of Northumberland in the parliament of 1461 meant that the young Henry Percy was prevented from inheriting his paternal estates; and while he did still stand to inherit the barony of Poynings from his mother, she was still alive and did not die until 1484.[26] Even if the attainder should be reversed at some point in the future, there was no guarantee that Tiptoft would gain custody of the estates during a minority; indeed, the Percy estates were so valuable and strategically important in the troubled north of England that it would be highly unlikely that Edward IV would grant them to a lord whose landed interests were in

---

[21] TNA, E404/73/1, no. 124B; *CPR*, 1461–7, p. 298.

[22] See for example the grant to John, Lord Wenlock, in 1462 of the custody of Anne, wife of the attainted Sir Edmund Hampden, and her estates: *CPR*, 1461–7, pp. 181, 184.

[23] The substantial profits Tiptoft made from his accumulation of royal offices are seen in entries on the issue roll of 1463: wages and a regard as treasurer of England totalled £366, and wages as constable of the Tower (£100), constable of England (£200), and as a royal councillor (200 marks) would have brought a total of £800 p.a. if paid fully and on time, and this did not include his fee as chief justice of North Wales: TNA, E403/828, mm. 6, 8; *CPR*, 1461–7, pp. 61, 62, 74.

[24] TNA, E404/72/3/85 (22 July 1463).

[25] 'John Benet's Chronicle', ed. Harriss and Harriss, 232. Frustratingly, the day in February mentioned in the warrant is illegible, but is likely to be 12 Feb. or else 26 Feb., the day of the earl's execution.

[26] *CP*, x. 665; Hicks, 'Career of Henry Percy', 8.

the Midlands, and was frequently at court. The two de Vere boys were also no catch; as younger sons of a traitor they had no prospects at all until their brother's restoration as earl, and then only their noble lineage made them of any significance. Their brother would have to look for advantageous marriages to provide them with landed estates of their own. Nor was Tiptoft in the market for possible husbands for daughters; even had he wished to marry any offspring to traitors' children, his two marriages to date had resulted in no surviving children, and both wives were dead.

In some respects, Tiptoft was a suitable custodian for noble boys, albeit ones without prospects. A nobleman himself, he would have been aware of what was appropriate for their upbringing – a rounded social, religious, linguistic and physical education;[27] furthermore, he was renowned for his learning and love of books, especially Latin classics and humanist works.[28] If the boys had access to his formidable book collection, they might have benefited substantially, although if they were immured within the Tower their access to books or physical activities such as hunting or training in arms were probably severely restricted. In other respects, the earl of Worcester was far from a suitable guardian. It cannot have been pleasant for the two de Vere boys to be under the governance of the man who had sat in judgment and ordered the execution of their father and eldest brother. Indeed, Tiptoft was a cruel man, whose character excited considerable hostile criticism in the late 1460s, and even more so when he added impalement to a sentence of hanging, drawing and quartering imposed on twenty men in 1470. Of particular pertinence in the present case, there are good grounds for the belief that while deputy governor of Ireland in 1468 Tiptoft was responsible for the deaths of the two young sons of Thomas Fitzgerald, earl of Desmond, whom he had also had executed. While the contemporary *Register of the Mayors of Dublin* just noted that 'this yeare the Earle of Desmond and his two sonnes were executed by þ^e Earle of Worcestre in Drogheda', the later 'Great Chronicle' of London noted the two boys were 'soo tendyr of age', and added circumstantial detail about the younger boy having a sore on his neck. Hall's chronicle described Tiptoft as exercising 'more extreme crueltie ... than princely pity or charitable compassion and in especial on ii enfantes, being sonnes to the erle of Desmond', while the later sixteenth-century *Book of Howth* added that such a shower of wind and rain followed the execution that those present thought 'that God was offended with shedding these innocents' blood'.[29] Perhaps the distance from Dublin to Westminster meant that he could get

---

[27] For aristocratic education in the later Middle Ages see Nicholas Orme, *From Childhood to Chivalry: The Education of the English Kings and Aristocracy 1066–1530* (1984), esp. 211–12.

[28] B.G. Kohl, 'Tiptoft, John, first earl of Worcester (1427–1470)', *Oxford DNB*; R.J. Mitchell, *John Tiptoft (1427–1470)* (1938), ch. 11.

[29] The eldest of the boys was perhaps 13 at this date. The *Register* is BL, Add. MS. 4791, f. 139; *The Great Chronicle of London*, ed. A.H. Thomas and I.D. Thornley (1938), 213; *Hall's Chronicle*, ed. Ellis, 286; 'The Book of Howth', in *Calendar of Carew MSS*, ed. J.S. Brewer and William Bullen (5 vols., 1871), v. 186–8. The story also made it to the Continent, being mentioned in Vespasiano de Bisticci's brief biography of Tiptoft: see David Rundle, 'Was there a Renaissance Style of Politics in Fifteenth-Century England?', in *Authority and Consent in Tudor England*, ed. G.W. Bernard and S.J. Gunn (Aldershot, 2002), 19–21. Some of these sources and the episode are discussed in Mitchell, *John Tiptoft*, 119–21; Art Cosgrove, 'The Execution of the Earl of Desmond, 1468', *Journal of the Kerry Archaeological and Historical Society,* viii (1975), 11–27, and in John Ashdown-Hill and Annette Carson, 'The Execution of the Earl of Desmond', *The Ricardian*, xiv

away with such shocking behaviour (though the Fitzgeralds of Munster rebelled and ravaged Meath and Kildare after Desmond's execution), whereas he could not in England under the closer supervision of King Edward; either way, it seems unlikely that he was a sympathetic guardian.

Another young son of an attainted father had a rather different experience. Henry Clifford was the eldest son of John, Lord Clifford, who was killed at Ferrybridge, the day before Towton. The Clifford estates in Westmorland, Cumberland, Durham and Yorkshire were valuable and strategically important in the troubled north and as such were a rich prize: Lord Clifford's primary residence at Skipton castle was granted to Sir William Stanley on 1 February 1462, while the earl of Warwick acquired the extensive Westmorland estates soon after.[30] Henry was aged about seven at his father's death, his brother Richard a year younger. A later story recounted that, on receipt of the news of Towton, their mother, Margaret, immediately sent her young sons away to the seaside, and on being interrogated about them by Yorkists she answered that she had sent them overseas and did not know whether they were alive or dead. When Lady Margaret thought it safe to do so, she brought Henry back in secrecy to her manor of Londesborough, Yorkshire, and placed him with a shepherd's family. There he remained in seclusion for several years, working as a shepherd boy. The story is noted in Hall's chronicle, and a later member of the family, Lady Anne Clifford, whose antiquarian work on the Cliffords was based on the family records, described how 'By which mean kind of breeding this inconvenience befell him, that he could neither write nor read; for they durst not bring him up in any kind of learning, for fear lest by it his birth should be discovered, yet after he came to his lands and honors, he learned to write his name only'.[31] However, she states that Henry lived with the shepherds until 1485; yet not only was he pardoned in 1472, but before that date he had been named as a recipient of a bequest in the will of one Henry Harlington, publically proved in the ecclesiastical court at York in 1466.[32] While R.T. Spence states that 'the story of Henry the shepherd boy has too much authenticity to be dismissed', Henry Summerson doubts it entirely, pointing out that 'Henry Clifford was later to be not just literate but even bookish, owning volumes on law and medicine, and developing a taste for astronomy and alchemy ... it may be that the Clifford heir

---

(2005), 70–93, esp. 79–81, 89–90. Mitchell notes the surprising silence of the Irish chroniclers on the subject, but concludes 'probability points to the truth of the accusation' (120). The absence of any reference to the execution of the boys from the later (1541) petition by the 13th earl of Desmond (the grandson of the executed earl) to Henry VIII's privy council casts some doubt on the veracity of the accusation: *Letters and Papers, Foreign and Domestic, of the Reign of Henry VIII*, ed. J.S. Brewer, R.H. Brodie and James Gairdner (23 vols. in 38, 1862–1932), xvi. 224.

[30] For some of the estates see *Cal. Inq. Misc.* vii. nos. 339–42; for the grants see *CPR*, 1461–7, pp. 115–6, 186, 189, 342. For the Clifford family, see R.T. Spence, *The Shepherd Lord of Skipton Castle: Henry Clifford, Tenth Lord Clifford, 1454–1523* (Skipton, 1994); Lady Anne Clifford, 'The Lives of the Cliffords...', abridged in *Clifford Letters of the Sixteenth Century*, ed. A.G. Dickens (Surtees Society, clxxxii, 1962), 127–34; J.W. Clay, 'The Clifford Family', *The Yorkshire Archaeological Journal*, xviii (1905), 355–411.

[31] Clifford, 'Lives of the Cliffords', 134.

[32] *CPR*, 1467–77, p. 327; T.D. Whitaker, *The History and Antiquities of the Deanery of Craven in the County of York*, ed. A.W. Morant (3rd edn., Leeds, 1878), 516.

thought it prudent to keep a low profile, but the fact that in 1466 Henry Harlington of Craven could bequeath him a sword and a silver bowl suggests that even then he stood in no perceptible danger.'[33] Even so, it would seem strange that, if Clifford's whereabouts were known, he was not taken into custody. He was a potential focus for Lancastrian resistance, his lands were valuable, and securing his person would give those in possession rather greater security of title. The bitter history between the houses of York and Clifford added a personal dimension to the political backdrop.[34] It may not have been with a shepherd, but surely Clifford was in hiding in secret somewhere.

Why did Edward IV keep these noble but landless boys in custody? Several reasons suggest themselves. It was politically and morally unacceptable to kill innocent children, especially for a king in the 1460s seeking to reconcile the political nation to his rule. If, as seems likely, Tiptoft executed two of the earl of Desmond's sons, he was popularly loathed for this and other cruelties; later, the public presumption that Richard III had murdered his young nephews was to be a major factor in his alienation of much of the Yorkist political elite and their defection to Henry Tudor in 1483 and after. The latter, as Henry VII, at least waited until the blameless Edward, earl of Warwick, was twenty-four before ordering a trial in which the outcome for Clarence's son was an inevitable execution. Moreover, for the Percy and de Vere boys the old saying that 'heirs of a noble race always have many heirs' was accurate; there were enough collateral heirs to make executing the boys almost pointless. Edward had already executed the twelfth earl of Oxford and his eldest son, but to exterminate the entire line he would have needed to execute another four boys, together with the late earl's brother and nephew, as well as the Cornish cadet line that eventually inherited the earldom in 1526.

Edward himself can scarcely have been unaware of the fact that he was the grandson of an earl executed for treason in 1415, whose son was allowed to succeed to the largest private inheritance of the day, so was perhaps inclined to benign treatment of such political orphans. More broadly, if he knew about recent political history, he would have been aware that the policy adopted by both Henry IV and Henry V, of allowing heirs ultimately to succeed their treasonous fathers, had been largely successful in building loyalty to the Lancastrian dynasty for families such as Percy, Mowbray and Montagu. While in the early 1460s, it may not have been obvious that the heirs of de Vere, Percy, Clifford and others would or should be restored to their titles, it remained a possibility.[35] Lord Herbert may well have thought this when he acquired the custody of Henry Percy in 1467.

---

[33] Spence, *Shepherd Lord*, 9; Henry Summerson, 'Clifford, Henry, tenth Baron Clifford (1454–1523)', *Oxford DNB*.

[34] York had led the army that killed the 8th Lord Clifford at the first battle of St. Albans in 1455; tradition has it that Clifford deliberately killed York's son, the young earl of Rutland, at Wakefield in 1460, and certainly York himself was killed there, and his severed head mockingly displayed on the walls of York.

[35] Michael Hicks has discussed the high rates of reversals of attainder that characterised the Wars of the Roses, but noted that few reversals occurred during the 1460s, with numbers increasing thereafter as a result of the upheavals of 1469–71 and 1483–5. Ultimately, of the 65 landholders attainted in 1461, as many as 59 secured restoration: M.A. Hicks, 'Attainder, Resumption and Coercion, 1461–1529', *Parliamentary History*, iii (1984), 16–31, esp. 17–18.

Michael Hicks has argued that 'perhaps he ... was also intended to marry a Herbert, as he later did' and that Herbert and others would have secured his restoration as earl to the detriment of their political enemies, Warwick, his brother John Neville, created Marquess Montagu in 1470, and Clarence.[36] Percy's restoration was not just considered desirable by a few of the nobility playing matrimonial politics. In 1469 the Yorkshire rebels led by Robin of Holderness demanded his restoration to the earldom of Northumberland, to which John Neville, then occupying that dignity, did not take kindly. In Cora Scofield's words 'at the first indication of danger to his earldom, Warwick's brother leapt into his saddle again, met the insurgents at the very gates of York, routed them and beheaded their leader'.[37] Nonetheless, it made good sense politically for such noble boys to be kept alive and treated reasonably well, as they might be of use in the future. For three of the families there was eventually a happy ending: the heirs achieved restoration to their estates and title – Percy in 1470, de Vere between 1464 and 1471 and more lastingly in 1485, and Clifford with the advent of Henry Tudor. While this might not have been readily anticipated in the 1460s, the possibility that the young men might do the king service in the future was not to be discounted.

Edward, brought up as the heir to a duke of royal lineage, was naturally sensitive to noble rank and status, and this might explain the generous payments for sustenance and other expenses, as well as an allowance for servants, he accorded to the de Vere boys, and more generously still to the Percy heir – payments that were only a little smaller than those granted to wards with unsullied prospects. The latter varied, and were not entirely dependent on rank. In 1423, the king's council had agreed to pay £100 p.a. for the expenses of the young earl of Oxford, a grant increased to 200 marks in 1429; Henry Beaufort, duke of Somerset, was assigned £200 for his sustenance in 1456; and Richard Neville, Lord Latimer, and George, duke of Bedford, received £100 and 200 marks respectively in 1470 and 1472.[38] Henry Percy was allowed four servants in the 1460s, nearly as many as the five attendant on the teenaged earl of Derby, Edward Stanley, while he was in the household of Cardinal Wolsey in the 1520s.[39] Thus, Percy was treated almost as if he was a 'normal' ward, to whom custom offered a guarantee of maintenance according to his or her station, while the de Vere boys were treated generously, even though they were not heirs to any estates at all.[40]

---

[36] M.A. Hicks, *False, Fleeting, Perjur'd Clarence: George Duke of Clarence 1449–78* (Gloucester, 1980), 26–7. The marriage between Percy and Maud Herbert had taken place by Mich. 1472: *Percy Bailiffs' Rolls of the Fifteenth Century*, ed. J.C. Hodgson (Surtees Society, cxxxiv, 1921), 59, 114.

[37] Scofield, *Edward the Fourth*, i. 391.

[38] TNA, E28/4, no. 101; E403/688, m. 11; *CPR*, 1452–61, p. 277; 1467–77, pp. 209, 335.

[39] Orme, *From Childhood to Chivalry*, 57.

[40] Both Bracton and Glanville note (in similar words) that custodians 'shall maintain the heirs honourably, as long as they are in wardship, in accordance with the size of the inheritance': *Bracton on the Laws and Customs of England*, ed. S.E. Thorne (4 vols., Cambridge, Mass., 1968–77), ii. 252; Ranulf de Glanville, *Tractatus de Legibus et Consuetudinibus Regni Angliae, tempore Henrici Secundi*, ed. Travers Twiss (RS, 1896), 196–7. Magna Carta, clauses 5 and 6, established the principle of marriage without disparagement and protected the estates of the heir from ruthless custodians, and while the latter custom was often observed in the breach, it did offer the possibility of legal redress: S.S. Walker, 'The Marrying of Feudal Wards in Medieval England', *Studies in*

It is worth noting that in the normal course of events these boys might have expected to be sent away from their family homes to serve in other noble households or even the royal court for a period; they would also have been aware that if their fathers died, even of natural causes, before they reached the age of twenty-one, this would also have resulted in their dislocation. Nonetheless, the impact of Towton on Henry Percy and Henry Clifford, or the conspiracy of 1462 on the de Vere boys, must have been profoundly shocking and traumatic, and involved the stigma of attainder on their family name and the loss of most or all of their future prospects. As children they had no legal voice, but the deprivation of their rights to 'their' property removed a level of protection as well. Custody in a royal prison (certainly the Fleet for Percy, probably the Tower for both him and the de Vere boys), or the likelihood of some degree of concealment or seclusion in Clifford's case, was also likely to have been far from pleasant. Perhaps only the fact that they were treated, to all intents and purposes, with due regard to their status would have softened the blow; deprivation of all or most of their future property, title and legal rights was not echoed in immediate social demotion or disparagement. This hints at a certain solidarity amongst the ruling elite in the midst of a bitter civil war that is not always readily visible to the historian.

Medieval Culture, iv (1974), 209–24; N.J. Menuge, *Medieval English Wardship in Romance and Law* (Cambridge, 2001), esp. ch. 3.

APPENDIX

TNA, PSO1/23, no. 1215A

The 'A' number indicates a more recent addition to the file; two pencil numerations of 28 and 60 on the document represent a numerical sequence not found anywhere else in the file and show its immediate provenance in another bundle, probably from a chancery series, as there is a chancery stamp on the dorse. However, no note of its original reference or when or by whom it was moved is found on the document. It was presumably already separated from the associated schedule when moved. The top left-hand corner of the document is lost, comprising the first third of the top four lines. Missing words and editorial suggestions (in modern English) are indicated by square brackets. Abbreviations have been silently expanded and some punctuation has been added. Capitalisation and the use of 'u', 'v', 'i' and 'j' have been retained as in the original.

[Endorsed] To oure Right trusty and welbeloued Clerc Maister Robert Styllington keper of our priuee seel

[Right trusty and well beloved we greet you] wele Lating you wit that wher Henry Percy son vnto Henry [Percy, earl of Northumberland, ?George Vere and] Thomas Veer, sones to John late Erle of Oxonford, sethen þe decesse of þeir [fathers ...] they might <haue> any sustentacion to leve by but oonly by oure comaundement [...] day of Feuer the [? second year] of our Reigne. that is to wit our right trusty and Right welbeloued cousin [the earl of] Worcestre hath prouided for the arraiement of theim and theirs vnto þe some of iiij^{xx}vij li. xj s. vj d., as it apperith in a sedule which we sende vnto you herein closede. We therefore wol and charge yov þat, vndre our priue seel being in your warde and keping, ye do make our lettres to bee directed vnto þe Tresorer and Chamberlains of our Eschequier for þe tyme beeing, charging them by the same to doo make due payement or suffisaunt assignement to þe said Erle of þe hole some conteyned in þe said sedule, and soo forth contynually after the Rate of þe same during the tyme þat it shal please vs that they or any of theym shal continue in þe gouernance of our said cousin, except oonly þat their dietts shal bee continued for ye same tyme as in forme folowing. That is to wit for þe dietts of þe said Percy, Veer and Veer eueryche of theim by the weke vj s. viij d. Item for ij Gentilmen of theirs by the weke vj s. viij d. Item for v yomen of theirs by the weke viij s. iiij d. And theis our lettres shal bee your suffisaunt warant and discharge in þat behalue. Yeuen vndre our signet at our Palaice of Westm' the ix day of Marche the third yere of our Reigne [1463].

[Signed] Craft

EDWARD IV AND BURY ST. EDMUNDS' SEARCH FOR SELF-GOVERNMENT

Anne F. Sutton

On 29 March 1461 men of Bury St. Edmunds fought at the battle of Towton for Edward IV, their banner flying alongside that of London, the white castle of Norwich, the harrow of Canterbury, the white ship of Bristol, the black ram of Coventry, the leopard of Salisbury, the wolf of Worcester, the dragon of Gloucester, the griffon of Leicester, the George of Nottingham, the boar's head of Windsor, and the wild rat of Northampton.[1] This was certainly a key moment of Bury's support for the house of York, orchestrated by Alderman John Smith – Bury had an alderman rather than a mayor. Though support for the king was mandatory when called for, the articulate leading burgesses, such as Smith, had organised their force under the captaincy of William Aleyn, one of their number, and it is probable they hoped that eventually they would receive some tangible reward.[2] This paper discusses the relations of Bury with Edward IV, in which the crucial role was played by John Smith, who earned the title of 'especiall lover and preferrer off the politik and comen well' of his town.[3] The chief aim of Smith and his fellows was to throw off the control of the abbey of Bury St. Edmunds, and for this the support of the king was essential. The Yorkist period was propitious for this campaign: both the kings and their lawyers favoured incorporating towns already responsibly ruling themselves by prescription. During his reign, Edward regularly showed he was willing to listen to requests from towns owned by clerics: Peterborough, Salisbury and Reading were all accorded his attention and favour in

---

[1] Frederic Madden, 'Political Poems of the Reigns of Henry VI and Edward IV', *Archaeologia*, xxix (1842), 318–47, esp. 342–7, which lists men and towns with emblems. The banner of Norwich is added on the last page of Bale's chronicle: Trinity College, Dublin, MS 604, f. 78v. Neither source mentions Bury, nor is Bury's banner known, although the three crowns (for the abbey) or the arrows (for the town) might be inferred. The author is greatly indebted to Margaret Statham, archivist at Bury St. Edmunds 1957–86, for reading this article and sharing her considerable knowledge of Bury and of John Smith in particular.

[2] TNA, C1/45/138, and see n. 17 below.

[3] This benefactor is frequently called Jankyn Smythe in Bury. Quotation is from the Benefactors' Book, cited in *Accounts of the Feoffees of the Town Lands of Bury St Edmunds, 1569–1622*, ed. Margaret Statham (Suffolk Record Society, xlvi, 2003), p. xix, which summarises the material. See also Margaret Statham and Sally Badham, 'Jankyn Smith of Bury St Edmunds and his Brass', *Transactions of the Monumental Brass Society*, xviii (2013), 227–50 and M.L. Merry, '"Special lover and preferrer of the polytike and common weal": John Smyth and Ideal Citizenship in Fifteenth-Century Bury St Edmunds', in *Negotiating the Political in Northern European Urban Society, c.1400–c.1600*, ed. Sheila Sweetinburgh (Tempe, Ariz., 2013), 17–44.

varying degrees, and are essential comparisons to augment and illuminate the under-documented struggle of Bury.

Edward IV, his Lordship of Clare and the Men of Bury St. Edmunds

Edward IV came to the throne in 1461 with popular support. For ten years before he did so there had been debate in England on how to cope with a king, Henry VI, who failed to direct government for the benefit of his people and allowed his household servants, gentry and nobles, to usurp his functions for their private gain. The reinstatement of good government had become the rallying cry of the Yorkists, led by Richard, duke of York, father of the future Edward IV, in accordance with the generally accepted idea that government should be conducted for the common good or weal of the people; the king was all powerful but he answered to God, a good king ruled for his people's welfare and he administered justice under God. Bills and manifestos on these themes circulated through England for a decade before Edward's accession. The best surviving collection of broadsides, newsletters and propaganda issued in these years was in fact made by a man from Bury St. Edmunds:[4] John Vale, secretary and man of affairs to Thomas Cook, draper, alderman and mayor of London (1462–3).[5] Vale placed the beginning of civil unrest in England in his home town: the first of the 'grete mischefes' of Henry VI's reign, as he called them, was the death (in his opinion, murder) of Humphrey, duke of Gloucester, while he was staying at St. Saviour's hospital during the parliament held at Bury St. Edmunds in 1447.[6]

A key aspect of the good government to which Edward was committed was that of his towns from the greatest city down to the smallest village. The inhabitants of many of them wanted to rule themselves, which they often already did by prescription, and eleven urban communities gained incorporation from the new king.[7] Certain towns, however, had difficult, specific problems which, despite the wealth of some of the townsmen and long years of self-government in practical terms, remained under the control of the lords who owned them, and the most troublesome of these lords were often clerics. Bury, owned by the abbey of Bury St. Edmunds, fell into this category, and Salisbury, whose lord was its bishop, was another; similarly, Peterborough and Reading fell under the lordship of their abbeys. In this study, the struggle of Salisbury against its lord, contemporary with that of Bury, is an essential comparison, as its extensive records of civic events and government compensate for the poverty of Bury's. Peterborough, not that far from Bury, is another useful, if more muted, comparison to the obstreperous urban centres of Bury and Salisbury, and shows that Edward was prepared to listen to the

---

[4] *The Politics of Fifteenth Century England: John Vale's Book*, ed. M.L. Kekewich, Colin Richmond, A.F. Sutton, Livia Visser-Fuchs and J.L. Watts (Stroud and London, 1995), esp. 103 (as a child he lived in the house of his father, Thomas, a dyer, in Mustow), 180–95, 204–15 (manifestoes).

[5] Cook was of the Suffolk family, prominent in the cloth industry of Lavenham and elsewhere. A.F. Sutton, 'Sir Thomas Cook and his "troubles": an Investigation', *Guildhall Studies in London History*, iii (1978), 85–108; M.A. Hicks, 'The Case of Sir Thomas Cook', *EHR*, xciii (1978), 82–96.

[6] *John Vale's Book*, ed. Kekewich *et al.*, 178–80 (ff. 119v–121: his chronicle 1431–71), 103.

[7] Martin Weinbaum, *The Incorporation of Boroughs* (Manchester, 1937), 132–3.

requests of a clerically-dominated town in a beneficent and intelligent way from the very beginning of his reign.

Peterborough Abbey boasted a large franchise of eight hundreds and full power over the borough which had been created by a twelfth-century abbot. The town obeyed the bailiff and under-bailiff, the feed officers of the abbot. It never had the economic success of Bury and, probably as a consequence, had a comparatively riot-free history, the discontent of the inhabitants vented by their grand jury's regular presentment of the abbot at his own court for his failure to maintain local amenities. In 1460 Henry VI permitted the abbot to make justices of the peace and gaol delivery at will on condition that one of them was of the county quorum, and this was confirmed by Edward IV in 1462, but on a stricter condition that one of them must be on the quorum or a person skilled in the law. As at Bury and Salisbury, the men of Peterborough had resorted to endowing their communal chantries and charities by the means of a guild or feoffees and it was through these bodies that they had come to manage their municipal affairs; it was the guild which solicited the king's favour. On 2 September 1464 Edward IV granted the brethren and sisters of the guild of Saints Mary, George and John in the parish church of St. John in the 'king's town' of Peterborough, 'in consideration of their good and faithful service' in the recent wars, a licence to acquire lands in mortmain worth £20 a year.[8] Peterborough's support for York during the wars therefore received a reward, and Bury's known military support for the new regime might be expected to provoke a similar response.

Bury had more than its military service to recommend it to Edward IV. John Smith, regularly alderman from 1443–4 until his death in 1481,[9] is likely to have had strong links to the duke of York's lordship of Clare, the great honour that stretched across East Anglia. There was also a tradition that the lords of Clare were willing opponents of the abbey of Bury St. Edmunds: for example they had taken a conspicuous part in the battle by the friars minor to set up a convent in Bury, in which popes and the king were involved. The abbey had finally and grudgingly allowed the friars a convent at Babwell, within easy walking distance of the town and outside its boundary and the abbey's direct control. Gilbert of Clare, earl of Gloucester (1262–95), was claimed as a founder of the friary (c.1263), and the townsmen unsurprisingly gave the convent their favour with many choosing to be buried there; nor were the friars slow to support the townsmen in their opposition to the abbey's rule. On 28 February 1447, Richard, duke of York, granted twenty acres of land to the friary at Babwell, and described himself as the friary's guardian. The impressive list of local notables who acted as witnesses to his grant was as much a challenge to St. Edmund's great abbey as his declaration of guardianship. Coincidentally, Humphrey, duke of Gloucester's body had been lying at the friary

---

[8] H.C. Darby, *Medieval Cambridgeshire* (Cambridge, 1977), 40; *Peterborough Local Adminstration: Parochial Government before the Reformation. Churchwardens' Accounts 1467–1573 with Supplementary Documents 1107–1488*, ed. W.T. Mellows (Northamptonshire Record Society, ix, 1937), pp. xxxii, 244; *VCH Northamptonshire*, ii. esp. 423–8.

[9] M.D. Lobel, 'A List of the Aldermen and Bailiffs of Bury St Edmunds from the Twelfth to Sixteenth centuries', *Proceedings of the Suffolk Institute of Archaeology and History*, xxii (1934), 17–28, esp. 26–7; his term of 1460–1 must be added, see TNA, C1/45/138.

for the past three days.[10] Most importantly, the king's assizes and probably also the east Suffolk musters took place at Henhowe, very close to Babwell; the area was close to Bury but *outside the banlieu* of the abbey's town.[11] At the more personal level, although John Smith's administrative role within the honour of Clare has not been established for certain, it is suggested by the lands he held throughout the county and the way he established his charity (described below). He had, for example, a good relationship with John Howard (the future duke of Norfolk), who was steward of the honour possibly from the late 1450s. The lord of Clare, the duke of York, was killed on 30 December 1460 at the battle of Wakefield, where it is known that London lost men and it seems likely that Bury and the honour of Clare did so too. Edward was acclaimed king in London on 4 March 1461 and his mother, Duchess Cecily of York, became the lady of Clare.[12]

The Yorkist party had become particularly popular among merchants. The mercantile elite of London had declared for York during 1460 and merchants and clothiers of cloth towns like Bury readily followed the lead of the Londoners, who bought their cloth and like themselves wanted peaceful and responsible government. London's civic freedoms were the envy of all lesser English towns. The men of Bury had followed the lead of London in earlier struggles for self-government, for example in the Barons' War, and had received specific aid from Londoners during their rising of 1327.[13] In 1461, as stated, Bury was among the provincial towns which are known to have sent men to fight for Edward 'at dyvers feldez and in especiall the kynges victorious feld of Touton' where their captain

---

[10] The records of the honour of Clare at this time are so poor that Smith's contacts with it are speculative and based on evidence in this note and n. 12. M.D. Lobel, *The Borough of Bury St Edmunds* (Oxford, 1935), 125; *VCH Suffolk*, ii. 124–5; John Gage, *The History and Antiquities of Suffolk: Thingoe Hundred* (1838), 240–51, 270–1; *CPR*, 1446–52, pp. 17 (licence), 231 (*inspeximus* and confirmation of licence and grant); P.A. Johnson, *Duke Richard of York, 1411–60* (Oxford, 1991), 66; *An English Chronicle*, ed. J.S. Davies (Camden Society, lxiv, 1856), 117–18.

[11] Antonia Gransden, 'John de Northwold, Abbot of Bury St Edmunds (1279–1301) and his Defence of its Liberties', *Thirteenth Century England III*, ed. P.R. Coss and S.D. Lloyd (Woodbridge, 1991), 92–7, for an essential explanation of the abbey's liberties and the boundary of the town. See also Gage, *Thingoe Hundred*, pp. ix–xi, and *Accounts of the Feoffees*, ed. Statham, p. xxxvi and n. 156. With thanks to Margaret Statham for advice on these points.

[12] See below for Howard heading the witnesses to Smith's grants to Bury. Anne Crawford, *Yorkist Lord: John Howard, Duke of Norfolk, c.1425–1485* (2010), 21, 145. The author is grateful for Margaret Statham's advice on Smith's career and personal ties to York, e.g. the information that Smith owned the manor of Swifts in Preston near Long Melford, part of the honour of Clare, and he was to endow his college or guild of the Holy Name with it. The final arrangements for this transaction were carried out by Thomas Ampe, Richard Yaxley, William Thwaytes and Clement Clerke, who received a licence to alienate this manor in perpetuity to benefit the guild of the Holy Name of Jesus (the then warden being Henry Hardman) from Duchess Cecily as lady of Clare, remembering her devotion to the Holy and Undivided Trinity and the most sweet Name of Jesus and the Mother of God; dated at her castle of Berkhampstead, 20 June 1482. This was copied into his 'Breviary of Suffolk' by Robert Reyce of Preston, while it was in his possession: Suffolk RO, Ipswich, HD 474/1, f. 164. For Wakefield see Caxton's continuation of the *Polychronicon* under 1460: *Polychronicon Ranulphi Higden monachi Cestrensis*, ed. Churchill Babington and J.R. Lumby (9 vols., RS, 1865–86), viii. 584.

[13] C.M. Barron, 'London and the Crown, 1451–61', *The Crown and Local Communities*, ed. J.R.L. Highfield and Robin Jeffs (Gloucester, 1981), 88–109; J.L. Bolton, 'The City and the Crown, 1456–61', *The London Journal*, xii (1996), 11–24; Lobel, *The Borough*, 131; *eadem*, 'A Detailed Account of the 1327 Rising at Bury St Edmunds and the subsequent trial', *Proceedings of the Suffolk Institute of Archaeology and History*, xxi (1933), 228.

William Aleyn 'was grevously hurte and wounded'.¹⁴ Its alderman was responsible for recruitment of the town's own forces and Alderman Smith's response to the king's order would have been taken with the advice of the twelve (or twenty-four) burgesses whose duty it was to advise him, and with full knowledge of what was toward in London.¹⁵ Trade contacts kept merchants abreast of the news and the Yorkist servant, John Howard, who was knighted by Edward at Towton, also passed through Bury at about this time. The abbey is known to have lent Edward £100 and another 100 marks 'by way of love' in March 1461, and both sums were transferred to him by Howard. It is not impossible that it was he and Smith who persuaded the abbot of the advisability of making the loans.¹⁶

In the aftermath of what was a very bloody battle fought in a snowstorm at Towton, the wounded William Aleyn and his companions waited on the victorious king at his command, as Aleyn later recounted. Edward was an impressively tall and handsome young man, who was to become famous for his ease of manner with his subjects and his ability to thank them for their service. Aleyn and his men relaxed in this congenial company a little too long, perhaps, and their expenses turned out to be £30 more than Bury and its alderman had expected.¹⁷ When they eventually came home, the stories of their exploits and the king's gracious behaviour no doubt lost nothing in the telling and would surely have encouraged yet more support for the new regime, and above all hopes of special favours for the town.¹⁸ Another encouragement for the townsmen of Bury was that early in 1462 Edward placed the abbot and three monks under arrest. Extensive Lancastrian activity was suspected and this led to the arrest of members of several East Anglian families, notably John de Vere, earl of Oxford, Aubrey his eldest son, Sir Thomas Tuddenham of Eriswell, John Clopton of Long Melford, John Montgomery of Great Tey in Essex, and William Tyrell of Gipping, Suffolk (the last three all brothers-in-law). Except for Clopton, all were executed. The abbot and monks of Bury had apparently posted up on the abbey door a notice publicising as fact that the pope had cancelled all the arrangements made by the papal legate with Edward IV, had absolved Henry VI's adherents of their sins, and excommunicated Edward's supporters. The royal pardon granted to the abbot and monks on 16

---

¹⁴ Quotations from TNA, C1/45/138.
¹⁵ Lobel, *The Borough*, 94, on number in council advising the alderman. The higher number was usual, to judge by the number of burgesses and feoffees in Smith's deeds, see below. For 'Bury' as the place of muster e.g. before Bosworth, see Crawford, *Yorkist Lord*, 131, or in 1471, see n. 46 below.
¹⁶ Edward received the money at 'Cambridge' on '17 March', according to C.L. Scofield, *Life and Reign of Edward the Fourth* (2 vols., 1923), i. 162, citing E404 warrants of '28 July' and '21 Dec.', but see Crawford, *Yorkist Lord*, 23 and n. 20, and p. 25 citing E404/72/1/80. Dr. Crawford has most kindly confirmed that there were two loans received via Howard on 27 March and 22 April, with repayment ordered by this warrant which is dated 21 December 1461.
¹⁷ TNA, C1/45/138; the case was scheduled to be heard in the octave of St. John the Baptist next, no year given but during the chancellorship of Robert Stillington, bishop of Bath and Wells [c.April 1471–June 1473], and Aleyn states that Smith began to prosecute him after the king had departed out of England. The fact that both men held the office of alderman may suggest that personal rivalry lay behind the suit.
¹⁸ Aleyn was to be alderman himself from Mich. 1464: Lobel, 'A List', 27. The list has so many gaps that he may have served in other years.

March cost their abbey as much as 500 marks (£333 6s. 8d.).[19] Any misfortune for the abbey meant jubilation (however privately expressed) among the townsmen of Bury. John Smith was still alderman – he seems to have been in office continuously from at least Michaelmas 1460 to Michaelmas 1464.[20] It is tempting to put the surviving undated 'Articles alleged against John, abbot of the monastery of Bury St. Edmunds, by the inhabitants of Bury aforesaid' in this year of an Abbot John's political disgrace; the articles included a complaint that he had used his veto against Smith to prevent him from taking office as alderman, which was especially likely if the forceful Smith had been elected by his fellow townsmen regularly over at least four years.[21]

As Smith seems to have been a close associate of John Clopton (1423–97) of Long Melford, and Clopton was the only one of the alleged conspirators not executed for treason at this time, it might be wondered whether Smith spoke on his behalf. Equally significant may be the fact that Clopton had also been one of the witnesses to the duke of York's grant to the friary of Babwell.[22] In May 1462, two months after the abbot's treason, Hugh Babington, Edmund Lorimer and other men of Bury were arrested for riot. This has prompted the speculation that they were 'heroes' of the town's struggle for self-government, perhaps seeking advantage from the abbot's recent error of judgment, but no details are known about the incident or the men involved. Sir John Howard, among others, and the abbot's bailiffs were ordered to make arrests and bring the offenders before the king's council. The matter had not been resolved by August when it was remitted to chancery, a clear indication that treason to the king was not considered an issue.[23]

---

[19] *Three Fifteenth Century Chronicles*, ed James Gairdner (Camden Society, 1st series, xxviii, 1880), 162; *CPR*, 1461–67, p. 178 (pardon for Abbot John 'Boon' and his convent for treasons and the consequent outlawry); Scofield, *Edward the Fourth*, i. 231–4. Scofield's source for the precise details of the abbot's offence is the letter of Antonio della Torre to the papal legate Coppini (*Cal. State Papers Milan*, *I*, ed. A.B. Hinds (1912), 107) where the offending abbey is not actually named. Scofield's assumption is likely to be correct given the arrest, pardon and heavy fine: James Ross, *John De Vere, Thirteenth Earl of Oxford 1442–1513* (Woodbridge, 2012), 38–49.

[20] Lobel, 'A List', 26–7; *Accounts of the Feoffees*, ed. Statham, p. xix, n. 34. Smith was also alderman 1460–1, taking William Aleyn's testimony into account.

[21] Printed in N.M. Trenholme, 'English Monastic Boroughs', *The University of Missouri Studies*, ii (1927), 102–4.

[22] Clopton was the major benefactor and rebuilder of his church, see e.g. David Dymond and Clive Paine, *Five Centuries of an English Parish Church: The State of Melford Church, Suffolk* (Cambridge, 2012), *passim* and 38 for Smith. There seems little doubt that Smith (like Clopton) contributed to the altarpiece of Long Melford in 1481 (the year of his death), Kim Woods, 'The Pre-Reformation Altarpiece of Long Melford Church', *Antiquaries Journal*, lxxxii (2002), 93–104, esp. 94 for inscription recording donors for the altarpiece. I am grateful to Margaret Statham for this reference. See above, n. 12 for Smith's property near Long Melford. Interestingly, Clopton was to be an executor of Margaret Leynham (*d*.1482), whose husband Sir John had been accused of treason in 1468 and may have been helped by William, Lord Hastings (she recorded in her will 'the grete secour that I have had of his gode lordeship in my lives daies'): Sutton, 'Thomas Cook', 99, n. 48. Sir John Leynham had made Hastings his overseer, TNA, PROB11/6, ff. 285v–86v. It is worth wondering if Clopton had benefited from similar aid in 1462. For Clopton's connections, see also Ross, *John De Vere*, 42.

[23] Lobel, *The Borough*, 159: 12 May 1462, commission headed by Sir John Howard, Richard Weldon esq., Richard George, king's serjeant-at-arms, and the bailiffs, to arrest Hugh Babington, Edmund Lorimer, John Wratton [*sic*; the local name was Watton], Robert Aylwyn, John Gye, William Butte, John White, John Porter and William Awfyn, and bring them before the king's council: *CPR*, 1461–7, p. 203; 25 Aug. 1462 commission headed by Sir John Wingfield, Richard Weldon, Arthur

Edward planned to take in Bury on a tour which began at the beginning of March 1462, dispensing justice to the surrounding area; Easter (Sunday 18 April) was to be spent there and would have included worship at the shrine of St. Edmund. The king's plans changed,[24] and it was not until June 1469 that he eventually visited Bury and went as a pilgrim to the shrine. Nothing else is known of his visit nor who was alderman at this time, although Abbot John Bohun (the same abbot as had been arrested in 1462), would have summoned the alderman and the greater men of the town to a council, the alderman and burgesses would have decided to wear scarlet to welcome the king, and lesser townsmen would have been garbed in red cloth. Edward saw an abbey that was still recovering from a disastrous fire on 20 January 1465 which had destroyed the wooden roof of the nave and the wooden structure of the tower.[25]

Bury and Salisbury: Clerical Controls and the Fight for Freedom

The inadequate survival of records of Bury's municipal life and events makes comparison essential to the well-documented struggles for self-government of the city of Salisbury, dominated by its bishop, during the reign of Edward IV: comparison provides some idea of the passion which lay behind civic aspirations. The abbey of St. Edmund's power and charters went back before the Conquest; it controlled a franchise of eight and a half hundreds (approximately half the county of Suffolk), and claimed absolute control of its town. The sacrist was the abbey's chief obedientiary for the town in all matters, he was rector of the two parish churches and had the probate of the townsmen's wills – there was no escape from the abbey's scrutiny. Ultimately, however, both town and abbey answered to the king – it was always the king's justice, not the abbot's. A sympathetic, interested king might be petitioned for favours, and if a leading man of a town had a personal link to the king, *he* might receive personal attention.

The administration of both Bury and Salisbury was essentially the same. Bury obeyed the abbot's bailiff or steward, who presided over the local courts, administered the borough and carried out orders from the royal chancery which would have been carried out by a sheriff elsewhere. The bailiff took an oath of office before the sacrist of the abbey, and beneath him were many lesser secular officers. In the mid to late fifteenth century the office of bailiff was often held by two men who might be local gentlemen or lawyers. Thomas Higham, from a well-to-do local family which also produced a serjeant-at-law, Richard Higham (*d*.1500), was bailiff probably continuously from 1436 to 1483. He and his fellow bailiff,

---

Greyson, Thomas Achambre and the bailiffs, to arrest John Gye, William Awfyn, John Dyer and Thomas Fletcher, son of Edmund Bowyer, and bring them before the king in chancery to answer for riots: *ibid.*, 206.

[24] *Paston Letters and Papers of the Fifteenth Century*, ed. Norman Davis (2 vols., Oxford, 1971, 1976), ii. 273–4; Scofield, *Edward the Fourth*, i. 244, n. 1, 245.

[25] Compare visit of Henry VI: Lobel, *The Borough*, 94. For the fire, see M.R. James, *On the Abbey of S. Edmund at Bury* (Cambridge Antiquarian Society, octavo series, xxviii, 1895), 150–212, esp. 205–12.

William Helperby, regularly associated with him from about 1468, were both accused more than once of improper use of their power of appointment of juries, and failure to obey the king's orders was not unknown.[26] Representing the town's interest was the alderman, who had originally been the head of the town's guild merchant (forfeited in 1327). Although elected by the townsmen, his election was subject to the abbot's veto and he took his oath before the sacrist; the same man could be re-elected, but that might invite opposition. He had supreme authority to raise taxes within the town, and the control of their finances was among the most basic desires of the townsmen. The alderman's duty was to keep the town peaceful and loyal to the abbey. He attended all the several courts of the town and the juries of townsmen rendered their judgments through him. He could take the place of an absent bailiff but he was not to interfere with the bailiff's office; he could arrest and imprison, he shared military duties with the bailiffs and held musters of the local militia and found arms, clothing, provisions and wages for soldiers, and was usually responsible for finding the gate-keepers (except for the east gate which the abbot kept under his direct rule) and watchmen, the keepers of the markets and the constables of wards. There were many officers under the alderman, as there were under the bailiff, and all of them were the abbey's servants, and the abbot could reject those elected at will.[27]

About 300 years younger than Bury, Salisbury was founded in 1225 by the bishop of Salisbury when he built his new cathedral. He granted a charter to *his* townsmen in 1225 and the king granted his first charter to the *bishop's men* in 1227 freeing them of tolls throughout the realm, a right that the townsmen of Bury had already enjoyed for over one hundred years. The bishops obtained royal privileges for the citizens of Salisbury, as did the abbots of Bury for their townsmen, yet although the citizens were allowed to elect their own mayor (by 1249), he was held to be subordinate to the bishop's bailiff, before whom he had to be sworn into office. As in Bury, there was a range of lower ranking officials including a coroner, clerks of the market, gate-keepers, down to scavengers or street cleaners; and both places were expected to run everyday affairs, often with little supervision, yet they had to abide by the original agreements of subordination to bishop or abbot. The sheer number of officials, however minor, shows that neither urban community lacked practical self-government. A study of Salisbury has shown that about 1% of householders were involved in local responsibilities each year.[28] Similarly, Bury was left almost entirely free to administer the practical affairs of the community,[29] but the townsmen remained servants. Whereas a town

---

[26] The records of Bury are largely in print: (HMC, *14th Report*, App. viii; Lobel, *The Borough* and Trenholme, 'English Monastic Boroughs'), as are a percentage of the wills: *Wills and Inventories from the Registers of the Commissary of Bury St Edmunds and the Archdeacon of Sudbury*, ed. Samuel Tymms (Camden Society, xlix, 1850). Lobel, *The Borough*, 60–72; eadem, 'A List', 17–28, esp. 27. For Higham pedigrees, *The Visitations of Suffolk 1561 Made by William Hervey*, ed. Joan Corder (2 pts., Harleian Society new series, xi, 1981), pt. 1, pp. 73–75; pt. 2, p. 394.

[27] Lobel, *The Borough*, 72–94; richer men tended to be given this role, 93–4, as in Salisbury.

[28] D.R. Carr, 'The Problem of Urban Patriciates: Office Holders in Fifteenth Century Salisbury', *Wiltshire Archaeological and Natural History Magazine*, lxxxiii (1990), 128, 133, n. 98, 135; *VCH Wiltshire*, vi. 98–9.

[29] *VCH Wiltshire*, vi. 94–136, esp. 95, 99, 100; Fanny Street, 'The Relations of the Bishops and Citzens of Salisbury (New Sarum) between 1225 and 1612', *Wiltshire Archaeological Magazine*, xxxix (1915–17), 185–257, 319–22.

as small as Orford had had a charter since the time of Henry III, enabling it to govern itself, and kings like Edward IV gave charters of incorporation or other privileges to towns that could prove responsible government by prescription, such concessions were denied to Bury and Salisbury, despite their prosperity.[30] The inhabitants were bitter about this discrimination. In Bury's case, its abbey acted as a screen between its townsmen and the king, sometimes literally, as when the abbot blocked the king's summons for representatives from the town to parliament, an act which, over the centuries, had had a cumulatively disastrous effect on the town's freedom. Salisbury did return MPs and had acquired a common seal, but Bury had neither of these privileges, and although the town may not have cared over much about MPs in the early fourteenth century, or even about a common seal, the lack of such privileges was painfully damaging to the town's self-esteem by the reign of Edward IV.[31]

Both towns had a guild merchant. Salisbury's was re-founded in 1306 in the religious and social guise of the guild of St. George, with about 300 members, and in due course this guild became a recipient of land and other bequests. The guild merchant at Bury dated from the twelfth century and was re-founded as the Candlemas Guild in exactly the same way as Salisbury's, probably shortly after the ferocious struggle with the abbey in 1327. These guilds provided the inhabitants with a means of meeting together socially and for worship. The landed estate of St. George's at Salisbury survived the dissolution of the guilds in 1548 as did that of the Candlemas Guild of Bury, because their property was held on behalf of the commonalty and not for superstitious religious uses. In Bury the guildhall was linked especially to the alderman and understood to be his preserve and in the convictions of the town's leaders the Candlemas Guild was identifiable with their commonalty.[32]

Bury prospered in the Yorkist period, although it was less wealthy than in the twelfth century. It had attracted outside investment in property, notably from Sir Thomas Cook, one of the wealthiest drapers of London, perhaps to house his cloth-workers, for his family had maintained strong contacts with the Suffolk cloth trade.[33] In 1477 its guild of weavers of woollen cloth and linen had twenty-nine

---

[30] Weinbaum, *Incorporation of Boroughs*, 132–3; A.F. Sutton, '"Peace, Love and Unity": Richard III's Charters to His Towns', in *The Yorkist Age: Proceedings of the 2011 Harlaxton Symposium*, ed. Hannes Kleineke and Christian Steer (Donington, 2013), 122–3 (examples of Edward's acknowledgement of prescriptive rights); HMC, *Reports on MSS in Various Collections*, iv (1907), 256–7.

[31] Lobel, *The Borough*, 129–30, 136, 146–7.

[32] Salisbury's guild of St. George: *VCH Wiltshire*, vi. 97, 132–3, and Street, 'Relations', 217–18. Members enjoyed the trading privileges of the town, and its fees were shared out, with the community receiving a quarter, the mayor an eighth, and the rest going to the bishop and bailiff. Bury's Candlemas Guild: Lobel, *The Borough*, 77–82, 147–9; *Accounts of the Feoffees*, ed. Statham, pp. xviii–xxix. Bury claims its guildhall as the oldest provincial civic building in England; the Guildhall Project, set up in 2012, hopes to elucidate its history and revivify the building.

[33] Sutton, 'Sir Thomas Cook', 107. Cook sold his Bury property to John Marlborough, the MP for Norwich in 1484 who had property at Clare, and who is probably to be identified as the son-in-law mentioned in the will of Margaret Odiham, benefactor of the Candlemas Guild, see Hannes Kleineke and Charles Moreton, 'A Disputed Election to Richard III's Parliament', *The Ricardian*, xix (2009), 32–5, and *Accounts of the Feoffees*, ed. Statham, p. xxi.

masters and this meant that twenty-nine households were major producers of cloth, employing not only their wives and children but also journeymen and apprentices. Each master was allowed no more than four looms, implying that a total of 116 looms could have been operating in the town in Edward IV's reign.[34] Bury was far below Salisbury in terms of wealth, for the city had twice as many master weavers (sixty-eight in 1474), and ranked in the top ten of English towns. It was famous for its fine woollen cloth and especially its ray.[35] How much political weight the guilds of Bury had is debatable: nothing is known of any guild other than the weavers', and yet it is likely there were tailors, as at Salisbury, and Bury's tailors may have numbered half the total members of that city's flourishing guild (forty-four in 1474; fifty-four in 1481).[36]

Salisbury had the wrong bishop to quarrel with in the reign of Edward IV. Richard Beauchamp (1450–81) was claimed as a kinsman by the king, he was rich and cultivated, and it was he who secured the canonization of St. Osmund of Salisbury after the campaign had ground to a halt in the bureaucracy of the papal curia. He became a great friend of Edward IV and it was they who designed and rebuilt St. George's Chapel at Windsor – Beauchamp's device of a snail crawls among the stone tracery. Out to fight this bishop was the wealthy wool merchant and property owner, John Hall, who cut his teeth negotiating a petition to Henry VI for a charter of incorporation.[37] The first trial of strength in the reign of Edward IV was actually won by the citizens of Salisbury although the bishop's rights over the city remained intact.[38] The next phase began in 1465 and was over property granted by the bishop to another merchant benefactor of the city, who was a personal rival of Hall, the wealthy tailor, William Swayn. The city claimed the land and petitioned the king against the bishop. This issue was soon overshadowed, however, by the demands that the city should govern itself and be freed of the bishop's veto over the appointment of its mayor. The royal council deliberated – and it is clear that Edward IV was prepared to listen. The bishop presented his case, and John Hall behaved so badly in front of the king and council that he was thrown into prison. The king ordered Salisbury to elect another mayor; the citizens delayed and sent new deputations to the king; months went by and a new mayor was at last elected, but Hall refused to stand down. The matter went before the king's council when Edward visited Salisbury in 1469, four years after the original petition, but the complexities were not resolved, and from October 1470 to April 1471 Edward was in exile. Negotiations re-opened when he returned. The sticking point was the

---

[34] For the ordinances of the weavers, 1477: HMC, *Fourteenth Report*, App. viii: *The Manuscripts of the Corporation of Bury St Edmunds* (1895), 133–8.

[35] John Hare, 'Salisbury: The Economy of a Fifteenth-Century Provincial Capital', *Southern History*, xxxi (2009), 3–8, 11; *VCH Wiltshire*, vi. 133, counts 66 weavers.

[36] For Tailors, Hare, 'Salisbury', 4–5, 22; Charles Haskins, *The Ancient Trade Guilds and Companies of Salisbury* (Salisbury, 1912), 105–8, 118–19 (1461 royal charter to tailors, confirmed by the bishop 1462), and *VCH Wiltshire*, vi. 134–5 (the Tailors were the only guild of sufficient wealth to have its own pageant, along with the Weavers).

[37] R.G. Davies, 'Richard Beauchamp', *Oxford DNB*, iv. 595–6; D.R. Carr, 'John Halle (d.1479)', *ibid.*, xxiv. 683; A.F. Sutton and Livia Visser-Fuchs, 'Edward IV's Tomb and Chantry', in A.F. Sutton, Livia Visser-Fuchs and R.A. Griffiths, *The Royal Funerals of the House of York at Windsor* (2005), 93–110.

[38] It partly concerned favours conferred by the king on the city in gratitude for its financial support at the beginning of his reign: Street, 'Relations', 229–30.

demand that the mayor be elected freely by the citizens and not be subordinated to the bishop's bailiff. The bishop was supported by his charters and the judgment of the king in council and his justices inevitably declared for the bishop in 1472. Salisbury's belligerents continued to fight and found themselves accused of contempt. They had to submit. The legal costs had been enormous, and the bishop was still lord of the city.[39] The regular involvement of the king's council shows Edward's concern that a rich and vocal town should be denied its self-government at a time when legal opinion held that prescriptive rights were valid; but prescriptive rights lost in the face of charters of lordship.

The legal situation of Salisbury was an object lesson for Bury, but the townsmen under the leadership of the rich and cultivated John Smith were not opposing an aristocratic and learned bishop but the rather commonplace men who were abbots of Bury at this date. Over his long career, Smith had undoubtedly learnt how to win arguments with the abbots and devise how to construct a charity to benefit his town despite the abbey's rule. It was taxation of the town by the abbey which sparked the first round of a significant campaign for greater independence. In the ten years between 1469 and 1479 three abbots died, and each new abbot cost the town a tribute of 100 silver marks (£66 13s. 4d.), known as 'cope-silver'. Abbot John Bohun died in February 1470 and by 2 March Robert Coote of Ixworth had been elected abbot in his place.[40] On 10 September John Smith made a conveyance of the first group of properties which he intended for his endowment of the alderman and burgesses, to Alderman Robert Gardiner and twenty-four feoffees, who undoubtedly represented the most wealthy and influential men of Bury, including several past aldermen. The properties were mostly in the area of Barton and the deed was made and dated at Barton – outside the boundary of the borough and the direct control of the abbey – where all these men were gathered along with a good number of the gentry elite of Suffolk who acted as witnesses. These witnesses were headed by Sir John Howard, now Lord Howard (so important in the Yorkist administration of East Anglia), Sir Thomas Waldegrave, Sir Robert Chamberlain and Sir Walter Trumpington, with a long list of esquires: John Broughton, John Clopton, Roger Drury and his son, John, Thomas Drury, William Allington, William Lee, Robert Harleston, Thomas Skargill, Henry Straunge, Thomas Hartshorne, Thomas Higham with his sons, Thomas and Clement, William Gedding, John Bokenham, Richard Coote, Roger and John Jerweys, along with the undesignated John Cocket of Ampton and his son, John, Walter Cockett of Ingham,

---

[39] In June 1474 the bishop met the citizens, they submitted and he made certain concessions. Rioting still troubled Salisbury but its mayors and rulers now knew that they must keep the king's peace or face punishment: Robert Benson and Henry Hatcher, *Old and New Sarum or Salisbury*, in *The History of Modern Wiltshire*, ed. R.C. Hoare (14 vols., 1822–44), iv. 161–84; Street, 'Relations', 237–55. One must reject Street's idea (p. 255) that Edward IV was 'unable to bring pressure to bear on so powerful a magnate' as Bishop Beauchamp – the charters represented the king's law.

[40] *CPR, 1467–77*, pp. 183, 186: John 'Boon' and Robert Coote or 'Ixworth'. The latter is also called Robert Schot on the south-east buttress of Ixworth church tower where he is recorded as a benefactor: Sylvia Colman, 'The Arcitecture, Fittings and Furnishings of St. Mary the Virgin, the Parish Church of Ixworth, Suffolk' (leaflet).

John Tillott, Roger Page, Robert Parman, John Bacon 'and others'.[41] The inclusion of John Clopton, the Highams and a Coote can be noted. The names reveal the extent of Smith's connections throughout East Anglia, and how he was buttressing his gifts against the abbey and taking no chances. The income from the lands was to assist in the payment of the cope-silver whenever it fell due, but as Smith was to receive this while he lived, it can be taken as certain that he alone paid the 100 marks due on Robert Coote's election as abbot.[42] He was about seventy years old at this time, he had already provided for his son and his daughter's family, and he could afford it.[43]

On *the same day* a document listing certain customs of Bury was finalised by Alderman Gardiner and his fellow townsmen – presumably the same townsmen that met at Barton. The document contained some wishful thinking, for it began by declaring Bury to be an 'ancient borough'. It went on to emphasise the role of the alderman as the annually-elected ruler of the town, chosen at the guildhall from among the greatest men of the town, and only then presented to the abbot, whose veto was not mentioned. Robert Gardiner and his fellows went on to assert that the guildhall was the preserve of the alderman along with its garden and tenements, and these with other rents and forfeits supported the office. His seat was at the right-hand of the bailiff, with all the burgesses present seated on the high bench; he could stand in for the bailiff in his absence. It was he, along with a body of at least twelve advisors, who admitted new burgesses to the freedom of the town; he summoned this advisory body and consulted it over all important matters concerning the community. And so on through all the rights they considered belonged to the town. The careful use of the word 'burgess' emphasised their insistence that Bury was still a borough. The most significant words of this document was the declaration that it was the alderman's duty to fight diligently against all usurpations and correct all violations and harms done to the liberty and status of the town (*Et aldermannus ... debet pugnare diligentes* [sic] *contra usurpationes et libertatum ac status dictae villae violationes seu laesiones et eas corrigere*).[44] Stirring words, but this is how Gardiner, Thurston, John Smith and all the other past aldermen saw themselves: heroic figures defending their liberties.

There has been some debate about the purpose of this document, and whether it was merely a declaration of rights and privileges made more as a reminder for the

---

[41] The feoffees were all Bury men and included John Ayleward (past alderman), Thomas Brette, William 'Thweyte' (past alderman), Henry Banyard, Clement Drury, John Foster, William Bunting and Andrew Skarbot: *Wills and Inventories*, ed. Tymms, 68. *Accounts of the Feoffees*, ed. Statham, p. xxi. I am most grateful to Margaret Statham for giving me a complete list of the witnesses.

[42] His payment of the cope-silver three times out of his pocket was set out in the bidding prayer for his obit, recorded in one of the Feoffees of Bury St. Edmund's books recording wills, etc., Bury RO, H1/2/1, f. 5; details kindly provided by Margaret Statham.

[43] Smith's age is based on the fact he first served as alderman in 1442–3; perhaps the John Smith who had been alderman in 1423–4 was his father: Lobel, 'A List', 26.

[44] The Customs of 1470 list the alderman's many duties: overseeing matters including street cleaning, weights and measures, the assize of bread and ale, the taking of all fines and forfeits, appointment of porters and gate-keepers. He also had rights of arrest and imprisonment and as constable he appointed the watch and assessed and collected all taxes – only he collected taxes, not the bailiff, unless the alderman, burgesses and constable were agreeable; and he presented the chaplain to the chantry of Robert Eriswell in the church of St. James. The Customs of 1470 only exist in an 18th-century copy, printed by Trenholme, 'English Monastic Boroughs', 98–102 (quotation at p. 99); his text is criticised by Lobel, *The Borough*, 159, n. 5, and she prints passages he omitted, 181.

burgesses themselves and not as a document to be used to demand further self-government from the new abbot. If there had been any definite plans to appeal to Edward IV at this time they came to nothing, for September 1470 was the worst possible date to choose for such a campaign. The king was forced to flee England in October and only regained his kingdom in April 1471. A more prosaic and likely interpretation of the document is suggested by the fact that the signature of Abbot Robert Coote was at its end alongside that of Alderman Robert Gardiner. If Abbot Coote accepted this rather belligerent document, the townsmen of Bury may have unwisely assumed they were beginning to have their own way, but what one mild abbot might weakly accept, a more militant successor could indignantly refuse.[45]

On 10 July 1470, after Edward was safely king again,[46] John Smith conveyed another portfolio of properties, mostly in Rougham, to the current alderman, John Forster, Robert Gardiner and many other townsmen who had figured in the deed of 1470; the grant was made at Rougham. A further tripartite deed of 10 August that year reinforced these two grants of Barton and Rougham, and was made at Bury. This set out in full Smith's intentions to relieve the alderman, burgesses and all inhabitants of Bury from the cope-silver and other taxes for ever. In return, his obit was to be kept in perpetuity.[47] Smith may have done this in anticipation of Abbot Coote's death. Coote died shortly before 14 September 1474, after scarcely five years in office, possibly a reflection of his age and frailty. Richard Hengham was elected and in office by the end of September, and another 100 marks, the great symbol of subjection, had to be found. It was John Smith who paid this sum, for the second of the three times carefully recorded in his epitaph.[48]

At some point there was a physical disturbance; certain townsmen may have been thirsting for a battle. Hengham seems to have been a more forceful character than Coote and as a doctor of canon law he may have been determined that the abbey should have all its dues. He could have felt threatened by the level of tension in the town and was looking for an excuse once more to try at law the issue of who was master. There was apparently some sort of riot led by Alderman Walter Thurston, who was put into prison by the abbot's men, along with two burgesses, William Sygo and William Clinton, and others unnamed.[49] It was now 1478.

---

[45] Lobel, *The Borough*, 159–60; her assessment that it was Bury's wealth and the unsettled nature of the country which provoked the document is not convincing: *Accounts of the Feoffees*, ed. Statham, p. xx.

[46] Whether any Bury men joined Edward's army before Barnet is not known. The town's position was complicated by the presence of the earl of Oxford, who called his muster of men to fight for Lancaster at Bury on 18 March, while Lord Howard went from Colchester to Edward at London and the route taken by his son, Thomas Howard, is obscure: Scofield, *Edward the Fourth*, i. 577; Crawford, *Yorkist Lord*, 62–3; Ross, *John de Vere*, 64.

[47] *Accounts of the Feoffees*, ed. Statham, p. xxi; *Wills and Inventories*, ed. Tymms, 55–64 (Smith's will), 64–8 (deed of 18 Dec. 1480), 68–73 (tripartite deed 10 Aug. 1473).

[48] *CPR*, 1467–77, pp. 470, 475 (licence to elect and release of temporalities); A.B. Emden, *A Biographical Register of the University of Cambridge to 1500* (Cambridge, 1963), 298. Hengham was D.Cn.L.

[49] All the following events come from the record of the hearing in the exchequer chamber: William Dugdale, *Monasticon Anglicanum*, ed. John Caley *et al.* (6 vols. in 8, 1817–30), iii. 168–9 (the only text that survives is in fact the exemplification of 1480, see n. 58); Lobel, *The Borough*, 160–2, but she misdates some of these events.

Salisbury had lost its case four years before, and such news cannot have failed to travel swiftly along mercantile and clerical lines of communication. In Michaelmas term, Abbot Hengham petitioned the king and his council asserting that Alderman Thurston, the burgesses Sygo and Clinton and other inhabitants of Bury whom he did not name were usurping his rights, had made riot and held illicit conventicles and damaged his franchise; Thurston had appointed keepers of the market, constables and watchmen without asking his consent. The use of the word 'conventicles' is also significantly accurate for that is exactly what had been going on: John Smith had conveyed property to his feoffees at meetings which might be misnamed as 'conventicles' by the suspicious. These conveyances were for the ultimate, impeccable purposes of founding a chantry for the provision of prayers for his soul, and to relieve the town of certain taxes, and the abbot was not, of course, complaining about these purposes, but only about the meetings and consequent plotting he understood by the word 'conventicle', a favourite word of the monks in accusations against the townsmen.[50]

Edward IV in council then ordered the chancellor Thomas Rotherham, bishop of Lincoln, John Russell, bishop of Rochester and keeper of the privy seal, Anthony, Earl Rivers, the queen's brother, John Morton, bishop-elect of Ely, Lord Howard and Sir Thomas Montgomery, the leading men of East Anglia, to summon the justices of England – all the justices of England – together with others learned in the law and examine the matter. This was a most prestigious assembly, and Edward was clearly aiming to have the best advice on the matter. He was not shirking and it can be wondered who was speaking for the town behind the scenes. Probably it was John Smith, who, as already suggested, had links to the king's dead father and to his mother Cecily, the dowager duchess of York and current lady of the honour of Clare. The justices of England sat on the matter in the exchequer chamber. This was where they were used to sit and discuss the most difficult points of law at their own volition, on the king's instructions, or on the orders of the chancellor. Important legal arguments and decisions survive, recorded in the Year Books and elsewhere.[51] On 6 November 1478 the petition of the abbot, the answer of the alderman and burgesses,[52] and the replication of the abbot were read, and the parties were ordered to produce their proofs. The answer of the townsmen dealt in detail with the abbot's twenty-one articles of complaint. The crux of the matter was that the abbot and his lawyers could show charters going back to Cnut and Edward the Confessor and produce accounts of all past trials of strength between the abbey and town, and the townsmen could only allege prescriptive custom and could 'not prove custom or use'. On 14 November the bishops and lords reported to the king and his council that the abbot was lord of the whole town with power of appointing

---

[50] E.g. 1385: Lobel, *The Borough*, 157.
[51] *Select Cases in the Exchequer Chamber Before all the Justices of England, II, 1461–1509*, ed. Mary Hemmant (Selden Society, lxiv, 1945), introduction, *passim*. Lobel, *The Borough*, 160, fails to appreciate the importance of the venue.
[52] Fourteen complaints against the abbey survive: Trenholme, 'English Monastic Boroughs', 102–4, undated and in the same late 18th-century MS which contains the 1470 Customs (see n. 44); these were identified by Lobel, *The Borough*, 161. The abbot's answer to these 14 complaints (and seven others) were also identified and printed by Lobel, *The Borough*, 162, 182–5 (found by her in TNA, STAC2/22/6). There are some reservations to be expressed about her identification and date of these complaints, see below n. 58.

and removing the alderman and all other officers, and 'the townsmen never had union of commonalty nor community incorporate; they have never had a common seal, and have no head or captain but the lord abbot'. They were duly barred from their claim.[53] Furthermore, Thurston and his fellows 'had made riot'. The king thereupon decreed that Sygo and Clinton, who were apparently representing the town in London, be put in the Fleet prison for riot until a fine had been paid to the abbot. Thurston, who was already in prison in Bury on the abbot's orders and had found security for his fine, was dismissed.[54]

Edward IV had done his best: the full panoply of the royal council and the justices in the exchequer chamber had sat upon the case but not even the finest judges of England could find a way round the abbey's charters. It was the same result as Salisbury's, but reached in an even more conspicuous manner. Every one of the rights and customs claimed by the townsmen derived from a grant of an abbot in the past for the convenience of the government of the town, and by the abbot's favour; the townsmen had no rights by themselves. Edward's support, however, had clearly shown that times had changed and that the received legal opinion was in favour of prescriptive right. The king could tell the abbot that although he might hold all the charters, he was to conduct himself well towards the king's townsmen.

Abbot Hengham died in 1478, the precise date unknown, and his successor was Thomas Rattlesden,[55] who presumably came from the village of that name, where John Smith owned property which he left to his daughter's family.[56] Nothing is known of Rattlesden's character, but it may be significant that he paid for an exemplification, dated 26 April 1480, of the judgment of 1478 in the abbey's favour to be entered on the patent rolls of chancery as a matter of record.[57] In general, however, it is likely that the town and the several contestants settled down once again,[58] and the new abbot could afford to take a more amenable line than his energetic predecessor, the doctor of canon law. John Smith wrote his will in December 1480 once more confirming his gifts to Bury. He died in June 1481 and in September of that year Edward IV licensed the foundation of his chantry and the college of priests in honour of the Holy Name of Jesus.[59] Smith left his best

---

[53] Compare the decision of 1305: Lobel, *The Borough*, 141.
[54] Sources as in n. 49.
[55] No dates of licence to elect or release of temporalities were recorded in the patent rolls.
[56] Smith left the property in Rattlesden to his son-in-law, Richard Yaxley: *Wills and Inventories*, ed. Tymms, 56.
[57] *CPR*, 1476–85, pp. 218–19, exemplification dated 26 April 1480.
[58] At Michaelmas 1479 or 1480, it has been suggested that John Smith, now about 80 years old, was elected alderman and was vetoed by the abbot; the town complained against the abbot's veto, but no further details are known – this is Lobel's interpretation (*The Borough*, 161), citing the 14 complaints printed by Trenholme, 'English Monastic Boroughs', 103, where the use of the veto is undated and the abbot's name is given as *John*. If these articles of complaint were part of the 1478 hearing, as Lobel claims, the veto against Smith must belong to Richard Hengham's abbacy, not Thomas Rattlesden's. It seems more likely, however, to refer to a veto of Smith by an earlier abbot called John (perhaps Bohun in the difficult years of 1460–2). Lobel complicates her reading of this matter by misdating the final judgment of the 1478 case and also Smith's death.
[59] *Wills and Inventories*, ed. Tymms, 55–64; *CPR*, 1476–85, p. 259.

standing cup of silver gilt to the prior of the abbey, who was given certain duties regarding the chantry and was made the overseer of his executors. This was a gift which underlined the probate powers of the sacrist, but also how elite townsmen might conceal their opposition – long years of compromise and argument – behind the courtesies of everyday life. The leading men all knew each other and some of them might be related to monks or to an abbot, for by this date the abbots were rarely men of rank or even great education but tended to be local men from the minor gentry (at best), such as Robert Coote, Richard Hengham and Thomas Rattlesden, or Abbot Bunting (*d*.1511) whose father may have been William Bunting, one of John Smith's feoffees.[60] The case of the men of Bury had been debated before the justices of England in the exchequer chamber with the king and chancellor closely involved. There had been a prestigious trial and although the judgment had replicated earlier decisions, they could now accept that a king, who recognised the value of prescriptive right, had heard their case sympathetically and had not permitted the abbey to cut his subjects off from his justice.

Edward IV continued to take an interest in those towns under the feudal lordship of clergy. In 1479–80, not long after the conclusion of the Bury case, bitter complaints reached his ears concerning Reading Abbey, which like the abbey at Bury dominated its town, its abbot having the power to select its mayor from names presented to him. The complaints were aimed at Abbot John Thorne (1446–86), who was old and ailing, and Edward was not unwilling to interfere. He placed the duties of an inquiry in the hands of Richard Beauchamp, bishop of Salisbury, who had powers of visitation over the abbey. This task was apparently assigned while they were riding together through Reading to Woodstock and it is possible that the complaints were handed to the king as he passed through the town. As with Peterborough, the complaints focused on the abbot's failure to maintain local amenities in his care despite ample endowments: roads, bridges including Caversham Bridge over the Thames, chapels and an almshouse.[61] Beauchamp conducted an energetic last tour of visitation in July and August 1481 and was at Reading Abbey on 10 August, but he died on 18 October, and nothing is known of any settlement of the differences between abbot and town. Beauchamp's successor, Lionel Wydeville, was not long in office and no register survives for him.[62]

Bury could not achieve a victory against its abbey despite the propitious climate of Yorkist England. The town's continued struggle for the technical emblems of self-government, which they largely possessed at a practical level, remains

---

[60] It may have been Thomas Rattlesden who made over certain properties to benefit the inhabitants of Bury in 1491: *Accounts of the Feoffees*, ed. Statham, p. xxi, re the gift of a 99-year lease.

[61] According to a recital of this complaint made in the 1490s nothing much had been done: Beauchamp's successor, Lionel Wydeville, did not apparently take up the challenge; Thomas Langton, Wydeville's successor, was an energetic administrator but nothing is known of his actions. *VCH Berkshire*, ii. 66–8; see A.F. Leach's disposal of the erroneous legends surrounding the town and abbey of this period, 245–9; the mention in the abbey's Almoner's Register, Cotton MS Vespasian E v, f. 48 makes it certain the event of 1479–80 happened. The document reciting the complaints is printed in full: Charles Coates, *The History and Antiquities of Reading* (1802), App. ix.

[62] Davies, 'Richard Beauchamp', *Oxford DNB*. Wiltshire RO, Reg. Beauchamp, vol. 2, f. 41, records his presence at Marlborough on 1 Aug. and Reading Abbey on 10 Aug. but no location for transactions recorded on 23 Aug. or 5 Sept. I am most grateful to Dr. Davies for these references and his advice. I am also grateful to Dr. Rosemary Hayes for her help.

significant and it should be firmly tied to the great endowment it received at this time from John Smith. Smith valued his town enough to endow it with freedoms that a rich man could provide, at the same time as the lawyers conspicuously failed in their challenge to the rule of the abbey. He removed the tyranny of the cope-silver, but the abbot's veto on the appointment of the alderman, the chief man elected by the town, remained.

THE EXCHEQUER INQUISITIONS *POST MORTEM*

Matthew Holford

This paper honours Michael Hicks's contribution to the understanding of the medieval English inquisitions *post mortem* (IPMs), both through his studies of aristocratic families and as director of *Mapping the Medieval Countryside*. This AHRC-funded research project created an online digital edition of the calendared IPMs from 1236 to 1447 and 1485 to 1509. It marked the culmination of almost two decades of recent work on the IPMs which had been initiated by the new series of calendars, for the years 1422–47, under the general editorship of Christine Carpenter. Professor Carpenter's project brought to light a great deal of new information about the production, use and value of the documents, much of which was summarised in her 'General Introduction' to the new series, and elaborated in more detail in the *Companion* volume edited by Professor Hicks.[1] Still more has been uncovered during those stages of *Mapping the Medieval Countryside* which collected supplementary information on jurors, writs and other items for the online edition of *CIPM*, xviii–xxi (covering 1399–1422). The present paper explores discoveries which shed new light on the exchequer files of inquisitions *post mortem*.

The exchequer IPMs are widely used by historians: as is well known, they are sometimes more legible than the main chancery series of IPMs and can be used to supply gaps where the latter are damaged or missing. They also contain some inquisitions not found in the chancery series, notably those taken by the escheator by virtue of his office (*ex officio* or *virtute officii*), without the warrant of a writ.[2] But the archival history of the documents – their origin, purpose and later use – is not well understood, with published sources offering brief accounts that are variously contradictory, confusing and mistaken.[3] Fuller understanding of that history has significant implications for our understanding of exchequer procedure and of the IPMs themselves.

---

[1] *CIPM*, xxii, 'General Introduction'; *The Fifteenth-Century Inquisitions Post Mortem: A Companion*, ed. Michael Hicks (Woodbridge, 2012).

[2] These do not, as is sometimes stated or implied, occur *exclusively* in the exchequer series. Practice was apparently as in the seventeenth century – 'the Escheater may at his choice return them either into the Chancery or Exchequer': James Ley, *A Learned Treatise Concerning Wards and Liveries* (1642), 73. For an example of an *ex officio* inquisition returned to chancery see *CIPM*, xxiii. 304.

[3] *Guide to the Contents of the Public Record Office*, ed. M.S. Giuseppi (3 vols., 1963–8), i. 59–60; below, n. 13. The most up-to-date information is contained in the detailed introductions to the typescript class lists housed (at the time of writing) in the Map and Large Document Reading Room; unfortunately, little of this information has been included in the National Archives online catalogue.

It is at times a complicated story, due both to the original nature of the records and to their later history, and an initial summary will clarify what follows. Escheators' records were radically reorganised by the Public Record Office in the early twentieth century in ways that have made it difficult to understand the original nature of the archive. It is clear, however, that from the second quarter of the fourteenth century the exchequer was usually supplied with texts of the inquisitions taken by an escheator, which were used to verify and audit his account. If these inquisitions had been ordered by a writ from chancery then the original inquisitions were returned to chancery and a copy was sent to the exchequer. If the inquisitions were taken *ex officio*, usually the original inquisition itself was returned to the exchequer. These inquisitions were stored in the exchequer with the escheator's particulars of account: the collection of accounts, inquisitions and related documents comprised the exchequer *escaetria* or escheators' records.[4] Their historical interest and importance is threefold. First, the documents shed light on the process by which escheators rendered account, and hence on the exchequer's oversight of royal officials and crown rights. Second, references to the use of the archive, principally for assessing relief and valuing wardship, again reveal the interest taken in feudal revenues, and how a documentary archive could be used to maximise them. Finally, the exchequer copies of IPMs illuminate the process by which inquisitions *post mortem* themselves were held and their findings written up. This is because a good number of them are not, in fact, exact copies. For most of the fourteenth and fifteenth centuries inquisitions were supplied to the exchequer from two sources. Some were precise transcripts made by chancery clerks from the original IPMs returned to chancery. Others were prepared by escheators or their staff, and while some of these are also exact copies, others are drafts or variant texts, often with important differences from the texts returned to chancery or with significant corrections. As we shall see, these corrections and variations make the exchequer inquisitions particularly valuable in this period.

I

We must begin by describing briefly the current organisation of escheators' records in the National Archives, even while emphasising that this does not reflect the original nature of the archive. For the period before 1485, there are four relevant record classes: escheators' accounts (E136), escheators' files: inquisitions *post mortem* (E149), enrolments of escheators' inquisitions (E152) and escheators' files (E153). This structure was created in the early twentieth century when the main series of *Calendars of Inquisitions Post Mortem* was begun,[5] and replaced an earlier arrangement produced by Joseph Hunter in the mid nineteenth century. By

---

[4] This sense of *escaetaria* is not recorded in the *Dictionary of Medieval Latin from British Sources*, ed. R.E. Latham *et al.* (17 vols., 1975–2013), *s.v.*, but see for example TNA, IND1/6992 (c.1444) headed '*Repertorium escaetr' de tempore regis Henrici sexti*'. All unpublished documents cited are in TNA.

[5] The first volume was published in 1904; the second series, for Henry VII, had commenced earlier, the first volume appearing in 1898.

1857 Hunter had sorted and calendared the extant inquisitions.[6] Using the evidence of escheators' accounts and a sixteenth-century inventory, he attempted to recreate the original structure of the archive, by grouping together all the extant exchequer documents associated with a particular escheator: accounts, inquisitions *post mortem*, other inquisitions, writs, indentures and so on. The twentieth-century rearrangement removed inquisitions *post mortem* to the new class E149, together with related documents such as assignments of dower and some writs.[7] The new class was organised according to tenant-in-chief rather than escheator: all the documents for a particular tenant were grouped together, in roughly chronological order. However, rolls and membranes containing more than one inquisition were, in general, filed separately, and organised according to escheator rather than tenant, in the new class E152.[8] The documents which remained in Hunter's files after the removal of items to E149 and E152 now form the escheators' files (E153). All three series (E149, E152, E153) have been added to as a result of subsequent cataloguing of unsorted records.[9] For the period after 1485, however, Hunter's arrangement was largely unchanged. The escheators' accounts for this period are also in E136, but the escheators' inquisitions (E150) are still organised by escheatry (not by tenant-in-chief), with IPMs alongside other 'miscellaneous' inquisitions.

An example will make the pre-1485 reorganisation clearer. Hunter gathered together six inquisitions associated with John Blount, escheator in Gloucestershire 1427–8: four IPMs and two 'miscellaneous' inquisitions. (Blount's account was missing.) The records are now dispersed among the three modern series:

No. in Hunter's arrangement	Content	Present location
1	IPM of John Berkeley, knight (*CIPM*, xxiii. 109)	E149/139/13, m. 1
2	IPM of Elizabeth who was the wife of Henry Fitzhugh, knight (*CIPM*, xxiii. 81)	E152/10/516, m. 1
3	IPM of Margery Dynghull (*CIPM*, xxiii. 7)	E152/10/517, m. 1
4	IPM of Elizabeth who was the wife of Richard Riall (*CIPM*, xxiii. 228)	E149/142/9, m. 1
5	Inquisition into vacancy of Abingdon Abbey	E153/874, m. 1
6	Inquisition into goods and chattels of outlaws	E153/874, m. 2

---

[6] *Annual Report of the Deputy Keeper of the Public Records*, i (1839), Appendix, 122, 130, 137, 139; iv (1843), 7; vi (1845), Appendix I, 7, 20; vii (1846), 12–13; viii (1848), 17; x (1849), Appendix II; xi (1850), 7; xii (1851), 13–14; xiii (1852), 13; xv (1854), 6; xvi (1855), 9; xvii (1856), 6; xviii (1857), 8. Hunter's calendars for the period before 1485 are TNA, OBS1/298–300, 301–4; an index, E501/15–18, is at the time of writing kept in the TNA Map Room at Kew.

[7] PRO4/9/31, 40.

[8] This series must originally have extended no later than 1485; a document from Henry VIII's reign (E152/10/565) was transferred at some point from E239.

[9] Knowledge of these additions must be gleaned from notes on the guards of the original documents or from obsolete class lists, which are often incomplete. For E153, see OBS1/1405. For E149, see OBS1/1410 and (e.g.) E149/85/11, m. 6, added 1925 (*CIPM*, xviii. 1062); E149/249/1–45. For E152, see OBS1/1408–9.

Although the modern arrangement can be convenient, it is much less satisfactory than Hunter's. The reorganisation of inquisitions was not always thorough, so that 'stray' exchequer IPMs are still sometimes to be found in the escheators' files (E153).[10] A few, in fact, are still attached to the escheators' original accounts (E136).[11] Many of the enrolments in E152, and some documents in E149, contain 'miscellaneous' inquisitions alongside IPMs.[12] And the creation of two classes of exchequer IPMS, E149 and E152, has caused needless confusion, leading some historians to assume erroneously that two distinct series of exchequer IPMs, with distinct origins and purposes, always existed.[13] It bears emphasis that the division of material between these different classes seems to have been based only on the documents' size and format and often involved separating documents that were previously associated, not only in Hunter's arrangement but in the medieval archive. Hunter, it is again worth emphasising, did attempt to reassemble the medieval archive and the accuracy of his work is often confirmed by other sources. In the case of the inquisitions of John Blount, escheator, listed above, a mid-fifteenth-century enrolment of escheators' records confirms that all the inquisitions were then stored 'in the bag of the particulars of account of the said John', and a sixteenth-century inventory records the same arrangement.[14] Both inventories also confirm that documents from the escheatry of Thomas Manningham (Bedfordshire and Buckinghamshire, 1426–7), again now divided between E149 and E152, were originally stored together.[15]

II

The enrolment and inventory suggest that the original context of the exchequer IPMs, at least by the fifteenth century, was with the escheators' accounts, and this is confirmed by other sources. By the middle of the fourteenth century (and probably, as we shall see, from an earlier date) the purpose of the exchequer escheators' inquisitions was to serve as a voucher for the escheator's account at audit. John Tretherf, for example, when making account for his office as escheator of Devon and Cornwall (1427–8) answered for £3 1s. 8d. from a third part and half of a third part of the manor of Ipplepen for the seventy-four days it had been in his custody.[16] This was a proportion of the £15 at which the manor had been extended in the IPM and was justified with reference to a transcript of the IPM: 'as is contained in a transcript of the inquisition and extent taken by writ of *diem clausit*

---

[10] *CIPM*, xxvi. 170 (see table above); E153/313, m. 30, damaged but apparently the exchequer copy of *CIPM*, xiv. 141.

[11] E136/74/7: seven membranes attached to the account, including exchequer copies of *CIPM*, xxii. 522, 654 and a copy of the IPM for John Lincoln, for which the chancery copy is no longer extant.

[12] Examples include E149/79/10, m. 1 (exchequer copy of *Cal. Inq. Misc.*, vii. 197 (p. 97); E149/82/15 (*ibid.*, 286); E149/92/14, mm. 1, 3 (*ibid.*, 393); E152/8/360, dorse, no. 1 (*ibid.*, 29).

[13] For example, *CIPM*, xxii, 'General introduction', 24, 27; *Cal. Inq. Misc.* iv. pp. vii–viii (arguing that the exchequer enrolments were created as estreats of chancery miscellaneous inquisitions); Mary McGuinness, 'Documents in the Public Record Office, II. Inquisitions Post Mortem', *The Amateur Historian*, vi (1963–5), 235–42 (at 237).

[14] E152/6/260; E164/48, f. 225.

[15] E152/6/260; 10/513; E164/48, f. 191v; E149/137/5, m. 2 (*CIPM*, xxii. 682, 728).

[16] E136/33/4, Cornwall, new escheats.

extremum and returned to chancery, which [transcript] remains with these particulars of account'. The account contained similar entries referring to transcripts of the other IPMs taken by Tretherf by royal writ and to a transcript of an inquisition into idiocy taken *ex officio* which had also been returned to chancery.[17] Also with the particulars of account were nine original inquisitions *ex officio* into the goods and chattels of outlaws. In total seventeen inquisitions, both transcripts and originals, were presented with the account and afterwards stored with it. All but one were still there about twenty years later when an enrolment of their contents was made, although all are now lost.[18]

The process recorded in Tretherf's account is well documented from the 1340s onwards. By the end of that decade the escheators' accounts almost always justified their valuations with reference to transcripts or original inquisitions presented with the account.[19] Before the 1340s, however, the situation is less clear. One possibility was put forward by Sir Henry Maxwell-Lyte, the deputy keeper of the Public Records, who suggested that transcript or duplicate IPMs had been supplied to the exchequer for accounting purposes from the very beginnings of the inquisition *post mortem* process in the thirteenth century.[20] If this was so, however, references to such transcripts are surprisingly scarce for most of the thirteenth century, as are transcripts themselves. Many of the early inquisitions now filed in E149 and E152 are not transcripts but original inquisitions forwarded to the exchequer from chancery, or taken by exchequer writ and returned to the exchequer.[21]

The requirement that inquisitions should be duplicated is apparently first mentioned in exchequer ordinances of 1325 and 1326. That of 1325 required some (but not all) escheators to make two copies of inquisitions *post mortem* taken according to writs of *diem clausit extremum*, each sealed by the jurors. One was to be returned to chancery 'as is customary', the other was to be kept by the escheator and presented at the exchequer when he made his account.[22] The ordinance of 1326, on the other hand, required escheators to supply the exchequer with enrolments of inquisitions and extents at their Easter and Michaelmas proffers, each enrolment containing copies of inquisitions taken up to that point.[23] These enrolments were to be used in auditing the escheators' accounts ('for the greater charging of the escheators on their accounts') and in determining reliefs. It is unclear, however, if these ordinances were intended to introduce new administrative practices, or to re-establish practices that had been disrupted by the reform of the escheatries in

---

[17] The chancery copy is *CIPM*, xxiii. 304.
[18] E152/6/260, rots. 11d–15. Apparently already missing by this date was a transcript of an inquisition before John Juyn and others into Tywardreath Priory.
[19] E357/2–4, *passim*.
[20] *CIPM*, i. p. viii.
[21] E.g. E149/5/2, 3, 7, 9, 11, 12; 8/11, m. 2 (*CIPM*, vii. 562).
[22] E368/97, rot. 101, cited (but not accurately summarised) in Mark Buck, *Politics, Finance and the Church in the Reign of Edward II: Walter Stapeldon, Treasurer of England* (Cambridge, 1983), 169.
[23] *The Red Book of the Exchequer*, ed. Hubert Hall (3 vols., 1896), iii. 944–7; *CFR*, iii. 405–6. Re-issued in 1327 when escheatries north and south of Trent were restored: *Calendar of Memoranda Rolls (Exchequer) Preserved in the Public Record Office: Michaelmas 1326–Michaelmas 1327* (1968), no. 1694 (22 July 1327).

1323.[24] Numerous exchequer enrolments of IPMs are documented from the 1290s, 1300s and 1310s, as well as one from the 1280s, each enrolment apparently containing an escheator's inquisitions for a regnal or accounting year, but the original purpose and archival context of these enrolments is not fully clear.[25] In the fifteenth century some at least seem to have been stored not with other escheators' records, but 'in the bag of evidences relating to relief'.[26] These are perhaps to be identified with the 'certificates for sureties of reliefs' mentioned in fourteenth-century sources which apparently contained transcripts of IPMs.[27] The memoranda roll for 1337–8 refers to 'a roll of inquisitions' taken before Malcolm de Harle, escheator, in 23 Edward I (1294–5), which was then in the lord treasurer's remembrancer, and another roll for 21 Edward I (1292–3), which was in the king's remembrancer: these were not presumably part of the same archive.[28]

The exchequer did, therefore, have copies of IPMs prior to the ordinances of 1325–6, typically enrolments rather than separate transcripts of individual IPMs. However it is presently unclear both when the practice of enrolment began, and exactly how the enrolments were used and archived. It was perhaps only after the ordinances of 1325–6 that copies of IPMs came to be filed with the escheators' accounts and a body of *escaetria* created. Only from the 1340s, as we saw above, is there clear documentation of how the exchequer IPM transcripts were used at the audit of account and afterwards stored, and even from this date there is some uncertainty about whether all escheators did in fact return copies to the exchequer, and about how complete the exchequer archive was.

In its present state the archive is undoubtedly fragmentary: the fifteenth-century enrolment mentioned above records whole series of inquisitions no longer extant, such as those of John Tretherf, mentioned above, or those from the escheatry of Guy Roucliff in Yorkshire (1426).[29] Many of these were still extant in the sixteenth century when they were recorded in an inventory or repertory of escheators' records which covers in detail the period from 1377 to the 1570s.[30] This inventory too reveals a much fuller archive than that which survives today, for example recording an exchequer copy of the Devon IPM for Warin Lercedekne, taken by William Hody, escheator, which is no longer extant.[31] Nevertheless the archive was still far from complete when the inventory was compiled: Hody's particulars of account were missing, as was the canvas pouch in which account and inquisitions were formerly stored, and there were no exchequer copies of other inquisitions taken by him. The archive was apparently in some disarray when the inventory was compiled – corrections and insertions are frequent. Probably, however, it had never

[24] S.T. Gibson, 'The Escheatries 1327–41', *EHR*, xxxvi (1921), 218–25.
[25] E.g. E368/177, rots. 88, 89, 95; 190, rot. 95; 200, Trin. fines, rot. 2. An extant roll of transcripts for 21 Edward I is E152/1/4, which refers to the roll for 22 Edward I on m. 15d (*quia est de anno xxijo et ibi irrotulatur*). The other extant roll is E152/1/1. The rolls for 23 and 24 Edward I are referred to in E368/110, rot. 61; 176, rot. 130d.
[26] E368/176, rot. 130 ('a roll of transcripts of various inquisitions *post mortem citra Trentam*, 32 Edward I, in the bag of evidences relating to relief', a similar roll, 6 Edward II, and another 1 Edward II).
[27] E.g. E368/103, rot. 74; 110, rot. 67.
[28] E368/110, rot. 61.
[29] E152/6/260, *passim*.
[30] E164/48, *passim*.
[31] *Ibid.*, f. 110v; cf. *CIPM*, xviii. 446.

been fully complete in the sense of containing a copy of every chancery IPM. A small number of escheators failed to account, like Robert Wolashull of Worcestershire, for whose office, unsurprisingly, no exchequer inquisitions are extant.[32] Nor can we be certain that duplicate inquisitions existed for all those who did account. While it seems to have been the ideal that transcripts should be made of all chancery IPMs, it remains uncertain how far this was realised in practice.

III

Even if it was never fully complete, the archive potentially formed a major source of information about the crown's feudal rights and revenues. Exactly how this potential was exploited needs further research, but the principal uses of the archive at least seem clear. First, there is some evidence that earlier IPMs were consulted when an escheator's account was audited (that is, in addition to the duplicate IPMs submitted by the escheator himself). John Tretherf, encountered above, was charged with an additional sum from the manor of Ipplepen; this was because an auditor believed that the valuation in the IPM he returned did not include twenty-six marks of assize rent mentioned in an extent of 1426.[33] Such corrections are, admittedly, uncommon, although it is unclear whether this indicates that earlier accounts were not routinely checked, or rather that discrepancies were not usually found.[34]

We can be more certain that the escheators' records were regularly consulted as part of the assessment of relief, from at least the reign of Edward III. Proceedings of 1337–8 used 'rolls of inquisitions' from 1292–3 and 1294–5, among other sources, to confirm the holdings of William Staunford.[35] Similar proceedings in 1418 used the transcript of an inquisition in the escheators' bags of account, again with other sources, to verify the holdings of Hugh Halsham.[36] The archive was similarly used to check information when wardships were valued. In 1404, for example, the Dorset lands of Roger Mortimer, earl of March, which had been granted to Hugh Waterton, were valued according to inquisitions and extents taken in 1398–9, of which there were transcripts in the escheator's bag of accounts. The same year when considering the wardship of the lands of Maud, widow of Sir Roger Clifford, the barons consulted an IPM transcript of 1344–5, which contained a higher valuation than the IPM returned in 1403, and used it to value the wardship.[37]

---

[32] For escheators' particulars of account missing c.1446, see IND1/6992. This relates to original, not enrolled accounts, as is clear from the references to 'bundles' for certain regnal years.

[33] E136/33/4 (attached membrane); cf. *CIPM*, xxii. 564.

[34] E136/58/1, corrected with reference to an extent taken by John Routh, escheator (cf. *CIPM*, xvii. 1062); so too E136/57/1; 125/1, where the values are corrected with reference to a 'schedule of the values of Margaret, duchess of Norfolk'.

[35] E368/110, rots. 61 (transcript of *CIPM*, iii. 221 in 'a roll of inquisitions' taken 1294–5, no longer extant), 64.

[36] E368/190, rot. 96 (the transcript is extant, E149/105/1, m. 3, but not noted in the printed calendar, *CIPM*, xx. 348).

[37] E368/177, rot. 19.

Yet the use made of the archive, particularly of the inquisitions, should probably not be exaggerated. It is clear that the transcripts were only one resource that the exchequer used during both procedures. For assessments of relief it was more common for exchequer officials to consult memoranda rolls or records of feudal aids, and it was perhaps most common for new extents to be made if the valuation of a wardship was in doubt.[38] Information in the *escaetria* was not highly 'discoverable': surviving detailed repertories of the records date only from the sixteenth century.[39] An enrolment of escheators' inquisitions for the years 1425–8 was produced early in Henry VI's reign, but it is unclear why. It was later annotated to record tenures in chief, but its contents are too miscellaneous for this to have been its original purpose.[40]

IV

We must now consider in more detail the processes through which the exchequer inquisitions were created: in particular, by whom and when were they copied? There are two related issues to consider here: the format of the documents and the clerks involved in writing them. The ordinances of 1325 and 1326 stipulated different kinds of transcript to be presented to the exchequer. The 1325 ordinance referred to duplicates of individual IPMs, sealed by the jurors just like the originals returned to chancery. That of 1326 referred to enrolments of all the IPMs taken by an escheator in a given period. Both formats of document do indeed survive in the archive: transcripts of single inquisitions, each on a separate membrane of parchment (although very rarely with seals attached), and enrolments of multiple inquisitions on one or more membranes. (As we have seen the former are now mostly in the series E149 and the latter in E152.) Sometimes these enrolments comprise lengthy membranes or collections of membranes and contain copies of all the inquisitions taken by an escheator.[41] Sometimes they are smaller, containing copies of only some inquisitions taken by a particular escheator, with copies of the others being found on separate single sheets.[42]

As to the writing of the documents, historians have suggested two alternatives: that the exchequer inquisitions were copied in chancery by chancery clerks, then forwarded to the exchequer, or produced and returned to the exchequer by escheators themselves.[43] Both alternatives seem in fact to have been practiced, possibly at different periods. The ordinances of 1325 and 1326 implied that both duplicates and enrolments of IPMs would be created by the escheator and his

---

[38] E.g. E368/151, *recorda*, Mich. rot. 1d, fines rot. 2d; 178, rot. 127 (reference to accounts of the escheator of Norfolk, 36 Edward III); 209, Mich. fines rot. 3, and Easter rot. 1d, where the escheators' accounts are used (cf. *CIPM*, xxiii. 366).

[39] The repertory, discussed above, is E164/48, ff. 45-end (ff. 1–42 contain a less detailed inventory covering Edward III to Henry VI). Its origins are no earlier than the mid sixteenth century. An earlier repertory of escheators' records for the years 1422–45 (IND1/6992) gives only the name of the escheator and his period of account.

[40] E152/6/260 (cf. Carpenter, 'General Introduction', 27).

[41] E.g. E152/9/433, 434.

[42] E.g. E152/9/438, copies of two inquisitions taken by Ralph Arches in Oxfordshire and Berkshire; copies of other inquisitions taken by him are E149/96/8, m. 4; 97/15, m. 2; 98/10, m. 1; 98/11.

[43] Carpenter, 'General Introduction', 24–6 (with references).

clerks. Palaeographical analysis of inquisitions from the early fifteenth century does indeed reveal instances where both chancery and exchequer copies were almost certainly produced in the escheator's writing office. Examples could be given from a number of counties,[44] but perhaps the most distinctive hand produced both chancery and exchequer copies of several Lincolnshire IPMs in the early 1400s.[45]

In other cases, however, handwriting suggests that the transcripts were produced by chancery clerks. These clerks certainly, on occasion, delivered transcripts to the exchequer: the transcript of an inquisition taken on 4 November 1407 was delivered by Simon Gaunstede on 16 May 1408; the transcript of another, taken on 26 January 1413, was delivered on 8 June that year by John Wakeryng, clerk of the rolls.[46] From the end of Edward III's reign, chancery clerks are also recorded as checking the exchequer transcripts for accuracy: from that period the inquisitions are often annotated with 'examined' (*'ex'* for *examinatus*), sometimes accompanied by the name of a chancery clerk. We have 'examined by Muskham' on a transcript of 1375, for example – that is Robert Muskham who was active in chancery in the period 1365–85.[47] By the sixteenth century it was recognised procedure for transcripts to be made in chancery and sent to the exchequer.[48]

What factors determined the format of the exchequer inquisitions and whether they were written 'locally' by escheators or 'centrally' in chancery? At present the answers are unclear, although a decisive development can be identified by the later fifteenth century, when it seems that all exchequer copies of IPMs were made by chancery clerks and as individual transcripts rather than enrolments. By perhaps the early 1480s at the latest there is a striking contrast between the variety of handwritings found in the chancery IPMs, mostly presumably still written locally by escheators and their clerks, and the uniformity of the practiced chancery hands which produced the exchequer transcripts. The exact chronology of this change, and the reasons behind it, again need further research. It is perhaps related to the increased interest in feudal revenues apparent in Edward IV's second reign from about 1476. Other aspects of the IPM process were reformed or clarified around this time, as with rules for livery of lands drawn up in 1477.[49]

From the later fifteenth century, the exchequer copies are therefore close transcripts of the chancery inquisitions, although they sometimes omit details, most notably the names of jurors, that were not considered necessary for the accounting process, and formulaic phrases may also be considerably abbreviated. Before this

---

[44] E.g. C137/59/6, m. 6 and E149/90/5, m. 2 (*CIPM*, xix. 177, Bucks.); C137/61/68, m. 11 and E149/88/13, m. 2 (*CIPM*, xix. 283, Cambs.).

[45] E.g. C137/58/48, m. 2 and E149/89/9, m. 1 (*CIPM*, xix. 212); C137/90/16, m. 6 and E149/99/1, m. 2 (*CIPM*, xix. 1038). E152/9/431 dorse is also in this hand, although the corresponding chancery IPM (C137/78/29, m. 9; *CIPM,* xix. 732) is not.

[46] E149/91/6 (*CIPM*, xix. 360); 99/11, m. 2 (*CIPM,* xix. 1015); E149/40/10, m. 1 (*lib... per manus Muskham*).

[47] E149/40/13; card index of chancery clerks in the Map Room, TNA.

[48] Ley, *Learned Treatise*, 72–3; Peter Osborne, *The Practice of the Exchequer Court, with its Severall Offices and Officers* (1658), 57, 99–100.

[49] C.D. Ross, *Edward IV* (1974), 382; J.H. Baker and J.S. Ringrose, *A Catalogue of English Legal Manuscripts in Cambridge University Library* (Woodbridge, 1996), 279–80.

period the situation is more complicated since the copies were made 'locally' by escheators and their clerks as well as in chancery. Indeed 'copies' is too imprecise a term. The inquisitions returned to the exchequer by escheators were indeed often fair copies of the IPMs returned to chancery, but they also included variant texts and corrected drafts, which make the exchequer inquisitions a particularly interesting source in this period.

The different sorts of text found in the exchequer IPMs in this period are easier to grasp if we outline, in a necessarily schematic way, the stages that might lead up to the creation of a chancery IPM.[50] This could after all be the product of a lengthy process. Certain information was, it seems, often supplied to the escheator by the family of the tenant or other interested parties. This might include information about the descent of properties, their tenure, the tenant's date of death and the identity of the heir. Other information had to be obtained by the escheator from local jurors or other sources, perhaps indeed earlier IPMs.[51] The jurors, at least in theory, had to be summoned to the inquisition itself and to attend; they might deliberate over competing claims and that deliberation, in some known cases, extended for some time. Finally, fair copies of the inquisition had to be written up: usually, one would assume, in the escheator's office, although the uniformity of the chancery IPMs for some tenants not infrequently suggests that inquisitions for a number of different counties were written up by a single scribe.[52] Even these fair copies could be altered or rewritten at a later stage: this is revealed not only in the well-known correspondence relating to William Paston's IPMs in 1444,[53] but by extant inquisitions where both chancery and exchequer copies have received identical corrections.[54]

Often, no doubt, a fair copy of the IPM to be returned to chancery was drawn up in the escheator's office, and the exchequer copy was then transcribed from this. Sometimes both chancery and exchequer texts seem to be fair copies but to have been drawn up independently from the same or a very similar set of notes. This would explain how the lists of jurors sometimes differ between chancery and exchequer versions and why the exchequer texts sometimes provide superior information.[55] One exchequer inquisition had an abbreviated jury list, with the name of only a single juror; but this supplied information about his residence that was not included in the chancery copy.[56]

Of particular interest are those exchequer IPMs which represent stages of the drafting process and which were returned by escheators because their contents

---

[50] For what follows see Carpenter, 'General Introduction', *CIPM*, xxii. 20–23; Matthew Holford, 'Notoriously Unreliable: the Valuations and Extents', in *The Fifteenth-Century Inquisitions Post Mortem*, ed. Hicks, 117–44 (at 120–2); *idem*, '"Thrifty men of the country?": the Jurors and their Role', *ibid.*, 201–21 (at 202–6).

[51] The question of whether escheators maintained local archives of IPMs and related documents requires fuller exploration on another occasion.

[52] E.g. C137/14/54, mm. 2, 4, 6 (*CIPM*, xviii. 207–9); C137/51/44, mm. 2, 4, 8, 10, 13, 14, *etc.* (*CIPM*, xviii. 1158–9, 1162–4).

[53] Holford, '"Thrifty men"', 203–4.

[54] C137/11/50, mm. 37–38 and E152/8/355, dorse nos. 2, 3 (*CIPM*, xviii. 145). In both copies information about Caldicot has been interlined in a different hand, and the same hand has added that the Barnsley advowson was held, presenting at every other vacancy.

[55] E.g. E149/72/5, m. 6 and C137/11/50, mm. 29–30 (*CIPM*, xviii. 141).

[56] E152/8/413, no. 1 (*CIPM*, xix. 112).

were close enough to the chancery IPMs that they could serve as duplicates. The earliest stages of this drafting process are rarely visible: the exchequer inquisitions are not typically roughly written drafts on paper, like those produced for the IPM of John Paston in 1466.[57] They mostly represent more advanced phases of composition, although there are a handful of exceptions. Isabel Dymmok's Bedfordshire IPM is extant in three forms: one with a bare minimum of information about the tenure and value of the manor of Clapham and Isabel's heir; the second, with interlineations relating to her life-estate and the grant by which she held it; and finally the fair copy returned to chancery.[58]

On several exchequer inquisitions we can see corrections being made as (presumably) improved information became available. Tenures and services might be specified: the manor of Didmarton in Gloucestershire, for example, held in 'socage' rather than 'service unknown'.[59] Another Gloucestershire inquisition was extensively annotated to indicate potential omissions and ambiguities relating, *inter alia*, to tenures, values and terms of rent payment.[60] It is rarely evident how such information was provided, although there are some occasional, tantalising indications. One Hampshire inquisition has been extensively interlineated to include details of grants made by Thomas Bonham and John Wykyng, and by Wykyng, John Fauntleroy and John Toper. It is endorsed '*A mon tresreverent amy Janekyn Fauntleroy*'; it seems a draft text had been sent to Fauntleroy, who had provided the relevant information.[61]

Less commonly we can see information being removed from a draft. This presumably occurred when escheator or family wished to avoid raising potentially awkward issues in an inquisition. One example relates to the 1416 IPMs of Sir Thomas West, in which details of enfeoffments in Somerset and Dorset appear in the exchequer texts but are struck through and do not appear in the chancery copies.[62] Perhaps these grants had taken place without royal licence and it was hoped to conceal them from scrutiny. But the reasons for many changes remain mysterious in the absence of more detailed information about the background of particular inquisitions. It is unclear, for example, why Maud Clifford's date of death was altered from 28 February 1403 to 1 November 1402 in her 1411 IPM.[63] Differences in valuations between chancery and exchequer versions can also be difficult to account for. In 1417 the manor of Morley in Norfolk was valued at £13 6s. 8d. in the chancery copy, but only £4 8s. 10½d. in the exchequer text. It is

---

[57] Paper: e.g. E149/105/11, m. 2; 106/1, m. 5. Paston: *Paston Letters and Papers of the Fifteenth Century*, ed. Norman Davis, Richard Beadle and Colin Richmond (3 vols., EETS, supplementary series xx–xxiii, Oxford, 2004–5), ii. 554–61.

[58] E149/103/3, m. 2 (*CIPM*, xx. 515). The first draft is on the dorse of the exchequer copy; the second is the exchequer copy; the fair text is the chancery copy.

[59] E149/93/9 (*CIPM*, xix. 617).

[60] E149/177/9 (*CIPM*, xxvi. 228).

[61] E149/83/10, m. 3 (*CIPM,* xviii. 959).

[62] E149/107/2, mm. 3–4 (*CIPM*, xx. 533, 535); see also E149/113/6, m. 1 (*CIPM*, xxi. 10), deleted information about an enfeoffment of the manor of Thurrock.

[63] 1411: Wednesday, the feast of All Saints, 4 Henry IV, rather than 28 Feb. 1403, the date that had been given in IPMs of 1403 (*CIPM*, xviii. 775–9; xix. 796). The exchequer copy of the 1411 inquisition had the 1403 date (Ash Wednesday, 4 Henry IV) before correction (E152/9/437, no. 2).

surprising that this difference, and others like it, was not noticed when the transcripts were examined for accuracy in chancery.[64] It is also unclear which (if any) valuation should be taken as authoritative: the exchequer sum, while conveniently lower, is also more precise, and it was this sum which was used to charge the escheator in his account.

At a final stage of drafting there is much evidence of stylistic corrections and attention to niceties of phrasing and word-order.[65] And it often seems to have been at a final stage that details of jurors were added. Sometimes this was done in a space left blank for the purpose, as with the Lincolnshire IPM of Juliana de Thoresby. The jurors' names were later inserted in what became the exchequer copy by the same clerk responsible for the chancery copy. This clerk wrote a number of other Lincolnshire inquisitions and can thus be identified as one of the escheator's staff. What became the exchequer copy was presumably a 'final draft' prepared before the inquisition took place: when the inquisition was held the names of jurors were added and a few other corrections made. A fair copy was returned to chancery and the 'final draft' to the exchequer.[66] In a similar case not only the names of the jurors, but the date and place of the inquisition, were added to a final draft which was then returned to the exchequer.[67] Like the chancery copy, the exchequer copy of this inquisition was indented, but the indentations do not match: indentation of itself is no sign that an exchequer copy was drawn up at the same time as the chancery copy, as the ordinance of 1325 had stipulated.

V

In summary, we have seen that the 'exchequer inquisitions *post mortem*' are a more complex subject than has usually been appreciated, with many possibilities for future research. Their current organisation does not reflect their original archival context, which is best recorded in early inventories and which Hunter attempted to recreate in the nineteenth century. The exchequer had copies of IPMs from at least the 1280s, but the purpose and use of these enrolments is not fully clear. Only from 1325–6, and especially from the 1340s, is there clear documentation of how inquisition transcripts were used to audit the escheators' accounts and afterwards filed with those accounts. And even from that date, the exchequer inquisitions comprise a rather bewildering variety of material: documents of different format, some copied by chancery clerks, some by escheators and their staff, and the latter including a variety of copies, drafts and variant texts. Only from the end of the fifteenth century do the exchequer inquisitions become more uniform, as all the transcripts were prepared in chancery.

Much of this picture is uncertain and will be subject to revision and correction as research on the IPMs and the late medieval exchequer continues. If correct, however, the above account does suggest some provisional conclusions regarding

---

[64] *CIPM*, xx. 834. The escheator was charged with the lower sum in his account: E357/25, rot. 14d.
[65] For a good example see E149/91/2, m. 4 (*CIPM*, xix. 463); also E149/111/5, m. 2 with C138/26/34, mm. 5–6 (*CIPM*, xx. 739).
[66] E149/101/2 (*CIPM*, xx. 33).
[67] E149/114/10, m. 3 (*CIPM*, xxi. 138); again the corrections are in the hand of the chancery IPM, C138/35/48, m. 6. I am grateful to my colleague Matthew Tompkins for this example.

the historical significance and value of the exchequer IPMs. First, the inquisitions and their associated archive evidence the exchequer's concern to record and maximise the crown's feudal revenues. There is a need for more research to explore how the archive was exploited and how changes in its use and development relate to fluctuating interest in feudal income. Second, in the period before about 1480, at least, the significant number of draft and variant texts in the exchequer IPMs also has much to reveal about how the inquisitions were drawn up. Perhaps the most important immediate conclusion, therefore, is that future editorial work on the IPMs, certainly in the period before the late fifteenth century, should pay greater attention to the exchequer copies. Details should be given not only of textual variations but of indentation, corrections, interlineations and annotations, and whether the hands of chancery and exchequer copies are similar. The exchequer IPMs are not only a means of establishing a full and accurate text, but an important witness to IPM procedure, and fuller description will lead to a fuller understanding of the documents and their significance. The new online edition of *CIPM*, xviii–xxi for *Mapping the Medieval Countryside* will incorporate such descriptions and provide a model for future work. It is one small way in which *Mapping* will stand as part of Michael Hicks's contribution to the history of late medieval England.

HAMS FOR PRAYERS: REGULAR CANONS AND THEIR LAY PATRONS IN MEDIEVAL CATALONIA[*]

Karen Stöber

In 1431 an earthquake shook the walls of the small Augustinian priory of Roca Rossa in eastern Catalonia.[1] The resulting damage only served to add to the deterioration of the monastic compound, part of which was already in a ruinous state even before the earthquake struck. In fact, in the years leading up to the disaster, complaints had been made regarding the state of the community and its buildings, which had previously been largely abandoned by its lay patrons and benefactors.[2] The loss of patronage was a key factor that contributed to the eventual collapse of the priory, reminding us just how crucial patronal support could be for a medieval religious community.

While in the British Isles interest in the subject of monastic patronage has been gathering speed since the 1950s,[3] in Iberia, the approach has to date been a

---

[*] The research for this study has been carried out within the framework of the research project 'Auctoritas – Iglesia, Cultura y Poder, s.XII–XIV' (HAR2012–31484), funded by the Spanish Ministerio de Economía y Competitividad.

[1] http://www.monestirs.cat/monst/mares/ma28roca.htm, accessed 18 Dec. 2013.

[2] Joan Bou i Illa and Jaume Vellvehí i Altimira, *Del Romànic al Gòtic. El Monestir de Santa Maria de Roca Rossa* (Mataró, 2010), 91.

[3] Susan Wood's ground-breaking study, *English Monasteries and their Patrons in the Thirteenth Century* (Oxford, 1955), set the pace on patronage studies, and despite its age it is still the main general study of the topic for thirteenth-century England. Several general works on aspects of the history of the medieval church, or on medieval monasticism, have sections on monastic patronage. Excellent outlines include R.W. Southern, *Western Society and the Church in the Middle Ages* (1970), esp. 228–30; also Janet Burton, *Monastic and Religious Orders in Britain, 1000–1300* (Cambridge, 1994), esp. ch. 10; C.H. Lawrence, *Medieval Monasticism: Forms of Religious Life in Western Europe in the Middle Ages* (2nd edn., 1989), esp. 69–77. And then there are the various studies dedicated specifically to the topic of monastic patronage, including notably work by Christopher Holdsworth, Benjamin Thompson, Emma Cownie and Marilyn Oliva, whose studies focus on different aspects of the topic: C.J. Holdsworth, *The Piper and the Tune: Medieval Patrons and Monks* (Reading, 1991); B.J. Thompson, 'From "Alms" to "Spiritual Services": the Function and Status of Monastic Property in Medieval England', *Monastic Studies, II*, ed. Judith Loades (Bangor, 1991), 227–61, and 'Monasteries and their Patrons at Foundation and Dissolution', *TRHS*, 6th series, iv (1994), 103–23; Emma Cownie, 'The Normans as Patrons of English Religious Houses, 1066–1135', *Anglo-Norman Studies*, xviii (1995), 47–62, and *Religious Patronage in Anglo-Norman England, 1066–1135* (1998); Marilyn Oliva, *The Convent and the Community in Late Medieval England* (Woodbridge, 1998); Karen Stöber, *Late Medieval Monasteries and their Patrons: England and Wales, c.1300–1540* (Woodbridge, 2007). In recent years, the study of monastic patronage has seen a rapid expansion of research on the topic, reflected in the production of a series of very competent doctoral theses, which are gradually appearing in print, covering a whole range of aspects of the subject and focusing on individual groups of people or types of patrons, different

different one, focusing less on the social history of the medieval church, that is the study of its social function, which is where I would mostly situate monastic patronage, and more on the institutional or economic history of religious communities.[4] There are exceptions, of course, appearing in increasing numbers, which are contributing to a growing body of work on issues related to socio-monastic studies. The work of Nikolas Jaspert, Ursula Vones-Liebenstein, Paul Freedman and Jill Webster, among others, has done much to enhance our understanding of the intricate interplay between church and society in medieval Iberia,[5] as have a series of (unfortunately often isolated) projects carried out in various research centres across the Peninsula, among them Flocel Sabaté's recent project at the University of Lleida on the Premonstratensian canons in medieval Catalonia,[6] or the work by Reyna Pastor, Esther Pascua and others on the social networks of several Galician monasteries.[7] But much more work remains to be done on the topic, and this paper aims to be a small contribution.

The relationship between a monastic patron and a religious community was a two-way liaison, in which the patron was the steward and protector of his community, while the monks, canons, or nuns, in turn, became the patrons and protectors of his soul and memory. In return for the spiritual (and other) benefits he derived from this host of praying men (and women), the patron provided financial and other support to his community. He (or she) was expected to protect the religious community against potential threats from outside, and occasionally from inside as well. A well-connected patron might be an important negotiator between

---

kinds of religious communities and regional and case studies, all of which are contributing greatly to our understanding of monastic patronage in the British Isles. My own Ph.D. thesis on medieval monastic patronage was supervised by Michael Hicks, and it was he who first inspired my interest in the topic. His own work on the subject includes the important study 'The Rising Price of Piety in the Later Middle Ages', in *Monasteries and Society in the British Isles in the Later Middle Ages*, ed. Janet Burton and Karen Stöber (Woodbridge, 2008), 95–109.

[4] Important to mention in this context are also the increasing number of editions of monastic documents, including cartularies, among them Josep Pons i Guri, *El Cartoral de Santa Maria de Roca Rossa* (Barcelona, 1984), and J.M. Marquès, *Escriptures de Santa Maria de Vilabertran (968–1300)* (Monografies Empordaneses, 1, Figueres, 1995).

[5] Nikolas Jaspert, *Stift und Stadt: Das Heiliggrabpriorat von Santa Anna und das Regularkanonikerstift Santa Eulàlia del Camp im mittelalterlichen Barcelona, 1145–1423* (Berlin, 1996); Ursula Vones-Liebenstein, *Saint-Ruf und Spanien: Studien zur Verbreitung und zum Wirken der Regularkanoniker von Saint-Ruf in Avignon auf der Iberischen Halbinsel (11. und 12. Jahrhundert)* (Turnhout, 1996); *Documenta Selecta Mutuas Civitatis Arago-Cathalaunicae et Ecclesiae Relationes Illustrantia*, ed. Johannes Vincke (Barcelona, 1936); Odilo Engels, 'Episkopat und Kanonie im mittelalterlichen Katalonien', *Spanische Forschungen, Gesammelte Aufsätze zur Kulturgeschichte Spaniens*, xxi (1963), 89–135. Note also J.J. Bauer, 'Die *Vita canonica* der katalanischen Kathedralkapitel vom 9. bis zum 11. Jahrhundert', in *Homenaje a Johannes Vincke* (2 vols., Madrid, 1962–3), i. 81–113, and *idem*, 'Die *vita canonica* an den katalanischen Kollegiatskirchen im 10. und 11. Jahrhundert', *Spanische Forschungen, Gesammelte Aufsätze zur Kulturgeschichte Spaniens*, xxi (1963), 54–83; P.H. Freedman, *The Diocese of Vic: Tradition and Regeneration in Medieval Catalonia* (New Brunswick, N.J., 1983), *idem*, *Church, Law and Society in Catalonia, 900–1500* (Aldershot, 1994); J.R. Webster, 'The Monastery of Val de Cristo in the Kingdom of Valencia: Relations, Economy and Significance to the Crown, 1410–50', *The Journal of Medieval Monastic Studies*, i (2012), 93–114.

[6] 'The Premonstratensian Order in the Crown of Aragon: Penetration, Development and Effects on Society' (HUM2005–03125/HIST).

[7] Reyna Pastor, E.P. Echegaray, A.R. López and P.S. León, *Transacciones sin Mercado: Instituciones, Propiedad y Redes Sociales en la Galicia Monástica, 1200–1300* (Madrid, 1999).

a religious community and an episcopal or royal contender, for example, or on occasions of internal strife.

Manifestations of monastic patronage are evident on many levels in the life of a religious community. The most visible demonstration of patronage, and the one for which our surviving evidence is perhaps most plentiful, was the granting of lands, properties, goods and objects, cash and so forth by a patron to a monastery or nunnery. The amount and nature of such donations naturally varied greatly and depended on the donor and on the time and place they were made. Trends also changed over time, depending on the requirements of a religious community and the financial capacity of its patrons, both of which developed as time went on: major grants of lands and property were normally made at an early stage in a house's history; these were later normally replaced by confirmations of earlier grants, as well as by smaller bequests, including various items such as vestments, books or furniture, or rents and cash donations.[8]

In return for their material, or other, support, monastic patrons naturally had certain expectations.[9] The prayers provided by a religious community during the patron's lifetime, as well as after his death, were central to the patron-monastery relationship.[10] But spiritual benefits aside, there were other, equally attractive, though sometimes perhaps less lofty, gains that might be enjoyed by patrons in return for their support of a community of monks, canons or nuns. The benefit of hospitality was one important way to indicate affiliation and commitment, as was the privilege of being laid to rest in the monastic church. Moreover, a patron might lay claim to the benefits from the assets of the religious house during a vacancy, and be involved in monastic elections. All of these types of contact and interaction have left traces in the written documentation, albeit to greatly varying degrees.

The sources for this present study, mostly kept at the diocesan archive in Girona and the Biblioteca de Catalunya in Barcelona, relate to two relatively moderate houses of Augustinian canons in Catalonia, the priory of Roca Rossa and the abbey of Vilabertran. Both houses, while remaining relatively unspectacular in the grander scale of things, were active participants in the life of their localities and constituted key elements in the wider social interaction that characterises the area, and therefore offer useful case studies in the study of monastic patronage and social networks in the region. The present study will consider both patrons, in the sense of the heirs of the founders of a monastery, and benefactors of the two communities in a wider sense, some of whom were involved with the religious communities over a long time, sometimes over several generations.

Roca Rossa Priory occupied what at first glance seems to be an isolated spot deep in the Montnegre massif, a hilly region of forests and arable land in the county and diocese of Girona in north-eastern Catalonia.[11] At a closer look, however, it emerges that despite its location in a sparsely populated mountain

---

[8] See Stöber, *Late Medieval Monasteries*, 80–93.
[9] J.T. Rosenthal, *The Purchase of Paradise: Gift Giving and the Aristocracy, 1307–1485* (1972).
[10] Cf. Wood, *English Monasteries*, 12–13; Stöber, *Late Medieval Monasteries*, 72–4.
[11] See the brief study of Roca Rossa by Bou i Illa and Vellvehí i Altimira, *El Monestir de Santa Maria de Roca Rossa*.

region, the priory lay at the heart of a network of paths that connected the house with the mills and farmhouses which it acquired over the centuries. In the medieval period the economy in the region was closely tied to its farmhouses and flour mills, of which the Roca Rossa canons owned several: at least three mills and eleven farmsteads in close proximity to Roca Rossa are known to have been in the possession of the priory by the later Middles Ages, as well as woodland, meadows and fields.[12] Politically the area was part of the patrimony of the viscounts of Cabrera, perhaps the greatest, certainly one of the most successful, and probably the most studied, of Catalonia's *cases vescomtals*.[13]

The monastery probably had its origins in an early hermitage, which was transformed into an organised community of some kind in the eleventh century. Though our knowledge of its beginnings is shadowy, its documented history starts in the mid twelfth century, with a charter dated 1145, from which date the documentation of the small priory becomes fairly extensive for about a century and a half. The identity of the founder of the priory has been contested, but certain evidence (an inscribed stone, which still survives) points to one Ramon Gausilus as *istius ecclesie primus fundator*.[14] Roca Rossa was from its beginnings, and remained throughout, a small community, which was closely involved with the neighbouring lay community, from which it drew both its brethren and its patrons. The editor of Roca Rossa's cartulary, Josep Pons i Guri, notes that 'the social influence of this little monastery in the region [*comarca*] was very intense; wills of important people who wished to leave their bodies for burial in its cemetery, and various monetary bequests, not collected in the cartulary, abound in our archives up to the end of the thirteenth century'.[15]

Despite Roca Rossa being, and remaining, a small and financially insignificant community, the network of families involved in one way or another with the canons of the priory – be that through benefactions, trade or family ties – included many names of local importance, as well as some of medieval Catalonia's leading families. Most prominent among them was the Cabrera family. The Cabrera, and foremost among them Viscount Guerau III (*d*.1180), were perhaps the most active of Roca Rossa's benefactors and were responsible for a great number of bequests to the canons from the earliest days of the priory.[16] But among the benefactors of the canons we come across several members of other known families from the region – the Queruç, Folgar, Cànoves, Riu and Palafolls families, for instance, their provenance often identifiable through their family name. These people provided the financial support so needed by the canons, they dealt and traded with them, and their sons joined the community as canons, pupils and servants; their donations, naturally, consisted of local produce. The Cabrera aside, Roca Rossa's benefactors

---

[12] *Ibid.*, 49–64; Pons i Guri, *Cartoral*, 20.
[13] On the Cabrera family note for instance Santiago Sobrequés, *Els Barons de Catalunya* (Barcelona, 1989), 35–8, 68–74, 105–8, 151–69. See also Alejandro Martínez Giralt, *El poder feudal, els seus agents i el territorio: El vescomtat de Cabrera (1199–1423)* (Santa Coloma, 2013).
[14] Pons i Guri, *Cartoral*, 10. An issue which merits further attention in this context, but which goes beyond the scope of this brief essay, is the vocabulary of patronage.
[15] Pons i Guri, *Cartoral*, 12.
[16] The main family monastery of this branch of the Cabrera family, however, and their dynastic mausoleum, was at the nearby Benedictine abbey of Sant Salvador de Breda; we therefore find no Cabrera burial at Roca Rossa Priory.

constituted the middling sort of Catalonia's society, men and women firmly rooted in their localities and socially influential on a moderate scale.

Turning to our second case study, the abbey of Vilabertran, we find that the patronal network was comparable to that of Roca Rossa in that it encompassed the local gentry and nobility, though it included a greater proportion of patrons of higher social standing, and even elements of royal patronage.[17] Santa Maria de Vilabertran stands at what was an important junction where the roads from Girona in the south and nearby Figueres in the west met with those that led north into the Pyrenees and east to the coast. Now a region which is, while still rural, dotted with hamlets and small towns, up until the eleventh century this was a sparsely inhabited area. The abbey was founded around the year 1065 by a certain Pere Rigau, who is perhaps better known for his activities surrounding the promotion of the early canonical movement in medieval Catalonia. In fact, he is considered to be one of three main instigators ensuring the success of the regular canons in the region:[18] from as early as its foundation, and through its founder, the community of Vilabertran was closely involved in the canonical reform movement in Catalonia.[19] In any case, the new community was a success. Fifteen years after its foundation, a new church was begun at the abbey of Vilabertran,[20] and ten years later, in 1090, Pere Rigau set about founding Vilabertran's first daughter house at Santa Maria del Camp in Roussillon.[21] The choice of location of this daughter house, beyond the Pyrenees, was a very meaningful one in the context of current border politics, and the consecration of the church was witnessed by a range of important clergymen from Catalonia, as well as clerics from Carcassonne and Narbonne.[22]

As houses of regular canons both communities were involved in a whole range of activities – including trade, education and hospitality – which made regular contact between the religious and the outside world, including their patrons and benefactors, not only possible, but indeed often unavoidable. In fact, for many a patron it was clearly this measure of contact and activity which made the regular canons such an attractive choice. From the start, both Roca Rossa and Vilabertran were closely involved with their local lay communities, from which they drew their patrons and their brethren. We know of the identities of some of these people thanks to the surviving archives of both houses and their plentiful charters, several

---

[17] On Vilabertran Abbey, note also P.H. Freedman and Flocel Sabaté, 'Two Twelfth-Century Papal Letters to the Collegiate Church of Vilabertran (Catalonia)', *Archivum Historiae Pontificiae*, xxxvii (1999), 39–59.

[18] There were three main centres held responsible for the development of the canonical movement in medieval Catalonia: first, a synod held in Vic under Bishop Berenguer Seniofred de Lluçà in 1087 to regulate the chapter of his cathedral led to the invitation of St. Ruf of Avignon; second, at around this time Barcelona came under the congregation of the same saint; and the third centre was at Girona under Pere Rigau of Vilabertran.

[19] Note Antoni Pladevall i Font, '*El moviment canonical a l'Església del segle XI o l'adopció de la regla de Sant Agustí a les canòniques catalanes*', in *Santa Maria de Vilabertan, 900 anys* (Figueres, 2002), 9–32.

[20] This church was to be consecrated on 11 Nov. 1100.

[21] Pladevall i Font, '*El moviment canonical*', 30.

[22] Miguel Golobardes Vila, *El Monasterio de Santa Maria del Vilabertran* (Barcelona, 1949), Appendix.

of which were explicitly granted by local lay folk to a family member who was a canon, or in one case, abbot, in one of the houses.[23] Beatriu d'Hortal, for example, asked in her will, dated 25 August 1221, to be buried in the precinct of Vilabertran Abbey, where her son was a canon,[24] and on 23 March 1218, a certain Lady Matheu made a bequest of a property and an olive grove to the abbot and canons of Vilabertran because a son of hers had earlier entered this monastery.[25] Where no such familial connections existed, a link might be consciously forged: In 1347, Viscountess Timbor de Cabrera requested episcopal permission to place a canon in Roca Rossa (although her main interest as a benefactress lay not with the canons of this priory, but with the female Cistercian community of Valldemaría).[26] The local connection of benefactors and brethren remained an important factor throughout for both houses. Josep Marquès has observed, in his analysis of Vilabertran's abbots, that the list of abbots reads like 'an exhibition of lesser nobles pertaining to the families of Llers, Cabanelles, Soler de Sant Climent, Sescebes, Solans, Camós, Darnius, Fortià, and other locally important families'.[27]

Not only the patrons and the abbots, priors and canons, but the lands and properties given to these monasteries likewise tended to be situated in the locality, and gifts were dominated by local produce. The patterns of benefactions in these two small Catalan Augustinian houses bear a striking resemblance to those of comparable religious communities elsewhere in Europe: initial grants to both houses consisted predominantly of lands and properties in the locality, sometimes with specification of how to use this. Thus, for instance, on 30 September 1180 a grant was made to Roca Rossa by Ponç, viscount of Cabrera, together with his wife Marquesa, of permission to build a mill by the farmhouse of Maiença in the nearby parish of Sant Andreu de Reminyó, next to another one already there.[28] And when in 1218 the small house of canons at Sant Corneli de Montells (founded in 1200) failed, its possessions were granted to Roca Rossa by another member of the same family, Guerau IV de Cabrera.[29] Most – though not all – of the lands and allotments granted to Roca Rossa and Vilabertran by members of the local communities were located within a ten-kilometre radius of the houses and lent a strong local flavour to the bequests. On 13 September 1221, Josbert de Cabanes, his wife Maria and their son Pere gave to Vilabertran a share of a nearby upland territory in return for provision of food for one year,[30] and on 20 February 1235 the canons of Vilabertran were the recipients of a farmhouse close to the abbey, left to them by Elicsendis, widow of Guillem Julià, in her will.[31] Not all transactions, however, were on such scale or of such value, and the sheer range of bequests indicates the inclusion in the patronal network of people of different social standing. As time

---

[23] On 10 July 1272 Dalmau de Darnius made a bequest to his brother, who was then abbot of Vilabertran: Marquès, *Escriptures de Vilabertan*, doc. 892.
[24] Arxiu Diocesà de Girona, perg. 33.
[25] Arxiu Biblioteca de Catalunya, perg. 5.523.
[26] Bou i Illa and Vellvehí i Altimira, *El Monestir de Santa Maria de Roca Rossa*, 45.
[27] J.M. Marquès Planagumà, 'Santa Maria de Vilabertran, els homes i l'edifici', in *Vilabertan, 900 anys*, 33-46, at 42.
[28] Cf. Pons i Guri, *Cartoral*, 330.
[29] *Ibid.*, doc. 150.
[30] Arxiu Biblioteca de Catalunya, perg. 9.612.
[31] Arxiu Biblioteca de Catalunya, perg. 9.789.

went on, the earlier larger grants were increasingly replaced by smaller gifts, often victuals and cash: thus in August 1257 the Roca Rossa canons, in return for their prayers, received from Ferrer Llobet and his wife Ermessenda two eighths of wheat, a ham, another eighth of wheat and a pair of hens.[32] Four years later, on 29 October 1261, a man named Bernat de Lladó gave to the canons of Vilabertran a bundle of hay, a couple of eggs and a quarter of oats.[33]

While the patterns of monastic patronage are distinctly similar in nature across medieval Europe, what gives the bequests a local flavour is the type of item given to a religious community. We have already noted the ham given to the canons of Roca Rossa by Ferrer and Ermessenda Llobet. Furthermore we find several donations of olive groves and of different quantities of olive oil among the charters of Catalan patrons to their monasteries. On 22 October 1177, for instance, a certain lady named Fresca, daughter of the late Pere de Menola and widow of Pere de Folgars, granted to the canons of Roca Rossa an annual allowance of oil;[34] and in a charter dated 10 December 1215 Guillelma de Sant Llorenç gave to the same community two cups of oil annually.[35] The grant of an olive grove made by Lady Matheu to Vilabertran has already been mentioned.

By the fourteenth century, the grants and sales to both houses gradually ceased, as they did elsewhere in medieval Christendom. Existing patronage ties, however, evidently continued to be honoured, as an inventory of 1337 from Roca Rossa confirms, which lists certain items kept at the priory by Viscount Bernat de Cabrera, one of Roca Rossa's principal benefactors. The inventory lists an impressive array of textiles, including bed linen, pillow cases and various vestments, as well as items of furniture (a table, for example) and items of domestic use, such as a pestle and mortar, and twenty-four beehives.[36]

Under normal circumstances, the patrons of a religious community were the fortunate beneficiaries of their house's hospitality, either on (more or less regular) visits to the community – depending on the individual relationship between a house and its patron, and also on the latter's place of residence – or on special occasions such as baptisms or funerals, which might be celebrated in the monastery. In their relationships with their patrons and other members of their local communities, the provision of monastic hospitality played an important part for the two Catalan houses, much in the way familiar from other parts of western Christendom. At Vilabertran we know about the existence of an almonry and certain 'lepers of the same place', which are referred to in a will of the year 1211.[37] The evidence from Roca Rossa, similarly, suggests that the much-frequented building known as the guest house was central to its role in the community, as was the regular provision

---

[32] Pons i Guri, *Cartoral*, 356.
[33] Arxiu Biblioteca de Catalunya, perg. 9.659.
[34] Pons i Guri, *Cartoral*, 330.
[35] *Ibid.*, 72.
[36] The inventory is now kept at the Arxiu Ducal de Medinaceli a Catalunya in the Cistercian abbey of Poblet (doc. 3730, roll 986, 559–61). It is reproduced in Bou i Illa and Vellvehí i Altimira, *El Monestir de Santa Maria de Roca Rossa*, 85.
[37] Marquès, *Escriptures de Vilabertan*, doc. 745.

of alms at the postern gate.[38] The popularity of this small priory with visitors was at least in part linked to the role we know it to have played as a local centre for Marian devotion.[39] We know of the extensive hospitality provided by the canons in part due to their failure to maintain such services during the later medieval period. In 1383 the prior of Roca Rossa was reprimanded by the episcopal visitor from Girona, Vicenç Carbonelli, for neglecting this duty and failing to adequately care for its by then inadequately maintained guest house.[40] Carbonelli recognised the provision of hospitality to be an important duty of the monastery even as late as the end of the fourteenth century, when the buildings of the priory were in a state of increasing decay.

Principal occasions that might bring visitors to religious houses like Roca Rossa and Vilabertran, and that made the provision of hospitality by the canons such an important matter, include business and diplomatic transactions, such as the witnessing and signing of documents, pilgrimage and the need for shelter for travellers passing through the region.[41] And then there were more solemn occasions such as weddings, baptisms and funerals. Anecdotes relating to patronal visits to religious houses show such events to have been both happy occasions and potential moments of crisis for a religious community, and an evidently cherished privilege in the eyes of patrons.[42] These were events that might bring whole gatherings of lay patrons and benefactors into the monastery. Weddings celebrated in the conventual church of a religious house might not be frequent occurrences, but in Vilabertran this happened in rather spectacular fashion when, in 1295, King James II of Aragon married Blanche d'Anjou, the daughter of King Charles II of Naples, James's adversary, at the abbey. The fourteenth-century chronicle of San Juan de la Peña is among the sources recording the occasion, noting that 'King Charles, with his daughter and the archbishops, and King James, with his barons and knights, arrived at Vilabertran on the day of the festival of All Saints, in the year of our Lord 1295'.[43] The scale of the event, on which the chronicler fails to elaborate further, focusing instead on the ensuing peace negotiations between the two kings, can only be surmised, but the mere mention of the presence of 'archbishops, barons and knights' hints at something more than humble celebrations. The meeting of such noble and important folk at a medium-sized Augustinian abbey shows that politics could be another factor in the relations between patrons and their religious

---

[38] J.A. Linage Conde, *La Vida Cotidiana de los Monjes de la Edad Media* (Madrid, 2007), 104–9.
[39] On the discovery of the miraculous statue of the Virgin of Roca Rossa that allegedly refused to be moved from the place where it was found in the woods, where a small chapel was eventually constructed for it (to be replaced later by the establishment of a confraternity of St. Mary within Roca Rossa Priory), see Pons i Guri, *Cartoral*, 9, 11.
[40] Cf. Carbonelli's report, dated 22 Jan. 1383, at the Arxiu Diocesà de Girona, Visites Pastorals, perg. 14, f. 46, where he criticised the poor state of the building called 'guest house' [*domus vocate 'dels ostes'*].
[41] Roca Rossa's confraternity dedicated to St. Mary, which had its own altar and priest, became a popular centre for Marian devotion in the area during the late twelfth to mid-thirteenth centuries, bringing visitors to the priory.
[42] Cf. Linage Conde, *La Vida Cotidiana*, 12.
[43] *The Chronicle of San Juan de la Peña: A Fourteenth-Century Official History of the Crown of Aragon*, trans. L.H. Nelson (Philadelphia, 1991), 91. Note also Ramon Muntaner, *Chrònica*, ed. Marina Gusta (2 vols., Barcelona, Edicions, lxii, 1979), ch. clxxxii, p. 44.

communities: a religious house might be regarded as a 'neutral' but adequately grand site for two opposing parties to meet to negotiate political matters.[44]

Interruptions to daily life of a less festive, but in other ways not dissimilar, kind were those caused by funerals held in religious houses. Initially hesitatingly granted, by the later Middle Ages burial of lay patrons and important benefactors in religious houses frequently enough took place either inside the conventual church, or in purpose-built chapels.[45] As time went on, monastic burials became both more frequent and more visible and this is perhaps especially striking in the case of royal patrons.[46] Both Roca Rossa and Vilabertran were popular choices for those patrons and benefactors who wished to make their stay among the canons rather more permanent. As Josep Marquès has pointed out, the fact that the abbey church of Vilabertran was chosen by a great number of nobles from the Empurdà region confirms the idea that burial and funerary services constituted one of the community's main duties for its lay patrons and benefactors.[47] One hundred and twenty-seven wills in which testators request burial in Vilabertran, dating from the eleventh to the thirteenth century, are included among the documents in the abbey's archive.[48] For the first four decades of the thirteenth century alone, the documents include almost a dozen wills with requests for burial in the abbey.[49] Among those asking to be laid to rest in Vilabertran were Berenguer d'Hortal (11 January 1203), Guillem de Terrades (9 June 1209), and other men and women (in fact, rather a remarkable number of women) from the area.[50] The testators were local gentry, both men and women, and all of them, as we might expect, made bequests to the house to accompany their bodies. These bequests ranged from cash to parcels of land or pieces of property, to vineyards and olive groves: in 1205 Pere Ferret gave to the canons of Vilabertran 100 *sous* for masses,[51] and in 1208 Guillem de Vilarig granted the canons, together with his body for burial, a farmhouse.[52] In 1242, Ramon de Figueres gave to the canons of Vilabertran certain lands near the town of Figueres.[53] On a number of occasions the abbot was named among the witnesses, as in the case of a lady named Berenguera, daughter of Berenguer de Figueres, who, in April 1202, asked to be buried in the conventual

---

[44] Compare this with the gathering in 1238 at the Welsh Cistercian abbey of Strata Florida of the princes of Wales, who had come together to swear allegiance to Dafydd ap Llywelyn ab Iorwerth: *Brut y Tywysogyon or The Chronicle of the Princes*, ed. Thomas Jones (Cardiff, 1955), 234.

[45] Bou i Illa and Vellvehí i Altimira, *El Monestir de Santa Maria de Roca Rossa*, 81–4. On monastic burial in the English context see for instance Rosenthal, *Purchase of Paradise*; Christopher Daniell, *Death and Burial in Medieval England, 1066–1550* (1997); Stöber, *Late Medieval Monasteries*, 112–46.

[46] Perhaps the most conspicuous example in medieval Catalonia is the Cistercian abbey of Poblet and the royal tombs of the kings of Aragón that dominate the church.

[47] Marquès, *Escriptures de Vilabertran*, p. xxxix.

[48] And there were undoubtedly more.

[49] For the earlier period, the surviving wills with requests for burial at Vilabertran Abbey include 29 from the eleventh century and 86 from the twelfth century. See Marquès, *Escriptures de Vilabertran*, p. xxxix.

[50] Cf. *ibid.*, 288–95.

[51] Arxiu Biblioteca de Catalunya, perg.9.947.

[52] Arxiu Biblioteca de Catalunya, perg.9.981.

[53] Arxiu Biblioteca de Catalunya, perg.9.987.

church of Vilabertran, to whose abbot and canons she bequeathed her field of Llinars, and whose abbot, Pere, was one of her executors.[54] The most prominent of Vilabertran's patrons, the Rocabertí family, chose the abbey as their family mausoleum, and in the fourteenth century built a beautiful little chapel adjacent to the north transept of the conventual church, which was consecrated on 17 April 1358 and which became the monumental focus of their presence in the house.[55]

Unlike Vilabertran, Roca Rossa never became the dynastic mausoleum of any one of its benefactors' families, but it was nonetheless a popular burial place for individual patrons and benefactors, or at least this is what the surviving wills suggest.[56] Among the testators requesting burial in Roca Rossa were Guillem Blancaç, knight at the court of the Palafolls family (patrons of Roca Rossa), who asked for burial there in 1204; in 1212 Bertran de Bescanó did likewise, and later in the same century two members of the Montpalau family also asked to be laid to rest in the priory (Simó in 1262 and Guillem in 1279).[57] In each case the request was accompanied by a donation, but we do not know whether the burials ever actually took place.[58]

One significant aspect to consider in this context is the wider impact such a generous provision of hospitality might have had on a religious community, even a 'less rigid' one (that is, of regular canons rather than of monks). This was the other side of the coin of monastic patronage, as it were. Each burial was preceded by the solemn celebration of a funeral, which in turn tended to signify the presence, potentially, of a whole host of lay folk around the conventual precinct, causing potential interruption to the monastic routine and an impact on the monastic accounts. Similarly, each wedding or christening brought groups of men and women into the close proximity of the religious community; the noise and upheaval caused by people gathering, and the provision of those people and their horses with sustenance meant that in each case there was a potential for disturbance of the monastic tranquillity, and strain on the monastic coffers.

The ties between the canons of Vilabertran and Roca Rossa and the local lay community continued over the generations and in more than one case family traditions developed, which saw successive members of the same extended families seeking burial within the monastic compound, as the Rocabertí family did at Vilabetran, and generally maintaining an active, occasionally personal patronage relationship. Family traditions are also discernible in the careers of canons within the two houses, especially during later centuries, when several members from the same families are recorded as heads of the Vilabertran abbey: Marquès refers to the Cruïlles in the fifteenth century, and the Domenècs in the sixteenth.[59]

---

[54] Arxiu Biblioteca de Catalunya, perg. 9.831. Successive abbots of Vilabertran appear in the charters as witnesses, or in the wills as executors. See Marquès, *Escriptures de Vilabertran*.

[55] The chapel is still in use today. Cf. Benet Cervera i Flotats, 'El conjunt arquitectònic de Santa Maria de Vilabertran', in *Vilabertan, 900 anys*, 63–91, at 78. Several members of the Rocabertí family are recorded to have been buried in the abbey.

[56] See Bou i Illa and Vellvehí i Altimira, *El Monaster de Santa Maria de Roca Rossa*, 81–4.

[57] *Ibid.*, 83.

[58] The remains of the priory are in too poor a state to allow identification of graves without extensive excavation on the site, which is not to my knowledge currently planned.

[59] Marquès, *Escriptures de Vilabertran*, 42–4.

Patronal ties and traditions of such constancy and frequency continued in both houses until at least the early fourteenth century, when various external factors – economic, political and demographic – were making themselves felt.[60] On the one hand, as elsewhere in western Christendom, lay benefactors increasingly moved away from monastic patronage and chose different options of expressing their piety and caring for their bodies and souls, notably in their local parish churches. On the other hand, political circumstances in the region had an impact on monastic patronage, too. The repercussions of King James I's great conquests of the thirteenth century, especially those of the Balearics and Valencia, magnified the territory of the crown of Aragon. One side-effect of this was the relocation of some of the Catalan nobility, who began to settle in the newly-conquered lands; they included actual and potential patrons and benefactors of both Roca Rossa and Vilabertran.[61] But although this loss of patrons did have an impact on the two communities, it did not signify the end of benefactor-monastery relationships at either of the two houses, as local landowners continued to give their support, albeit greatly reduced and much more sporadic, to the canons. In fact, Vilabertran Abbey continued to exist as an active house of regular canons until it was secularised under Pope Clement VIII in 1592.[62] Roca Rossa, being a much smaller, poorer house, had by that time declined almost to the point of disintegration; during its final years there had been practically no resident canons left at the priory.[63]

Because of their often close involvement with lay society, in part due to their emphasis on pastoral care and their role in the parish and the community, the regular canons in medieval Catalonia had no option but to be drawn into the wider social life, the politics and conflicts which affected its surrounding lay community as well as lay society more widely. The extent to which this was the case, and to which this had a direct, noticeable impact on the life of the religious community, varied from house to house, as these communities took on particular roles for particular people in particular times and contexts. The documents seem to indicate that the canons of both communities were on the whole popular with the local lay community, at least until the fourteenth century. Records of discord or, worse, violence against the canons, are rare indeed in the documents relating to the two houses. There was the exceptional case at Vilabertran in November 1133 of a certain man named Ramon Erimball de Palol, according to his name a local man (Palol is some three kilometres south-east of Vilabertran), who was fined for his unruly behaviour at the abbey, where he was accused of sacrilege, of having seized the priest and spilt the canons' wine, after breaking the truce established between him and the canons.[64] And in 1247 another local man killed the horses ridden by Jacob, prior of Vilabertran, and a canon of the abbey, named Ponç of Vilatenim.[65] But these cases are exceptions, as far as the documentation goes, and in neither

---

[60] Moreover, external circumstances coincide with the decrease in available documentation: the cartulary of Roca Rossa, for instance, breaks off in 1310.
[61] See Golobardes Vila, *Vilabertran*, 116–26.
[62] Marquès, *Escriptures de Vilabertran*, 44.
[63] Pons i Guri, *Cartoral*, 16.
[64] Arxiu Biblioteca de Catalunya, perg. 9.756.
[65] Marquès, *Escriptures de Vilabertan*, doc. 907.

case do we have further information about the origins of the conflict. But clearly, from monasteries like Vilabertran and Roca Rossa we learn not only about the religious men who lived in them, but also about the lay community outside their walls.

It seems clear, then, that just as in their observance of a common rule and the use of a common liturgy, the different religious communities across medieval Europe followed certain common patterns of patronal relations.[66] Roca Rossa and Vilabertran are just two examples – and there were many like them. These were religious communities that were firmly rooted in their community, negotiating and interacting with the world outside and the wider locality, with which they were connected through their patrons and benefactors. So what do these findings tell us about monastic patronage more generally, about motivations, belief systems, orders of society, priorities and traditions? It seems fair to say that, when looking at motivations and practices, we are looking at a common phenomenon, and that monastic patrons in different regions were acting in very similar ways. We can discern certain common elements, relating to the nature of bequests, and the nature of patrons' expectations or demands, notably concerning spiritual services and funerals, but also more tangible benefits, such as a house's hospitality, the safekeeping of property or valuable items, the compilation of genealogies. Among monastic patrons across western Christendom there was evidently a shared basis of common experiences and commonly held beliefs, fears and ideas; a common education, in the most basic sense, and outlook on life; something we might perhaps call a common western Christian attitude, with certain fairly clearly defined ideas of conduct and expectation, reflected for instance in the different legal codes of individual countries and their use of a shared canon law; and also a shared concern for changing fashions and a keen awareness of changing developments across countries.[67]

We can, on the other hand, identify particular regional characteristics, which tell us about particular circumstances of one society or another – politically, socially, economically – and which had an impact on the nature of monastic patronage at a given moment in time. Regional characteristics or particularities, which differentiate one area from another, are also evident in the most ordinary bequests by patrons to religious communities. The nature of the bequest itself can reveal much about a region's produce or agricultural activities, as is reflected, for instance, in bequests of typical local items, such as olive oil and hams, to Roca Rossa and Vilabertran. External circumstances aside, what we see are shared motivations and belief systems, very similar ideas about the very essence of what patronage meant to both parties, namely that it was a two-way process in which the two parties effectively patronised each other, and how this might be expressed.

It seems adequate to conclude by emphasising that the findings presented here are moderate in scale and unlikely to cause a sensation; however, to cause a sensation was not the aim of this essay, nor (perhaps more importantly) was it the aim of the religious communities at the heart of this study; concerned, as it is, with

---

[66] The research of this present study is based on the evidence from regular canons in Catalonia only, but the patterns of patronage are more generally applicable to other religious orders also.

[67] This last point, not elaborated in the present essay, refers in particular to the emergence of new religious orders, or new fashionable additions to medieval burial culture such as chantry chapels.

relatively small monastic communities, which is where evidence for patronage relations with lay folk tend to be most commonly found, the kind of material this study is considering is by definition concerned with quite the opposite. It relates rather to the kind of mundane, unspectacular aspects of lay-monastic relations that tell us so much about the ways in which these two worlds interacted, often on a personal level.

PRODUCTION, SPECIALISATION AND CONSUMPTION IN LATE MEDIEVAL WESSEX*

John Hare

The later Middle Ages has frequently been seen through a glass darkly: as a world still dominated by mental and demographic traumas of the Black Death. Here was a retreat from the thirteenth-century demographic and commercial peak, with a shrunken GNP. But the period may also be seen in a much more optimistic light. The demographic slump opened up enormous opportunities. More land could be acquired as tenants or lessees, tenants were able to free themselves from the burdens of serfdom, there were greater opportunities for mobility, and for choices within a consumer economy. Labour shortages paradoxically allowed wage earners to benefit, through higher payments.[1] But the surpluses which were generated were there to be spent. Historians have shown a growing interest in consumption and a consumer economy. Christopher Dyer has written of a more varied diet and of generally increased consumption of clothing, housing, goods and services, and of the impact of consumption in stimulating the rest of the economy, emphasising that the growth of consumerism in the eighteenth century had 'a modest precursor in the late Middle Ages'.[2] Maryanne Kowaleski has written more dramatically of a 'consumer revolution' of the later Middle Ages.[3] This period was to see a growth in consumption per head, and growing specialisation and professionalism. Such developments would have generated more new jobs, in a population that was essentially static. We must be careful not to exaggerate these positive elements, but the commercial elements of the early modern world of the sixteenth century were already established as a natural part of everyday life. This was not restricted to London and had percolated the provinces. Commerce, choice and specialisation

---

* The area of study has selected itself as a result of my own earlier and current work, but it seems singularly appropriate in view of the honorand's support for local and regional history during his distinguished career at Winchester. I am grateful to Dr. Winifred Harwood for all her work in preparing the database from the Southampton Brokage Books, and for reading and commenting on a draft of this paper.

[1] Although for a cautionary reassessment of some of our assumptions about wages see John Hatcher, 'Unreal Wages: Long-run Living Standards and the "Golden Age of the Fifteenth Century"', in *Commercial Activity, Markets and Entrepreneurs in the Middle Ages*, ed. Ben Dodds and C.D. Liddy (Woodbridge, 2011), 1–24.

[2] Christopher Dyer, *An Age of Transition: Economy and Society in England in the later Middle Ages* (Oxford, 2005), 147–57; idem, *A Country Merchant, 1495–1520: Trading and Farming at the End of the Middle Ages* (Oxford, 2005), 14–19, quote from p. 18.

[3] Maryanne Kowaleski, 'A Consumer Economy', in *A Social History of England, 1200–1500*, ed. Rosemary Horrox and W.M. Ormrod (Cambridge, 2006), 238–59.

were now more widespread. We must beware of assuming that what was visible was necessarily new, and commercial growth was evidently already a feature of the generations around 1300. But the increase in consumption per head generated by such specialisation would have stimulated the whole economy.[4]

For the economic historian, this period remains a time of difficulties, as our sources become much less useful. Demesne agriculture was already in decline by the end of the fourteenth century, and had generally ceased by the middle of the following century. With the retreat to leasing, the manorial account rolls, which have so much to tell us about the lord's agriculture, become much less useful. It was a century later before the probate inventories offer a different core source and open a new phase in the study of agriculture. Meanwhile, throughout the period urban sources in this area remain very fragmentary in their survival. The absence of a major source that allows systematic coverage means that it is ever more important to examine matters on a local and regional level where the scanty available, but varied, documentation can be integrated with greater confidence. Somehow manorial records, taxation, wills, buildings and the unique record of Southampton's internal trade recorded in the port's brokage books have to be linked into a coherent whole. In this paper, the area chosen for examination has been that of the old Wessex, centred on Wiltshire and Hampshire but incorporating the neighbouring counties. This was an area that was prospering, rising in relative terms among the regions of England. It saw a clear rise in the relative growth of tax between 1334 and 1514, with dramatic rise in the ranking of Wiltshire.[5]

The Cloth Industry

One of the most important changes of the period was the growth of the cloth industry, and this produced a particularly noteworthy expansion of jobs and economic surpluses in southern England. England changed from being an exporter of wool to one of manufactured cloth. This was a process that was already clearly underway by the end of the fourteenth century, but it continued to rise in the course of the fifteenth century. Cloth exports had risen by 55% by 1500 and this continued to expand in the first half of the following century (Table 1). The figures mark the various peaks before recession and then continued expansion took over. In each period of growth, industry extended beyond that of its predecessor.

Cloth production, however, was not just required for export, but also for a more demanding domestic market. Although we have no precise figures of internal consumption, it was evidently large. Dyer has argued that, 'The number of cloths woven each year cannot have been less than 200,000',[6] suggesting that exports in the early sixteenth century occupied less than half of national production. There would have always been a demand for textiles of some sort, often locally produced, but cloth was now being produced in specialist regions or areas and distributed throughout the country.

---

[4] Dyer, *An Age of Transition*, 156.
[5] R.S. Schofield, 'The Geographical Distribution of Wealth in England 1334–1649', *EcHR*, xviii, pt. 2 (1965), 504.
[6] Dyer, *An Age of Transition*, 149.

Table 1: Cloth Exports (decennial averages)

Date	Cloth exports
1351–60	6,413
1391–1400	[40,291]
1441–50	[49,421]
1491–1500	[62,361]
1531–40	106,110

Source: A.R. Bridbury, *Medieval English Clothmaking* (1982), 116, 122.

Salisbury cloth would find its way to other parts of England as well as abroad.[7] Cloth was being produced and consumed on a national and international standard. But this concentration on production minimises the economic impact of such industrial growth. Increased production would have generated personal surpluses that could be applied to a more selective choice of food and demand for consumer goods or specialist services, thus further emphasising regional contrasts and prosperity.

Types of cloth varied from region to region, but England was noted abroad as a producer of mid-range fabrics, both dyed and undyed.[8] In west Wiltshire the emphasis was on the large heavily-fulled broad cloth, while other areas concentrated on smaller, lighter and coloured fabrics, the straights and dozens of Somerset or the kersies of Hampshire and the valleys of the Thames and Kennet. The industry became part of a much wider European market. Goods were imported to help produce cloth of a higher European quality: dyestuffs like woad and madder, alum, oil and soap, whose distribution to some of the main specialist cloth centres of England is recorded in remarkable detail in the brokage books of Southampton.[9] This included the period when Southampton was at the peak of its importance as the most important cloth-exporting provincial port. In return, cloth was exported to the Mediterranean, France and Flanders and beyond.

Industrial growth was concentrated in particular geographic areas and above all in the area covered by this paper, which had become the industrial heartland of England, producing much more cloth than its population would warrant.[10] This

---

[7] As with King's College Cambridge: J.S. Lee, *Cambridge and its Economic Region, 1450–1560* (Hatfield, 2005), 146–7.
[8] E.g. in Toulouse: Philippe Wolffe, 'English Cloth in Toulouse (1380–1450)', *EcHR*, 2nd series, ii (1950), 290–4.
[9] John Hare, 'Commodities: the Cloth Industry', in *English Inland Trade 1430–1540: Southampton and its Region*, ed. M.A. Hicks (Oxford, 2015).
[10] Excluding Berkshire and Oxfordshire, 14% of the population in 1377 produced 54% of the cloth in the 1390s: John Hare, *A Prospering Society: Wiltshire in the Later Middle Ages* (Hatfield, 2011), 193.

importance is clear in the aulnage accounts (a tax on cloth that was marketed),[11] but it emphasises the importance of this area, with about half of the national production coming from central southern England.

Table 2: Aulnage

	1390s	1460s
Somerset	25.1	12.7
Wiltshire	14.8	11.0
Hampshire	4.7	3.7
Dorset	0.9	1.8
Berkshire and Oxfordshire	4.3	4.0
Gloucestershire and Bristol	9.0	9.0
Central Southern England	58.3	42.2

Source: calculated from H.L. Gray, 'The Production and Exportation of English Woollens in the Fourteenth Century', *EHR*, xxxix (1924), 34; Herbert Heaton, *The Yorkshire Woollen and Worsted Industries* (Oxford, 1920).

The percentage drop in the, albeit less reliable, figures of the 1460s may have resulted from the growth of the textile industry in Suffolk and Essex, or from the increased domination of London over the wholesale marketing of cloth, rather than an actual fall in production. In the fourteenth century the major growth had been in and around the great towns like Bristol, Salisbury and Winchester. Salisbury was a major centre of production. In 1421, 396 city weavers and fullers attended a meeting, suggesting that something like a third of the adult male population was then engaged in the cloth industry.[12] But it was also the trading centre for the industry beyond, as seen in the brokage books. Elsewhere in the region other urban centres dominated the industry: in the 1390s, Sherborne was responsible for 87% of Dorset's production, and Winchester 77% of that of Hampshire, while in Somerset traditional cloth producing towns like Bath, Wells and Frome were less important but were still responsible for over a third of the total. Moreover, around the cities lay regions of clothing activity, such as the Wyle Valley, west of Salisbury, where there was already a concentration of weavers and fullers in 1379 in Heytesbury hundred. But the industry also opened up new ground in rural areas, as at Pensford in Somerset, a new settlement on the fringe of two adjacent parishes which by the 1390s marketed about 40% of the cloth traded in Somerset, itself by far the largest cloth producing county in England.[13]

---

[11] On the aulnage accounts see J.N. Hare, 'Growth and Recession in the Fifteenth-Century Economy: the Wiltshire Textile Industry and the Countryside', *EcHR*, lii. pt. 1 (1999), 2.

[12] *The First General Entry Book of the City of Salisbury*, ed. D.R. Carr (Wiltshire Record Society, liv, 2001), 100–3; Hare, *A Prospering Society*, 180.

[13] On the industry in Wiltshire and Somerset, see Hare, *A Prospering Society*, 176–94; E.M. Carus-Wilson, 'The Woollen Industry Before 1550', *VCH Wiltshire*, iv. 115–47; John Hare, 'Pensford and

At the same time we need to be aware of the varied chronology of cloth production and impact on industrial distribution. Table 1 highlights the successive phases of expansion: the dramatic late fourteenth century growth, the early fifteenth century recession followed by expansion to a new peak in the 1440s, the mid-fifteenth-century recession, followed by sustained growth from the 1470s to the mid sixteenth century. While expansion often occurred in areas of existing production, each phase also opened up new areas of importance. This process was clearly apparent in Wessex. The industrial expansion which continued in the first half of the fifteenth century opened up rural industry in the countryside of west Wiltshire such as at Castle Combe, in Stroudwater (Gloucestershire), or in eastern Hampshire as seen in the growing importance of Basingstoke and Alton. The last phase of cloth expansion occurred in the revival of the later fifteenth century and into the boom-time conditions of the sixteenth century. In some areas, expansion was built on earlier industrial areas as in west Wiltshire although with a renewed focus on London. But some of the greatest growth was in the Thames and Kennet basin and in kersey production. It is noticeable that those southern towns that showed the greatest growth by the early sixteenth century were all in this area and were noted as cloth producers: Marlborough, Reading, Basingstoke, Alton and Newbury.[14]

One of these towns, Basingstoke in north-east Hampshire, provides a useful and unfamiliar case study, as a town which rose to prominence on the back of this industrial growth. By 1524/5 it was among the top fifty-five towns in the country by population and taxable wealth. It was not assessed separately in the aulnage accounts of 1394/5, but by 1466/7, with neighbouring Odiham, it was responsible for 4.8% of the county's production, with an industry dominated by Nicholas Draper *alias* Bayley.[15] The Basingstoke courts fined men for infringement of trading regulations with a regularity that suggests that such fines were effectively a registration charge for all traders in a particular occupation. Such fines show the cloth industry's continuing growth. By 1470, eleven men were charged for activity in this industry, nineteen in 1491, thirty in 1503 and fifty-six in 1524.[16] In the 1520s, 42% of those fined were involved in cloth production and marketing, and this industry dominated the rich financial elite in the subsidy assessments of the 1520s.[17] There were evidently textile craftsmen among the urban population, as seen in the twenty-three weavers who were fined in 1524, but they tended to be among the poorer or mid-range assessments, representing small-scale independent producers. Many more were engaged in trading and finishing the cloth – much

---

the Growth of the Cloth Industry in late Medieval Somerset', *Procs. Somerset Archaeological and Natural History Soc.* cxlvii (2003), 173–80.

[14] Hare, 'Commodities: the Cloth Industry', in *English Inland Trade*, ed. Hicks; Margaret Yates, *Town and Countryside in Western Berkshire, c.1327–c.1600* (Woodbridge, 2007), 67–124. These towns are mapped in Alan Dyer, 'Urban Decline in England, 1375–1525', in *Towns in Decline*, ed. T.R. Slater (Aldershot, 2000), 283; reproduced in Richard Britnell, *Britain and Ireland 1050–1530* (Oxford, 2004), 349.

[15] TNA, E101/344/17, m. 18; the reference to these being the same person is in Sheila Himsworth, *Winchester College Muniments* (3 vols., Chichester, 1976, 1984), ii. 186.

[16] Hants RO, Basingstoke borough records, 148M71/2/7/7, 9, 16, 18.

[17] *Ibid.*, 148M71/2/7/18; 3/4/2.

more than would be needed to service the urban weavers. Thus there were three mercers, five drapers, twenty-eight fullers and five dyers compared with the twenty-three weavers. The town, its rich merchants and townsmen evidently depended on the production of the countryside beyond.

It is difficult to establish the presence of substantial cloth production in the countryside without a painstaking trawl through a wide variety of sources in many villages, but a cursory and preliminary survey shows that this was already occurring in the surrounding villages. There was a dye works at Sherborne St. John in 1473.[18] There were fulling mills, especially in the valleys of the rivers Lodden, Lyde and Whitewater, at Andwell, Newnham and Stratfield Saye, Bramley, Hook and Heckfield.[19] Nor were these mere relics of earlier activity, as can be seen in regard to the Milton family of Andwell. They were already tenants of the manor in 1447.[20] John Milton was recorded as a clothman in the period 1493–1500 and died in 1521.[21] Another John Milton (perhaps his son) was among the leading figures in the village, with the fourth highest assessed wealth there in 1525. He died in 1541,[22] but his widow continued the business. She was subsequently recorded among those makers of fine kerseys.[23] She leased the fulling mill with her son Roger in 1542, by herself in 1545, and with her son Nicholas in 1560. Shortly before her death in 1573 she was still dwelling in the mill.[24] Elsewhere at Greywell, Robert Chapman was described as a clothier when he died in 1524, and his wealth was reflected in the large number of wealthy Chapmans in the subsidy assessment.[25] When Thomas Chapman died in 1558, his inventory valued his goods and debts at over £300 including £123 in the wool loft.[26] At Mattingley, there were at least three clothier families.[27] Moreover, once inventories become available, they provide further evidence of rural industry as at Mapledurwell and Up Nately, with shops containing looms and fulling equipment, debts for wool and oil, and a significant number of spinning wheels.[28] This area figures prominently among the list of 'clothiers that make fine kerseys' from the mid sixteenth century, including Overton (four names), Kingsclere (three), Whitchurch (four), Odiham (three), Greywell (one), Mattingley (three), Basingstoke (eight), and Andwell (two).[29] Thomas Kitson, a London merchant trading on a large scale, bought cloth extensively from two Odiham clothiers in 1531.[30] There was also a movement of merchant families from Basingstoke into the adjacent countryside, as with the

---

[18] Montagu Burrows, *The Family of Brocas of Beaurepaire and Roche Court* (1886), 393.
[19] Winchester College Muniments, 3092, 25757–63; *VCH Hampshire*, iv. 47, 107, 142, 157. For John Lyde of Newnham, fuller see Hants RO, Jervoise of Herriard MSS, 44M69/D1/6; *CIPM*, xviii. 360.
[20] Winchester College Muniments, 2917, k. William Milton held two half-virgates when he died.
[21] *Ibid.*, 29218 a; TNA, C1/216/7.
[22] Hants RO, Wills unclassified, 1541U/52.
[23] TNA, E101/347/17.
[24] Winchester College Muniments, 25757; Hants RO, Wills bishopric, 1573B/090.
[25] TNA, E179/173/183.
[26] Hants RO, Winchester Diocese MSS, 21M65/D3/80.
[27] Richards, Turners, and Hill: Hants RO, Wills and Inventories, 1545, 1552, 1576, 1580, 1582.
[28] John Hare, Jean Morrin and Stanley Waight, *The Victoria History of Hampshire*, New Series: *Mapledurwell* (2012), 42; see also draft articles on Up Nately and Andwell in www.victoriacountyhistory.ac.uk/counties/hampshire.
[29] TNA, E101/347/101.
[30] P.H. Ramsey, 'The Merchant Venturers in the First Half of the Sixteenth Century' (Oxford Univ. D.Phil. thesis, 1958), 184.

Kingsmills to Ashe and Sydmonton, the Belchambers to Cliddesden, and the Deanes into Newnham. This migration of industrial wealth to the countryside is familiar elsewhere, as with the Dolmans from Newbury to nearby Shaw.[31] But it was an interaction that could be continuous. The Canners remained important tenants and freeholders of Mapledurwell while becoming temporarily important townsmen. As late as 1594, the demesne lessee of neighbouring Andwell reflected these dual urban and rural family traditions. In his will, Gilbert Locker, a rich gentleman from a family of wealthy Basingstoke fullers, who possessed land in both places, left his body to be buried in Basingstoke itself, in, unusually, the school house, which before the Reformation had been the Holy Ghost chapel, on which the townsmen had lavished considerable wealth.

The growth of the industry would have had an enormous impact in the cloth centres themselves, although the documentation is difficult. It generated new jobs, whether among the individual craftsmen fined in Basingstoke or the individual workers paying chevage at Castle Combe when the number rose from nineteen in 1394 to seventy in 1443. The influx of outsiders is difficult to quantify precisely but occasionally can be assessed using a minority group, those recorded in the alien subsidies. Thus in Wiltshire, the cloth towns and their area figure prominently in the distribution of aliens: of 369 individuals recorded in the Wiltshire records for the 1440 subsidy 214 were Frenchmen and 125 Irish. This is likely to be an underestimate but is also likely to represent a small proportion of those coming from elsewhere in England.[32]

Housing needed to be provided. In some cases this was reflected within buildings scattered in towns and villages, but sometimes we can see more specific and large-scale examples. At Castle Combe there were fifty-five tenants in 1340. But between 1409 and 1454, as the industry made its breakthrough, fifty new or rebuilt houses appeared. One clothier rebuilt his own house and erected nine new dwellings.[33] At Mells, Abbot Selwood of Glastonbury built a new street which still survives. At North Warnborough (Hampshire) a terrace of nine houses was created in 1478 and another seven built in 1535.[34] Lords and tenants invested in capital equipment. At Castle Combe, William Haynes added a gig mill (which mechanised the process of raising the nap of the cloth) to his existing fulling and corn mills.[35] Elsewhere, lords invested in new fulling mills, as at Heytesbury, Mere, Boynton, Warminster,[36] Bentworth (Hampshire),[37] and Overton.[38] Fulling mills became an increasing focus within the industry, with business being increasingly concentrated

---

[31] Yates, *Town and Countryside*, 94.
[32] Hare, 'Growth and Recession', 15–16.
[33] E.M. Carus-Wilson, 'Evidences of Industrial Growth on Some Fifteenth-Century Manors', in *Essays in Economic History*, ed. *eadem* (2 vols., 1962), ii. 165; G.P. Scrope, *History of the Manor and Ancient Barony of Castle Combe* (1852), 249–50.
[34] Edward Roberts, *Hampshire Houses, 1250–1700: Their Dating and Development* (Winchester, 2003), 238. Interestingly, only one of the houses possessed a fireplace.
[35] Carus-Wilson, 'Evidences', 163.
[36] E.M. Carus-Wilson, 'The Woollen Industry before 1550', *VCH Wiltshire*, iv. 129.
[37] Hants RO, Manors of Bentworth and Boxhead MSS, 25M75 M2, mm. 18, 19.
[38] Hants RO, Bishop of Winchester's estate records, Overton, 11M59/ B2/27/2.

around them, as developed by the Miltons, Thomas Horton at Westwood, or Alexander Langford.[39]

Industrial growth generated considerable wealth. Clothiers like Horton were assessed much more highly than those who were the rich lessees of the great demesnes.[40] They spent some of their surpluses in buying consumer goods, as in the purchases made in the sale of goods of John Grene, the former rector at Castle Combe.[41] Parts of the newly-generated surpluses went on building churches, some of which, such as Steeple Ashton, Castle Combe, Seend and Westwood, can be documented to have had heavy investment from clothiers.[42] In other cases, their high cost and elaboration reflects the generation of considerable financial surpluses which in turn were spent on the buildings and craftsmen, and thus on their food and consumer goods. Elsewhere, and on a much more modest scale, among the small chapels around Basingstoke, the men of Mapledurwell re-roofed and re-windowed the nave and invested in a new bell tower and bell.[43]

Industrial growth encouraged the rise in rents and seigneurial incomes, particularly in the cloth-producing centres but also in the surrounding villages, where it helped generate agricultural prosperity. Castle Combe was probably exceptional for the scale of its growth, and its lords were able to gain enormously from the high fines charged on changes of landholding. Moreover, here we possess the exceptional records kept by William Worcestre, the steward. In nineteen years, the courts rendered over £318 on a manor whose annual rental was about £26.[44] But the cloth industry also generated increased demand and thus higher rentals or court returns from the villages beyond, at Durrington and Bromham, whose efforts fed the food demands of the cloth industry. In Wiltshire rents in the rural area beyond remained artificially high only to fall during the mid-century recession in the industry.[45] At Castle Combe, butchers, bakers and fishmongers brought their products from substantial small towns such as Chippenham and Malmesbury, as well as a wide range of smaller places within a ten-mile radius.[46] The growth of such industry and its dependent population also generated problems as well as benefits, as with the social control of an expanding industrial proletariat. Thus at Castle Combe, the court sought to regulate the opening time of taverns, and thus to control gambling. Basingstoke also sought to fix opening hours and to regulate the carrying of knives and daggers, and the brawling between apprentices, serving men and outsiders.[47] Moreover, a more widespread breakdown of law and order could

---

[39] Hare, *A Prospering Society*, 182–4; G.D. Ramsay, *The Wiltshire Woollen Industry in the Sixteenth and Seventeenth Centuries* (2nd edn., 1965), 16–19, Carus-Wilson, 'The Woollen Industry', 143–4.
[40] Horton was assessed at £450, while other lessees of major demesnes were assessed at figures between £50 and £100. The only exception was provided by the Goddards and their high assessment may have resulted from an unproven involvement in cloth trading (TNA, E179/197/155, 156, 161).
[41] Scrope, *History of Castle Combe*, 227–8.
[42] Hare, *A Prospering Society*, 189–90; BL, Add. Ch. 18478, 22 June 1436.
[43] Hare, Morrin and Waight, *Mapledurwell*, 76–8.
[44] BL, Add. MS 28208; Ramsay, *Wiltshire Woollen Industry*, 16; Scrope, *History of Castle Combe*, 250 (the annual rental is that for 1458–9).
[45] Hare, *A Prospering Society*, 195–211.
[46] Carus-Wilson, 'Evidences', 166.
[47] *Ibid.*, 165; John Hare, 'Church-Building and Prosperity on the Eve of the Reformation: Basingstoke and its Parish Church', *Procs. Hants Field Club*, lxii (2007), 191; F.J. Baigent and J.E. Millard, *A History of the Ancient Town and Manor of Basingstoke* (Basingstoke, 1889), 311, 320, 322.

arise when recession struck the industry, as it did in 1450 when industrial difficulties led to troubles in the centres of the cloth industry and played a part in the murder of Bishop Aiscough.[48]

Consumption and Choice: Agriculture and Food

A study of the agrarian markets has also to be built up from scattered fragments, but it shows a buoyant market with growing specialisations, in particular in grain, livestock and cheese. Again the fragmentary nature of the evidence needs to be emphasised. As long as demesne farming continued we have some evidence of its produce, but we rarely know where such produce was marketed, and our evidence of urban marketing is poor. Wessex shows that by 1400 there were already pronounced regional variations in agriculture.[49] The chalk downlands which ran through this area were characterised by great sheep flocks, many of which continued well into the fifteenth century, with flocks of over 1,000 sheep.[50] Nor were such large flocks restricted to the lord. Thus at Warminster there were over 1,000 non-seigneurial lambs compared with ninety for the lord, while individual peasant flocks of up to 120 were found at Coleshill (Berkshire) and up to 300–400 at Eastrop.[51] The great demesne flocks constituted a relatively small proportion of the total number of sheep. At Downton, demesne lambs constituted about a fifth of the total issues of the tithe, and as lords increasingly replenished their stocks by purchase, peasant land flocks became ever more important.[52]

Here was a very mixed economy with sheep and arable cultivation closely linked. Meanwhile a different pastoral sector was emerging in the Hampshire basin, the Thames basin, and the clay-lands of Wiltshire. This can clearly be seen by comparing a largely chalk-land great estate (Winchester Cathedral Priory) with an estate most of whose land lay within the clay-lands of Hampshire (Titchfield Abbey). Such a comparison is made possible by the fortunate survival of listings of livestock on each whole estate in 1390. Titchfield was a much smaller estate (in the 1530s, it was valued at 17% of that of the cathedral priory), as well as being less dominated by the lord's demesne,[53] and the figures for each estate contain a few manors not on the primary land type (thus clay-land Titchfield included the chalk-

---

[48] Hare, *A Prospering Society*, 202–8; J.N. Hare, 'The Wiltshire Risings of 1450: Political and Economic Discontent in Mid-Fifteenth-Century England', *Southern History*, iv (1982), 13–31.
[49] Hare, *A Prospering Society*, 59–82; John Hare, 'The Bishop and the Prior: Demesne Agriculture in Medieval Hampshire', *Agricultural Hist. Review*, liv (2006), 190–209; Edward Miller, 'Farming Practices and Techniques: I. The Southern Counties', in *The Agrarian History of England and Wales*, ed. idem (Cambridge, 1991), 285–303; John Hare, 'Agriculture and Rural Society in the Chalklands of Wiltshire and Hampshire from c.1200 to c.1500', in *The Medieval Landscape of Wessex*, ed. Michael Aston and Carenza Lewis (Oxford, 1994), 159–69.
[50] Hare, *A Prospering Society*, 53–70; idem, 'The Bishop and the Prior', 198–9, 206.
[51] Hare, *A Prospering Society*, 78–9; Rosamond Faith, 'Berkshire: Fourteenth and Fifteenth Centuries', in *The Peasant Land Market*, ed. P.D.A. Harvey (Oxford, 1984), 172.
[52] Hare, *A Prospering Society*, 70, 78–9.
[53] Calculated from *Valor Ecclesiasticus*, ed. Joseph Hunter and John Caley (5 vols., 1810–34), ii. 3, 21.

land manor of Inkpen), but the ratio of stock of different types between the two estates is revealing.

Table 3: Livestock on Two Wessex Estates: Titchfield Abbey and Winchester Cathedral Priory (1390)

	Titchfield Abbey (a)	Cathedral Priory (b)	a/b %
total horses	80	195	41.0
oxen	187	405	46.2
cows	91	189	48.1
total cattle	438	911	48.1
total sheep	2130	20367	10.5
total pigs	378	1809	20.9

Source: Hare, *A Prospering Society*, 6; Hants RO, DC/J Stockbook (uncatalogued, since removal of the cathedral archives to Hants RO); BL, Add. MS 70507, ff. 46v–47.

Titchfield's sheep flock was particularly low (10.5% of that of the cathedral priory) and most other animals were on a similar scale by comparison. But by contrast its cattle numbers were 48.1% of that of the priory estates. When the demesne was leased, regional characteristics were retained: thus the larger downland sheep flocks were often leased with the demesne, and the same was occasionally done with the cattle herd, as at Bitterne where the bishop of Winchester had kept over fifty-one cows in 1393.[54] Already by 1400, the Wiltshire clay lands had showed clear evidence of concentration on the pastoral sector, in an area where demesnes tended to be small and tended to be broken up when they were leased. This was already an area of family farms and the pastoral economy: in the 1379 poll tax the distribution of butchers shows a concentration in the vale as at Cricklade, Ashton, Malmesbury, Bradford, Rowde, Bromham and Chippenham. The relatively few demesne accounts we possess from this area also show the importance of a cattle-breeding herd and of cheese and pigs.[55] There were also areas where cattle and pastoral farming dominated in the Thames basin to the north and in the Hampshire basin to the south. In north-east Hampshire at Crondall there were twenty-four adult cows in 1391. At Coleshill in Berkshire, as the demesne arable was replaced, cattle numbers increased: they trebled between the 1390s and the mid fifteenth century.[56] By the mid sixteenth century the evidence is clearer, as in the clay lands

---

[54] Hare, 'The Bishop and the Prior', 208.
[55] Hare, *A Prospering Society*, 80–1.
[56] Faith, 'Berkshire: Fourteenth and Fifteenth Centuries', 171.

of Wiltshire and in north-east Hampshire, at Crondal, Up Nately and Newnham.[57] Earlier, Leland had described the area between Southampton and Winchester as one more suitable for cattle breeding than growing grain or vegetables.[58]

The chalk lands also offered opportunities for specialisation other than for sheep. In some cases rich, broad river valleys, as at Chilbolton and Downton, provided opportunities for significant dairy herds. Large pig herds were also found on some of the ecclesiastical estates such as Edington or Wootton (and other manors of Winchester Cathedral Priory).[59] Rabbit warrens developed and made specialist use of the poorer chalk downland, at a time when the arable acreage had shrunk with the resultant changes in land use, releasing additional better pastures for sheep and allowing poorer pastures to be put to these new uses. The man-made warrens generated large quantities of rabbits for meat and fur. Rabbit fur was not exotic and as parliament commented in 1532 was suitable for 'serving men and yeomen taking wages', adding a further element to the mix of choices, and they were also worth exporting to the Baltic in the sixteenth century.[60] At Aldbourne, on the great duchy of Lancaster manor, the warren generated a third to a half of the revenue of the manor and in some years produced over 5,000 rabbits. In Hampshire the bishopric of Winchester warrens at Overton, Longwood could produce over 1,000 rabbits a year.[61]

The growing demand for meat helped to enhance the position of butchers who might join the ranks of the great men of the towns, perhaps not among the very greatest but following close behind. Two examples should suffice. John Chippenham (*d*.1479) was a Salisbury butcher. He was a regular member of convocation, the ruling body of the city. He served as steward of the butchers' craft in 1449, and warden in 1474, and paid to be excused the role of alderman and reeve. Two of the three witnesses to his will were among the leading merchants of the time, both being mayor on several occasions.[62] William Grete of Basingstoke came from a family of butchers known in Basingstoke from at least 1409.[63] He himself was fined as a butcher between 1503 and 1539, and subsequently became bailiff (the main official of the town) in 1530, and warden of the chapel of the Holy Ghost, the main gathering place of the town's elite, in 1536.[64] He imported salt, and another Grete became a leading fishmonger in Southampton.

But the reduced population also offered opportunities to shift the production of arable crops to reflect the changing and more exacting demands of the market.

---

[57] Eric Kerridge, 'Agriculture c.1500–c.1793', in *VCH Wiltshire*, iv. 43–4; 'Up Nately and Andwell: Tenant Agriculture 1599–1700', www.victoriacountyhistory.ac.uk/counties/hampshire; Nigel Bell, *Newnham, a History of the Parish and its Church* (n.d.), 22–3; Joan Harries, *Farnham in the Time of Elizabeth* (Farnham, 1986), 28, 31, 34–7.

[58] John Leland, *Itinerary*, ed. John Chandler (Stroud, 1993), 202.

[59] Hare, *A Prospering Society*, 50–1; idem, 'The Bishop and the Prior', 206–7.

[60] E.M. Veale, *The English Fur Trade in the Later Middle Ages* (Oxford, 1966), 176–9.

[61] Hare, *A Prospering Society*, 72–4; idem, 'The Bishop and the Prior', 208–9.

[62] There were two John Chippenhams. The earlier one was a rich clothier. The first reference to the butcher is in 1436: *The First General Entry Book of Salisbury*, 157; Wiltshire and Swindon RO, Salisbury ledger bk. 2, G23/1/2, ff. 72v, 84v, 107v; TNA, PROB11/7, f. 2.

[63] Hants RO, Basingstoke borough records, 148M7 2/1/10. See also e.g. 148M71/2/7/1–5, 7, 12, 16.

[64] *Ibid*., 148M71/2/1/65–7; 2/7/16, 18, 19, 21; 71/3/4/2.

Demesne acreages did not just shrink, they applied an increasing proportion of the land to wheat and barley, and a decreasing amount to oats. Consumers increasingly wanted the better quality bread and ale and the market responded. Moreover, smaller landowners and tenants, under certain circumstances, shifted even further to barley production. This was very obvious at Downton where at one point, the rectory or parsonage estate was almost exclusively given over to barley production.[65] Even lords were adding value by converting the barley to ale as at Urchfont and Bishops Sutton.[66] The ale industry was also being transformed by the use of hops. This was initially focused on the towns where large-scale production in larger units became possible using the greater longevity of hop beer. This was already spreading among the small towns of south-east England,[67] and there was a growing import through Southampton for use among the towns. As the brokage books show, the trade expanded further during the 1490s and in the sixteenth century, when, in addition to Winchester and Salisbury, smaller, but still substantial, towns such as Andover, Basingstoke, Romsey and Hungerford also traded in hops with Southampton.[68]

As producers, the rural tenantry could benefit from the demands for such wider choice, but as consumers they could also benefit from the wider available options. They could accumulate land and, where relevant, could free themselves from the burdens of serfdom. They were better fed and no doubt benefited from the accessibility of relatively cheaper higher-quality cloth. They had higher expectations of housing. More and more rural housing has been dated to the fifteenth century in this area thanks to tree-ring dating. Both the surviving houses and the occasional surviving documentation make it clear that these were well constructed buildings, and the product of skilled professionals rather than unskilled amateurs. We can already see something of this in the substantial number of carpenters scattered throughout the Wiltshire villages in the poll tax figures for 1379.[69] We can also see this in the building of tenant properties carried out by various landlords. Winchester College built new houses on some of its estates. They were erected on well-made stone foundations, which in some cases used imported stone rather than flints from the field. The structures were timber-framed, and in one case brought from elsewhere, from nearby Bulford, and then re-erected on site at Durrington.[70] They included several rooms, thus a new house at Coombe Bissett in 1434 comprised a hall, upper and lower chamber, kitchen and outer buildings.[71] An inventory from 1525 of Robert Weylott, a rich tenant of Durrington, showed he possessed a house with kitchen, alehouse, hall, chamber and upper chamber, with painted cloth and furnishings.[72]

---

[65] Hare, *A Prospering Society*, 78.
[66] Hants RO, Bishop of Winchester's estate recs., 11M59//B2/22/6; 13.
[67] M.E. Mate, *Trade and Economic Development, 1450–1550: The Experience of Kent, Surrey and Sussex* (Woodbridge, 2006), 60–80.
[68] Hare, *A Prospering Society*, 141–2; idem, 'Miscellaneous Commodities', in *English Inland Trade*, ed. Hicks.
[69] *Ibid.*, 124–30, 141.
[70] Winchester College Muniments, 5989–91.
[71] *Ibid.*, 4400bb.
[72] *Ibid.*, 4359.

Towns and Trade

There has been continuing debate on the fortunes of the urban sector: were towns in the midst of decline? There has been, and no doubt will continue to be, debate on the nature and handling of the evidence of tax assessments, in the quest to establish national trends. Yet the problems of these sources mean that we are unlikely to discover a clear and coherent trend.[73] The sources need to be examined, not in isolation but in the context of the wider economy, and this brings in new problems. Somehow we both need more local studies and to find a means of handling the variety of local evidence and experiences. One good example of the problems is provided by the well-studied city of Winchester, the old capital city of Wessex. Here was a classic picture of decline with much of the former built-up area now empty. Yet it was an important hub of trade for the county beyond, as is shown in the brokage books of Southampton. It saw major capital investment in housing along the High Street in the course of the fifteenth century and its industrial eastern suburb grew and made up an increasing part of the city's tax assessment.[74] It retained this importance well into the sixteenth century.[75] As the brokage books remind us, there was an evident hierarchy of towns and markets, with provincial capitals like Salisbury and county towns like Winchester at the head. There were also a huge variety of lesser towns, many of which were themselves subject to long-term and short-term fluctuations. Whether or not towns were growing or shrinking, we are evidently viewing a well-established and mature pattern of towns, great and small, offering the institutional structure for increasing choice, for example, between local and imported products.[76]

The exceptional brokage books of Southampton show a complex of near and distant trade routes from the port, and a hierarchy of markets, that would have all generated jobs in transport, purchase and sale. Different types of goods showed different patterns of trade. Fish could be brought into ports and showed a more restricted pattern of trading. But specialist goods that came into Southampton travelled much further inland. Relatively bulky goods like wine could be transported overland even to Bristol, itself a major port. Such trade depended on a satisfactory infrastructure of bridges, roads and inns. The brokage books provide a unique view of the trade from 1430 to 1540, both enabling the construction of a

---

[73] The longstanding debate is summarised in Alan Dyer, *Decline and Growth in English Towns, 1400–1640* (Basingstoke, 1991) and continues most recently in *idem*, 'Urban Decline', 266–88; and S.H. Rigby, 'Urban Population in Late Medieval England: the Evidence of the Lay Subsidies', *EcHR*, lxiii, pt. 2 (2010), 393–417, which makes clear the difficulties of generalising.

[74] Derek Keene, *Survey of Medieval Winchester* (2 vols., Oxford, 1985), i. 87–195; T.B. James and E.V. Roberts, 'Winchester and Later Medieval Development: from Palace to Pentice', *Medieval Archaeology*, xliv (2000), 181–200.

[75] A.B. Rosen, 'Economic and Social Aspects of the History of Winchester, 1520–1670' (Oxford Univ. D.Phil. thesis, 1975); *eadem*, 'Winchester in Transition, 1580–1700', in *County Towns in Pre-Industrial England*, ed. Peter Clark (Leicester, 1981), 144–55, 174–5; J.N. Hare, 'Symonds, Peter' in *Oxford DNB*.

[76] Dyer, *An Age of Transition*, 190–4.

snapshot of trade in the period as a whole and glimpses of short-term trends.[77] The varied nature of Southampton's trade has a relevance beyond the trade of the port itself. Southampton's decline in the sixteenth century did not reduce trade, but merely served to redirect it, as the region's goods were increasingly concentrated on the London market. The brokage books show clearly both the hierarchy of towns, and common patterns throughout the century after 1430, as well as the presence of short-term fluctuations.

The timing of their transportation depended on when goods came into Southampton rather than on weather conditions, and reflected the capacity of the road system to cope with the demands of the economy. In many ways the pioneering period of bridge-building had occurred in the thirteenth and early fourteenth century but bridge-building and road improvement continued. Occasionally, there were major schemes, such as that across the Thames at Abingdon, or to a lesser extent a new bridge to the east of Salisbury. Elsewhere it could be a relatively small bridge that removed an awkward bottleneck, as at Quemerford, outside Calne on the main Bristol–London route, or in the investment in many smaller packhorse routes across the Wiltshire clay lands.[78] In addition to the need for a structure of roads and bridges, transport and trade was also developing a specialist support system for travellers in the form of inns.[79] In the fifteenth century there was already a well-established network of inns with most small towns having several. The value of such institutions depended partly on the traders and carters who carried the goods. There would have always been a need for merchant bases or shelter but now this was being professionalised. The wealthy would have made use of the private chambers which inns now provided, while carters no doubt slept on the hall floor. Inns could be of high value, with at the upper end of the market *The Angel* at Andover in which Winchester College was prepared to invest £400, while in Salisbury *The George Inn* on a plum High Street site briefly produced a rental of £15 p.a. Inns and innkeepers offered shelter and a range of professional services relating to marketing. The high revenues of this trade were reflected by the innkeepers themselves who, in small towns like Andover and Basingstoke, were among the elite of the town, and even in Salisbury could lay claim to being among the urban elite, albeit a second tier.

The brokage books provide evidence of a range of trade. Salisbury was a provincial capital and was frequently the largest trading partner of Southampton and traded much beyond Wiltshire itself. London was its only rival, and its trade was largely monopolised by the London–Italian distance trade. Nevertheless, Salisbury's importance can be seen in the way in which it dominated Wiltshire's trade. From a sample of years from 1430/1 to 1539/40, Salisbury was the trading destination for 94% of the herring brought into the county, 91% of its woad and 89% of its wine. This ratio was not constant – the city's dominance was reduced in the later fifteenth century as traders from the small towns of Wiltshire shifted from

---

[77] This section is based on the work of the Inland Trade Project and on the work on the database. I am grateful to my co-authors: see *English Inland Trade*, ed. Hicks.

[78] David Harrison, *The Bridges of Medieval England: Transport and Society, 400–1800* (Oxford, 2004); *Royal Commission on Historical Monuments, City of Salisbury* (1980), i. 52; Hare, *A Prospering Society*, 173.

[79] This paragraph summarises some of the conclusions of John Hare, 'Inns, Innkeepers and the Society of Later Medieval England, 1350–1600', *Journal of Medieval History*, xxxix, pt. 4 (2013), 477–97.

using the Salisbury market to taking goods to and from their home town. They had a choice and circumstances led to short-term shifts. The figures for Salisbury would be exaggerated by including products whose ultimate point of sale would be beyond the county, nevertheless, the importance of the city as the marketing centre of the county is clear. As a provincial capital Salisbury received a much wider range of goods than any other town outside London. This can be seen particularly in the amounts and range of spices sent to the city.[80]

Hampshire provides a different model of trade, with Winchester playing a dominant role, but much less so: 95% of the carts going to Wiltshire went to Salisbury, but only 53% of Hampshire goods went to Winchester. The towns of Hampshire traded directly with Southampton in a way which was much less usual in Wiltshire. But Winchester remained pre-eminent and served as a transit point for the towns beyond. Thus fish was taken from Southampton and other south-coast harbours, but two Andover men were fined for purchasing fish secretly in Winchester in 1427.[81] Andover itself was a major fish market, exceeded in its trade from Southampton only by Salisbury and Winchester. Its import of barrels of herring per number of taxpayers in 1524 was greater than that of Winchester itself, emphasising its wider trading role. It also seems to have been a major regional market for Spanish iron, being the fourth largest market after Salisbury, Winchester and Romsey. Much depended on the changing fortunes of these Hampshire towns. The growth of Basingstoke and its cloth industry led to a growth in direct trade from Southampton: in the fifteenth century the maximum was thirteen carts in a single year, but in the two years 1539 and 1540 it averaged forty-six carts. Newbury in Berkshire provided an even more striking example of the growth of trade by an expanding cloth town. In the 1440s it had averaged twenty-six carts per year, but in 1539 and 1540 this had risen to ninety-eight, and it had achieved a virtual monopoly over Southampton's woad trade.[82]

But the region was also criss-crossed by carters taking goods to more distant centres. Coventry was a familiar but surprising major destination for Southampton's trade. In seven years between 1439/40 and 1477/8 an average of thirty-five carts each year travelled the distance, with mainly dyestuffs for the city's textile industry but also with substantial quantities of wine. Surprisingly, the latter commodity went from Southampton to Midland towns when closer ports like Bristol would have seemed to have made more sense. The port even traded extensively with Bristol which was the seventh most important destination for carts from Southampton. Distance was thus not an insurmountable problem. These more distant towns and cities also served as hubs for trade to the lesser towns beyond, as seen in the trading activity of such centres as Northampton, Chesterfield, Shrewsbury, Gloucester and Cirencester.[83]

---

[80] Hare, 'Southampton's Trading Partners: Salisbury' and 'Southampton's Trading Partners: the Small Towns of Hampshire and Wiltshire'; Winifred Harwood, 'Luxury Goods and Spices', in *English Inland Trade*, ed. Hicks.
[81] Keene, *Survey of Medieval Winchester*, i. 260, 277.
[82] Hare, 'Commodities: the Cloth Industry', in *English Inland Trade*, ed. Hicks.
[83] Hare, 'Beyond Hampshire and Wiltshire', in *ibid*.

The towns provided a wide range of specialisations, occupations and guilds. The range varied according to the status of each town, being much more extensive at a provincial capital like Salisbury when compared with a large but essentially industrial, or largely single industry, town like Basingstoke. It is difficult to be precise about numbers of specialists, since individuals might have divided loyalties and groups might be subdivided or merged from one year to the next. But these occupational groupings were evidently felt to be useful divisions for the authorities in large towns to use in order to organise their responsibilities. At Salisbury lists of crafts in 1441 provide us with thirty-nine occupations, while later the order of crafts specified for the procession by the city corporation provide eighteen occupations in 1480 and thirty-three in 1527.[84] At Basingstoke, the number of occupations was smaller and although they rose from fifteen in 1409 to twenty-one in 1524, many of these groups were represented by very few people. In 1524, outside the cloth industry and the brewers and tapsters, no occupation had more than four people fined.[85] With these few exceptions occupational divisions would have been an inadequate means of organisation.

One growth area was the tailoring industry. 'A tailoring revolution of the later middle ages was occurring.' Costume became more complicated, more tight-fitting in cut, with bias cutting, more extravagant use of cloth and much more fine stitching. All of this required more training, more employment and greater specialist skills.[86] Fashion and style were important among the Salisbury elites. We find references to gowns and fashions, 'in the style of the citizens of the city', 'in this year's style', 'in my own style', and 'in the style of Walter Nandre'.[87] The upshot was a great growth in the numbers of tailors in Salisbury, where they rose from six (1381) to forty (1451), fifty-four (1481) and ninety-four (1517).[88] At Basingstoke, which had much less of a role as a consumer centre, the number of tailors' fines was far fewer and showed some, but not systematic growth. In 1422 there were four, in 1524 there were seven.[89] There were also signs of growing specialisation within the leather industry.[90] In Salisbury the glovers and sadlers had already emerged in 1441 as part of groups of small crafts, and by 1527 had their own place within the civic processions.[91] In Basingstoke, as befitted its different size and role, the development was slower and the numbers small, but by the end of the century, glovers and sadlers had emerged as specific occupations among the fines.[92]

Urban buildings also show evidence of a vibrant economy. An exhaustive survey of Salisbury's buildings published in 1980 ascribed about fifty houses to the

---

[84] *The First General Entry Book of Salisbury*, 185; A.D. Brown, *Popular Piety in late Medieval England: the Diocese of Salisbury, 1200–1550* (Oxford, 1995), 147.
[85] Hants RO, Basingstoke borough records, 148M7/2/1/10, 18.
[86] Dyer, *An Age of Transition*, 150–1; Kowaleski, 'A Consumer Economy', 247.
[87] Bridbury, *Medieval English Clothmaking*, 76.
[88] C.C. Fenwick, *The Poll Taxes of 1377, 1379 and 1381, Vol. III: Wiltshire to Yorkshire* (Oxford, 2005), 110–19; Charles Haskins, *The Ancient Trade Guilds and Companies of Salisbury* (Salisbury, 1812), 113–14; Wilts. and Swindon RO, Salisbury ledger bk. 2, G23/1/2, f. 120v; Swayne's ledger, G23/1/251, f. 10.
[89] Hants RO, Basingstoke borough records, 148M71/2/7/1, 18.
[90] Kowaleski, 'A Consumer Economy', 251.
[91] *The First General Entry Book of Salisbury*, 185; Brown, *Popular Piety*, 147.
[92] Hants RO, Basingstoke borough records, 148M71/2/1/64.

fifteenth century, many more than to the fourteenth or the sixteenth centuries. They ranged from spectacular double-jettied buildings in the central expensive area to more ordinary houses around.[93] This study preceded the dating accuracy achieved by tree-ring dating. The latter has, however, been applied particularly extensively in Hampshire, where despite the destruction of so many timber-framed buildings during the redevelopment of Andover and Basingstoke in the 1960s, the surviving buildings in north Hampshire show a marked prevalence of fifteenth-century dates.[94] Carpenters tended to be recognisably based in a single centre but their activities ranged much more widely and they would have competed with each other. Salisbury had its own group of carpenters, and these can be found outside the town, supplementing the pattern of village craftsmen. Thus Winchester College used carpenters from Salisbury to construct a new grange and a porch, and to supervise work on the mill at Coombe Bissett.[95] But the city also used the services of others. When William Ludlow wanted to build a new range at his Blue Boar Inn in 1444, he employed a carpenter from Bishopstrow, a village distant from Salisbury, although, perhaps significantly, near Ludlow's own residence at Hill Deverill.[96] John Lewys was a Winchester carpenter who can be seen employed in local projects as in that at St. John's Hospital. But he also operated more widely. He was Cardinal Beaufort's principal carpenter in the 1440s at Bishop's Waltham, Wolvesey and Marwell palaces, probably at his new work at St. Cross, and probably also at Kimpton.[97]

Conclusion

The fifteenth century thus saw the presence of a consumer market that was dependent on increased specialisation and professionalism. New jobs in growing industries like cloth manufacturing increased specialist production and production for a wider market. The greater range of choices meant that a more complex economy was emerging, based on a sophisticated hierarchy of towns, linked by the professional services of innkeepers and merchants. These developments were built on earlier changes and commercial expansion, and further evolution would take place. But already we can see the gradual emergence of a recognisably consumer

---

[93] *Royal Commission on Historical Monuments, City of Salisbury*, i. p. lxii.
[94] Roberts, *Hampshire Houses*, 193, 197; John Hare, 'Regional Prosperity in Fifteenth-Century England: some Evidence from Wessex', in *Revolution and Consumption in Later Medieval England*, ed. Michael Hicks (Woodbridge, 2001), 113.
[95] Winchester College Muniments, 4630, 4684.
[96] L.F. Salzman, *Building in England Down to 1540* (Oxford, 1952), 516–17.
[97] On Lewys, see Keene, *Survey of Medieval Winchester*, i. 283; John Harvey, *English Medieval Architects* (Gloucester, 1984), 184; Richard Warmington, 'Appendix', in J.N. Hare, 'Bishop's Waltham Palace, Hampshire: William of Wykeham, Henry Beaufort and the Transformation of a Medieval Episcopal Palace', *Archaeological Journal*, cxlv (1988), 250; Hants RO, Bishop of Winchester's pipe rolls, 11M59/B1/179, 180. The St. Cross rebuilding has no documentation, but the hall roof can now be dated to the Beaufort period and the roof structure of the chambers shows clear structural similarities to that of the chambers at Bishop's Waltham: *Vernacular Architecture*, xli. 107; *Newsletter of Hampshire Field Club*, lvi (2011), 17.

economy. The Wessex evidence does much to support the view that 'the "early modern" consumer revolution actually began in the later Middle Ages'.[98]

---

[98] Kowaleski, 'A Consumer Economy', 239.

A BUTT OF WINE AND TWO BARRELS OF HERRING: SOUTHAMPTON'S TRADING LINKS WITH RELIGIOUS INSTITUTIONS IN WINCHESTER AND SOUTH CENTRAL ENGLAND, 1430–1540[*]

Winifred A. Harwood

Fifteenth-century Southampton was a vibrant and successful port engaged in national and international trade. The incoming trade which was distributed from the port by land was recorded in the Southampton brokage books. These are a remarkable and unique source, which have allowed the port's inland trade to be analysed in a variety of different ways – chronologically, geographically, by goods and by towns – considered in a recent book.[1] This essay examines an aspect of trade not covered in that volume, namely the role played by the port of Southampton in the supply of religious institutions.[2] Although Southampton was just one link in the network of supply for these establishments, this essay will focus specifically on the port's part in supplying the religious houses of Winchester. Beginning with an overview of Southampton's overland trade system, it then considers the patterns of consumption in religious institutions in Southampton's hinterland, and uses two commodities, fish and wine, to illustrate the extent to which such houses were reliant on this particular port.

On Friday 15 November 1538 a carter named John de Huse left Southampton bound for St. Swithun's Cathedral Priory, Winchester, with a butt of wine and two barrels of herring.[3] This was just one cart of many which left the port in the fifteenth and early sixteenth centuries, and an entry typical of the many thousands of others in the brokage books. Southampton was a thriving port for much of this period and, situated centrally on England's south coast, was in a key position to

---

[*] This topic was selected because it combined aspects of the honorand's expertise which have shaped my own research interests – from his inspiring undergraduate lectures on monasticism, to his careful supervision while investigating consumption and purchasing patterns in religious institutions, and, more recently, his direction of the Overland Trade Project.

[1] *English Inland Trade 1430–1540: Southampton and its Region*, ed. M.A. Hicks (Oxford, 2015).

[2] For this paper, as for the volume, data from 13 brokage books has been analysed and used. This data is available online via the Overland Trade Project GIS at Winchester University (www.overlandtrade.org). The 13 brokage books, covering 12 accounting years (Michaelmas to Michaelmas), are Southampton Archives Services, SC5.5.1, 3, 8, 13, 14, 22, 23, 28–30, 33, 37, 38. Books 22 and 23 are for one accounting year. All references to data appear as on the geodatabase: e.g. SC5.5 followed by the number of the book, the folio number and whether recto or verso, followed by the number of the entry on that folio, e.g. SC5.5.13.89r5. Where more than one reference applies to a total quantity, just one example is offered.

[3] Southampton brokage books, SC5.5.37.8v2. www.overlandtrade.org

engage in England's inland trade. Drawing on both coastal and international trade, the arrival of goods at the port was the first stage in the process. Small coastal vessels arrived laden with cargoes of slates from Devon, tin from Cornwall, and fish from places ranging from Penzance in Cornwall to Southwold in Suffolk. Ships from France, Spain and the Mediterranean frequented the port for much of the century, along with Venetian galleys and Genoese carracks,[4] of which as many as ten or eleven visited each year between 1421 and 1458.[5]

Among the wide range of goods brought ashore were shipments of boots and shoes, herring and salt fish from the Low Countries; furs from the Baltic; millstones, salt and wine from France; iron, leather and wax from Spain; sweet wines – malmsey, muscadel and rumney – from the eastern Mediterranean; and dyes, glass, silks and other luxury goods from Italy.[6] Some of the commodities were mundane essentials required for work and daily living. Dyes – grain, madder and woad, and mordants such as alum – were staples for the cloth industry; Caen stone, wainscots and tiles were needed for the building trade, while fish, fruit and wine were imported for household consumption. Alongside these commodities, many of which arrived on Italian vessels, were exotic, highly-priced luxury goods destined for the capital: armour and weapons from Milan, cloth of gold from Lucca and Florence, saffron, olive oil and liquorice from southern Italy, and prunes, raisins, silk and sugar from Sicily.[7]

Southampton was a well-organised port; at the waterfront there were efficient systems both for handling goods and for the collection and recording of national and local customs and other tolls. The water bailiff collected levies such as anchorage, cranage, custom and wharfage.[8] Small coastal vessels moored alongside the wharf to unload their cargoes and paid 'wharfage', but the carracks and galleys were too large to do so and anchored offshore, from where small 'lighters' ferried the goods to land. These bigger vessels paid anchorage fees. Goods from the many vessels entering the port were then either transferred to smaller boats to be distributed along the coast to destinations such as Lymington, Chichester and Arundel and, more relevant here, directly to religious houses such as Christchurch Priory to the west of Southampton and Quarr Abbey on the Isle of Wight, or else they were brought ashore by hand or using the town crane.[9] The crane needed to be deployed for heavier items such as the great tuns of wine.[10] Once ashore, porters assisted in taking some goods for storage in the many stone cellars or vaults, some

---

[4] *The Southampton Brokage Book 1447–48*, ed. W.A. Harwood (Southampton Records Series, xlii, 2008), pp. x–xi.

[5] A.A. Ruddock, *Italian Merchants and Shipping in Southampton 1270–1600* (Southampton Records Series, i, 1951), 61.

[6] *Ibid.*, 77–8; Colin Platt, *Medieval Southampton: The Port and Trading Community, AD 1000–1600* (1973), 157–8.

[7] See Olive Coleman, 'Trade and Prosperity in the Fifteenth Century: Some Aspects of the Trade of Southampton', *EcHR*, 2nd series, xvi (1963–4), 9–22; Platt, *Medieval Southampton*, 154–63; Ruddock, *Italian Merchants*, 71–93.

[8] The records kept by the water bailiff are known as the port books.

[9] *The Local Port Book of Southampton for 1435–36*, ed. Brian Foster (Southampton Records Series, vii, 1963), 9, 28, 34, 45.

[10] These were large casks which contained as much as 252 gallons of wine, the maximum load for a cart to carry.

of which can still be seen today. The remaining commodities were carted out of the town, passing through Bargate, Southampton's north gate.

As goods were carted in or out of the town through Bargate, a town official, the Bargate broker, collected three tolls, namely, local custom, brokage,[11] and pontage,[12] meticulously recording them in a series of books. The Southampton brokage books are extremely detailed accounts, providing information such as the carter's name, the items being carried, their quantity, the owner and the town to which the cart was heading,[13] and it is thanks to these that so much is known about the merchandise carted out of Southampton and the people involved. The Overland Trade Project was established to extract information from the books into a Geographical Information System (GIS), and this has made it possible for researchers to analyse and visualise the data in detail.[14] The data shows that a variety of commodities were taken by cart to a wide range of places, but the greatest number of carts left Southampton for three core markets: London, for which it acted as an 'out-port'; Salisbury, which was a major trading and marketing centre for a huge area; and, to a lesser extent, Winchester, an important ecclesiastical centre and a notable market in Hampshire.

Despite the richness of their detail, the brokage books have limitations and need to be used with care. Twenty-two monastic houses, or twenty-seven religious institutions (listed in Table 1 and shown on the map),[15] are mentioned in the books entered on the database. However, it is possible that even more religious institutions traded via Southampton, albeit in years not included on the database or were recorded in books which have not survived. On other occasions, unidentified agents, dealing on behalf of a monastery, may have been named in the accounts but without being specifically associated with that institution. Similarly, on occasion commodities left Southampton for a small settlement situated close to an important religious establishment, such as Wherwell Abbey, where the final destination or consumer is not specified. Although some goods were sent directly to the abbey yet more were sent to individuals in Wherwell who may have been commissioned to act as 'middlemen' and make a sale to the convent, but the records simply do not confirm this information.[16] Therefore, it is possible, though by no means certain, that figures for such households have been underestimated. Many other religious establishments outside Hampshire were within trading distance of Southampton, although their location in relation to the coast or to other ports, such as Bristol, would have had a bearing on their supply networks. Using this source with caution, the supply of religious institutions in Southampton's hinterland, particularly those of Winchester, may be examined.

---

[11] A fee levied for arranging the haulage of goods.
[12] A one-penny toll levied on all vehicles as they entered or left the town.
[13] W.A. Harwood, 'The Customs System in Southampton in the Mid-Fifteenth Century', *Hampshire Studies*, liii (1998), 191–200.
[14] See note 3. The GIS combines spatial data in the form of maps with attribute data held in a relational database.
[15] Monastic houses refers to households of canons, monks or nuns living under religious vows; the term religious households here includes colleges and hospitals as well.
[16] See John Hare and W.A. Harwood, 'Assessment', in *English Inland Trade*, ed. Hicks.

Situated just twelve miles from the port, Winchester, as county town of Hampshire, was a notable provincial capital and market for the area beyond. It supported a sizeable, though declining, cloth industry. An important ecclesiastical centre, its religious institutions included three wealthy Benedictine monasteries – Hyde Abbey, the nunnery known as St. Mary's Abbey and St. Swithun's Cathedral Priory – and the large and impressive foundation of Winchester College. In addition there were hospitals, other colleges and houses for four orders of friars, as well as Wolvesey palace where the bishop of Winchester resided occasionally.[17] Studies of patterns of consumption at Winchester College and other religious institutions have demonstrated that these large households drew on a range of suppliers from a variety of locations.[18] Analysis of the purchasing practices of Richard Mitford, bishop of Salisbury, provides some insight into networks of supply in this period. In 1406–7 the bishop made both local and national purchases while staying at his Wiltshire manors of Potterne and Woodford. Forty-one per cent of his total expenditure related to items ordered from London; he also used the ports of Bristol and Southampton which, along with the markets at Salisbury, accounted for a further 39% of his purchases. While the bulk of his expenditure focused on the large centres of supply, further goods were acquired locally. Interestingly, when sourcing wine for these two Wiltshire manors, that for Potterne, situated centrally in the county, was brought from Bristol, but the wine for Woodford, further south and close to Salisbury, originated from Southampton.[19] Thus the evidence suggests that the bishop relied on a complex network of national, regional and local suppliers depending on a number of factors including availability and convenience of supply.

Of the religious institutions which were supplied through Southampton (see Table 1), fourteen (of which the most important trading partner was Reading Abbey) were located in counties beyond Hampshire. Eight monastic houses, or a total of thirteen religious households (when colleges and hospitals are included), were situated in Hampshire.[20] Those in Hampshire (but outside Winchester) were the two wealthy houses of Benedictine nuns at Romsey and Wherwell (approximately nine and twenty-five miles from Southampton) and the Augustinian canons at Christchurch, Mottisfont and Southwick (approximately twenty-four, fourteen and twelve miles from the port).

While evidence shows that, on occasion, some commodities were carried as far as Evesham in Worcestershire, some 120 miles away, and rather more frequently to institutions in the counties of Berkshire, Dorset and Wiltshire, closer to Southampton, most of Southampton's deliveries for religious institutions were destined for elsewhere within Hampshire. Some of the institutional households mentioned in the brokage books may have used the port on only one or two

---

[17] The bishop of Winchester also sometimes resided at his palace at Bishop's Waltham, at Farnham Castle and at Marwell, about ten, twenty-eight and twelve miles respectively from the port.

[18] See W.A. Harwood, 'The Pattern of Consumption of Winchester College c.1390–1560' (Southampton Univ. Ph.D. thesis, 2003).

[19] John Hare, *A Prospering Society: Wiltshire in the Later Middle Ages* (Hatfield, 2011), 169–70; Christopher Dyer, *Standards of Living in the Later Middle Ages: Social Change in England c.1200–1520* (Cambridge, 1989), 74–5.

[20] John Hare, *The Dissolution of the Monasteries in Hampshire* (Hampshire Papers, xvi, 1999), 1.

occasions but for the three great Benedictine houses in Winchester, the port of Southampton was of far greater importance.

Table 1: Religious institutions trading through Southampton.[21]

Religious institutions in Hampshire	no. of carts	Religious institutions beyond Hampshire	no. of carts
Christchurch (A. canons)	5	Abingdon, Berks. (B. monks)	5
Hyde Abbey, Winchester (B. monks)	87	Amesbury, Wilts. (B. nuns)	5
Mottisfont (A. canons)	3*	Battle, Sussex (B. monks)	2
Romsey (B. nuns)	13	Bramber, Sussex (B. monks)	2
St. Cross hospital, Winchester	7	Cirencester, Glos. (A. canons)	1
St. Elizabeth's College, Winchester	8	Evesham, Worcs. (B. monks)	1
St. John's hospital, Winchester	1	Gloucester, Glos. (B. monks)	2
St. Mary's Abbey, Winchester (B. nuns)	21	Milton, Dorset (B. monks)	1
St. Swithun's, Winchester (B. monks)	129	Osney, Oxon. (A. canons)	1
Southwick (A. canons)	3	Reading, Berks. (B. monks)	12
Wherwell (B. nuns)	17	Shaftesbury, Dorset (B. nuns)	1
Winchester College	23+2	Sherborne, Dorset (B. monks)	1
		Tarrant, Dorset (C. nuns)	1
		Waverley, Surrey (C. monks)	3
Bishopric of Winchester	44+11		

Key: A: Augustinian; B: Benedictine; C: Cistercian
* forty-five carts went to the priory at Mottisfont after it had been dissolved and when the buildings were being converted into a private residence.
Figures for the bishopric include forty-four carts which went to Winchester and eleven others: one each to Alresford, Bishop's Waltham, Farnham and Hursley; two to London and Overton and three to Twyford (Marwell). Figures for Winchester College include two carts taking millstones for their estate at Harmondsworth.

---

[21] Based on the twelve years on the database: 1430–1, 1439–40, 1447–8, 1461–2, 1462–3, 1477–8, 1491–2, 1492–3, 1493–4, 1527–8, 1538–9, 1539–40.

Table 1 shows the number of carts which went to each religious institution in the twelve years examined. As in ten of those years 2,255 carts left Southampton for Winchester,[22] the 315 carts destined specifically for the religious institutions in the city amounted to 14% of the total. These establishments therefore represent a significant proportion of Southampton's direct overland trade to Winchester.[23]

It is surprising how infrequently major religious establishments, other than those in Winchester and, to a lesser extent, Reading, appear to have used Southampton. Dorset, which contained some old and wealthy monasteries, had remarkably few overland trading links with Southampton. This was no doubt because as well as having its own ports – Bridport, Melcombe Regis and Poole – the county was served by the Devon ports of Exeter and Dartmouth further west. Although the canons at Christchurch Priory took advantage of goods arriving from Southampton, both by road and by sea,[24] they only used the port to a limited extent. Perhaps this is not surprising since Christchurch had its own harbour and the priory was situated a similar distance from Salisbury, from where supplies could also be bought, and closer still to the port of Poole (about eleven miles away) from where direct purchases could be made. In addition, Salisbury, an important redistribution centre, was probably a source of supply particularly for specific commodities such as wax. Thus, despite Winchester's proximity to Southampton, in three successive years between 1492 and 1496 Winchester College sourced wax from Salisbury, even though it had originally been imported through Southampton.[25]

Quantities purchased depended on the size of the household. Small religious houses may have had no need to buy in large amounts, and no wish to set up a system for purchasing in bulk from the port, thereby avoiding the large-scale costs associated, and preferring instead to buy locally in the town as required. Hospitality was an expectation of medieval society, and the presence of visitors was not unusual, with the result that numbers to be catered for fluctuated from day to day. For example, St. Swithun's Cathedral Priory was responsible not just for feeding the religious community, which numbered forty-two in 1409, thirty-nine in 1447, thirty-five in 1500 and forty-three in 1533,[26] but also for feeding numerous others including corrodians, guests and servants.[27] Likewise, servants, guests and craftsmen would have had to be added to the basic household of twenty-one religious at Hyde Abbey in 1539, and the twenty-six at St. Mary's in 1536, in order to arrive at a more realistic figure of the number of people for whom provisions were needed. Winchester College regularly housed approximately 130 people,

---

[22] The two years excluded are 1430–1, when the figures are not reliable, and 1493–4, when the records are incomplete. See Harwood, 'Winchester' in *English Inland Trade*, ed. Hicks.

[23] The numbers of carts shown on Table 1 is the total for all twelve of the years examined, of which the figure for Winchester carts is 320.

[24] For example, on 9 May 1440 a boat belonging to the prior of Christchurch left Southampton with one pipe of wine for the prior: *The Local Port Book of Southampton for 1439–40*, ed. H.S. Cobb (Southampton Records Series, v, 1961), 45. Unfortunately, the years of the extant port books seldom coincide with those of the brokage books.

[25] See Harwood, 'The Pattern of Consumption', 315.

[26] Figures from David Knowles and R.N. Hadcock, *Medieval Religious Houses in England and Wales* (2nd edn., 1971), 80–1.

[27] A corrody was a type of pension, in the form of clothing, food and/or lodging granted to a lay person, frequently for life, by a religious house, often as a reward for services rendered. A corrodian was an individual who received such benefits.

including the warden, ten fellows, a schoolmaster and an usher, three chaplains, seventy scholars, ten commoners, three lay clerks, sixteen choristers and several servants. Household numbers fluctuated when the scholars went home, generally at Pentecost, or when visitors, advisors, carters, craftsmen and estate officials dined in hall. The number of visitors increased at specific times of the year, such as at religious festivals and at the time of the college elections, the fair, and the quarter sessions and assizes.[28]

The income of the establishment, as well as its size, helped determine its purchasing practices. As a benchmark, the wealthiest religious house in England during this period was Westminster Abbey with a net income of £2,800 in 1535.[29] This was almost twice the income of St. Swithun's Priory which, with a net income of £1,507, was slightly more than Durham Cathedral Priory's income of £1,328, and substantially more than Hyde Abbey's £865.[30] It is not possible to give figures for St. Mary's Abbey since those documented in the *Valor Ecclesiasticus* were seriously distorted. For this error the abbey was fined, and consequently lost two of its richest manors. St. Swithun's Cathedral Priory, Hyde Abbey and St. Mary's Abbey were all Anglo-Saxon foundations which over the centuries had benefited from generous grants of land and, like Romsey and Wherwell, they were all rich monasteries.[31] Winchester College, a school for seventy adolescent boys, had a modest standard of living and by adopting prudent purchasing practices ensured that by 1535 it had become the third wealthiest institution in Hampshire.

The supplies required by religious houses ranged from basic staples of the monastic diet through to luxurious delicacies served on important occasions. What was enjoyed at the abbot's table at Hyde Abbey, the prior's table at St. Swithun's or indeed at the warden's table at the college would not, almost certainly, be the same as the more basic food the monks, scholars or servants were offered. At Westminster Abbey conger eel and fresh salmon, which were commonly served to the abbot, were considered a treat by the other monks.[32] Similarly, at Winchester College the warden had a food allowance of 2*s.* per week, compared with the page whose allowance was 6*d.*; the warden did not consume more of the same food as the page, rather, the increased allowance demonstrates that he enjoyed a diet of

---

[28] W.A. Harwood, 'The Household of Winchester College in the Later Middle Ages 1400–1560', in *Proceedings of the Hampshire Field Club and Archaeological Society*, lix (2004), 163–79.

[29] This figure includes the income of the abbot, unlike at the cathedral priories where there was no abbot. In such cases, the bishop assumed the role of titular head of the community, though his income remained separate.

[30] Figures for Westminster Abbey in Barbara Harvey, *Westminster Abbey and its Estates in the Middle Ages* (Oxford, 1977), 26 (which amends the net income given by David Knowles). Figures for St. Swithun's priory and Hyde Abbey from *Valor Ecclesiasticus temp. Henry VIII, Auctoritate Regia Institutus*, ed. John Caley and Joseph Hunter (6 vols., Record Commission, 1810–34), ii. 2–4. For data relating to Durham Cathedral priory see David Knowles, *The Religious Orders in England* (3 vols., Cambridge, 1948–59), iii. 473–4.

[31] Hare, *Dissolution of the Monasteries*, 3.

[32] Barbara Harvey, *Living and Dying in England 1100–1540: The Monastic Experience* (Oxford, 1993), 49.

different, more expensive food.[33] Even so, the warden's 2s. per week was modest when compared to the 4s. per week allowed to an ordinary monk at Westminster Abbey.[34]

Table 2 shows the type of commodities that were taken from Southampton to religious institutions in different counties. Wine was carted to such institutions in ten counties; millstones and fish to five. Generally, it would appear that most religious establishments relied on the port for ordering such basic goods, but on only few occasions. Not surprisingly, a greater variety of goods was taken to Hampshire and neighbouring Berkshire which were closer to the port. Hampshire, specifically the Winchester houses, took the greatest range of goods but even this was restricted when compared with the total range of commodities which left Southampton for Winchester generally. For most other counties fish and wine were the main commodities of trade.

Table 2: Commodities delivered to religious institutions arranged by county

County	*Commodities*
Berkshire	fish, fruit, household goods, iron, millstones, oil, wine
Dorset	fruit, 'spruceware', wine
Gloucestershire	furnishings (beds), utensils and equipment, wine
Hampshire, excluding Winchester	coal, condiments/preservatives (salt), fish, fruit, furnishings (wainscots), hops for brewing, metalware (iron), oil, spices, stone, tar, wine
Middlesex	fish
Oxfordshire	millstones, wine
Somerset	wine
Surrey	millstones, wine
Sussex	fish, hops for brewing, metalware (iron), wine
Wiltshire	fish, fruit, millstones, tiles, wine
Worcestershire	wine
Winchester	boards, cider, condiments/preservative (salt), fish, fruit, furnishings (beds, wainscots), grain (wheat), hops for brewing, metalware (iron), millstones, nails, wax, slates, spices, stone, tar, tiles, vegetables, wine

Although spices and wax feature in Table 2 they were not often sent in bulk to the religious houses; more frequently consignments of these commodities were delivered to the chandlers and retailers of Winchester from whom the religious institutions could purchase small quantities. For many years of the fifteenth century,

---

[33] See C.M. Woolgar, *The Great Household in Late Medieval England* (1999), 10, in which he has shown that within a household there could be at least three dietary regimes – for the lord, those of gentle rank, and those who were not of gentle rank – and in some households possibly as many as five or six.

[34] Harvey, *Living and Dying*, 36.

Winchester College used the services of a local chandler whose supplies originated from Southampton, although later the college turned to London for bulk purchases of wax when it was more expedient to do so. It also purchased spices in small quantities in Winchester, and in bulk from the capital and Southampton. Financially, purchasing in bulk was found to be beneficial even when transport costs were taken into consideration. It was clearly more expensive to buy smaller quantities locally than in bulk.[35] Availability, convenience and the prevailing price of commodities balanced against household purchasing power and preference were factors which determined where goods were sourced.

While many of the religious institutions were quite restricted in the bulk orders made directly from the port of Southampton, Table 3 shows that a greater variety of commodities was taken to the monks and nuns in Winchester, with items of food and drink, particularly fish and wine, dominating the list.

Table 3: Number of commodity transactions for fish, wine and other goods from Southampton to the main religious institutions in Winchester

Institution	Number of transactions fish	Number of transactions wine	Number of transactions other than wine or fish
Hyde Abbey	46	35	32
St. Mary's Abbey	11	–	14
St. Swithun's Priory	74	36	31
Winchester College	8	9	12

Although the results are somewhat crude, Table 3 shows clearly that within a single city different institutions might adopt different purchasing policies. All used Southampton for a variety of transactions, but St. Mary's Abbey and Winchester College were less involved in the direct bulk trade through the port than Hyde Abbey and St. Swithun's Cathedral Priory. St. Mary's Abbey received mainly fish from the port, but among the bulk purchases were seven consignments of slates delivered there during April and May 1462, which suggests a project to reconstruct the roof. In addition to fish and wine, Winchester College received fruit and salt; Hyde Abbey ordered fruit and vegetables, marble, millstones, salt and a small quantity of spices, while St. Swithun's Priory received fruit, iron, salt, wainscots and, on one occasion, hops. Items of food and drink were the most numerous. Two key items carried direct to religious establishments – fish and wine – need to be examined in more detail.

---

[35] Harwood, 'The Pattern of Consumption', 230, 310.

Fish

Fish was a fundamental component of the diet for everybody in the Middle Ages, and the religious orders were no exception. Everyone, whether inside the cloister or outside, was expected to eat fish on Wednesdays (until the fifteenth century), Fridays, Saturdays, on the eves of important feasts and during Lent.[36] In her study of the monks of Westminster Abbey, Barbara Harvey estimated that fish was consumed by the monks there on about 215 days a year.[37] Fish, both freshwater (from rivers and monastic fish ponds) and saltwater, was an extremely important component of the monastic diet. It was eaten fresh, dried, pickled in brine, salted or smoked. The most commonly mentioned fish in the accounts were herring, which were carried in barrels and sold ready-processed. Those that had been salted and pickled were referred to as 'white herring' while those that had been smoked were known as 'red herring'.[38] So important was fish to the diet that up to the fourteenth century the monks of Beaulieu Abbey in Hampshire sent their ship to collect consignments of herring which had been dried and kippered in their own depot at Great Yarmouth.[39] Clearly, households were prepared to source their supplies from a distance. The cellarers of Battle Abbey in Sussex were using a London fishmonger as early as 1385–6, despite the abbey's proximity to the coast. Although they bought fish at the fair at Faversham as well as sourcing fresh catches from Hastings (six miles away) and herring from Winchelsea (thirteen miles), the abbey's salt fish, salmon and stock fish came from London nearly seventy miles away.[40] Similarly, in the second half of the sixteenth century, Winchester College was buying large quantities of fish from the capital, which already had a highly developed fish market.[41]

It is not surprising, then, that with such high demands for fish, Southampton, too, played a significant role in its distribution during the period. Analysis of the brokage books shows that substantial quantities of fish left the port. Some of these loads were destined for counties beyond Hampshire; for instance, herring, salt fish and salmon were taken to Abingdon Abbey in Berkshire, and herring were among the products sent to Bramber Priory, in Sussex. However, most of the destinations were in Hampshire and Wiltshire, and chief among them were the ecclesiastical centre of Winchester and the major redistribution hub of Salisbury,[42] from where religious institutions in Dorset and Wiltshire could augment their supplies. The records show that fish from Southampton was carted to locations in Wiltshire such as Amesbury Abbey, and to the bishop and friars of Salisbury,[43] albeit only infrequently.

---

[36] P.W. Hammond, *Food and Feast in Medieval England* (Stroud, 1993), 18.
[37] Harvey, *Living and Dying*, 46.
[38] Woolgar, *Great Household*, 119.
[39] Hammond, *Food and Feast*, 21.
[40] *Accounts of the Cellarers of Battle Abbey: 1275–1513*, ed. Eleanor Searle and Barbara Ross (Sydney, 1967), 87, 97.
[41] Harwood, 'The Pattern of Consumption', 165; Harvey, *Living and Dying*, 47.
[42] See Hare, 'Fish', in *English Inland Trade*, ed. Hicks.
[43] In the brokage books, the species of fish is not always noted.

Within Hampshire the priors of Christchurch,[44] Mottisfont and Southwick[45] all received occasional cartloads of fish from Southampton. Despite its proximity to the sea and to the rivers Avon and Stour, the prior of Christchurch sourced fish from Southampton both by sea and by land.[46] In the case of Mottisfont, fish was carted there on three occasions in two years.[47] In some cases the records specify the type of fish delivered. Herring, red and white, were among the consignments taken to the nuns of Romsey, while hake, herring and salt fish were included in the deliveries to Wherwell. Since fish was so important in the monastic and medieval diet it is surprising that it was not carried directly to these religious houses more frequently. A probable explanation lies in the fact that Southampton fish was distributed to a group of lesser towns which included both Andover (five miles from Wherwell) and Romsey,[48] and with convenient supplies of fish close by it is likely that the nuns were also buying Southampton-sourced fish indirectly via local suppliers.

Winchester itself was an important regional centre for the sale of fish, much of which originated from Southampton. Conger, herring, ling, mulwell and salmon were the fish most commonly sold, with bass, bream, mackerel and mullet to a lesser extent. By the fifteenth century hake and sprat were also marketed there.[49] Evidence from the brokage books shows that most of these types of fish were taken to Winchester from Southampton in the years examined. Generally, the range of fish consumed in England was influenced by local supplies; salmon was relatively plentiful in the north-east, hake, conger and dogfish in the south-west, and oysters and whiting in the south-east.[50] In the brokage book for 1492–3 we see that hake, herring, mulwell, salmon, saltfish (stockfish) and sprat were carted to Winchester as well as eight consignments of unspecified types of fish. In February and March that year numerous cartloads of oysters were taken to unknown destinations, which would almost certainly have included Winchester.[51]

Quantities of fish were also taken from the port directly to Winchester's four main religious institutions, as shown in Table 4, which once again highlights the different purchasing strategies adopted by them, with Hyde Abbey and St. Swithun's Priory depending far more on bulk purchasing of fish from Southampton than St. Mary's Abbey and Winchester College. Whether gender can account for the marketing decisions made at St. Mary's nunnery is impossible to tell. However, St. Swithun's Priory received a limited range of fish, including salt fish and salmon, direct from the port.

[44] Southampton Archives Services, SC5.5.28.21r4.
[45] *Ibid.*, SC5.5.23.2r10.
[46] Salmon was taken by boat to the prior of Christchurch in 1436 as well as by land: *Port Book for 1435–36*, ed. Foster, 68–9; Southampton Archives Services, SC5.5.28.21r4.
[47] Fish was taken to Mottisfont in 1447–8, 1491–2, 1527–8 and 1538–9. It was only taken there in February, probably for Lent, and in February 1491–2 and 1527–8 the fish was specifically for the prior, see for example Southampton Archives Services, SC5.5.28.19v10 and SC5.5.33.33v3.
[48] See Hare, 'Fish'.
[49] Derek Keene, *Survey of Medieval Winchester* (2 vols., Winchester Studies ii, Oxford, 1985), i. 260.
[50] Dyer, *Standards of Living*, 67.
[51] These carts, owned by the carters, were not required to pay brokage and therefore were not required to state their destination.

Table 4: Fish sent from Southampton to various religious institutions in Winchester

Year of account	Hyde Abbey	St. Mary's Abbey	St. Swithun's Priory	Winchester College
1430–1	–	–	unspecified, salmon, salt fish	–
1439–40	red herring, salt fish	–	salt fish, red and white herring	white herring
1447–8	unspecified, herring, salmon, stockfish, sturgeon	unspecified, herring	unspecified, herring, salt fish	unspecified, herring
1461–2	unspecified, herring	herring	unspecified, herring, salmon	–
1462–3	–	herring	herring, salmon	mackerel
1477–8	conger eels, salmon	–	conger eels, herring, salmon, salt fish	herring
1491–2	herring, salt fish	–	herring, salt fish	herring
1492–3	unspecified	–	herring, salt fish	–
1493–4	–	herring	–	–
1527–8	cod, unspecified, herring, salmon	unspecified, herring	unspecified, herring, salmon	–
1538–9	herring, hake	–	unspecified, herring	herring
1539–40	–	–	unspecified, herring	–

Most important for the community at St. Swithun's was its supply of herring. In the year 1538–9 as many as thirty-two barrels of herring were taken to the priory, of which just five were dispatched from Southampton in November and December. The remaining twenty-seven were delivered during the first three months of the year: nine in January, fifteen in February and three in March. One explanation for such seasonality is that preserved fish, dried, salted or smoked, could be purchased in advance and stored in readiness for Lent. Records show that the fish trade generally was at its busiest in these months, but particularly in February. Similarly, fish was the principal commodity required when Winchester College purchased victuals for Lent each year, although figs and raisins were two other Lenten favourites for the warden's table. However, in two years when the origin of these goods was specified they had been sourced in London.[52]

Table 5: Number of barrels of herring taken to Winchester institutions

	Hyde Abbey	St. Mary's Abbey	St. Swithun's Priory	Winchester College
1439–40	6 (red)	–	13.5+	2 (white)
1447–8	22	7+	11	9.5
1461–2	21	3	3	–
1462–3	–	?	?	–
1477–8	–	–	6.5	6
1491–2	7	–	14	4
1492–3	–	–	?	–
1493–4	–	1	–	–
1527–8	9.5	5.5	25	–
1538–9	16	–	32.5	3
1539–40	–	–	17+	–

Two extant diet rolls from St. Swithun's Priory reveal that during Lent 1493, eels, flounders, herring, lampreys, ling, mulwell, minnows, plaice, salmon, stockfish, whiting and a whole range of shellfish, including oysters, were consumed in the refectory. By correlating the brokage books with the diet rolls it becomes clear that at St. Swithun's the monks were adding to the varieties of fish received direct from Southampton by obtaining other species from at least one other source. It is likely that this source was the market at Winchester. An analysis of the fish sent from Southampton to Winchester to be marketed there demonstrates that many of the types of fish consumed in St. Swithun's, but not sourced directly from the port, would have been available for purchase locally.

The brokage books show that fish, mainly herring, was sent to Winchester College direct from the port at Southampton, while the manciple's book of 1555–60 shows weekly purchases.[53] In one week alongside two gallons of ale, which cost 3*d*., was listed one penny's worth of butter, half a porker, two flounders costing 6*d*. and bass and whiting costing 4*s*.[54] Another week the manciple accounted for butter, herring, larks, onions, two pigs, puddings, one penny's worth of raisins, two thornback,[55] and a pint of wine.[56] These purchases on a small scale were surely

---

[52] The cost varied from £38 in the accounting year 1542–3 to £67 in 1553–4. See Harwood, 'The Pattern of Consumption', 231.
[53] Winchester College Muniments, 22875 (manciple's book 1555–60).
[54] *Ibid.*, week 4, term 1 in 1559.
[55] A species of ray found in coastal waters of Europe.

made locally in Winchester. The manciple's shopping list suggests that fish orders in bulk carried directly from Southampton were supplemented with fish such as bass, bream, carp, flounder, gurnard, plaice, salmon and whiting bought in the market-place, thereby adding variety to the menu for those at the top table beyond the basic fundamentals, herring and stock-fish, which were surely for the consumption of the ordinary monks and scholars.

Evidently, Southampton was never the only source of supply for the Winchester institutions. In the earlier years the college estates, and doubtless monastic estates, too, supplied some fish to the religious households. Archaeological evidence of fish bones recovered from the site of St. Mary's Abbey shows that at least twenty different species of fish were consumed there, including sturgeon and porpoise.[57] In the accounting year 1414–15, porpoise, which had originated from the college estate of Hamble, on Southampton Water, was also consumed at Winchester College; and Hamble sent regular supplies of other fish (including conger eels, hake, herring, ling, mackerel and mulwell) to the college between 1412–13 and 1423–4, although after that such consignments became less frequent. The London fish market was a further source for the religious institutions. St. Elizabeth's College purchased one barrel of salt salmon and 100 stock-fish from the capital in 1468–9;[58] and by about 1540 Winchester College was also buying fish in bulk in London: dried cod or ling, salt cod, conger eels, salt eels, smoked and salted herring, sprat, stock-fish and sturgeon.

By comparing evidence from the brokage books with available sources for consumption of the ecclesiastical establishments it is possible to build up some idea of the significance of Southampton to these institutions. It is clear that, just as Winchester College changed suppliers in order to obtain a more competitive price, so, too, for the larger and financially viable establishments in particular, the ability to order bulk quantities direct was surely beneficial. Nevertheless, such large orders were frequently supplemented with smaller ones, probably at a higher cost, which came indirectly from Southampton via local markets and traders. Furthermore, on occasion, fish supplies from other sources, such as the monastic estates and the London market, were also significant.

Wine

Wine was consumed widely in this period and Southampton was the third most important importer of this commodity in England, surpassed only by Bristol and London. This was Southampton's principal import in the fifteenth century, most of the wine shipped into the port being the basic red which came from the Gascon region of France. Although sweet wines, such as malmsey, muscadel and rumney, were also shipped in through Southampton, the quantities were small, representing

---

[56] Winchester College Muniments, 22875, week 11, term 1 in 1559.
[57] In this period a porpoise was classed as fish rather than mammal to conform with fasting rules: D.K. Coldicott, *Hampshire Nunneries* (Chichester, 1989), 77–8.
[58] Winchester College Muniments, 986. A barrel of salmon generally contained twenty-four fish: *The Brokage Book of Southampton 1443–44*, ed. Olive Coleman (2 vols., Southampton Records Series, iv, vi, 1960–1), ii. 329.

only about 2.5% of the total.[59] These sweet wines, coming from the eastern Mediterranean, were both fashionable and expensive. They were made from grapes that had been picked late in the season when the fruit was sweeter, making the final product more alcoholic and giving it a longer shelf life. In November 1527 one pipe, or 126 gallons, of malmsey was carted to the abbot of Hyde in Winchester and, in the same month, one barrel (thirty-two gallons) of muscadel and two pipes of rumney (252 gallons in total) were delivered to the bishop.

Unlike fish which was generally distributed to places within a fifty-mile radius of the port, the basic red wine was carted considerable distances from Southampton and to a wide range of towns; on three occasions it was delivered to Manchester, a significant journey of approximately 235 miles. The three principal destinations were Winchester, Salisbury and London. It was dispatched inland for a variety of recipients including merchants and vintners for further redistribution and sale. Again, as was the case with fish, wine could have been sourced from many of these local suppliers, instead of directly from the port. It was also sent to important dignitaries and large households. Between 1538 and 1540 as many as 1,638 gallons or 6.5 tuns of wine were carted to William, Lord Sandys, the new owner of the former Augustinian priory at Mottisfont.[60] As one of the lesser religious houses, Mottisfont had been suppressed in 1536,[61] and Sandys, who had acquired the former priory in exchange for land at his two villages of Chelsea and Paddington, was newly in residence, overseeing alterations to the buildings.[62] Throughout the whole period wine was carted to many other religious institutions, such as colleges, hospitals and monasteries, where, as asserted by Margery James in her study of the wine trade, 'The yearly consumption of wine by these religious houses must have been very considerable and their demand was as steady as it was important to the wine trade of the port.'[63]

Ale was the usual beverage provided for monks, and at Westminster Abbey the basic allowance per monk was a gallon of ale per day. In addition, wine was served on about a hundred feast days and anniversaries a year.[64] The brokage books demonstrate that wine from Southampton was taken to religious institutions which included the abbeys at Abingdon, Amesbury, Battle, Gloucester, Milton, Reading and Waverley. Waverley Abbey, the first Cistercian house in England and about forty miles from Southampton, sourced wine from the port in three of the years in my sample.[65] Reading Abbey, about forty-eight miles away, relied on variable supplies of wine from the port, taking as much as 882 gallons (3.5 tuns) of wine during the accounting year 1439–40.[66] Abingdon Abbey, like Reading a large wealthy house, bought less wine direct from the port in these years. However, the

---

[59] This figure depends on the broker's ability to be able to distinguish consistently between the barrels of sweet wine and the barrels of ordinary wine.
[60] See for example Southampton Archives Services, SC5.5.27.28v2.
[61] Smaller houses, with an income of less than £200 per year, were suppressed in 1536.
[62] 'House of Austin Canons: Priory of Mottisfont', in *VCH Hampshire*, ii. 172–5.
[63] M.K. James, *Studies in the Medieval Wine Trade* (Oxford, 1971), 183.
[64] Harvey, *Living and Dying*, 44, 58.
[65] One tun (252 gallons) each in the years 1447–8 and 1493–4, but half that quantity in 1462–3.
[66] One tun in each of the years 1447–8, 1491–2 and 1493–4, but two in 1462–3.

brokage books show that Southampton merchants sent wine to the towns of both Abingdon and Reading in most of the years examined.[67] This suggests that in those years when the monks of Abingdon and Reading did not order wine direct from the port, they either topped up their supplies using local vintners or agents or chose to purchase it in Bristol or London. The cellarer of the great Benedictine abbey at Gloucester had 252 gallons of wine carted there from Southampton on two occasions, the first being in July 1492 and the second in May 1494. This is curious, given that the important wine port of Bristol lay just forty miles away, in comparison with the approximately one hundred-mile journey between Gloucester and Southampton. It is also difficult to understand why, in February 1493, the carter Thomas Helyer came to Southampton from Battle Abbey, only to return with 252 gallons of wine for the abbot; again this was a distance of over eighty miles and this one entry for wine was unusual.

In the case of Salisbury, approximately 3,024 gallons or twelve tuns of wine was carted to religious institutions there in seven of the twelve years examined. This does not, of course, include any wine purchased by the religious houses from the markets in the city, much of which would also have originated from Southampton. In terms of direct orders, wine was taken from Southampton to the bishop of Salisbury and the dean and canons of the cathedral;[68] as much as 726 gallons went to the dean in 1440;[69] 536 gallons were taken to Master Cranbourne and Master Chaunter, canons of the close in 1462;[70] one pipe (126 gallons) of the expensive, sweet wine known as sack was sent to the bishop in June 1448,[71] and 819 gallons of wine were delivered to Salisbury cathedral environs in 1539–40.[72]

In the twelve years examined, wine from Southampton was only carted to two religious institutions within the county of Hampshire, excluding those in Winchester. These were Christchurch Priory and Wherwell Abbey. Christchurch Priory received a pipe (half a tun) in 1462–3, one tun in 1477–8 and another in 1491–2.[73] A pipe went to Wherwell Abbey in 1477–8,[74] and a hogshead, half that amount (63 gallons), in both 1491–2 and 1492–3. Wine was carted to other recipients in the towns of Christchurch and Wherwell in some years and could have been purchased by the monks and nuns locally through these intermediaries. In addition, as the port books show, some goods that arrived in Southampton were transferred to coastal vessels and sent to religious houses within easy access of the sea. Wine, therefore, was not only taken by cart to Christchurch Priory but the

---

[67] Men such as Christopher Ambrose, John Bentham, Walter Fetplace, Harry Huttoft and Robert Ronager to Abingdon, and Robert Aylward, John Bentham, Robert Blewet and Walter Fetplace to Reading.

[68] Salisbury cathedral was an old foundation, a secular cathedral, staffed by clergy who were not members of a religious order; at Winchester there was a cathedral priory staffed by Benedictine monks, where the prior was the head of the religious community and entrusted with the care of the cathedral church, and the bishop was the titular head of the community.

[69] Southampton Archives Services, SC5.5.3.73v6, for example.

[70] *Ibid.*, SC5.5.13.34v7, 268 gallons each.

[71] *Ibid.*, SC5.5.8.73v7.

[72] Wine, 252 gallons, was also delivered to an unnamed canon of the cathedral in 1448 (*ibid.*, SC5.5.8.34v10); 126 gallons in 1494, to the close at Salisbury (SC5.5.30.20r5); and 126 gallons to the black friars in 1527–8 (SC5.5.33.45r11).

[73] *Ibid.*, SC5.5.28.15r1; SC5.5.35.15v15.

[74] *Ibid.*, SC5.5.22.14v1.

priory also tapped into the coastal trade. In September 1435, three butts containing 378 gallons of wine were taken by sea to the prior of Christchurch; at the end of February 1436 a further tun was shipped; in June yet another butt of wine (the equivalent of half a tun) together with one tierce of lamp oil; and in September one pipe of wine and one butt of salmon was received by the prior. Similarly, in February, one pipe of wine was taken by sea to the abbey of Quarr, on the Isle of Wight.[75]

Throughout the period, large amounts of wine were carted to the city of Winchester from Southampton. Although it could not rival London and Salisbury in terms of quantity, Winchester was a significant market for Southampton's wine, receiving as much as 14% of the total amount of wine distributed by land, compared with the 23% which was sent to London and 44% to Salisbury.[76] Here again, the religious institutions adopted contrasting purchasing strategies when acquiring wine for their households. For those that preferred not to buy in bulk (Winchester College and St. Mary's Abbey), wine was certainly available for purchase in smaller quantities in the city, from merchants or vintners such as John Coteler whose stock originated from Southampton.[77] So, while the nuns of an institution such as St. Mary's Abbey did not receive any wine direct from the port in the years examined, it is likely that they were still consumers of Southampton wine, albeit indirectly, preferring to buy locally as required. Other Winchester institutions did purchase wine in bulk. It was delivered to St. Elizabeth's College for secular priests, which was situated close to Winchester College in the Kingsgate suburb: a pipe in 1439–40, thirty-two gallons in 1461–2 and considerably more, 504 gallons or two tuns, in 1477–8.[78] In the same accounting year of 1477–8, 567 gallons were sent to St. Cross Hospital, which lay outside the walls, about one mile from the centre of the city.[79]

Table 6 shows the quantities of wine sent from Southampton in bulk to the bishop of Winchester, Hyde Abbey, St. Swithun's Priory and Winchester College. Analysis shows that Winchester College received bulk consignments of wine in fewer years than these other religious institutions, and, overall, a much smaller quantity of wine was sent direct from the port, less than a quarter of the amount sent to St. Swithun's Priory or the bishop of Winchester. Successive bishops of Winchester and the priory took the greatest quantity of wine and, in addition to the wine ordered for Wolvesey, the bishop's palace in Winchester, the bishops had wine sent to their other, more favoured, residences. For Bishop William Waynflete 252 gallons of wine were carted to Farnham in 1447–8,[80] and Bishop Stephen Gardiner received 189 gallons at Bishop's Waltham in 1539–40,[81] presumably for their households at the castle and palace respectively. The largest quantity to be

---

[75] *Port Book for 1435–36*, ed. Foster, 8, 32, 38, 50, 68.
[76] This figure is based on the 12 years on the database but excluding 1430–1 and 1493–4, see Harwood, 'Winchester' in *English Inland Trade*, ed. Hicks.
[77] eadem, 'Wine' in *ibid*.
[78] Southampton Archives Services, SC5.5.3.77v6; SC5.5.13.89v1; SC5.5.22.35r4.
[79] *Ibid*., SC5.5.8.56v1.
[80] *Ibid*., SC5.5.8.4r5.
[81] *Ibid*., SC5.5.38.58v3.

carried to a bishop's residence was that sent to Bishop Richard Foxe at Wolvesey in 1527–8, which amounted to 3,686 gallons – over fourteen tuns.

Table 6: Annual quantity of wine in gallons delivered from Southampton to select religious institutions in Winchester

	Bishop	Hyde Abbey	St. Swithun's Priory	Winchester College
1430–1	–	504	–	–
1439–40	504	1323	252	32
1447–8	504*	914	819	63
1461–2	252	684	504	–
1462–3	–	–	–	126
1477–8	–	504	1575	189
1491–2	–	378	1134	–
1492–3	–	252	441	–
1493–4	–	–	–	63
1527–8	3182	630	756	–
1538–9	756	756	1985	504
1539–40	2016*	252	252	756

*includes 252 gallons for the treasurer of Wolvesey and 252 gallons sent to Farnham in 1447–8; and 189 gallons which were sent to the bishop at Bishop's Waltham in 1539–40.

Even among those institutions which used the port, the absence of wine entries for some institutions in some years is significant. It is possible that in those years the wine was either purchased elsewhere, which seems unlikely, or else that it was sourced by an agent and passed through the accounts in the name of that agent rather than the institution.[82] It is unfortunate that the channels through which the monks of Winchester purchased their wine from the port and the agents involved are unknown. Hospitality would have required wine to have been served to certain guests, and records demonstrate that these larger institutions, even though purchasing direct from Southampton, bought small amounts locally as well. Though less economic to do so, purchase on an *ad hoc* basis certainly occurred, including at institutions like Winchester College which also imported direct; the college manciple accounted for wine purchased locally in small quantities, three pottles,[83] or occasionally a gallon of wine at a time.[84] The college also bought

---

[82] Whether John Coteler, vintner and wine merchant, acted as an agent in the port on behalf of any of the Winchester institutions is difficult to ascertain, but, described as '*serviens*' of the priory, he was awarded the office of doorkeeper with a room, corrody and livery on account of his past and continuing good services. Dated 1447, this was in the same period that Coteler, vintner, was active but there was another of the same name in Winchester at that time: *The Register of the Common Seal*, ed. Joan Greatrex (Hampshire Record Series, ii, 1978), 92, no. 292.

[83] Winchester College Muniments, 22875, week 2, term 1 in 1555. A pottle equalled half a gallon.

communion wine locally rather than directly from the port. In 1453–4, for example, a small amount was purchased in the city specifically to enable the boys and servants to take communion at Easter.[85] The brokage books show that this practice continued into the sixteenth century, with wine being purchased in small quantities for the chapel from other local suppliers such as Thomas Bedam and John Serle, both of whom received their stock from Southampton.[86]

Analysis of the supply of wine to the religious institutions taken in conjunction with household size provides some insights into patterns of consumption. For Westminster Abbey, Barbara Harvey calculated the average daily consumption of wine per monk to be just over a quarter of a pint.[87] At Durham Priory, Miranda Threlfall-Holmes estimated the much higher average daily consumption of just over a pint of wine per monk;[88] while the allowance at Battle Abbey, based on figures for 1412–13 only, was 1.4 pints per day, higher still.[89] Figures at Battle and Durham were rather more than the 'reasonable consumption' recommended by St. Benedict.[90] Unfortunately, the same methodology employed for Durham Priory cannot be used to estimate the consumption of wine of the monks of Winchester Cathedral Priory, since it is impossible to know how much of the wine imported through Southampton was for the consumption of the monks, and how much was used for communion and guests.[91] Therefore, calculations for the cathedral priory and Hyde Abbey, based solely on bulk supplies purchased directly from the port, give an estimate of the institutional consumption of wine. However, it is conceivable that stocks were supplemented from the city, as happened at Winchester College, using vintners such as John Coteler, so such estimates should be treated with caution and are likely to be underestimates of the total amount of wine consumed.

Referring to Table 6, at Hyde Abbey a total of 24.6 tuns (6,197 gallons, or 49,576 pints) was purchased in the twelve years examined. This indicates an average of 4,131 pints per year. There were thirty-three monks at Hyde in 1447 which gives an estimated allowance per monk of 125 pints per year or one third of a pint per monk per day. The same calculations were made for the allowance of wine at St. Swithun's which had 7,718 gallons delivered from the port and, based on the number of monks – thirty-nine in 1447 – the daily allowance per monk calculates to just over a third of a pint. However, the allowance at both St. Swithun's Priory and Hyde Abbey would have been considerably less when the wine was shared with visitors and when some was also assigned for use at the mass.

[84] *Ibid.*, week 11, term 1 in 1559.
[85] *Ibid.*, 22128.
[86] See for instance Southampton Archives Services, SC5.5.33.48r8; SC5.5.38.67v12.
[87] Wine was not necessarily consumed on a daily basis, but calculations for comparison are for a daily average throughout the year.
[88] Miranda Threlfall-Holmes, *Monks and Markets: Durham Cathedral Priory, 1460–1520* (Oxford, 2005), 64–71.
[89] Figures for Battle Abbey were based on one account and were not necessarily typical. See *ibid.*, 69 and n. 82.
[90] *Ibid.*, 68, in which it is suggested that half a pint of wine was deemed sufficient.
[91] The bursar at Durham priory purchased 7.7 tuns of wine per year between 1464 and 1520 (wine for the mass and for visitors was purchased and accounted for separately).

Based on wine from Southampton alone, and taking consumption at mass and by visitors into account, the Winchester monks had a reasonable, though somewhat smaller, daily allowance than those at both Battle and Durham. However, it should be noted that daily allowance is calculated as a flat average across the year; in reality there would have been fluctuations in daily consumption, as on some days wine would not be permitted at all, on others a 'normal' amount would be consumed, and on special feast days and anniversaries greater quantities would be imbibed. Furthermore, the daily allowance figure does not take into account additional wine which might have been bought locally to supplement the bulk purchases from Southampton.

Through a detailed exploration of the supply and consumption of two key components of the monastic diet, fish and wine, this paper has demonstrated the significance of Southampton's trading links with religious institutions in Winchester and south-central England during the period 1430–1540. It has highlighted the complexity of supply networks used by establishments in Winchester and its hinterland, showing that purchasing decisions were based on availability and convenience of supply, the quantity required and the ability to agree a favourable price, as well as personal choice. Origin of supply was also governed by the commodity itself, wine being distributed greater distances than fish, which tended to be limited to about a fifty-mile radius of the port. Purchasing strategies also varied by institution; for some reason St. Mary's and Winchester College preferred not to undertake bulk purchasing through agents from Southampton to the same extent as Hyde Abbey and St. Swithun's Priory. Although Southampton clearly played an important role, Winchester's religious houses did not confine themselves to purchasing directly from the port. Rather, they employed a range of buying schemes which included purchasing from distant London and small-scale purchases in the locality. Yet evidence shows that even where religious houses in Southampton's hinterland acquired goods through other channels, such as local traders and markets, the commodities concerned had often originated from Southampton. Winchester's religious institutions used Southampton for the direct supply of goods to a much greater extent than religious institutions elsewhere in south-central England. Such direct purchases were a significant portion of the trade emanating from Southampton. Even though Southampton did not meet all the needs of the Winchester religious houses, the fact that at least 14% of carts travelling from Southampton to Winchester were destined for them, is testament to the significance of these establishments to Southampton's trade.

By contrast, the religious houses of Dorset depended less on direct trade from Southampton by land than was expected. A likely reason for this is their closeness to Salisbury and to ports such as Poole. Proximity to the coast certainly opened up the coastal trade as a convenient source of supply for religious houses such as Christchurch Priory and Quarr Abbey, but this seaborne trade would not have been included in the brokage books, which only recorded the trade carried by land. Salisbury was an important market to institutions in Wiltshire and, as one of Southampton's main trading partners, many of the goods sold there would have originated from Southampton, meaning it played a significant indirect, rather than direct, role in these networks. For the same reason Southampton's overland trading links were relatively important to Reading Abbey in Berkshire. In terms of direct overland trade, however, this paper has shown that of all the religious institutions in Southampton's hinterland it was for the wealthy religious houses of Winchester, particularly Hyde Abbey and St. Swithun's Priory, that the wharves of Southampton were of key importance.

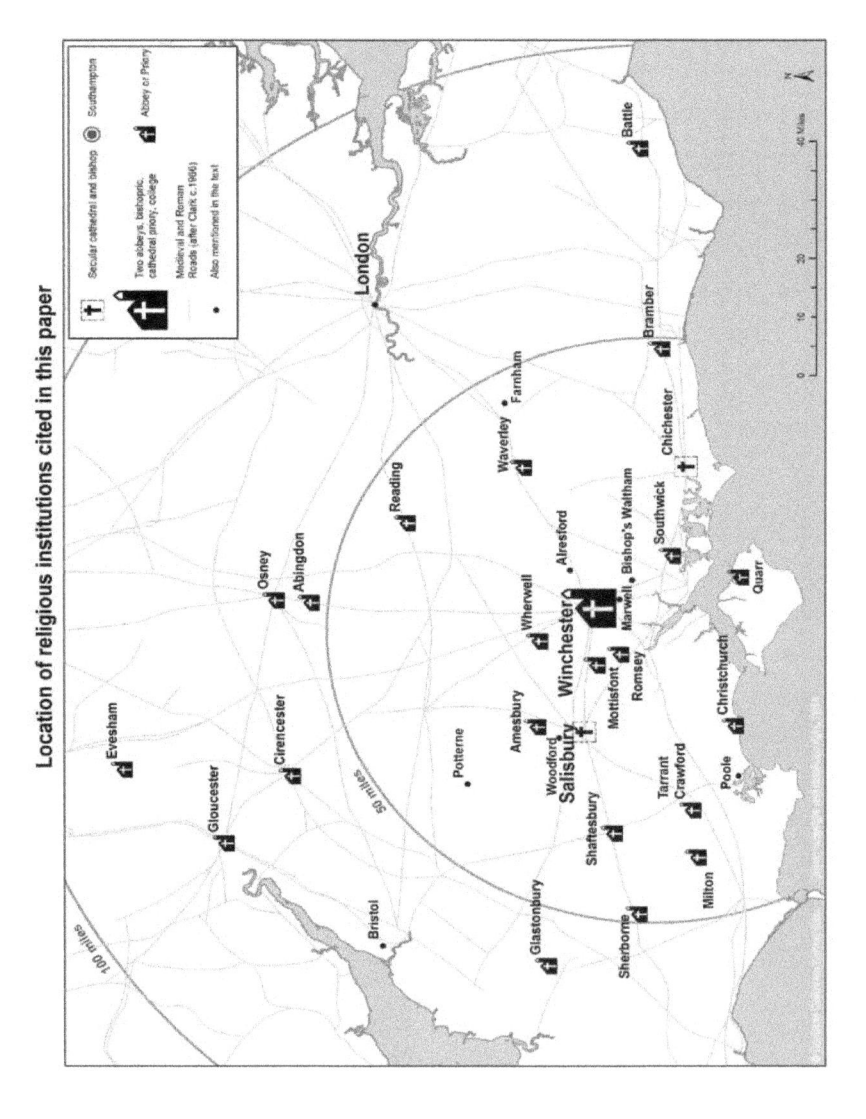

Map (Andrew Murdock, APM geo ltd.)

INDEX

Abbotstone, Hants 44–7
Abergavenny, Lady, see Beauchamp
Abingdon, Berks. 202, 222
    Abbey 163, 211, 216, 221, 222
Achambre, Thomas 149
Acts of Parliament
    Accord (1460) 98
    electoral (1406) 64
        (1429–30) 59, 64
    livery (1390) 55, 56, 60
        (1399) 61
        (1429) 55–65
        (1468) 56, 65
        (1504) 56, 65
    Praemunire 111
    Resumption 87
    Titulus Regius (1483) 104
Agincourt, battle of (1415) 1
agriculture 197–200
Aiscough, William, bishop of Salisbury 197, 222
Aldbourne, Wilts. 199
ale 219, 221
Aleyn, William, of Bury St. Edmunds 143, 147
Allington, William 153
    William (*d*.1446), *trésorier général* of Normandy 4, 6
Alresford, Hants 44, 46, 211
    deanery 42
Alton, Hants 44, 45, 193
    deanery 42
Alwyn, Robert, of Bury St. Edmunds 148
Ambrose, Christopher, of Southampton 222
Amesbury Abbey, Wilts. 211, 216, 221
Ampe, Thomas 146
Andover, Hants 200, 202, 203, 205, 217
    deanery 42
Andwell, Hants 194, 195
Annales Rerum Anglicarum 106–7
Ansculf, William fitz 13
arable crops 197–200
Archdeacon family, of Ruan Lanihorne 105
    see also Lercedekne
Arches, Ralph, escheator of Oxon. and Berks. 168
Argentan 3
Arundel, Suss. 208
Arundel, earl of, see Fitzalan
Ashe, Hants 195
Ashill, Som. 120
Ashton, Hants 198

Astley, Elizabeth, probable wife of Andrew Sackville 88
    Margaret, see Malefaunt
    Thomas (*d*.1432) 79, 86, 87
        Jane, wife of, nurse to Henry VI, see Gresley
        Henry, son of 88
        Joan, daughter of, wife of John Clay 88
        Sir John, son of 87, 88, 90
        Katherine, daughter of 88
        Richard, son of 87, 88
        Thomas, son of 85–8, 90
        William, son of 88
    Sir William 88
Athelhampton, Dorset 120
Awfyn, William, of Bury St. Edmunds 148, 149
Aylburton, Glos. 15
Aylward, John, of Bury St. Edmunds 154
    Robert, of Southampton 222

Babington, Hugh, of Bury St. Edmunds 148
Babwell, Suff. 146
    friary 145, 148
Bacon, John 154
Badminton, Glos. 15
Baglan, Glam. 78, 80, 81, 90
Balearics, the 185
Banyard, Henry 154
Barcelona, Biblioteca de Catalunya 177
Barnard Castle, Co. Durham 70
Barnet, battle of (1471) 155
Barre, Sir John 122
    Elizabeth, daughter of, wife of Humphrey, Lord Stafford 122, 127
Barton, Lancs. 120
Barton, Suff. 153, 154
Barton Blount, Derbys. 103
Barton Regis, Glos. 93
Basin, Thomas, *Histoire de Charles VII* 73
Basing, Hants 45
Basingstoke, Hants 44–6, 193–6, 199, 200, 202, 205
    deanery 42
bastard feudalism 55, 59, 60, 65, 67
Bath, Som. 98
    cloth production 192
Battle Abbey, Suss. 211, 216, 221, 222, 225, 226
Baugé, battle of (1421) 6
Bayeux 4
Bayne, Rawlyn 119, 128

Index

Bean, J.M.W. 56
Beauchamp, Anne, countess of Warwick, wife of Richard Neville 93
   Henry, earl of Warwick 84, 87
   Joan, Lady Abergavenny 15, 16, 64, 107
   Richard, bishop of Salisbury 109, 149, 152, 158
   Richard, earl of Warwick 16, 19, 77, 83, 84, 87, 89
     Elizabeth, daughter of, wife of George Neville, Lord Latimer, and Thomas Wake 112
     Isabel, wife of (*d*.1439) 84
Beaufort, duke of, muniments of 15
Beaufort, Edmund 135
   Edmund, duke of Somerset 94
   Henry, cardinal and bishop of Winchester 58, 205
   Henry, duke of Somerset 95, 97, 98, 113, 123, 131, 135, 139
     Eleanor, sister of, countess of Wiltshire 105
   Joan, daughter of John of Gaunt, countess of Westmorland 68–70, 75
   Margaret, countess of Richmond, mother of Henry VII 62, 105
   Thomas, duke of Exeter 5
Beaulieu Abbey, Hants 216
Beckinsall, Lancs. 120
Bedam, Thomas 225
Bedford, dukes of, see John of Lancaster, Plantagenet
Bedminster, Som. 93
Bekensawe, John (two) 128
   Roger 118, 120–3, 127, 128
   Roger (another) 128
Belchamber family 195
Bentham, John, of Southampton 222
Bentworth, Hants 195
Beresford, Maurice 47
Berkeley family 13–37
   Sir John 163
   Sir Maurice [14th cent.] 15
     Katherine, wife of, see Botetourt
   Sir Maurice (*d*.1464) 13, 15–19, 23, 25, 27, 28
     Eleanor, wife of, see Mountfort
   Sir William (*d*.1501) 15, 16, 18, 19
     Anne, wife of, see Stafford
Berkhampstead castle, Herts. 146
Bescanó, Bertran de 184
Bewdley, Worcs. 18
Bewsey, Lancs. 85
Bideford, Devon 128
Bidston, Cheshire 85
Bilton, Stephen, rector of Combpyne 121
Birkenhead, Cheshire 85
Birmingham, Warws. 15, 18, 22, 64
Bishop's Waltham, Hants 205, 211, 223, 224

Bishopstrow, Wilts. 205
Bitterne, Hants 198
Black Death, the 27, 39, 41, 43, 46–8, 189
Blancaç, Guillem 184
Blewet, Robert, of Southampton 222
Blisworth, Northants. 112
Blore Heath, battle of (1459) 95
Blount, John, escheator of Glos. 163, 164
   Walter, Lord Mountjoy 103, 104, 117
     Anne, wife of, see Neville
Boconnoc, Cornw. 124
Bohun, John, abbot of Bury St. Edmunds 147–9, 153, 157
Bokenham, John 153
Bonham, Thomas 171
Bonville, Cecily, Lady Harington 122, 125–6
   John, the younger 122, 123, 128
     Florence and Elizabeth, daughters of 123
   Thomas 122, 123
   William, Lord (*d*.1461) 118, 120–5
     Elizabeth, wife of, see Courtenay
     John, bastard son of 121–3
      Alice, wife of, see Denys
     William (*d*.1460), son of 121, 122
     William (*d*.1460), Lord Harington, 122, 123
      Katherine, wife of, 123
Book of Howth 136
Booth family, of Barton 120
Bordesley, Worcs. 16
Bosworth, battle of (1483) 16
Boteler, Sir John
   Isabel, wife of, see Haryngton
Botetourt family 13, 16, 33
   Katherine, wife of Sir Maurice Berkeley 15
Bothe, John 129
Botiller, Thomas 89
Bourgchier, Henry, earl of Essex 62
   Humphrey, Lord Cromwell 129
   Thomas, archbishop of Canterbury 121
Bourn Brook, Worcs. 15, 23
Bowyer, Edmund 149
Bradley, Glos. 15
Bradley, Hants 43, 44
Bradshaw, William 61
Bramber Priory, Suss. 211, 216
Bramley, Hants 194
Brandon, Frances, duchess of Suffolk, niece to Henry VIII 126
Breamore, Hants 46
Brereton family 57
Brest 6
Brette, Thomas, of Bury St. Edmunds 154
Bridgtown Pomeroy, Devon 120
Bridgwater, Som. 120
Bridport, Dorset 212
Brigham, John 124

Bristol 18, 23, 92–4, 96–101, 143, 201–3, 209, 210, 220, 222
    cloth production 192
    Earl's Court 93
    Red Books 92
Brit, Ralph 72
Brodsworth, Yorks. 68, 74
Bromham, Wilts. 196, 198
Bromsgrove, Worcs. 19, 31, 36
Broughton, Hants 42
Broughton, John 153
Broun, John, parker 25, 29, 36
    Richard 64
Browning, William 120
Buckingham, duchess of, see Neville
    dukes of, see Stafford
Bulford, Wilts. 200
Bunting, William, abbot of Bury St. Edmunds 158
    William 154, 158
Burgh, Elizabeth de, lady of Clare 63
    John, gauger of Bristol 96
    John, of Surr. 87
Burgundy, Bastard of 119
Burley, William, of Salop 93, 94
Burton Bradstock, Dorset 121, 127, 128
Bury St. Edmunds, Suff. 143–59
    Candlemas guild 151
    St. Saviour's hospital 144
    Abbey 143–9
        abbots of, see Bohun, Bunting, Coote, Hengham, Rattlesden
        shrine of St. Edmund 149
Butler, Ralph, Lord Sudeley 104
    Sir Thomas, Eleanor, wife of, see Talbot
Butler, James, earl of Ormond (*d.*1452) 16
    James, earl of Wiltshire, 16, 17, 19, 99, 120, 123
        Eleanor, wife of, see Beaufort
        Elizabeth, countess of Shrewsbury 103, 109
    Thomas, wife of, see Hankford
Butte, William, of Bury St. Edmunds 148
Byconnell, John 120

Cabanes, Josbert de 180
    Maria, wife of 180
    Pere, son of 180
Cabrera, Bernat, viscount de 181
    Guerau III, viscount de 178
    Guerau IV, viscount de 180
    Ponç, viscount de 180
        Marquesa, wife of 180
    Timbor, viscountess de 180
Cade, Jack 123
Caen 4, 8, 12
Calais 125
Calendars of Inquisitions Post Mortem 161, 162, 173

Calne, Wilts. 202
Cambridge 60
Canner family 195
Cànoves family, of Catalonia 178
Canterbury, Kent 143
Canterbury, archbishop of, see Bourgchier
Canynges, William, of Bristol 93, 98
Carbonelli, Vicenç 182
Carcassonne 179
Cardiff 83
Carpenter, Christine 131, 161
Cassy, William, rector of Corscombe 128
Castle Combe, Wilts. 193, 195, 196
Catalonia, monastic patronage in 175–87
Catesby, Sir John 111
Caundel Marsh, Dorset 72
Chaddesley Corbett, Worcs. 19
Chamberlain, Sir Robert 153
Champernowne, William, of Modbury 125
Chapman family 194
Charles II, king of Naples 182
    Blanche d'Anjou, daughter of 182
Charles VI, king of France 5, 8
Charles VII, king of France 58
Chedworth, John, bishop of Lincoln 109
Chelsea, Mdx. 221
Cheshire, palatinate of 63
    illegal retaining in 57, 58, 61
Chester 57, 85
Cheyne, John 120
Chichester, Suss. 208
Chilbolton, Hants 199
Chilworth, Hants 46
Chineham, Hants 45
Chippenham, Wilts. 196, 198
Chippenham, John, of Salisbury 199
Christchurch, Hants 42, 43, 222
    Priory 208, 210–12, 217, 222, 223, 226
Cirencester, Glos. 98, 119, 203
    Abbey 211
Clapham, Beds. 171
Clare, Gilbert of, earl of Gloucester (*d.*1295) 145
Clare, honour of 144–6
    lady of, see Burgh, Neville
Clarence, dukes of, see Thomas of Lancaster, Plantagenet
Clavilsey, [–] 119
Clay, John 88
    Joan, wife of, see Astley
Clement VIII, pope 185
Clerke, Clement 146
    John 128
Cliddesden, Hants 195
Clifford, Anne, Lady 137
    John, Lord 137
        Henry, son of 137–40
        Margaret, wife of 137
        Richard, son of 137

232 Index

Clifford (cont.)
   Sir Roger 167
      Maud, wife of 167, 171
Clinton, John, Lord 97
   William, of Bury St. Edmunds 155–7
Clopton, John, of Long Melford 147, 148, 153, 154
cloth industry 190–7, 208
   aulnage accounts 192, 193
   exports 190, 191
Cnut, king of England 156
Cockett, John, of Ampton 153
   Walter, of Ingham 153
Colchester, Essex 155
Colcombe, Devon 123, 128
Coleshill, Berks. 197, 198
Coleshill, Warws. 19
Colly, John 128
Combpyne, Devon 121
consumption 197–200, 207, 210
Cook, Sir Thomas, mayor of London 144, 151
Coombe Bissett, Wilts. 200, 205
Coote, Richard 153
   Robert, abbot of Bury St. Edmunds 153–5, 158
Coppini, papal legate 148
Corhampton, Hants 45
Cornwall, duchy of 123
Corscombe, Dorset 128
Coteler, John, of Winchester 223, 225
Cotentin, the 3
Courtenay family, earls of Devon 118, 126
   Edward, earl of Devon (*d*.1419) 121
      Elizabeth, daughter of, wife of John, Lord Harington, and William, Lord Bonville 121, 123
   Edward, earl of Devon (*d*.1509) 124
   Edward, earl of Devon (*d*.1556) 126
   Henry (*exec*.1469) 124
   Hugh, of Boconnoc 124
   John 124
   Sir Philip (*d*.1463), of Powderham 125
      Humphrey, son of 125
      Peter, son of, bishop of Exeter 125
      Sir Philip the younger, son of 125
      Walter, son of 125
      Sir William, son of 125
   Thomas, earl of Devon (*d*.1458) 125
   Thomas, earl of Devon (*d*.1461) 97, 98, 123, 124
   William, earl of Devon (*d*.1511) 126
      Katherine, wife of, see Plantagenet
Coventry, Warws. 18, 36, 91–3, 95–102, 143, 203
   Leet Book 92, 96
Cradley, Worcs. 16
Cressy, Sir John 70
Cricklade, Wilts. 198
Cromwell, Ralph, Lord 64

Cromwell, Lord, see also Bourgchier
Crondall, Hants 198, 199
Croston, Lancs. 120, 122, 128
Cruïlles family 184
Crux Easton, Hants 44

Dacre, Thomas, Lord 70
   Sir Thomas 70
Dallington, Northants. 104, 106, 110
Dalton, Yorks. 67
Danvers, Robert, j.c.p. 110
   Thomas, lawyer 104, 108–13
Darell family 67, 68
   Sir Edmund (*d*.1436) 67–75
      George, son of 73
         Margaret, wife of, see Plumpton
      Isabel (*d*.1448), wife of 69, 73
   George 69
   John (*d*.1438), 68
   Marmaduke (*d*.1423) 68
      Joan, wife of 68
   William (*d*.1365) 68
   William (*d*.1450/1), 68, 69
Dartford, Kent 94
Dartmoor, Devon 119
Dartmouth, Devon 212
Dawnay family 67
Deane family 195
Deeping, Lincs. 71
Denys, Alice, daughter of William, wife of John Bonville 121
Derby, earls of, see Stanley
Derbyshire 56
   illegal retaining in 61
deserted settlements 39, 40, 41, 44–7
Desmond, earl of, see Fitzgerald
Devereux, Walter, Lord Ferrers of Chartley 117, 134
Devon, earls of, see Courtenay, Stafford
Devon, mines in 87
Didmarton, Glos. 171
Dinefwr 79
Doding, John, bailiff of Gloucester 101
Dolman family 195
Domenècs family, of Catalonia 184
Domesday Book 33
Dorset, marquess of, see Grey
Downton, Wilts. 197, 199, 200
Draper *alias* Bayley, Nicholas, of Basingstoke 193
Drogheda 136
Drover, Edmund, of Coventry 36
Droxford, Hants, deanery 42
Drury, Clement 154
   John 153
   Roger 153
   Thomas 153
Dublin 136
Dudley, Worcs. 21

Dunham, W.H. 56, 118
Dunraven, Glam. 89
Dunstanburgh castle, Northumb. 113
Dunstaple, Beds. 99
Durham 69, 70
    Cathedral Priory 213, 225, 226
Durham, bishop of, see Langley
Durrington, Wilts. 196, 200
Dyer, Christopher 189, 190
    John 149
dyes 208
Dymmok, Isabel 171
Dynghull, Margery 163

Easingwold, Yorks. 68
East Meon, Hants 40, 47
East Parley, Hants 42, 43
Easton-in-Gordano, Som. 93
Eastrop, Hants 43, 45
Eastrop, Wilts. 197
Eborall, John, rector of Paulerspury 106
    Thomas, master of Whittington College 106
Edgecote, battle of (1469) 119, 125, 133
Edington, Wilts. 199
Edmond, Master Thomas 129
Edward III, king of England 2, 15, 167, 169
Edward IV, king of England (previously earl of March and duke of York) 16, 56, 65, 69, 87, 91–4, 97–101, 104, 106, 107, 113–15, 117–19, 122–4, 127, 143–59, 169
    clemency of 131–41
Edward of Lancaster, prince of Wales 97, 99
Edward the Confessor, king of England 156
Egerton family 57
Eling, Hants 47
Ellisfield, Hants 45
Elton, William 99
Ely, bishop of, see Morton
Empshott, Hants 45
England,
    chancellors, see Kemp, Neville, Rotherham, Stillington
    chancery, clerks 162, 168, 169, 173
        writs 161–5
        diem clausit extremum 164–5
    exchequer, files of inquisitions *post mortem* 161–73
        ordinances 165, 168, 172
    Parliaments
        (1390) 56
        (1411) 57
        (Apr. 1414) 59
        (1427–8) 39, 57, 58, 61
        (1429–30) 58–61, 63– 65
        (1433) 72
        (1437) 84–6
        (1439–40) 77, 79, 81, 86, 89
        (1447) 144
        (1450–1) 93
        (1455) 93
        (1459) 95, 97
        (1460) 103, 107, 114
        (1461) 132, 135
        (1467–8) 56
    parliamentary elections, disputed 59
    privy seal, keepers of, see Russell, Stillington
Erimball de Palol, Ramon 185
Eriswell, Suff. 147
escheators 161–73
Essex, cloth production 192
Essex, earl of, see Bourgchier
Estcote, Robert 128
    William 128, 129
Eure, Robert 69
    Sir William 69, 72
Everingham, Sir Henry 99
    priest of 99, 100
Evesham, Worcs. 98
    Abbey 210
Ewenni Priory, Glam. 79, 89, 90
Exeter, Devon 212
    cathedral, chancellor of, see Gosse
Exeter, bishops of, see Courtenay, Neville
Exeter, dukes of, see Beaufort, Holand

Fardel, Devon 125
Farnham, Surr. 211, 223, 224
Fauconberg, Lord, see Neville
Fauntleroy, John 171
Faversham, Kent 216
Fécamp 73
Ferrers of Chartley, Lord, see Devereux
Ferret, Pere 183
Ferrybridge, Yorks. 137
Fetplace, Walter, of Southampton 222
Fèvre, Jean le, chronicler 1
Fiennes, James 90
    Sir Roger 88–90
    William, Lord Say and Sele 110
Figueres 179, 183
Figueres, Berenguer de
    Berenguera, daughter of 183
    Ramon de 183
Filoll, John 120
fish, trade and consumption 201–3, 207, 208, 213–20
Fitzalan, Thomas, earl of Arundel 62
Fitzgerald family, of Munster 137
    Thomas, earl of Desmond 136, 137
    sons of 136, 138
Fitzhugh, Sir Henry 163
    Elizabeth, wife of 163
Fitzlewis, Sir Henry 105, 108–13
    Mary, daughter of, wife of Anthony Wydeville, Earl Rivers 105

Fitzwaryn, Sir Ivo 72
Fletcher, Thomas 149
Florence 208
Fogge, Sir John 117
Folgar family, of Catalonia 178
Folgars, Pere de
    wid. of, see Menola
Fordingbridge, Hants, deanery 42
Forest of Dean 101
Forster, John, alderman of Bury St. Edmunds 154, 155
    William 119
Foster, Robert 88
Foxe, Richard, bishop of Winchester 224
Frankelen, Thomas, abbot of Margam 89
Frankley, Worcs. 19
Freedman, Paul 176
Freefolk, Hants 45
Frome, Som., cloth production 192
Fulford, Sir Baldwin 98
    Sir Humphrey 123
        Florence, wife of, see Bonville
Fyfield, Hants 43, 44

Gainsborough, Lincs. 105
Gardiner, Robert, alderman of Bury St. Edmunds 153–5
    Stephen, bishop of Winchester 223
Gaunstede, Simon 169
Gausilus, Ramon 178
Gedding, William 153
George, Richard 148
Gest family 36
Gipping, Suff. 147
Girona 177, 179
    diocese 177
Glamorgan 77, 78, 81–4, 89
Glastonbury Abbey, abbot of 195
Gloucester, Glos. 92, 97–101, 143, 203
    Abbey 101, 211, 221, 222
    Llanthony Priory, prior of 100
Gloucester, dukes of, see Humphrey of Lancaster, Plantagenet
    earl of, see Clare
Glyn, Simon 119
Gosse, Master Nicholas, chancellor of Exeter cathedral 119, 122
Gower, s. Wales 77–9, 81–4, 90
Grafton, Worcs. 19
Great Harrowden, Northants. 105
Great Tey, Essex 147
Great Yarmouth, Norf. 216
Greatham, Hants 45
Green, Henry, of Drayton 105
Greenham, Nicholas 62
    Robert 62
Gregory, William, mayor of London 106
Grene, John, rector of Castle Combe 196
Grenville, William 121

Gresley, Sir Thomas 86–8, 90
    Jane, daughter of, wife of Thomas Astley, nurse to Henry VI 78–80, 83, 86–8
Grete, William, of Basingstoke 199
Grey, Edmund, earl of Kent 110
    Henry, duke of Suffolk (*exec*.1554) 126
    Jane, queen of England 126
    Sir John 104
    Thomas, marquess of Dorset 126
Grey of Codnor, Richard, Lord 3
Grey of Powys, Richard, Lord 94
Grey of Ruthin, Reynold, Lord 88
Greyson, Arthur 148–9
Greywell, Hants 194
Griffiths, R.A. 95
Groby, Leics. 104
Gye, John, of Bury St. Edmunds 148, 149
Gyldon, Richard 120, 123

Hake, Henry 119
Hale, Hants 46
Halesowen, Worcs. 18, 36
Hall, Edward, chronicle of 132, 136, 137
    John, of Salisbury 152
    Roger 133
Halsham, Hugh 167
Hamble, Hants 220
Hambledon, Hants 47
Hammoon, Dorset 120
Hampden, Sir Edmund 135
    Anne, wife of 135
Hampshire, cloth production 191
    parish tax 39–53
Hankford, Anne, wife of Thomas Butler 105
Hanley Castle, Worcs. 22
Harborne, Worcs. 19, 25, 27
Hardman, Henry 146
Harfleur, Normandy 1, 12
Harington family 121
    Cecily, Lady, see Bonville
    John, Lord (*d*.1418) 121
        Elizabeth, wife of, see Courtenay
    William, Lord (*d*.1458) 121
        Elizabeth, daughter of 121
Harle, Malcolm de, escheator 166
Harleston, Robert 153
Harlington, Henry, of Craven 137, 138
Hartcliffe, Som., hundred of 93
Hartley Mauditt, Hants 45
Hartshorne, Thomas 153
Harvey, Barbara 216, 225
Haryngton, Isabel, wife of Sir John Boteler 85
    Thomas 86
Hastings, Suss. 216
Hastings, William, Lord 16, 111, 118, 124, 148
Haybarn, Worcs. 16
Haynes, William 195
Headbourne Worthy, Hants 45

Index

Heckfield, Hants 194
Hedgeley Moor, battle of (1464) 132
Helperby, William, bailiff of Bury St. Edmunds 150
Helyer, Thomas, carter 222
Hengham, Richard, abbot of Bury St. Edmunds 155–8
Henhowe, Suff. 146
Henley in Arden, Warws. 36
Henmershe, William 17
Henry III, king of England 151
Henry IV, king of England 60, 61, 138
Henry V, king of England 1–3, 5–11, 58, 60, 61, 65, 138
Henry VI, king of England 8, 39, 58, 72, 78, 82–4, 86, 89, 93–5, 97, 106, 107, 118, 125, 144, 145, 147, 152, 168
Henry VII, king of England 56, 62, 65, 138, 139
Henry VIII, king of England 126
Herbert, William, Lord Herbert and earl of Pembroke 117, 133, 134, 138, 139
Hereford, Herefs. 97, 99
Hexham, battle of (1464) 132
Heytesbury, Wilts. 195
  hundred 192
Hicks, Michael 40, 56, 67, 74, 95, 104, 112, 131, 134, 139, 161, 173
  Edward V 104
Higham, Richard, serjeant-at-law 149
  Thomas, bailiff of Bury St. Edmunds 149, 153
Hill Deverill, Wilts. 205
Hody, William, escheator of Devon 166
Holand, Henry, duke of Exeter 94, 97, 123
  John, earl of Huntingdon and duke of Exeter 60, 70, 100, 104, 110
  Anne, wife of, see Montagu
  Thomas, illegitimate son of 100
Holderness, Robin of 139
Holt, John, of Aston 19
  Richard 101
Honfleur, Normandy 73
Hook, Hants 194
Hooke, Dorset 122, 127
Hopton, Walter 114
Hore, Thomas, of Solihull 19
Horrox, Rosemary 131
Hortal, Beatriu d' 180
  Berenguer d' 183
Horton, Thomas 196
Hotoft, John 70
housing 195, 200, 201, 204, 205
Howard, John, Lord Howard and duke of Norfolk 118, 119, 146–8, 153, 155, 156
  Thomas, earl of Surrey 62
Hull, Henry, of Ashill 120
Humburton, Yorks. 70

Humphrey of Lancaster, duke of Gloucester 3, 57, 58, 77, 86, 87, 89, 144, 145
Hungerford, Wilts. 200
Hungerford, Robert, Lord 123
Hunter, Joseph 162–4, 172
Huntingdon, earl of, see Holand
Hurdleton family 122
  Robert 127, 128
  Thomas 128, 129
Hurn, Hants 43
Hursley, Hants 211
Huse, John de, carter 207
Huttoft, Harry, of Southampton 222

Iberia 175, 176
Ilchester, Som. 82
Ingrave, Essex 110
Inkpen, Berks. 198
inns 202, 204
Ipplepen, Cornw. 164, 167
Isle of Wight 41, 42
Italy 208
Itchen Stoke, Hants 45
Itchen, valley 44
Ixworth, Suff. 153

Jakkes, Robert, sheriff of Bristol 98
James I, king of Aragon 185
James II, king of Aragon 182
James, Margery 221
Jaspert, Nikolas 176
Jervoise family 15
  Richard 15
Jerweys, John 153
  Roger 153
Jewe, John, of Ilchester 119, 120
Joan of Arc 58
John of Gaunt, duke of Lancaster 68
John of Lancaster, duke of Bedford 3, 8
John, Sir Lewis 104
  Anne, wife of, see Montagu
  Henry, son of, see Fitzlewis
  Margaret, daughter of, wife of Sir William Lucy, John Stafford and Thomas Wake 103–15
Judde, John, master of the king's ordnance 98
Julià, Guillem 180
  Elicsendis, wife of 180
Juyn, John 165

Katherine de Valois, queen to Henry V 5
Kayleway, William, of Sherborne 120
Kemp, John, archbishop of York and chancellor 59
Kempshott, Hants 42, 45
Kendale, John, of Bridgwater 120
Kenilworth, Warws. 91, 95
Kennet, valley, cloth production 191, 193
Kent, illegal retaining in 62

236   Index

Kent, earl of, see Grey
Kildare 137
Kilkhampton, Cornw. 119, 121, 122, 127
Kilmainham, prior of 3
Kimpton, Hants 205
Kings Norton, Warws. 31, 36
Kings Weston, Glos. 15
Kingsclere, Hants 194
Kingsmill family 195
Kitson, Thomas, of London 194
Kleineke, Hannes 59
Knights Enham, Hants 44
Koeur, Lorraine 124
Kowaleski, Maryanne 189
Kyrkeby, Isabel 121

Lambeth, Surr., parish church 122, 127, 128
Lancaster 85, 86
   county palatine of 57, 86
Lancaster, duke of, see John of Gaunt
Langford, Alexander 196
Langley, Thomas, bishop of Durham 72
Langton, Thomas, bishop of Salisbury 158
Latimer, Lord, see Neville
Laughton, Jane 51
Lavenham, Suff. 134, 144
Lee, William 153
Leicester, Leics. 143
Leland, John 199
Leominster, Herefs. 99
Lercedekne (Archdeacon), Warin 166
Lewys, John, of Winchester 205
Leynham, Sir John 148
   Margaret, wife of 148
Leyshon family, see also Lleision
Leyshon *alias* Gethin, Lewys, 77–82, 84, 89, 90
   William 90
Lichfield, Staffs. 17, 18, 23
Lincoln, bishops of, see Chedworth, Rotherham
Litchfield, Hants 44
Littlecote, Wilts. 69
Liverpool, Lancs. 85
livestock 197–9
Lladó, Bernat de 181
Llandaff, Glam. 89
Lleida, university of 176
Lleision family 78, 80, 81, 83, 89, 90
Llobet, Ferrer 181
   Ermessenda, wife of 181
Locker, Gilbert 195
Lomer, Hants 43, 45
Londesborough, Yorks. 137
London 17, 18, 22, 23, 62, 68, 77–9, 81, 90–2, 95–7, 99, 100, 102, 122, 143, 146, 147, 189, 202, 203, 209–11, 221–3, 226
   cloth marketing 192
   fish market 216, 219, 220

Fleet prison 132, 133, 135, 140, 157
'Great Chronicle' of 136
St. Bartholomew's hospital 81, 87, 88
Tower of 93, 96, 111, 132, 133, 135, 136, 140
Long Melford, Suff. 146–8
Longford, Henry 61
Longwood, Hants 199
Lorimer, Edmund, of Bury St. Edmunds 148
Lucca 208
Lucy, Sir William (*d*.1460), 104–7, 114
   Elizabeth, wife of, see Percy
   Margaret, wife of, see John, Sir Lewis
Ludford Bridge, battle of (1459) 95
Ludlow, Salop 94, 97
Ludlow, William 205
Luttrell, Sir Hugh, seneschal of Normandy 4
Lymington, Hants 208
Lyttleton, Thomas, of Frankley 19

Maiença in Sant Andreu de Reminyó 180
Maine, county 7
maintenance 57, 58, 60, 96
Makworth, Thomas 64
Malefaunt, Edmund 80, 87–90
   Katherine (née Mathew) wife of 89, 90
   Henry son of 81, 87, 88
   Sir Thomas (*d*.1438) 77–9, 81, 86–9
      Margaret (née Astley), wife of 77–90
Malmesbury, Wilts. 196, 198
   deanery 47
Malory, Robert 135
Manchester, Lancs. 221
Manningham, Thomas, escheator of Beds. and Bucks. 164
Mansell, Philip 81, 84, 89
Mantes 2, 12
Mapledurwell, Hants 42, 45, 194–6
Mapping the Medieval Countryside 161, 173
March, earls of, see Edward IV, Mortimer
Margam Abbey, Glam. 89
Margaret of Anjou, queen to Henry VI 91, 92, 95–7, 99, 101, 105, 121, 124
Marlborough, Wilts. 193
Marlborough, John, of Norwich 151
Marquès, Josep 180, 183, 184
Marshfield, Glos. 18
Martin, Thomas, of Athelhampton 120
Marwell palace, Hants 205
Matheu, Lady 180, 181
Mathew family, of Llandaff 89
   David 88–90
      John the younger, son of 90
         Katherine, daughter of, wife of Edmund Malefaunt 89, 90
   John the elder 89
   Lewis 89
Mattingley, Hants 194
Mauntell, Sir William 110

Maxstoke castle, Warws. 16, 18
Maxwell-Lyte, Sir Henry 165
May, Henry, of Bristol 98
McFarlane, K.B. 55, 67
Meath 137
Melbury Sampford, Dorset 120
Melcombe Regis, Dorset 212
Menola, Pere de
  Fresca, daughter of, wid. of Pere de Folgars 181
Mere, Wilts. 195
Micheldever, Hants 43
Middleham, Yorks. 69
Middleton, Warws. 27, 29
Middleton, George 120
Milan 208
Milford Sound 78
Milleholme, Robert 128
mills, fulling 194, 195
Milton Abbey, Dorset 211, 221
Milton family, of Andwell 194, 196
Mitford, Richard, bishop of Salisbury 210
Modbury, Devon 125
Mohun, John, of Hammoon 120
Molyneux family 122
  John 122–3, 128
Monstrelet, Enguerran de, chronicler 1
Montagu family 138
  John, earl of Salisbury (*d*.1400) 104
    Anne, daughter of, wife of Sir Lewis John and John, duke of Exeter 104, 112
  Thomas, earl of Salisbury 7, 8
Montagu, marquess of, see Neville
Montgomery, John, of Great Tey 147
  Sir Thomas 156
Montpalau family 184
More, John, chaplain 129
  Sir Thomas 104
  History of Richard III 115
Morley, Norf. 171
Mortimer, Roger, earl of March 167
Mortimer's Cross, Herefs., battle of (1461) 91–102
Morton, John, bishop-elect of Ely 156
Mottisfont Priory, Hants 210, 211, 217, 221
Mountfort family, of Coleshill 19
  Sir Edmund 99
  Eleanor, wife of Sir Maurice Berkeley 17–19
Mountjoy, Lord, see Blount
Mowbray family 138
  John, duke of Norfolk (*d*.1432) 60
  John, duke of Norfolk (*d*.1461) 77, 79, 81, 84
  John, duke of Norfolk (*d*.1476) 56
Munster 137
Muskham, Robert 169
Musson, Anthony 82

Narbonne 179
Nechells, Warws. 19
Neville family 69, 133
  Cecily, duchess of York, lady of Clare 146, 156
  George, bishop of Exeter, archbishop of York and chancellor 108, 109, 111, 112, 134
  George, Lord Latimer 112
    Elizabeth, wife of, see Beauchamp
  John, earl of Northumberland and marquess of Montagu 117, 132, 134, 139
  Sir John 2
  Margaret, wife of John de Vere 134
  Ralph, earl of Westmorland (*d*.1425) 63, 68, 70
    Anne, daughter of, duchess of Buckingham and wife of Thomas Wake 103
    Elizabeth, Lady, daughter-in-law of 63, 64
    Joan, wife of, see Beaufort
  Richard, earl of Salisbury 67–75
  Richard, earl of Warwick 16, 91, 93, 96–101, 108, 111–13, 117, 125, 133, 134, 137, 139
    Anne, wife of, see Beauchamp
  Richard, Lord Latimer 139
  William, Lord Fauconberg 69
New Forest, Hants 40, 47
Newbury, Berks. 193, 195, 203
Newhall, R.A. 4
Newhay, John, of Nechells 19
Newnham, Hants 194, 195, 199
Nicholas, Gruffudd ap 79–81, 89, 90
Norfolk, dukes of, see Howard, Mowbray
Normandy, duchy of 1, 2, 7–10, 59, 73
  chambre des comptes 4
  Estates 6, 8
  lieutenant of 5, 9, 11
  ordinances for garrisons in 1–12
  seneschal of 4, 6
  trésorier-général of 4, 6
North Charford, Hants 46
North Warnborough, Hants 195
Northampton, Northants. 143, 203
Northampton, battle of (1460) 97, 103, 106, 107, 118
Northfield, Worcs. 13–37
Northington, Hants 40, 46
Northumberland, countess of, see Poynings
  earls of, see Neville, Percy
Norwich, Norf. 143
Nottingham, Notts. 143
Nutley, Hants 46

Odiham, Hants 193, 194
Odiham, Margaret 151

Oldswinford, Worcs. 16
Olyver, Robert, vicar of Powerstock 119, 128
Orford, Suff. 151
Orléans, siege of 58
Ormond, earl of, see Butler
Osney Abbey, Oxon. 211
Oswaldkirk, Yorks. 74
Overton, Hants 40, 44, 194, 195, 199, 211
Oxford, earl of, see Vere
Oxfordshire, deserted villages 39
    illegal retaining in 62

Pachet, Thomas, lawyer 110, 111, 113, 114
Paddington, Mdx. 221
Page, Roger 154
Palafolls family, of Catalonia 178, 184
Palol 185
Parc le Breos, Gower 79, 81, 84
Paris 4, 5, 86
Parman, Robert 154
Pascua, Esther 176
Paston, John (*d*.1466) 133, 171
    Margaret, wife of 133
    William (*d*.1444) 170
Pastor, Reyna 176
Paul II, pope 109
Paulerspury, Northants. 106
Paulet family, of Basing 45
Payling, Simon 131
Paynel family 13, 21
Pembroke 77, 78, 89
    earls of, see Herbert, Tudor
Penrith, Cumb. 70
Pensford, Som. 192
Penzance, Cornw. 208
Percy family 138
    earls of Northumberland 68
    Henry, earl of Northumberland (*d*.1455) 70, 73–74, 132
    Henry, earl of Northumberland (*d*.1461) 132, 135
        Elizabeth, wife of, see Poynings
    Henry, son of 131–3, 135, 138–41
    Henry, earl of Northumberland (*d*.1527) 62
    Sir Henry (*d*.1432), Elizabeth, daughter of, wife of Sir William Lucy 105
    Ralph 132
Peterborough, Northants. 143–5, 158
    Abbey 145
Petersfield, Hants 45
Peyto, Sir William 19
Pickering, Sir Richard, of Oswaldkirk 74
    William 74
Pierrepoint, Sir Henry 61
Pill, Pemb. 77
Pinchbeck, Lincs. 71
Pittleworth, Hants 42
Pius II, pope 103

Plantagenet, Edward, earl of Warwick 138
    George, duke of Bedford 139
    George, duke of Clarence 117, 125, 139
    Katherine, countess of Devon 126
    Richard, duke of Gloucester 134
    Richard, duke of York 69, 72, 91, 93, 94, 96–8, 101, 144–6
Plumpton, Sir William 74
    Margaret, daughter of, wife of George Darell 74
Plush, William 119
Pole, John de la, duke of Suffolk 56
Polhampton, Hants 44
Pons i Guri, Josep 178
Pontefract, Yorks. 70
Poole, Dorset 212, 226
Poore, Richard, bishop of Salisbury 150
Popham, Sir John 4
population levels 39, 40–7
Portbury, Som., hundred of 93
Porter, John, of Bury St. Edmunds 148
Potterne, Wilts. 210
Powderham, Devon 125
Powell, Edward 83
Powerstock, Dorset 119, 128
Poynings, barony of 135
    Elizabeth, Lady, countess of Northumberland 135
Prallingworth, Hants 41
Premonstratensian canons 176
Preston, Suff. 146
Pulle (or del Pole), William, of Birkenhead 85, 86
Purdeney, William 129
Pyrenees, the 179

Quarr Abbey, Isle of Wight 208, 223, 226
Quemerford, Wilts. 202
Queruç family, of Catalonia 178
Quidhampton, Hants 44

rabbit warrens 199
Raglan 89
Raleigh, Walter (*d*.1464), of Fardel 125
Raskelf, Yorks. 69–71, 75
Rattlesden, Thomas, abbot of Bury St. Edmunds 157, 158
Reading, Berks. 77, 143, 144, 193, 222
    Abbey 158, 210–12, 221, 222, 227
Redesdale, Robin of 119
Register of the Mayors of Dublin 136
Reyce, Robert 146
Rheims 58
Riall, Richard 163
    Elizabeth, wife of 163
Richard II, king of England 1, 56, 60, 61, 67
Richard III, king of England 16, 138
Richard's Castle, Herefs. 105
Richmond, countess of, see Beaufort

Richmondshire 68
Rigau, Pere 179
Riu family, of Catalonia 178
Rivers, Earl, see Wydeville
roads 201, 202
Roca Rossa Priory 175, 177–86
    cartulary of 178
Rocabertí family, of Catalonia 184
Rochester, bishop of, see Russell
Rockhampton, Glos. 15
Rodney, Walter, sheriff of Somerset 82
Roger, Thomas, mayor of Bristol 98
Romsey, Hants 46, 200, 203, 217
    Abbey 210, 211, 213, 217
Ronager, Robert, of Southampton 222
Roos, Thomas, Lord 70, 103
Ross, Charles 131
    James 55
Rotherham, Thomas, bishop of Lincoln 156
Roucliff, Guy, escheator of Yorks. 166
Rouen, Normandy 3–9, 11
    captain of 10
    lieutenant of 5
Rougham, Suff. 155
Roussillon,
    Santa Maria del Camp Abbey 179
Routh, John, escheator 167
Rowde, Wilts. 198
Ruan Lanihorne, Cornw. 105
Rugles 3
Russell, John, bishop of Rochester and keeper of the privy seal 156
Rutland, illegal retaining in 62

Sabaté, Flocel 176
Sackville, Andrew 88
St. Albans, first battle of (1455) 132
St. Albans, second battle of (1461) 91–102, 104, 121, 124
St. Donats, Glam. 89
St. George, Glam. 77, 78
St. Mewan, Cornw. 121
Saints
    Benedict 225
    Osmund 152
Salisbury, Wilts. 99, 143–5, 149, 150–3, 156, 157, 199–203, 205, 209, 210, 212, 216, 221–3
    cathedral, dean and canons 222
    cloth production 191, 192
    guild of St. George 151
Salisbury, bishops of, see Aiscough, Beauchamp, Langton, Mitford, Poore, Wydeville
Salisbury, earls of, see Montagu, Neville
San Juan de la Peña, chronicle of 182
Sandys, William, Lord 221
Sant Andreu de Reminyó 180
Sant Corneli de Montells 180

Sant Llorenç, Guillelma de 181
Say and Sele, Lord, see Fiennes
Schoyer, John 100
Seend, Wilts.196
Selly, Worcs. 15, 27, 29, 31, 33
Serle, John 225
Sessay, Yorks. 67–9, 71, 73, 75
Severn, river 18, 101
Shaftesbury Abbey, Dorset 211
Shaw, Wilts. 195
Sheffield castle, Yorks. 103
Sherborne, Dorset 72, 120
    Abbey 211
    cloth production 192
Sherborne St. John, Hants 194
Sheriff Hutton, Yorks. 68, 70
ships
    Marie of Bayonne 97
    Marie of La Rochelle 97
Shrewsbury, Salop 92–9, 101, 203
Shrewsbury, earls of, see Talbot
Sicily 208
Simond, John 127
Sizergh, Cumb. 73
Skarbot, Andrew 154
Skargill, Thomas 153
Skipton castle, Yorks. 137
Smith, John, of Bury St. Edmunds 143, 145–8, 153–7, 159
Solers, John 87
Solihull, Warws. 19
Somborne, Hants, deanery 42
Somerset, cloth production 191, 192
    sheriff of 81, 82
Somerset, dukes of, see Beaufort
Somery family 13, 21, 25, 33, 35
Sopworth, Wilts. 47
South Charford, Hants 46
South Tidworth, Hants 44, 46
Southampton, Hants 46, 199
    Bargate 209
    brokage books 190–2, 200–2, 207, 209, 210, 216, 217, 219–22, 225, 226
    deanery 42
    port 207–28
    trade 201–3, 207–28
Southampton Water 220
Southwick, Hants 42
    Priory 210, 211, 217
Southwold, Suff. 208
Spalding, Lincs. 71
Spence, R.T. 137
Spencer family 13, 37
Stafford family, of Grafton 19
Stafford, earls of 118
Stafford, Edward, duke of Buckingham 62
    Fulk 19
    Henry, duke of Buckingham 124
    Henry, earl of Wiltshire (*d*.1523) 126

Stafford (cont.)
　Humphrey, duke of Buckingham 16, 18, 94, 107
　　Anne, wid. of, see Neville
　　Henry, son of 105
　　John, son of 105
　Humphrey, Lord Stafford of Southwick and earl of Devon 117–26
　　Elizabeth, wife of, see Barre
　Sir Humphrey, Anne, daughter of, wife of Sir William Berkeley 19
　John (*d*.1421) 107
　John (*d*.1461) 106, 107, 110, 114
　　Margaret, wife of, see John, Sir Lewis
　William (*d*.1450) 118, 120, 123
Staffordshire, illegal retaining in 57, 61
Stalbridge, Dorset 72
Stallworth, Simon 124
Standen, Hants 46
Stanley, Edward, earl of Derby 139
　Sir Thomas 85, 86
　Thomas, earl of Derby 62
　Sir William 137
Staunford, William 167
Steeple Ashton, Wilts. 196
Stillington, Robert, bishop of Bath and Wells, chancellor 147
　keeper of the privy seal 131, 141
Stoke Gifford, Glos. 15, 17–18, 23, 27
Stonor, Sir William 124
Stourton, William, Lord 123
Stradling, Sir Edward 89
Stratfield Saye, Hants 194
Stratfield Turgis, Hants 47
Straunge, Henry 153
Strickland, Walter (*fl*.1448), of Sizergh 73
　Walter (*d*.1569) of Sizergh 73
Stroudwater, Glos. 193
Styng, Henry 7
Suffolk, cloth production 192
Suffolk, dukes of, see Grey, Pole
Summerson, Henry 137
Surrey, earl of, see Howard
Sussex, illegal retaining in 62
Swansea 83
Swarraton, Hants 43, 46
Swayn, William, of Salisbury 152
Sydmonton, Hants 195
Sygo, William, of Bury 155–7

Talbot family, of Richard's Castle 105
Talbot, John, earl of Shrewsbury (*d*.1453)
　Eleanor, daughter of, wife of Sir Thomas Butler 104
　John, earl of Shrewsbury (*d*.1460) 94, 103, 106
　　Elizabeth, wife of, see Butler
Tarrant Abbey, Dorset 211
Taunton castle, Som. 119

Teffont Evias, Wilts. 119
Terrades, Guillem de 183
Tewkesbury, battle of (1471) 124
Thames, valley 197, 198
　cloth production 191, 193
Thirkleby, Yorks. 68
Thirsk, Yorks. 68
Thomas of Lancaster, duke of Clarence 2, 5–7
Thomas, Sir William ap 89
Thoresby, Juliana de 172
Thornbury, Glos. 16, 18
Thorne, John, abbot of Reading 158
Threlfall-Holmes, Miranda 225
Throckmorton, John 19
Thurston, Walter, alderman of Bury St. Edmunds 155–7
Thwaytes, William, of Bury St. Edmunds 146, 154
Tillott, John 154
Tiptoft, John, earl of Worcester 103, 118, 132–6, 138, 141
Titchfield, Hants 41
　Abbey 197, 198
Tiverton, Devon 118, 119, 122–5, 128
Topcliffe, Yorks. 68
Toper, John 171
Torre, Antonio della 148
Towton, battle of (1461) 69, 91, 99, 100, 102, 107, 111, 124, 132, 137, 140, 143, 146, 147
Tretherf, John, escheator of Devon and Cornw. 164–7
Troyes, treaty of (1420) 5
Trumpington, Sir Walter 153
Tuddenham, Sir Thomas, of Eriswell 147
Tudor, Jasper, earl of Pembroke 94, 97, 99, 101
Tunstall, Sir Richard 133
　William 133
Turberville family 81, 83, 89, 90
　Gilbert 80, 89
Tutbury, Staffs. 91, 95
Tyrell, William, of Gipping 147
Tythegston, Glam. 79, 80, 82
Tywardreath Priory, Cornw. 165

Uley, Glos. 13, 15, 16
Up Nately, Hants 194, 199
Upton Castle, Pemb. 77–9
Upton Grey, Hants 45
Upton, Nicholas, *De Studio Militari* 7, 8
Urchfont, Wilts. 200

Vale, John, of Bury St. Edmunds 144
Valencia 185
Valldemaría Abbey 180
Valor Ecclesiasticus 213
Vampage, John 19
Vaux, William, of Great Harrowden 105, 114

Venor, John 19
    William 132
        Elizabeth wid. of 132, 133
Vere, John de, earl of Oxford (*exec*.1462) 131, 133–5, 138, 139, 141, 147
    Elizabeth, wid. of 134, 135
    sons of 132–4, 136, 138–40
        Aubrey 133, 136, 138, 147
        George 134, 141
        Richard 134
        Thomas 134, 141, 155
    John de, earl of Oxford (*d*.1513) 62, 134–6, 139, 155
Vernon, Sir Richard 64
Vilabertran Abbey 177, 179–86
    abbots of 180, 183, 184
Vilarig, Guillem de 183
Vones–Liebenstein, Ursula 176

Wake, Thomas 108–12
    Elizabeth, wife of, see Beauchamp
    Margaret, wife of, see John
    John, son of 110
Wakefield, battle of (1460) 91, 98, 122, 138, 146
Wakeryng, John, clerk of the rolls 169
Waldegrave, Sir Thomas 153
Walker, David 94
Wallsworth, Hants 42, 46
Walsh, Odomar 28, 29, 36
Walsshe, John 128
Wanstead, Hants 42
Ware, Herts. 70
Warminster, Wilts. 195, 197
Warwick, Warws. 93
    castle 112
Warwick, earls of, see Beauchamp, Neville, Plantagenet
Warwickshire, illegal retaining in 62
Waterstock, Oxon. 112
Waterton, Hugh 167
Watton, John, of Bury St. Edmunds 148
Waurin, Jean de, chronicler 1
Waverley Abbey, Surr. 211, 221
Waynflete, William, bishop of Winchester 108, 109, 120, 223
Webster, Jill 176
Weeke, Hants 42, 45
Wehelok, Richard 61
Weldon, Richard 148
Wells, Som., cloth production 192
Wenlock, John, Lord 135
Wenvoe, Glam. 77, 78
Weoley castle, Worcs. 13, 15–23, 25, 26
    park 23–26, 28, 29, 33
Werle, George 61
West Horndon, Essex 110
West Worldham, Hants 44, 45
West, Sir Thomas 171

Westbury, Hants 40
Westminster 17, 86, 91, 95, 96, 136
    Abbey 58, 213, 214, 216, 221, 225
Westmorland, countess of, see Beaufort
    earl of, see Neville
Weston Colley, Hants 43, 46
Weston Corbett, Hants 45
Westwood, Wilts. 196
Weylott, Robert, of Durrington 200
Whatcrofte, John 36
Wherwell, Hants 209, 222
    Abbey 209–11, 213, 217, 222
Whitchurch, Hants 194
White, John, of Bury St. Edmunds 148
    Piers, priest 129
Whitsbury, Hants 46
Widley, Hants 42
Wigmore, Herefs. 99
Wilgrise, William, mayor of Coventry 96
Willoughby, Sir John 120
    Robert, Lord 5
Wilson, John 133
Wiltshire, cloth production 191
Wiltshire, earls of, see Butler, Stafford
Winchelsea, Suss. 216
Winchester, Hants 45, 199, 200, 201, 203, 209, 210, 217, 220, 223
    cloth industry 192, 210
    deanery 42
    religious institutions in 207–28
        Hyde Abbey 210–13, 215, 217–19, 221, 223–7
        St. Cross hospital 205, 211, 223
        St. Elizabeth's College 211, 220, 223
        St. John's hospital 211
        St. Mary's Abbey 210–13, 215, 217–20, 223, 226
        St. Swithun's Cathedral Priory 197–9, 207, 210–13, 215, 217–19, 223–7
    Winchester College 200, 202, 205, 210–13, 215–20, 223–6
    Wolvesey palace 205, 210, 223, 224
Winchester, bishop of 223, 224, and see Beaufort, Foxe, Gardiner, Waynflete, Wykeham
Winchfield, Hants 45
Windsor 143
    St. George's Chapel 152
wine, trade and consumption 201–3, 207, 208, 210, 214, 215, 220–6
Wingfield, Sir John 148
Winkton, Hants 43
Winslade, Hants 42
Wiscombe park, Devon 128, 129
Wiston, Pemb. 89
Wode, John, priest 122, 128
Wodecok, Richard 27, 29
Wogan, Sir Henry 89
Wolashull, Robert, escheator of Worcs. 167

Wolsey, Thomas, cardinal 139
Woodcott, Hants 44
Woodford, Wilts. 210
Woodstock, Oxon. 158
Wootton, Hants 199
Worcester, Worcs. 23, 26, 31, 143
Worcester, earl of, see Tiptoft
Worcestre, William 106, 196
Wormleighton, Warws. 13, 28, 29, 36
Worting, Hants 45
Wydeville, Anthony, Earl Rivers 105, 156
     Mary, wife of, see Fitzlewis
  Elizabeth, wid. of Sir John Grey, queen to Edward IV 104, 106
  Lionel, bishop of Salisbury 158
  Richard, Earl Rivers 117
  Richard, seneschal of Normandy 5–6
Wykeham, William of, bishop of Winchester 42, 47, 198
Wykyng, John 171
Wyle, valley 192
Wyntor, Walter 133

Yaxley, Richard 146
York 68, 137, 139
York, archbishops of, see Kemp, Neville
York, duchess of, see Neville
York, dukes of, see Edward IV, Plantagenet
Yorkshire, illegal retaining in 57, 61, 62
Young, Thomas, of Bristol 93, 94, 96

THE PUBLISHED WORKS OF MICHAEL HICKS, 1977–2015

Compiled by Jessica Lutkin

Given Michael's immense productivity and the range of his interests, the following list may not be exhaustive, but it should at the very least give an indication of his contribution to historical scholarship.

1977
'*Draper* v. *Crowther*: The Prebend of Brownswood Dispute 1664–92', *Transactions of the London and Middlesex Archaeological Society*, xxviii. 333–45.

1978
'Dynastic Change and Northern Society: The Career of the Fourth Earl of Northumberland, 1470–89', *Northern History*, xiv. 78–107. *
'The Case of Sir Thomas Cook, 1468', *EHR*, xciii. 82–96. *

1979
'The Changing Role of the Wydevilles in Yorkist Politics to 1483', in *Patronage, Pedigree and Power in Later Medieval England*, ed. C.D. Ross (Gloucester), 60–86. *
'Descent, Partition and Extinction: The "Warwick Inheritance", 1471–5', *BIHR*, lii. 116–28. *

1980
False, Fleeting, Perjur'd Clarence: George, Duke of Clarence, 1449–1478 (Gloucester).
'Friern Barnet', in *VCH Middlesex*, vi. 6–37.
'Hornsey, including Highgate' (with T.F.T. Baker), *ibid.*, 101–205.
'The Neville Earldom of Salisbury, 1429–71', *Wiltshire Archaeological Magazine*, lxxii–lxxiii (1980 for 1977), 141–7. *

1981
'The Beauchamp Trust, 1439–87', *BIHR*, liv. 135–49. *
'The Middle Brother: "False, Fleeting, Perjur'd Clarence"', *The Ricardian*, v. 302–10.
'Clarence's Calumniator Corrected', *The Ricardian*, v. 399–401.

1982
'Ealing and Brentford', in *VCH Middlesex*, vii. 100–72.

'"False, Fleeting, Perjur'd Clarence": A Further Exchange. Richard and Clarence', *The Ricardian*, vi. 20–1.

1983

'St. Katherine's Hospital, Heytesbury: Prehistory, Foundation and Refoundations, 1408–1472', *Wiltshire Archaeological Magazine*, lxxviii (1983–4), 62–9. *

'The Warwick Inheritance – Springboard to the Throne', *The Ricardian*, vi. 174–81.

'Restraint, Mediation and Private Justice: George, Duke of Clarence as "Good Lord"', *Journal of Legal History*, iv. 56–71. *

'Romsey and Richard III', *Hampshire Field Club Local History Newsletter*, i (7), 151–3. *

1984

'Attainder, Resumption and Coercion, 1461–1529', *Parliamentary History*, iii. 15–31. *

'Edward IV, the Duke of Somerset and Lancastrian Loyalism in the North', *Northern History*, xx. 23–37. *

'Nether Wallop Parsonage after the Reformation', *Hampshire Field Club and Archaeological Society Section Newsletter*, new series, ii. 9–10.

1985

'Chantries, Obits and Almshouses: The Hungerford Foundations 1325–1478', in *The Church in Pre-Reformation Society: Essays in Honour of F.R.H. Du Boulay*, ed. C.M. Barron and Christopher Harper-Bill (Woodbridge), 123–42. *

1986

Richard III as Duke of Gloucester: A Study in Character (Borthwick Papers lxx, York). *

'Piety and Lineage in the Wars of the Roses: The Hungerford Experience', in *Kings and Nobles in the Later Middle Ages: A Tribute to Charles Ross*, ed. R.A. Griffiths and J.W. Sherborne (Gloucester), 90–108. *

'Richard, Duke of Gloucester and the North', in *Richard III and the North*, ed. Rosemary Horrox (Studies in Regional and Local History, vi, Hull), 11–26.

'Counting the Cost of War: The Moleyns Ransom and the Hungerford Land-Sales 1453–87', *Southern History*, viii. 11–35. *

'The Yorkshire Rebellion of 1489 Reconsidered', *Northern History*, xxii. 39–62.

'What Might Have Been: George Neville, Duke of Bedford 1465–83: His Identity and Significance', *The Ricardian*, vii. 321–6.

'"Landlady sells up – businessman turns country gent": The Sale of the Botreaux Lands in Hampshire in the 1460s', *Hampshire Field Club and Archaeological Society Section Newsletter*, new series, v. 5–6.

'An Intermittent Abbot of Quarr', *Hampshire Field Club and Archaeological Society Section Newsletter*, new series, vi. 5–6.

1987

'The Piety of Margaret, Lady Hungerford (d.1478)', *Journal of Ecclesiastical History*, xxxviii. 19–38. *

'Further Comments on Richard III and Romsey', *Hampshire Field Club and Archaeological Society Section Newsletter*, new series, viii. 5. *

1988
'The Last Days of Elizabeth, Countess of Oxford', *EHR*, ciii. 76–95. *

1989
'Walter, Lord Hungerford (d.1449) and his Chantry in Salisbury Cathedral', *Hatcher Review*, iii. 391–9.

1990
Richard III and His Rivals: Magnates and Their Motives in the Wars of the Roses (London).[1]
Profit, Piety and the Professions in Later Medieval England (Gloucester), edited with an introduction by Michael Hicks.
'The English Minoresses and Their Early Benefactors, 1281–1367', in *Monastic Studies: The Continuity of Tradition*, ed. Judith Loades (Bangor), 158–70.
'Did Edward V Outlive His Reign or Did He Outreign His Life?', *The Ricardian*, viii. 342–5.
'John Nettleton, Henry Savile of Banke, and the Post-medieval Vicissitudes of Byland Abbey Library', *Northern History*, xxvi. 212–17.
'Lessor v. Lessee: Nether Wallop Rectory 1700–1870', *Proceedings of the Hampshire Field Club and Archaeological Society*, xlvi. 145–56.
'Wallop House: The Rectory House at Nether Wallop', *Hampshire Field Club and Archaeological Society Section Newsletter*, new series, xiii. 9.
'Bastard Feudalism: Society and Politics in Late Medieval England', in *Richard III and His Rivals*, 1–40.
'Idealism in Late Medieval Politics', in *Richard III and His Rivals*, 41–59.
'Lord Hastings' Indentured Retainers?', in *Richard III and His Rivals*, 229–46.
'Richard III's Cartulary in British Library MS Julius BXII', in *Richard III and His Rivals*, 281–90.

1991
Richard III: The Man Behind the Myth (London).
Who's Who in Late Medieval England, 1272–1485 (London).
'Four Studies in Conventional Piety', *Southern History*, xiii. 1–21.
'The 1468 Statute of Livery', *HR*, lxiv. 15–28.
'Unweaving the Web: The Plot of July 1483 against Richard III and its Wider Significance', *The Ricardian*, ix. 106–9.
'Warwick – the Reluctant Kingmaker', *Medieval History*, i. 86–98.
'Presentations to the Vicarage of Nether Wallop, 1460–1865', *Hampshire Field Club and Archaeological Society Section Newsletter*, new series, xv. 29–30.

---

[1] Various articles previously published in edited volumes and journals. These are marked * above. Original pieces in *Richard III and His Rivals* are listed separately.

1993

'Richard, Duke of Gloucester: The Formative Years', in *Richard III: a Medieval Kingship*, ed. John Gillingham (London), 21–37.

'One Prince or Two? The Family of Richard III', *The Ricardian*, ix. 467–8.

'Rectors and Vicars in the Eighteenth Century: The Case of Nether Wallop', *Hampshire Field Club and Archaeological Society Section Newsletter*, new series, xx. 17–18.

1994

'Hampshire and the Isle of Wight', in *English County Histories: A Guide. A Tribute to C.R. Elrington*, ed. C.R.J. Currie and C.P. Lewis (Stroud).

1995

Bastard Feudalism (London).

'The Sources', in *The Wars of the Roses (Problems in Focus)*, ed. A.J. Pollard (revised edn., Basingstoke and New York), 20–40, 224–6.

1996

'Lawmakers and Lawbreakers', in *An Illustrated History of Late Medieval England*, ed. Christopher Given-Wilson (Manchester and New York), 206–28.

1997

'The Forfeiture of Barnard Castle to the Bishop of Durham in 1459', *Northern History*, xxxiii. 223–31.

1998

Warwick the Kingmaker (Oxford).

'Art, Attainder and Forfeiture', in *Medieval England: An Encyclopedia*, ed. P.E. Szarmach, M.T. Tavormina and J.T. Rosenthal (New York), 94–5.

'An Escheat Concealed: The Despenser Forfeitures 1400–61', *Proceedings of the Hampshire Field Club and Archaeological Society*, liii. 183–9.

'Cement or Solvent?: Kinship and Politics in Late Medieval England: The Case of the Nevilles', *History*, lxxxiii. 31–46.

1999

'A Minute of the Lancastrian Council at York, 20 January 1461', *Northern History*, xxxv. 214–21.

'Between Majorities: The "Beauchamp Interregnum", 1439–49', *HR*, lxxii. 27–43.

'From Megaphone to Microscrope: The Correspondence of Richard, Duke of York, with Henry VI in 1450 Revisited', *Journal of Medieval History*, xxv. 243–56.

2000

'Bastard Feudalism, Overmighty Subjects and Idols of the Multitude During the Wars of the Roses', *History*, lxxxv. 386–403.

'Propaganda and the First Battle of St. Albans, 1455', *Nottingham Medieval Studies*, xliv. 167–83.

2001

Revolution and Consumption in Late Medieval England (Woodbridge), edited by Michael Hicks.
'Richard, Lord Latimer, Richard III and the Warwick Inheritance', *The Ricardian*, xii. 314–20.

2002

English Political Culture in the Fifteenth Century (London).
Richard III (revised edn., Stroud) – originally published as *Richard III: The Man Behind the Myth* (1991).

2003

Edward V: The Prince in the Tower (Stroud).
The Wars of the Roses 1455–1485 (Oxford).
'Richard III, the Great Landowners and the Results of the Wars of the Roses', in *Tant d'Emprises – So Many Undertakings: Essays in Honour of Anne F. Sutton*, ed. Livia Visser-Fuchs, *The Ricardian*, xiii. 260–70.
'The Early Lords: Robert Fitzhamon to the de Clares', and 'The Later Lords: The Despensers and their Heirs', in *Tewkesbury Abbey: History, Art and Architecture*, ed. R.K. Morris and Ron Shoesmith (Almeley), 11–18, 19–30, 291–2.

2004

Edward IV (London and New York).
Oxford DNB: Anne [*née* Neville] (1456–1485); Ashley, Sir Anthony, baronet (1551/2–1628); Bigod, Sir Francis (1507–1537); Dale, Valentine (*c.*1520–1589); Davis [Davys], John (*c.*1550–1605); Dynham, John, Baron Dynham (*c.*1433–1501); Elizabeth [*née* Woodville] (*c.*1437–1492); George, duke of Clarence (1449–1478); Hallam, John (*c.*1495–1537); Heneage, Sir Thomas (*b.* in or before 1532, *d.*1595); Holland, Henry, second duke of Exeter (1430–1475); Hungerford, Robert, second Baron Hungerford (*c.*1400–1459); Hungerford, Robert, third Baron Hungerford and Baron Moleyns (*c.*1423–1464); Hungerford, Sir Walter (*b.* in or after 1441, *d.*1516); Lisle [de Lisle] family (*per. c.*1277–1542); Neville, George (1432–1476); Neville [Fauconberg], Thomas [*called* the Bastard of Fauconberg] (*d.*1471); Norton, Richard [*called* Old Norton] (*d.*1585); Paulet, Sir Amias (*c.*1532–1588); Pole, John de la, second duke of Suffolk (1442–1492); Speed, John (1703–1781); Stafford, Humphrey, earl of Devon (*c.*1439–1469); Stafford, Thomas (*c.*1533–1557); Stanhope, John, first Baron Stanhope (*c.*1540–1621); Stillington, Robert (*d.*1491); Talbot, Gilbert, seventh earl of Shrewsbury (1552–1616); Waad [Wade], Armagil (*c.*1510–1568).

2005

'King in Lords and Commons: Three Insights Into Late-Fifteenth-Century Parliaments 1461–85', in *People, Places and Perspectives: Essays on Later Medieval and Early Tudor England in Honour of Ralph A. Griffiths*, ed. Keith Dockray and Peter Fleming (Stroud), 131–53.
'Crowland's World: A Westminster View of the Yorkist Age', *History*, xc. 172–90.

2006

Anne Neville: Queen to Richard III (Stroud).
'Out of Session: Edward Guildford of Halden, Justice of the Peace for Kent, 1436–43', *Southern History*, xxviii. 24–45.

2007

'The Second Anonymous Continuation of the Crowland Abbey Chronicle 1459–86 Revisited', *EHR*, cxxii. 349–70.

2008

'A Story of Failure: The Minority of Edward V', in *The Royal Minorities of Medieval and Early Modern England*, ed. Charles Beem (Basingstoke), 195–210.
'Heirs and Non-heirs. Perceptions and Realities Amongst the English Nobility c.1300–1500', in *Making and Breaking the Rules: Succession in Medieval Europe, c.1000–c.1600* (*Etablir et Abolir les Normes: la Succession dans l'Europe Médiévale, vers 1000–vers 1600*), ed. Frédérique Lachaud and M.A. Penman (Turnhout, Belgium), 191–200.
'The Rising Price of Piety in the Later Middle Ages', in *Monasteries and Society in the British Isles in the Later Middle Ages*, ed. J.E. Burton and Karen Stöber (Studies in the History of Medieval Religion, xxxv, Woodbridge), 95–109.

2009

'The Yorkshire Perjuries of Henry Bolingbroke in 1399 Revisited', *Northern History*, xlvi. 31–41.

2010

The Wars of the Roses (New Haven, Conn., and London).
'Edward IV's *Brief Treatise* and the Treaty of Picquigny of 1475', *HR*, lxxxiii. 253–65.

2011

'Henry VI: A Misjudged King?', *History Today*, lxi. 31–4.
'The Fifteenth Century Inquisitions Post Mortem: The Newest Calendars 1432–47', *Southern History*, xxxiii. 113–18.

2012

The Fifteenth-Century Inquisitions Post Mortem: *A Companion* (Woodbridge), edited with an introduction by Michael Hicks, and including 'Crossing Generations: Dower, Jointure and Courtesy', 25–46.
'The Precedence of the Earldom of Devon, 1335–1485', *Coat of Arms*, 3rd series, viii. 85–90.

2013

'English Monasteries as Repositories of Dynastic Memory', in *Monuments and Monumentality Across Medieval and Early Modern Europe: Proceedings of the 2011 Stirling Conference*, ed. M.A. Penman (Donington), 224–38.

'The Yorkist Age?', in *The Yorkist Age*, ed. Hannes Kleineke and Christian Steer (Harlaxton Medieval Studies, xxiii, Donington), 1–17.

2014
'What was Personal about Personal Monarchy in the Fifteenth Century?', in *Image and Perception of Monarchy in Medieval and Early Modern Europe*, ed. Sean McGlynn and Elena Woodacre (Cambridge), 8–22.

2015
The Family of Richard III (Stroud).
False, Fleeting, Perjur'd Clarence: George, Duke of Clarence, 1449–1478 (2nd edition, Oxford).
English Inland Trade 1430–1540: Southampton and its Region (Oxford), edited with an introduction by Michael Hicks and Winifred A. Harwood and including 'The Trading Calendar', 'The Freight Transport of Southampton', and 'The Brokage Books as Sources for Local and Family History'.

Reviews: in *Albion*, *EHR*, *History*, *Northern History*, *Southern History*, *Speculum*, *The Ricardian* and several other publications.

TABULA GRATULATORIA

Martin Allen
Lorraine Attreed
Caroline Barron
Michael Bennett
Alexander R. Brondarbit
Clive Burgess
Christine Carpenter
Howard Choppin
Angela Clark
Linda Clark
Julia Cruse
Anne Curry
Keith Dockray
Christopher Dyer
Peter Fleming
David Green
Ralph Griffiths
John Hare
Winifred A. Harwood
Rosemary Hayes
Matthew Holford
Rosemary Horrox
Michael Jones
Maureen Jurkowski

Nicholas Kingwell
Hannes Kleineke
Jessica Lutkin
Jonathan Mackman
Gordon McKelvie
John Milner
Philip Morgan
Rebecca Oakes
Mark Ormrod
Mark Page
Simon Payling
Lynda J. Pidgeon
C. Anne Pike
A. J. Pollard
Edward Powell
Nigel Ramsay
Sarah Rose
James Ross
Brendan Smith
Christian Steer
Karen Stöber
Anne F. Sutton
John Watts
Barbara Yorke

CONTENTS OF PREVIOUS VOLUMES

I
Concepts and Patterns of Service in the Later Middle Ages
ed. Anne Curry and Elizabeth Matthew (2000)

P.J.P. Goldberg	What was a Servant?
Chris Given-Wilson	Service, Serfdom and English Labour Legislation, 1350–1500
Virginia Davis	Preparation for Service in the Late Medieval Church
Jeremy Catto	Masters, Patrons and Careers of Graduates in Fifteenth-Century England
David Morgan	The Household Retinue of Henry V and the Ethos of English Public Life
R.A. Griffiths	'Ffor the myght off the lande, aftir the myght off the grete lordes thereoff, stondith most in the kynges officers': the English Crown, Provinces and Dominions in the Fifteenth Century
Kathleen Daly	Private Vice, Public Service? Civil Service and *chose publique* in Fifteenth-Century France
Michael Jones	The Material Rewards of Service in Late Medieval Brittany: Ducal Servants and their Residences
Alexander Grant	Service and Tenure in Late Medieval Scotland, 1314–1475

II
Revolution and Consumption in Late Medieval England
ed. Michael Hicks (2001)

Christopher Woolgar	Fast and Fast: Conspicuous Consumption and the Diet of the Nobility in the Fifteenth Century
Alastair Dunn	Exploitation and Control: The Royal Administration of Magnate Estates, 1397–1405
Shelagh M. Mitchell	The Knightly Household of Richard II and the Peace Commissions
Alison Gundy	The Earl of Warwick and the Royal Affinity in the Politics of the West Midlands, 1389–99
T.B. Pugh	The Estates, Finances and Regal Aspirations of Richard Plantagenet (1411–60), Duke of York
Jessica Freeman	Middlesex in the Fifteenth Century: Community or Communities?

John Hare	Regional Prosperity in Fifteenth-Century England: Some Evidence from Wessex
John Lee	The Trade of Fifteenth-Century Cambridge and its Region
Miranda Threlfall-Holmes	Durham Cathedral Priory's Consumption of Imported Goods: Wines and Spices, 1464–1520
Winifred Harwood	The Impact of St. Swithun's Priory on the City of Winchester in the Later Middle Ages
P.W. Fleming	Telling Tales of Oligarchy in the Late Medieval Town

III
Authority and Subversion
ed. Linda Clark (2003)

Keith Dockray and Peter Fleming	Authority and Subversion: A Conference on Fifteenth-Century England
Alastair Dunn	Henry IV and the Politics of Resistance in Early Lancastrian England, 1399–1413
James Ross	Seditious Activities: The Conspiracy of Maud de Vere, Countess of Oxford, 1403–4
Clive Burgess	A Hotbed of Heresy? Fifteenth-Century Bristol and Lollardy Reconsidered
Ian Forrest	Anti-Lollard Polemic and Practice in Late Medieval England
Hannes Kleineke	Why the West was Wild: Law and Disorder in Fifteenth-Century Cornwall and Devon
Peter Booth	Men Behaving Badly? The West March Towards Scotland and the Percy-Neville Feud
Frank D. Millard	An Analysis of the *Epitaphium Eiusdem Ducis Gloucestrie*
J.L. Laynesmith	Constructing Queenship at Coventry: Pageantry and Politics at Margaret of Anjou's 'Secret Harbour'
David Grummitt	Public Service, Private Interest and Patronage in the Fifteenth-Century Exchequer
James Lee	Urban Recorders and the Crown in Late Medieval England

IV
Political Culture in Late-Medieval Britain
ed. Linda Clark and Christine Carpenter (2004)

Christine Carpenter	Introduction: Political Culture, Politics and Cultural History
Simon Walker	Remembering Richard: History and Memory in Lancastrian England
Maurice Keen	Early Plantagenet History Through Late Medieval Eyes
Alan Cromartie	Common Law, Counsel and Consent in Fortescue's Political Theory

Benjamin Thompson	Prelates and Politics from Winchelsey to Warham
Miri Rubin	Religious Symbols and Political Culture in Fifteenth-Century England
Caroline M. Barron	The Political Culture of Medieval London
Christopher Dyer	The Political Life of the Fifteenth-Century English Village
John Watts	The Pressure of the Public on Later Medieval Politics
Jenny Wormald	National Pride, Decentralised Nation: The Political Culture of Fifteenth-Century Scotland

V
Of Mice and Men: Image, Belief and Regulation in Late Medieval England
ed. Linda Clark (2005)

Jon Denton	Image, Identity and Gentility: The Woodford Experience
S.A. Mileson	The Importance of Parks in Fifteenth-Century Society
Alasdair Hawkyard	Sir John Fastolf's 'Gret Mansion by me late edified': Caister Castle, Norfolk
Jenni Nuttall	'*Vostre Humble Matatyas*': Culture, Politics and the Percys
Clive Burgess	A Repertory for Reinforcement: Configuring Civic Catholicism in Fifteenth-Century Bristol
Anne F. Sutton	Caxton, the Cult of St. Winifred, and Shrewsbury
Thomas S. Freeman	'*Ut Verus Christi Sequester*': John Blacman and the Cult of Henry VI
P.R. Cavill	The Problem of Labour and the Parliament of 1495
Colin Richmond	Mickey Mouse in Disneyland: How Did the Fifteenth Century Get That Way?

VI
Identity and Insurgency in the Late Middle Ages
ed. Linda Clark (2006)

Anthony Goodman	The British Isles Imagined
Andrea Ruddick	Ethnic Identity and Political Language in the King of England's Dominions: A Fourteenth-Century Perspective
Katie Stevenson	'Thai War Callit Knychtis and Bere the Name and the Honour of that Hye Ordre': Scottish Knighthood in the Fifteenth Century
Jackson Armstrong	Violence and Peacemaking in the English Marches towards Scotland, c.1425–1440
Matthew Tompkins	'Let's Kill all the Lawyers': Did Fifteenth-Century Peasants Employ Lawyers When They Conveyed Customary Land?

Simon Payling	Identifiable Motives for Election to Parliament in the Reign of Henry VI: The Operation of Public and Private Factors
David Grummitt	Deconstructing Cade's Rebellion: Discourse and Politics in the Mid Fifteenth Century
Jacquelyn Fernholz and Jenni Nuttall	Lydgate's Poem to Thomas Chaucer: A Reassessment of its Diplomatic and Literary Contexts
Maureen Jurkowski	Lollardy in Coventry and the Revolt of 1431
Carole Hill	Julian and her Sisters: Female Piety in Late Medieval Norwich

VII
Conflicts, Consequences and the Crown in the Late Middle Ages
ed. Linda Clark (2007)

Christine Carpenter	War, Government and Governance in England in the Later Middle Ages
Anne Curry	After Agincourt, What Next? Henry V and the Campaign of 1416
James Ross	Essex County Society and the French War in the Fifteenth Century
Michael Brown	French Alliance or English Peace? Scotland and the Last Phase of the Hundred Years War, 1415–53
J.L. Bolton	How Sir Thomas Rempston Paid His Ransom: Or, The Mistakes of an Italian Bank
Catherine Nall	Perceptions of Financial Mismanagement and the English Diagnosis of Defeat
Hannes Kleineke	'Þe Kynges Cite': Exeter in the Wars of the Roses
Lucy Brown	Continuity and Change in the Parliamentary Justifications of the Fifteenth-Century Usurpations
Peter Fleming	Identity and Belonging: Irish and Welsh in Fifteenth-Century Bristol
Anthony Goodman	The Impact of Warfare on the Scottish Marches, c.1481–c.1513
G.M. Draper	Writing English, French and Latin in the Fifteenth Century: A Regional Perspective

VIII
Rule, Redemption and Representations in Late Medieval England and France
ed. Linda Clark (2008)

Carole Rawcliffe	Dives Redeemed? The Guild Almshouses of Later Medieval England
Kathleen Daly	War, History and Memory in the Dauphiné in the Fifteenth Century: Two Accounts of the Battle of Anthon (1430)

Lucy Rhymer	Humphrey, Duke of Gloucester, and the City of London
Jonathan Mackman	'Hidden Gems' in the Records of the Common Pleas: New Evidence on the Legacy of Lucy Visconti
Colin Richmond	Sir John Fastolf, the Duke of Suffolk, and the Pastons
David King	Reading the Material Culture: Stained Glass and Politics in Late Medieval Norfolk
Anne F. Sutton	An Unfinished Celebration of the Yorkist Accession by a Clerk of the Merchant Staplers of Calais
Ruth Lexton	Henry Medwall's *Fulgens and Lucres* and the Question of Nobility Under Henry VII

IX
English and Continental Perspectives
ed. Linda Clark (2010)

Christine Carpenter	Henry VI and the Deskilling of the Royal Bureaucracy
Sarah Rose	A Twelfth-Century Honour in a Fifteenth-Century World: The Honour of Pontefract
Frederik Buylaert and Jan Dumolyn	The Representation of Nobility and Chivalry in Burgundian Historiography: A Social Perspective
Vincent Challet	*Tuchins* and '*Brigands de Bois*': Peasant Communities and Self-Defence Movements in Normandy During the Hundred Years War
Juliana Dresvina	A Heron for a Dame: A Hitherto Unpublished Middle English Prose Life of St. Margaret of Antioch in BL, Harley MS 4012
Andy King	Sir William Clifford: Rebellion and Reward in Henry IV's Affinity
Jessica Lutkin	Luxury and Display in Silver and Gold at the Court of Henry IV
Alessia Meneghin	Nursing Infants and Wet-Nurses in Fifteenth-Century Florence: Piero Puro di Francesco Da Vicchio and his Wife, Santa di Betto Da San Benedetto

X
Parliament, Personalities and Power:
Papers Presented to Linda Clark
ed. Hannes Kleineke (2011)

A.J. Pollard	The People and Parliament in Fifteenth-Century England
Simon Payling	'A Beest envenymed thorough ... covetize': An Imposter Pilgrim and the Disputed Descent of the Manor of Dodford, 1306–1481

Charles Moreton and Colin Richmond	Henry Inglose: A Hard Man to Please
J.L. Bolton	London Merchants and the Borromei Bank in the 1430s: The Role of Local Credit Networks
James Ross	'Mischieviously Slewen': John, Lord Scrope, the Dukes of Norfolk and Suffolk, and the Murder of Henry Howard in 1446
Carole Rawcliffe	A Fifteenth-Century *Medicus Politicus*: John Somerset, Physician to Henry VI
Elizabeth Danbury	'Domine Salvum Fac Regem': The Origin of 'God Save the King' in the Reign of Henry VI
Matthew Davies	'Monuments of Honour': Clerks, Histories and Heroes in the London Livery Companies
Hannes Kleineke	The East Anglian Parliamentary Elections of 1461
David Grummitt	Changing Perceptions of the Soldier in Late Medieval England
Caroline M. Barron	Thomas More, the London Charterhouse and Richard III

XI
Concerns and Preoccupations
ed. Linda Clark (2012)

Christopher Allmand	The English Translations of Vegetius' *De Re Militari*. What Were their Authors' Intentions?
John Milner	The English Commitment to the 1412 Expedition to France
Rhun Emlyn	Serving Church and State: the Careers of Medieval Welsh Students
Peter D. Clarke	Petitioning the Pope: English Supplicants and Rome in the Fifteenth Century
Frederick Hepburn	The Queen in Exile: Representing Margaret of Anjou in Art and Literature
Anthony Smith	The Presence of the Past: The Bokkyngs of Longham in the Later Middle Ages
Dean Rowland	The End of the Statute Rolls: Manuscript, Print and Language Change in Fifteenth-Century English Statutes
S.P. Harper	Divide and Rule? Henry VII, the Mercers, Merchant Taylors and the Corporation of London

XII
Society in an Age of Plague
ed. Linda Clark and Carole Rawcliffe (2013)

J.L. Bolton	Looking for *Yersinia Pestis*: Scientists, Historians and the Black Death
Karen Smyth	Pestilence and Poetry: John Lydgate's *Danse Macabre*

Sheila Sweetinburgh	Pilgrimage in 'an Age of Plague': Seeking Canterbury's 'hooly blisful martir' in 1420 and 1470
Elizabeth Rutledge	An Urban Environment: Norwich in the Fifteenth Century
Samantha Sagui	Mid-Level Officials in Fifteenth-Century Norwich
Elma Brenner	Leprosy and Public Health in Late Medieval Rouen
Neil Murphy	Plague Ordinances and the Management of Infectious Diseases in Northern French Towns, c.1450–c.1560
Jane Stevens Crawshaw	The Renaissance Invention of Quarantine
John Henderson	Coping with Epidemics in Renaissance Italy: Plague and the Great Pox
Samuel K. Cohn, Jnr.	The Historian and the Laboratory: The Black Death Disease

XIII
Exploring the Evidence: Commemoration, Administration and the Economy
ed. Linda Clark (2014)

S.J. Payling	The 'Grete Laboure and the Long and Troublous Tyme': The Execution of the Will of Ralph, Lord Cromwell, and the Foundation of Tattershall College
Christian Steer	A Royal Grave in a Fifteenth-Century London Parish Church
Matthew Ward	The Livery Collar: Politics and Identity During the Fifteenth Century
David Harry	William Caxton and Commemorative Culture in Fifteenth-Century England
Euan C. Roger	Blakberd's Treasure: A Study in Fifteenth-Century Administration at St. Bartholomew's Hospital, London
Sheila Sweetinburgh	Placing the Hospital: The Production of St. Lawrence's Hospital Registers in Fifteenth-Century Canterbury
Maureen Jurkowski	Were Friars Paid Salaries? Evidence from Clerical Taxation Records
Susanne Jenks	Exceptions in General Pardons, 1399–1450
Martin Allen	The English Crown and the Coinage, 1399–1485
Christopher Dyer	England's Economy in the Fifteenth Century

The Fifteenth Century aims to provide a forum for the most recent research into the political, social, religious and cultural history of the fifteenth century in Britain and Europe.

Contributions are invited for future volumes. Draft submissions or informal inquiries should be sent to The General Editor, Dr. Linda Clark, at 18 Bloomsbury Square, London WC1A 2NS, e-mail lclark@histparl.ac.uk. Authors should submit one copy of their contribution typed on A4 paper (double spacing throughout), with notes set as footnotes, as well as an electronic version. Contributions should not be longer than 10,000 words. 'Notes for Contributors' are available on request. Typescripts will not normally be returned if not accepted for publication.

Authors submitting manuscripts do so on the understanding that the work has not been published previously. Neither the General Editor nor the publisher accepts responsibility for the views of the authors expressed in their contributions. Authors wishing to include illustrations in their articles should contact the General Editor prior to submission. It is the author's responsibility to obtain the necessary permission to use material protected by copyright.